Coming Home after Disaster

Multiple Dimensions of Housing Recovery

Coming Home after Disaster

Multiple Dimensions of Housing Recovery

Edited by
Alka Sapat
Ann-Margaret Esnard

Routledge
Taylor & Francis Group
LONDON AND NEW YORK

First published 2017 by Routledge
2 Park Square, Milton Park, Abingdon, Oxon OX14 4RN
605 Third Avenue, New York, NY 10017

First issued in paperback 2021

First issued in hardback 2019

Routledge is an imprint of the Taylor & Francis Group, an informa business

ISBN 13: 978-1-03-224228-6 (pbk)
ISBN 13: 978-1-4987-2286-5 (hbk)

DOI: 10.4324/9781315404264

Dedication

We dedicate this book to the memory of Dr. William (Bill) Averette Anderson (1937–2013) for his support of disaster research and his commitment to understanding and mitigating hazard risks for vulnerable populations.

All royalty proceeds from this book are donated to the William Averette Anderson Fund.

THE William Averette Anderson **FUND**

Expanding inclusive hazard disaster planning for communities of color

The William Averette Anderson Fund, fondly called the Bill Anderson Fund (BAF), was developed in honor of William Averette Anderson who, for 50 years, was a hazard and disaster mitigation scholar, researcher, and policy developer. Bill served as a mentor and role model to countless new researchers and practitioners in the field. He also worked tirelessly to ensure that funding be dedicated to studying vulnerable populations and ensuring that women and people of color be recruited into all hazards professions—from frontline hazards management to critical hazards research.

BAF's mission is to support members of its student fellows program, who are individuals from underrepresented groups pursuing a graduate degree related to hazards, disasters, engineering, emergency management, or related fields, to graduation and beyond to placement in an academic or other professional position.

BAF students are supported through a suite of activities designed to enhance their professional development, academic progress, and sense of connectivity to the broader hazards and disaster management community including their BAF student peers and mentors. Included with this suite is a mentoring program that formally matches BAF fellows one-to-one with an academic or other professional mentor working in the field of hazards, disasters, and/or emergency management.

Contents

SECTION IV Multiple Dimensions of Housing Recovery

List of Figures

List of Tables

Foreword

In 1982 Enrico (Henry) Quarantelli, the longtime director of the Disaster Research Center (DRC), presented a gift to the hazard and disaster research community. In a DRC report that was later published in a shortened version in the journal *Disasters,* he conceptualized housing recovery as involving four phases: emergency shelter, temporary shelter, temporary housing, and permanent housing. Around that same time, several early pioneering students of recovery, such as Robert Bolin, Claire Rubin, and Robert Kates, had made seminal contributions regarding family and community recovery issues. However, Quarantelli was focusing upon housing recovery, discussing the social, organizational, and policy factors associated with the four phases, and championing the need for extensive research in this critical area. Mary Comerio's significant contributions would come in the next decade. Quarantelli's gift, a thoughtful, useful, conceptually parsimonious framework, has proven to have great staying power. It is still a referenced and fundamental component of our knowledge base about disaster housing recovery.

With this book, Alka Sapat and Ann-Margaret Esnard offer up another gift, one that has come at the right moment in the development of our understanding of housing recovery in post-disaster settings. Research on recovery in general could be charitably labeled as sparse from the mid-1980s into the 1990s. The literature could fit comfortably on one or two shelves of a bookcase. Specific research on the more limited area of housing recovery was even rarer. However, since 2000, the volume of research has rapidly expanded. Perhaps, this increased attention to housing recovery was stimulated by major, large-scale disasters, both in the United States (such as Hurricanes Katrina, Sandy, and Ike, and other large flooding events) and internationally (such as the Indian Ocean tsunami; earthquakes in China, Haiti, Chile, Japan, New Zealand, and Nepal; and tropical storm Haiyan). Funding agencies proposed solicitations to support research on a number of these extreme events. Also, the research community has paid far greater attention to the topic, resulting in a monumental increase in our knowledge. One less than optimal indicator of this trend is that of the 1000 or so references in this volume, roughly 82% have been produced in the last 15 years. (About 12% of the references were published from 1990 to 2000, and only about 6% were published before 1990.)

This book does a masterful job of summarizing this body of knowledge. What are some of the major strengths of this work? First, the authors of these 19 chapters are some of the finest scholars and researchers focusing upon housing recovery in the world. In addition, the collection of authors is appropriately multidisciplinary in nature and includes such expertise as anthropology, architecture, economics, engineering, geography, law, psychology, public policy and public administration, sociology, and urban and regional planning and science. They have all produced outstanding chapters that make significant contributions to the knowledge base and should be utilized. Second, the breadth of the topics and discussion is impressive, without sacrificing needed depth. The book is multinational and multicultural in its analysis. It deals with housing policies and processes at local, regional, and national levels. It is also comparative in its considerations of a variety of natural hazard situations. A variety of diverse and critically important topics are discussed, such as social and physical vulnerability; governance structures and processes; financial factors, including insurance; displacement and relocation; the role of the private sector and nongovernmental organizations (NGOs); comparative legal structures; affordable housing; informal settlers; perceptions of recovery effectiveness and satisfaction by victims; time compression; social networks and capital; and community involvement. The reader is given a detailed tour of the intricacies and complexities of housing recovery both in the United States and throughout the world.

There is no reason for me to discuss the individual chapters. Sapat and Esnard provide an insightful overview in the introductory chapter. However, it can be noted that the book is divided into four sections. Section I presents careful reviews of such topics as scalar housing approaches, socially vulnerable populations, relocation and resettlement, financing recovery through insurance, and displacement policies. Section II of the book presents case studies of housing recovery in the United States following Hurricanes Ike and Dolly in Galveston and the Colonias region of Texas, the Colorado floods of 2013, the Joplin tornado of 2011, Hurricane Sandy, and a nationwide survey of housing recovery for disabled populations. Section III presents four case studies of recovery based upon research in Haiti, South India, China, and the Philippines. Section IV covers such issues as problematic patterns in reconstruction and recovery, housing for informal settlers, the role of NGOs and the private sector in recovery, the importance and utility of pre-disaster recovery planning, critical legal elements that influence the recovery process, and guidelines on how the recovery process can be improved.

Reading the chapters results in a few take-aways or themes. First, there is no "magic bullet," no panacea for solving the myriad difficulties inherent in the complex recovery process. It is obvious that "one size fits all" does not fit the recovery process. This theme applies quite clearly when comparing different cultural and national experiences, but it also applies internally within societies. Second, although there is no magic bullet, it is obvious that successful recovery processes must facilitate, empower, and utilize strong community involvement in recovery policy, planning, and activities. Bottom-up approaches result in higher levels of perceived satisfaction on the part of housing victims. Third, developing successful permanent housing for socially vulnerable populations involves including them in the process, targeting their functional needs, and utilizing their capabilities. It is obvious that a slipshod recovery process under the impact of time compression can result in increasing vulnerability to future hazards, rather than reducing it. Fourth, housing recovery is a holistic process that involves much more than just building houses. It includes the strengthening of neighborhoods, social networks, and social capital. Fifth, land-use issues involving land tenure and location are extremely important in recovery in all countries, and should be addressed through pre-disaster recovery planning. Sixth, it is apparent that individuals, NGOs, governments, and market forces cannot individually or independently undertake a successful housing recovery process for major disasters. This book could make significant contributions in improving the recovery process. Hopefully, the ideas presented here will find their way into policy and decision making.

There is another area in which this book can make a significant contribution, and that is in the construction of mid-range theory. There is nothing more useful than a sound theory. There have been calls for a "grand theory" of disaster recovery for more than 30 years. The current version of that plea is for a grand theory of resilience. One of the problems with grand theories is that they are often founded upon mid-range theory, such as the sound theory of housing recovery. The chapters in this book have the potential to be used as building blocks for the construction of a solid theory of disaster housing recovery, which means that these are building blocks for resilience.

Enjoy and benefit from this gift that has been provided to hazard and disaster scholars and practitioners. Use its lessons to contribute to our knowledge base and theoretical development. Implement and utilize its recommendations for improving the housing recovery process. It has the potential to impact future research and policy. Henry will be proud.

Dennis Wenger
Former Program Director
Infrastructure Management and Extreme Events
National Science Foundation

Chair
Scientific and Technical Advisory Group
UNISDR

Acknowledgments

We are deeply grateful to Dr. Dennis Wenger and the United States National Science Foundation's Infrastructure Management and Extreme Events in the Division of Civil, Mechanical and Manufacturing Innovation (CMMI) for funding research projects that have allowed us to explore various facets of disaster mitigation, housing recovery, and long-term post-disaster recovery over the past 18 years. The four research projects funded by NSF's CMMI Division that planted the ideas for and influenced this book on post-disaster housing are: *State Regulation of Building Safety: Policy Choices, Institutions, and Interests.* (NSF Grant No. CMS-9813611); *Displacement Due to Catastrophic Hurricanes: Assessing Potential Magnitude and Policy Implications for Housing and Land Development* (NSF Grant No. CMMI-0726808); *Haitian-Americans as Critical Bridges and Lifelines for Long-Term Recovery in Haiti* (NSF Grant No. CMMI-1034667); and *Diaspora Advocacy Coalitions and Networks: A Focus on Haiti's Disasters* (NSF Grant No. CMMI-1162438). Our academic institutions, Florida Atlantic University (FAU) and Georgia State University (GSU), provided the necessary institutional infrastructure to pursue these research efforts.

However, this book project was truly a collaborative effort and we are very grateful to our 31 colleagues and coauthors who contributed their knowledge and insights, and invested their time and resources despite very busy schedules to prepare various chapters. We are a group of scholars and practitioners from various parts of the world with insights, perspectives, and field experiences that have shaped our efforts to tackle the multiple dimensions of post-disaster housing recovery. We thank each of them sincerely for all their efforts and for responding to our emails and requests. The quality of the chapters reflects their scholarly knowledge and expertise and has helped broaden the vision and depth of this book. During the course of this book project, we also learned that funding from the National Science Foundation supported the research in several chapters in this book and a large portion of this funding is from the CMMI Division.*

We owe a special thanks to Jennifer Abbott, Associate Editor, Homeland Security of CRC Press who supported this book project from the start, patiently and swiftly responded to our queries, and guided and mentored us throughout the process. Stephanie Morkert, Project Coordinator, Editorial Project Development and Kari Budyk, Senior Project Coordinator of CRC Press were also instrumental in providing prompt feedback and in helping us to navigate the editing and publishing process. They passed over the reins to Natalja Mortenson, Senior Editor, Political Science Research of Routledge Press and Lillian Rand, Editorial Assistant, Politics of Routledge Press, who made the transition seamless. They provided us with quick guidance, feedback, and helped us with the numerous elements needed to bring this

* While this support has been critical to this research, any opinions, findings, and conclusions or recommendations expressed in this material are those of the author(s) and do not necessarily reflect the views of the National Science Foundation.

book to completion. Thank you for entrusting us with this important project. We wish to also express our sincere thanks to the CRC editorial board and reviewers who supported our book proposal.

This book project required a lot of work behind the scenes and we are grateful to one key individual, Lorena Schwartz, a doctoral candidate in the School of Public Administration and recipient of the Provost's Fellowship at Florida Atlantic University. Her stellar assistance in organizing and gathering materials and completing the cumbersome tasks related to reference lists, citations, and formatting was invaluable in helping us meet our deadlines. She helped tremendously in meticulously organizing and keeping track of all the multiple tasks related to the book. Thank you, Lorena, for your thoroughness and professionalism.

Last but not least, we speak on behalf of all our coauthors when we say that this book would not have been possible without the steadfast support, love, and patience of our spouses, partners, significant others, children, immediate and extended families, friends, research assistants, and pets for their support and patience as we worked on various book chapters.

Bill Anderson was an invaluable mentor and guide to us and to many authors in this book; his legacy continues to inspire us and live on through the work presented in these chapters. We dedicate the book to his memory and the fund created in his name which encourages and assists the next generation of students and researchers to carry on his legacy of serving vulnerable populations and ensuring diversity in the hazards and disaster field.

We also dedicate this book to those communities, their advocates, and others who have strived tirelessly in their quest to find solutions to post-disaster housing dilemmas. We hope that the work presented in this book will inspire and encourage all who work in disaster management and related fields to continue to find safe, humane, just, and equitable solutions to help people come back to a home after disaster.

Editors

Alka Sapat is an associate professor of public administration at Florida Atlantic University. Her expertise includes disaster and crisis management, vulnerability and resilience assessment, environmental policy governance, environmental justice, and social network analysis. She was a research fellow with the National Science Foundation's "Next Generation of Hazards Researchers" program and has been involved in a number of initiatives including serving as principal investigator and co-principal investigator on National Science Foundation funded projects on topics of building code regulation, disaster-induced population displacement and implications for housing and land development, and the role of the Haitian diaspora in disaster recovery and resilience. Sapat is currently working on projects funded by the National Science Foundation on the role of nongovernmental organizations and diaspora-led coalitions in disaster recovery and on a collaborative research project on interdependencies in critical infrastructure resilience. Her work has been published in the *Natural Hazards Review, Public Administration Review, the International Journal of Mass Emergencies and Disasters, Policy Studies Journal, Risks, Hazards, and Crises in Public Policy*, and other scholarly venues. She is the coauthor of the book *Displaced by Disasters: Recovery and Resilience in a Globalizing World* published by Routledge Press and is editor of a forthcoming book, *The Routledge Handbook of Environmental Governance*. She is an editorial board member of the journals *Risk, Hazards and Crisis in Public Policy* and *Environmental Hazards*. She has served on a number of state committees, including the Florida State Disaster Housing Task Force and the Governor's Hurricane Conference committee, along with serving on local committees on post-disaster housing initiatives. Since June 2015, she serves on the William Averette Anderson Foundation's Feeder Advisory Council as a member and faculty mentor. She earned an MA and PhD in political science (with a specialization in political economy and public policy) from the State University of New York-Stony Brook.

Ann-Margaret Esnard is a distinguished university professor in the Andrew Young School of Policy Studies at Georgia State University (GSU) hired in 2013 as part of the University's Second Century Initiative cluster hire on *Shaping the Future of Cities*. She served as the chair of GSU's Council for Progress of Cities and is affiliated with the university's global partnership for better cities research initiative. Prior to joining GSU, Esnard held tenure appointments in the Department of City and Regional Planning at Cornell University and in the School of Urban and Regional Planning at Florida Atlantic University. Her expertise encompasses urban planning, disaster planning, hazard and vulnerability assessment, and GIS/spatial analysis. Esnard has been involved in a number of related research initiatives, including National Science Foundation funded projects on topics of population displacement from catastrophic disasters, long-term recovery, and the role of diaspora groups in disasters with transnational impacts. She is the coauthor of the book *Displaced by Disasters: Recovery and Resilience in a Globalizing World* published by Routledge Press. Esnard has served on a number of local, state, and national committees including: the Steering Committee for Evaluation of the National Flood Insurance Program; the Disasters Roundtable of the National Academy of Sciences; the National Research Council's committee on Private–Public Sector Collaboration to Enhance Community Disaster Resilience, and the State of Florida Post-Disaster Redevelopment Planning initiative. She also served as a mentor for the fourth round of the NSF-funded Enabling the Next Generation of Hazards & Disasters Fellowship Program, and currently serves on the William Averette Anderson Foundation's Feeder Advisory Council as a member and faculty mentor. Esnard is a native of the Caribbean island of Saint Lucia, and earned degrees in agricultural engineering (BSc, University of the West Indies-Trinidad), agronomy and soils (MS, University of Puerto Rico-Mayaguez), and regional planning (PhD, UMASS-Amherst). She also completed a 2-year postdoc at UNC-Chapel Hill as part of the Carolina Postdoctoral Program for Faculty Diversity.

Contributors

Simon A. Andrew is an associate professor in the Department of Public Administration at the University of North Texas. His research focuses on metropolitan governance and urban management—the role of governance institutions and human behavior/interactions in solving institutional collective action problems. He studies the challenges of developing and sustaining multi-stakeholder collaborations in the context of disaster planning and management. He is an expert in social network analysis (SNA) and quantitative research methods.

Sudha Arlikatti is an associate professor in the Integrated Emergency Management and Business Continuity Management Program at Rabdan Academy in Abu Dhabi, United Arab Emirates. Her research interests include disaster warnings and risk communication, protective action decision making, post-disaster sheltering and housing recovery, and organizational and community resiliency to disasters. Her field research has been funded by the US National Science Foundation, the Texas Department of State Health Services, and Dallas Area Habitat for Humanity.

Jennifer Duyne Barenstein holds a PhD in social anthropology. She specialized in socio-cultural dimensions of disaster risk management, post-disaster housing, and settlement reconstruction and has extensive field experience in Asia and Latin America. Between 1999 and 2008, she was a senior lecturer at the Department of Social Anthropology of the University of Zurich and was the founder of the World Habitat Research Centre at the University of Applied Sciences of Southern Switzerland, which she directed until 2015. At present she is a senior researcher at the Centre for Research on Architecture, Society and the Built Environment (CASE) and the Institute of Science, Technology and Policy (ISTP) of the ETH Zurich.

Samuel D. Brody is a professor and holder of the George P. Mitchell '40 Chair in Sustainable Coasts in the Departments of Marine Sciences and Landscape Architecture and Urban Planning at Texas A&M University. He is the director of Center for Texas Beaches and Shores and the co-director of the Institute for Sustainable Coastal Communities. Dr. Brody's research focuses on coastal planning, flood mitigation, climate policy, and natural hazards mitigation.

Mary C. Comerio is a professor of the Graduate School in the Department of Architecture at the University of California, Berkeley. Her research focuses on housing resilience, post-disaster recovery and reconstruction, and loss modeling. In 2011, she received the Green Star Award from the United Nations for her work in post-disaster reconstruction. In 2013, she received the UC Berkeley Chancellor's Award for Public Service for Research in the Public Interest.

Zhen Cong is currently an associate professor in the Department of Human Development and Family Studies at Texas Tech University. She is interested in disaster preparation and human responses, changes in family relationships and social networks, and mental health in the setting of natural disasters. Her expertise in family mechanisms helps to strengthen the understanding of disaster resilience from the family level.

William Drake is a doctoral candidate in the Planning, Governance, and Globalization Program at Virginia Tech. His research focuses on climate change adaptation planning.

Ann-Margaret Esnard is a distinguished university professor in the Andrew Young School of Policy Studies at Georgia State University (GSU). She has been involved in a number of research initiatives, including National Science Foundation-funded projects on topics of population displacement from catastrophic disasters, and the role of diaspora organizations in long-term recovery. She is the coauthor of the book *Displaced by Disasters: Recovery and Resilience in a Globalizing World* published by Routledge Press.

Mahmood Fayazi is a PhD candidate affiliated to the IF Research Group at the School of Architecture of the Université de Montréal. He has been involved in important projects after earthquakes in Iran including; Bam (2003), Lorestan (2005), and Semnan (2009). He worked at the Research Department of the Housing Foundation of the Islamic Republic. He earned a master's degree from the University of Shahid Beheshti.

N. Emel Ganapati is an associate professor in public administration at Florida International University. Her articles have appeared in leading journals, including the *Journal of American Planning Association*, *Public Administration Research*, *Natural Hazards Review*, *Natural Hazards, and Disasters*. Dr. Ganapati has served as the principal investigator of several grants funded by the National Science Foundation. Her areas of interest include disaster recovery, citizen participation, and social capital.

Brian J. Gerber is an associate professor at the College of Public Service and Community Solutions, Arizona State University, where he is director of the Emergency Management and Homeland Security Program. His research specialization areas include disaster policy and management, homeland security policy and administration, and environmental regulatory policy; and his work has been published in a wide variety of academic journals. He also has an extensive experience in executing applied projects with local, state, and federal agencies, as well as with nonprofit sector organizations, on hazards-related policy and management issues.

Souparno Ghosh's research interest lies in Bayesian hierarchical models. His current research is focused on developing mechanistically motivated statistical models for analyzing plant demography. His further interest lies in developing models for facilitating sequential learning in sensor network data. He received his PhD in Statistics from Texas A&M University. He joined the Department of Mathematics and Statistics at Texas Tech University as an assistant professor in Fall 2012.

Wesley E. Highfield is an assistant professor in the Department of Marine Sciences at Texas A&M University at Galveston and Associate Director of the Center for Texas Beaches and Shores where he teaches courses in GIS and spatial sciences. Dr. Highfield's research interests focus primarily on the impacts and mitigation of natural hazards and spatial sciences.

Kanako Iuchi is an associate professor at the International Research Institute of Disaster Science, Tohoku University. She specializes in disaster management planning in international settings. Her past and current planning practices include projects run by international development agencies, including the World Bank and JICA. She earned a BS from Tsukuba University, an MRP from Cornell University, and a PhD from the University of Illinois, Urbana-Champaign, all in urban and regional planning.

Faten Kikano is a PhD student affiliated to the IF Research Group at the School of Architecture of the Université de Montréal. She worked for 20 years as a designer and a consultant for various types of architecture and interior architecture projects and has taught at the Lebanese American University (LAU), the American University of Science and Technology (AUST), and Académie Libanaise des Beaux-Arts (ALBA) in Lebanon. She earned a master's from ALBA.

Adrienne La Grange is an associate professor in the Department of Public Policy at the City University of Hong Kong. She has worked as planner and researcher in the public, private, and nonprofit sectors in South Africa, Australia, and Hong Kong. Her research focuses on housing studies, neighborhood studies, and urban policy in Hong Kong and South East Asia. Her specific research interests include urban redevelopment, gentrification, gated communities, and public housing policy.

Daan Liang joined Texas Tech University in 2004 and has been active in interdisciplinary research on disaster impact assessment and mitigation. He directed post-storm damage assessment efforts after Hurricane Katrina (2005), Super Tuesday Tornado (2008), Joplin Tornado (2011), Tuscaloosa Tornado (2011), and Moore Tornado (2013). In August 2014, Dr. Liang was appointed as the Interim Director of National Wind Institute (NWI), overseeing about two dozen staff members along with more than 40 faculty affiliates from various academic departments.

Michael K. Lindell is an affiliate professor, University of Washington and emeritus professor, Texas A&M University. Over the past 45 years, he has conducted research and provided technical services on the management of a wide range of natural and technological hazards for over 40 public and private sector organizations. He has been a member of three National Research Council committees, made over 230 presentations in the United States and abroad, and is the author of 80 technical reports, 140 journal articles and book chapters, and nine books.

Gonzalo Lizarralde is a professor at the School of Architecture of the Université de Montréal. He has long experience in consulting for architecture and construction projects. Dr. Lizarralde is the director of the IF Research Group (grif) and lead researcher of Œuvre Durable. He is a founding member of i-Rec, coauthor of the book *Rebuilding after Disasters* and author of the book *The Invisible Houses: Rethinking and Designing Low-Cost Housing in Developing Countries.*

Dr. Carrie Makarewicz is an assistant professor in the Department of Planning and Design at the University of Colorado, Denver. Her research focuses on how the physical and social aspects of communities interact with public policies for education, housing, transport, and development to affect everyday life and economic mobility. Prior studies include estimating household transportation expenditures, promoting equitable transit-oriented development, and understanding the effects of the urban environment on parent engagement.

Elizabeth Maly is an assistant professor at the International Research Institute of Disaster Science (IRIDeS), Tohoku University. With the theme "people-centered housing recovery," her research focuses on post-disaster housing and community recovery. Before IRIDeS, she worked at the Disaster Reduction Institute (DRI) and the International Recovery Platform (IRP) in Kobe. She earned a BA from Reed College, M.Arch from the University of Washington-Seattle, and PhD in Architecture from Kobe University.

John Travis Marshall is an assistant professor of law at Georgia State University, where he teaches environmental law and land use law and serves as associate director of the Center for the Study of Comparative Metropolitan Growth. From 2007 to 2011, he was a counsel and project manager with the New Orleans Redevelopment Authority (NORA). In that role, he advised NORA on post-Hurricane Katrina implementation of the Authority's urban revitalization efforts, including land acquisition, development, and disposition programs. Prior to New Orleans, he was a partner with Holland & Knight LLP.

Ali Nejat joined Texas Tech University in 2011 and since then he has been involved in a variety of multidisciplinary research on post-disaster housing recovery encompassing a wide range of disasters including Hurricanes Katrina and Sandy as well as the Moore, OK Tornado. His research was recently recognized by a National Science Foundation's CAREER grant in which he intends to develop RECOVUS which is an agent-based model of collective post-disaster housing recovery.

Brenda D. Phillips, PhD, is an associate dean and professor of sociology at Ohio University in Chillicothe. She is an author of *Disaster Recovery, Introduction to Emergency Management, Qualitative Disaster Research* and *Mennonite Disaster Service.* She has coedited *Social Vulnerability to Disasters* and *Women and Disasters.* Dr. Phillips has earned the Blanchard Award for excellence in emergency management education and the Myers Award for work on the effects of disasters on women.

Guitele J. Rahill is an associate professor and interim associate director of Social Work at the University of South Florida. Her work is published in journals such as *AIDS Care*, *American Journal of Public Health*, *Journal of Ethnicity and Health*, *Disasters*, and *Journal of Health Care for the Poor and Underserved*. She has received a presidential fellowship, awards for academic and research excellence, service awards, and most valuable mentor awards.

Andrew Rumbach is an assistant professor in the Department of Planning and Design at the University of Colorado, Denver. His research centers on disaster risk reduction and community resilience, in the United States and India. He is especially interested in the role that urban and regional planning can play in creating safer and more equitable cities.

Alka Sapat is an associate professor of public administration at Florida Atlantic University. She has been involved in a number of initiatives including NSF-funded projects on topics of building code regulation, disaster-induced population displacement, and the role of diasporas and nongovernmental organizations in disaster recovery. She is the coauthor of the book *Displaced by Disasters: Recovery and Resilience in a Globalizing World* published by Routledge Press.

Susanna Seeley is a certified emergency manager who specializes in the coordination of disaster human services at the state and federal levels. Seeley is a US Army Veteran and a past chairperson of the New York City Voluntary Organizations Active in Disaster and the Missouri Voluntary Organizations Active in Disaster. Seeley was deployed to many notable disasters including the 2011 Joplin Tornado, and the 2012 Super Storm Sandy response. She is currently serving as the chairperson of the Conference Committee of the International Association of Emergency Managers-USA Council and is attending the Harvard National Preparedness Leadership Initiative Executive Education program.

Madison Sloan is the director of the Disaster Recovery and Fair Housing Project at Texas Appleseed. Her work focuses on ensuring that low-income and minority communities can rebuild after disasters, and fair housing advocacy. She joined Texas Appleseed in 1997 as an Equal Justice Works Katrina Legal Fellow and received the *2011 Impact Award* from the State Bar of Texas Poverty Law Section for her work. Sloan received a Juris Doctor from Michigan Law School and a Master of Public Affairs from the LBJ School at University of Texas. Her previous experience includes over 5 years as a legal services attorney.

Gavin Smith is the director of the US Department of Homeland Security's Coastal Resilience Center of Excellence, located at the University of North Carolina at Chapel Hill, where he is also a research professor in the Department of City and Regional Planning. In 2011, he completed the text, *Planning for Post-Disaster Recovery: A Review of the United States Disaster Assistance Framework*. Dr. Smith has worked for Governor Hunt in North Carolina following Hurricane Floyd and

Governor Barbour in Mississippi following Hurricane Katrina, leading hazard mitigation and disaster recovery efforts, respectively.

Isabelle Thomas is a professor at the School of Urban Planning and Landscape architecture of the Université de Montréal. She has been working on many projects related to rebuilding after disasters, especially in New Orleans, Honduras, and France. She is an associate researcher at Œuvre Durable and has published numerous articles on resilience, vulnerability, and sustainable rebuilding. She recently organized an international conference on adaptations to climate change. https://territoiresvunerablesvillesresilientes.wordpress.com/.

Shannon Van Zandt is a professor of Landscape Architecture & Urban Planning at Texas A&M University. She holds the Nicole & Kevin Youngblood Professorship in Residential Land Development, directs the College of Architecture's Center for Housing & Urban Development, and coordinates the professional graduate program in urban planning. As a faculty fellow in the Hazard Reduction & Recovery Center, Van Zandt's research focuses on the role of housing in mitigating or exacerbating social vulnerability to disaster.

Yang Zhang is an associate professor of Urban Affairs and Planning at Virginia Tech. His research interests include hazards mitigation planning and disaster recovery. Subscribing to the international comparative approach, his work includes case studies in United States, China, Haiti, Japan, and Korea. His research has been funded by the National Science Foundation, the Virginia Sea Grant, HUD, the Lincoln Institute of Land Policy, the Peking University-Lincoln Institute Center, the Wilson Center, and the Korea Council of Humanities.

Introduction

> Disasters tear into the safety and security that a home symbolizes. Displacement from our homes can be a disorienting experience, disrupting our ties to the places that provide relationships with meaning and identities with substance. When we lose the familiarity and comfort of a home, it can take time to regroup and recover socially and psychologically. Losing a home can also result in significant financial harm. The journey from temporary post-disaster lodging to permanency can be time-consuming, enervating, and discouraging. But the housing recovery process, with the support of family, neighbors, recovery leaders, and nongovernmental and governmental organizations, can also restore hope, stabilize families, support the economy, and point a community toward a new future (Phillips 2016, p. 196).

Housing issues are critical to the disaster recovery process but are some of the most complex aspects of disaster recovery (Arendt and Alesch 2015; Bates and Peacock 1987; Bolin 1986; Bolin and Stanford 1991; Comerio 1998; Peacock et al. 2007, 2014; Phillips 2016; Quarantelli 1982; Sapat et al. 2011). Housing issues are also inextricably intertwined with social, economic, and political considerations, yet post-disaster housing continues to be an under-studied area in disaster research. Past disasters in the United States such as the 1993 Midwest floods, Hurricanes Hugo and Andrew in 1989 and 1992, respectively, Hurricane Katrina in 2005, and Hurricane Sandy in 2012 led to catastrophic damage to residential housing units. In October 2012, Superstorm Sandy affected 24 states and more than three quarters of a million people in the United States were forced to leave their homes (Internal Displacement Monitoring Centre [IDMC] 2013, p. 17). A major problem after Sandy was the lack of post-disaster housing, given the limited housing (and affordable housing) options specifically in New York City; one of the most difficult housing markets, with low vacancy rates and high rents. The problem of post-disaster housing is equally challenging in other countries, particularly in increasingly urbanized, resource-strapped cities that have often been built in hazard-prone areas. Relocation of communities in rural areas affected by disasters, such as the 2004 Indian Ocean tsunami has also proven to be a complicated and difficult phenomenon. The 2010 Haiti earthquake affected almost 3.5 million people, with displacement of more than two million at its peak, as well as the damage and destruction to hundreds of thousands homes (International Federation of Red Cross and Red Crescent Societies [IFRC] 2012). The early sheltering recovery dilemmas are addressed in Chapter 11 by Emel Ganapati and Guitele Rahill.

WHY READ THIS BOOK?

Post-disaster housing concerns and dilemmas cannot be adequately captured via a single disciplinary lens or profession. Housing recovery has far too many facets and needs a holistic approach that accounts for its multiple dimensions and contours that are best captured with multidisciplinary, multi-scalar, and multi-hazard approaches. However, while the impact of disasters on housing is large and complex, housing continues to be an under-studied area in disaster research and in-depth, systematic analysis of post-disaster housing recovery is limited (National Research Council [NRC] 2011; Zhang and Peacock 2009).

This book attempts to fill that gap by exploring several concerns, concepts, and challenges with respect to post-disaster housing.

Among them are:

- Variable rates of housing recovery: a number of factors affect housing recovery, including levels of social and physical vulnerability, levels and types of social capital, community resources, housing markets and demand and supply, the presence of leadership, legal and institutional factors, political will, adaptive flexibility, the severity of the disaster, and the extent of dislocation and displacement.
- Technical challenges to finding appropriate and sustainable building materials for transitional and permanent post-disaster housing and for retrofitting and repairs.
- The role played by financial institutions and insurance.
- Problems related to land tenure, home ownership, property rights, planning, and zoning.
- Issues related to rebuilding affordable housing, and the potential effects of gentrification and redevelopment.
- Cross-sector coordination and collaboration, and the role of the nonprofit sector.

WHAT'S AHEAD

SETTING THE STAGE: CONTEXT AND CONCEPTS

Mary Comerio's seminal work on disaster housing (Comerio 1998) stimulated a large body of work on this subject in 1998. Almost two decades later, her work continues to explore issues of housing recovery and its connection to community recovery. Section I of this book begins with Mary Comerio's contribution, in which she outlines some of the key issues and concerns in recovery such as the lack of planning at the individual and agency level, lack of adequate insurance, lack of local implementation capacity, lack of funding, inflexible government programs, poverty, and the lack of institutions. Comerio also sets the stage for the discourse that follows in the other chapters of the book, by discussing an array of issues critical to housing recovery ranging from the individual and community level to the role played by national and subnational levels of government. She situates this discussion through a cross-country comparison that examines the role played by governments (from limited to more involved) and the extent of community participation.

Disasters are caused by the accumulation of physical, social, economic, and political vulnerabilities and the lack of capacity to withstand or respond (Blaikie et al., 1994; Bogard 1988; Bohle et al. 1994; Cutter et al. 2003; Dow 1992; Dow and

Downing 1995; Downing 1991; Laska and Morrow 2006; Peacock et al. 2012). The discussion of vulnerability and its link to post-disaster housing is one of the central themes of this book. In Chapter 2, Brenda Phillips explores this concept in more detail, focusing on social vulnerability and addressing the different ways in which various populations (women, children, the elderly, lower-income populations, and the disabled) experience the return to permanent post-disaster housing. Through several examples, she explores the ways in which marginalization of certain populations and social, cultural, and environmental contexts create dilemmas for those attempting to return home. Drawing from this discussion, Phillips provides recommendations for those working with historically marginalized populations.

The theme of vulnerability is carried forward in Chapter 3, in which Ann-Margaret Esnard discusses how displacement, particularly when layered upon urbanization patterns and existing societal vulnerabilities, complicates post-disaster recovery trajectories and outcomes. She examines in-situ, cultural-economic, and protracted displacement, their intangible, overlapping, and intractable nature and their ramifications for housing and for second levels of vulnerability and insecurity for displaced persons. Problems related to relocation and resettlement, and the impact of community social ties, sheltering and housing policies on displacement timelines and outcomes are discussed using examples from various disasters and countries to elucidate pathways from displacement to return and relocation.

Other key issues in post-disaster housing concern the all-important question of financial resources and who pays for housing reconstruction. Financial and natural disasters combine to exacerbate housing dilemmas, particularly for vulnerable populations.* In Chapter 4, Michael Lindell, Wesley Highfield, and Samuel Brody address these issues by focusing on how housing solutions are financed. They specifically focus on hazard insurance and how adverse selection, moral hazards, charity, and concurrent hazards affect the viability of insurance programs. Using the example of the National Flood Insurance Program in the United States, they argue that policy makers need to replace superficial assumptions about "economically rational" decision makers with empirical data by understanding the ways in which people actually decide whether to purchase hazard insurance, how much coverage to buy, and how long to retain their policies. Since personal savings, peer relief, and government funds are generally insufficient to rebuild, hazard insurance needs to be reformed to effectively accelerate post-disaster housing and community recovery.

Addressing pre- and post-disaster vulnerabilities and developing better financing solutions for housing require more effective policies and governance mechanisms. Policies to address post-disaster housing are, however, complex and often difficult to achieve. In Chapter 5, Alka Sapat focuses on several overarching policy challenges in improving housing recovery outcomes using examples from various disasters and countries. Some of the more critical and crosscutting challenges include problems of coordination, silos, and fragmented governance, political considerations, including the salience of pre-disaster planning, time compression, administrative

* Financial crises, such as the 2008 recession which was itself caused by malpractices in the housing finance industry have a large impact on housing; however, since the impact of natural disasters itself is a very large topic, we confine the focus of this book solely to the effects of natural disasters on housing.

accountability, location, and land ownership. Renters, who are often most affected by disaster outcomes are routinely neglected in disaster housing policies and programs. Sapat argues that the effectiveness of actions taken by disaster managers and policy makers are critical to achieving successful housing and community recovery outcomes.

Understanding Housing Recovery in the United States

Chapters in this book also explore how some of the key concepts, concerns, and challenges discussed in Section I play out in different community settings and disasters. Case studies are particularly useful in providing more in-depth understanding of complex issues. The case study approach is increasingly used to understand multifaceted phenomena in their real-life settings (Crowe et al. 2011; Miles et al. 2014) and illuminate factors that facilitate or hinder individual and collective decisions. The case studies in Section II focus on housing recovery in the United States using an eclectic collection of primary and secondary data incorporating the perspectives and lived experiences of those who face the daunting challenges of returning home.

In Chapter 6, Shannon Van Zandt and Madison Sloan compare and contrast housing recovery in a highly physically vulnerable, tourism-based coastal community in Galveston, Texas with an economically depressed, heavily minority area, the Lower Rio Grande Valley in Texas after Hurricanes Dolly and Ike. They find that households most vulnerable to disasters must overcome higher levels of initial damage, have fewer and less dependable forms of assistance, face greater obstacles to using such assistance, and are dependent on a rental housing market that is often blind to low-income housing needs. Social and economic vulnerabilities lead to inequities in the pace and completeness of housing recovery for low-income and minority residents. They argue that more effective pre-disaster land-use and capital-investment planning prioritized by demonstrated need, including assessments of physical and social vulnerability, can improve housing and community recovery outcomes.

Inequities in housing recovery are also manifested in the availability of affordable housing prior to and after disasters. Whether and how much affordable housing gets built following disasters and the factors that influence decision making with respect to reconstruction of affordable housing are explored in Chapter 7. Andrew Rumbach and Carrie Makarewicz examine affordable housing through a case study of the 2013 Colorado floods and focus on three flood-affected communities that lost a significant amount of affordable housing. Using interviews with local, county, and state officials involved in the recovery process, as well as direct observations of recovery housing meetings and events, they find that decisions about affordable housing are driven by local actors and institutions as well as by external grant programs. They also find that a host of factors, including local conditions, land availability, the housing market, government priorities and capabilities, resident support of affordable housing, and the resources, reputations, and commitments of local agencies, affect the reconstruction of affordable housing.

Due to the volume of debris generated, recovery after tornadoes may be different from housing recovery following floods, hurricanes, and storm surge as discussed in the previous two chapters in this section. Nonetheless, the importance of the role played by government agencies and differential levels of vulnerability remains the same regardless of the area or the type of hazard. In studying housing recovery after the 2011 Joplin, Missouri tornado in Chapter 8, Brenda Phillips and Susamma Seeley find that the role of government agencies working in concert with multiple partners was important in facilitating housing recovery. Partners in the recovery process included nongovernmental agencies, volunteer organizations, universities, long-term recovery committees, and faith-based organizations working with governmental agencies. Phillips and Seeley point out that this array of multiple partners and resources are crucial in resolving unmet needs, particularly for more vulnerable segments of the population such as seniors and the disabled. In discussing these issues, Phillips and Seeley also highlight the psychological impacts of losing a home and having to cope with the aftermath of its destruction.

Individual and household perspectives on the impact of disasters on housing are the focus of the case studies presented in the next two chapters. In Chapter 9, Ali Nejat, Souparno Ghosh, Zhen Cong, and Daan Liang use an innovative combination of face-to-face surveys and a vignette questionnaire to elicit household decisions on whether they would rebuild/repair, wait, or relocate, from highly affected households in Staten Island following Hurricane Sandy. They find that individual reactions differed depending on whether they were making decisions based on hypothetical scenarios for others as compared to decisions for their own households. Their findings also reveal the importance of place attachment and the marginal significance of neighborhood recovery actions in affecting household recovery decisions.

Decision-making and individual level preparedness are also the focus of the analysis presented by Brian Gerber in Chapter 10, who uses data from a nation-wide survey of various communities to understand factors affecting preparedness levels and evacuation experiences of those with disabilities. He finds that the presence of disability in a household, Assisted Daily Living limitations, and personal support networks can affect household readiness to deal with sheltering or temporary housing demands during a disaster. These individual experiences can in turn, provide insights into improving emergency management through more inclusive whole community planning approaches, and inform the nature of service assistance needs during large-scale dislocations from disaster.

Housing Recovery in a Global Context

Housing recovery in other countries is often beset by similar problems. However, there are different and myriad other challenges that arise depending on various factors such as the power and resources of the state, levels of economic development, levels of centralization and decentralization of power, and opportunities for community participation. The case studies in Section III provide a more in-depth understanding of housing recovery after earthquakes, tsunami, and typhoon disasters in a sample of communities across the globe—Haiti, India, China, and the Philippines at individual and community levels.

In Chapter 11, Emel Ganapati and Guitele Rahill explore the challenges that disaster survivors face in fragile states like Haiti during early shelter recovery. Using data collected from in-depth interviews, focus groups, participatory site observations, and secondary documents in three socioeconomically diverse communities (Pétion-Ville, Delmas, and Canapé Vert) in Port-au-Prince following the 2010 Haiti earthquake, they find that leadership, social capital, faith, and adaptive flexibility mechanisms helped Haitians overcome their shelter-related challenges.

Perceptions of recovery are also the focus of the discussion presented in Chapter 12 by Sudha Arlikatti and Simon Andrew. They focus on post-disaster rural housing recovery by analyzing the physical improvements to housing and perceptions of recovery in seven coastal villages in South India following the 2004 Indian Ocean tsunami. They used data collected from surveys in 2005 and 2008, and information gleaned from informal conversations with occupants in 2011. They find that while housing reconstruction and rehabilitation programs have provided stronger core-housing units in safer locations, there were marked differences in beneficiaries' perceptions of recovery by housing programs—owner driven *in situ* repair and rebuilding versus donor driven new resettlement housing. Involving beneficiaries in the rebuilding process and explaining the need for mitigation and land-use regulations matter.

The need for greater more inclusive housing recovery planning and more participation by beneficiaries to engender more successful recovery outcomes is also a key finding in a study of post-disaster housing following the Wenchuan earthquake in China, presented by Yang Zhang and William Drake in Chapter 13. Using government documents and interviews collected after the earthquake in Sichuan Province and a case study on housing recovery in two inner city neighborhoods in the city of Dujiangyan, they find that the Chinese Government's fast-paced and intense investment in recovery and redevelopment did lead to quick large-scale housing recovery and significant improvements in physical reconstruction, structural safety, and infrastructure. However, they argue that the pace of social recovery, especially in the face of the Chinese Government's aggressive resettlement and replacement of traditional rural development with high density, urban forms of "modern" living, casts doubts on the success narrative of the Wenchuan earthquake housing recovery. They advocate a more deliberate, immersive, and participatory process would have aided recovery.

Increasing participation also involves more holistic efforts in housing recovery. The impact of disasters on livelihood systems and cultural lifeways is often underemphasized, but these elements are critical to recovery processes (Companion 2015). Housing recovery, particularly relocation, often fails due to the neglect of livelihood systems and socio-cultural factors. In Chapter 14, Kanako Iuchi and Elizabeth Maly look at housing relocation efforts in Tacloban City after the 2013 Typhoon Yolanda (internationally named Haiyan). Through semi-structured interviews and informal conversations with government officials and community members, they find that while there are several steps that governments can take to facilitate housing relocation, relocated populations become more vulnerable over time. Often, housing construction is the central focus in rebuilding and relocation, while the provision of other infrastructure and livelihood support is overlooked. Yet, preventive relocation can only be successful if residents are able to recover their quality of life. They argue then, that it is critical that relocation is treated as a holistic effort; one that includes the development of tight-knit communities as well as housing and infrastructure.

Multiple Dimensions of Recovery

Housing recovery is multifaceted and inextricably linked with other dimensions of community recovery and a multitude of issues, actors, and institutions that can critically affect outcomes for individuals and communities.

The myriad dimensions of housing recovery receive more attention in Section IV, which begins with Chapter 15 by Gonzalo Lizarralde, Fayazi Mahmood, Faten Kikano, and Isabelle Thomas who explore how post-disaster housing reconstruction can either improve living conditions of affected families and decrease their vulnerabilities or it can deteriorate local livelihoods, social fabric, governance structures, household economic conditions, and reduce infrastructure efficiency while increasing urban sprawl. Through a detailed review of case studies conducted by the Canadian Disaster Resilience and Sustainable Reconstruction Research Alliance (Œuvre Durable by its French name) in six countries of the Global South, they reveal drawbacks and opportunities in housing reconstruction after disasters. They discuss nine meta-patterns in the planning and transformation of the built environment that emerge, and argue that key stakeholders often ignore the complexity of the relationships that exist between the natural, socioeconomic, and built environments. Among other aspects that need attention, they point out that the informal sector needs to be considered as an important (and unavoidable) stakeholder in housing development before, during, and after disasters.

The informal sector is also addressed in Chapter 16 by Jennifer Duyne Barenstein who explores how disasters impact informal settlers and their rights to housing. She critically reviews the extent to which various international policies and instruments are reflected in national post-disaster reconstruction practices in supporting informal settlers displaced by disasters. Through case studies using data from secondary sources and field research in various countries including India, Sri Lanka, Indonesia, Argentina, Haiti, and Nicaragua, she examines the achievements and challenges of a wide range of organizations in addressing the housing needs of informal settlers after disasters. The capacity to support informal settlers at all stages of the recovery process is often constrained by insufficient funding and by national governments unwilling to recognize the housing rights of the urban poor. Duyne Barenstein contends that whether and how informal settlers are supported in attaining durable and sustainable housing solutions often depends not so much on the international humanitarian and development community, but on national reconstruction policies, municipal authorities, the capacity of informal communities to organize and struggle for their rights, and on the actions of local nongovernmental organizations (NGOs) and civil society organizations.

The voluntary sector and NGOs have always played an extensive and critical role in disaster response and recovery (Arlikatti et al. 2012; Eikenberry et al. 2007; Flatt and Stys 2013; Jenkins et al. 2015; McCurry 2009; Simo and Bies 2007; Stys 2011). In Chapter 17, Alka Sapat explores the role of voluntary sector organizations in post-disaster housing and focuses on their contributions and the challenges they face in addressing the myriad and multifaceted complexities of disasters and resultant housing dilemmas using examples drawn from various disasters and countries. She contends that while variations exist across NGOs and communities, the critical role played by NGOs in housing recovery can be more effective when they develop long-term sustainable partnerships; understand local political and economic environments, societal and cultural norms, accompanying infrastructure needs, and end-user preferences; and, when they build their own organizational and resilience capacities.

Building organizational capacities to deal with the challenges and dilemmas requires planning. In Chapter 18, Gavin Smith discusses how planning for disaster recovery can help address a number of pre- and post-disaster conditions that influence recovery processes and outcomes at the household and community level and how a review of plan quality elements that comprise good plans provides a contextual vehicle to discuss how post-housing-related issues can be effectively managed. Using case studies, he provides examples of ways to better catalyze the value of recovery planning, and recommends that building and sustaining the collective capacity of networks during the recovery planning process as well as developing actionable pre-disaster recovery plans can proactively tackle housing issues.

The focus on planning is also emphasized in Chapter 19 by John Marshall, Adrienne LaGrange, and Ann-Margaret Esnard who argue that a community's existing laws and law-based programs greatly influence its long-term recovery trajectory. They explore the importance of understanding the critical linkage between "pre-disaster" housing impediments, programs, and policies, and the legal and regulatory challenges urban and coastal communities may face. They discuss examples of legal and regulatory issues as well as considerations and approaches such as residential relocation and "clear" land titles from various countries. While they shed light on how legal tools and strategies can be deployed to promote effective and equitable housing redevelopment decisions, they warn that there is no "one size fits all" approach to ensuring successful housing and recovery.

Key Features of This Book

This book encompasses 19 chapters written by 33 academics and practitioners discussing housing and recovery issues following various types of disasters in different countries across the globe. There is a diversity of disciplines represented in this book based on the backgrounds of the authors, and the intended audience to benefit from the book's content: anthropology, architecture, economics, emergency management, engineering, geography, law, political science, psychology, public administration, public policy, social work, sociology, and urban and regional planning. There are also several types of data collected and used by authors. Primary data collected and utilized include data from interviews, surveys, focus groups, field research, vignette studies, and participant observation. Secondary data include those from academic sources, government reports, media coverage, and other documents. Multiple analytical approaches have been used by various authors, which encompass statistical approaches, content and document analysis, and geographic information systems analysis.

While there is a multitude of perspectives and approaches voiced in this book, there are nonetheless several common themes and threads running across many of the chapters. Among them are the emphasis on *vulnerability and marginalized populations*, including often ignored homeless persons and informal settlers. Socioeconomic vulnerability, housing status, exposure to fast and slow-onset hazards, and repeated disasters in some regions of the world have implications for the type of policies used to address post-disaster housing recovery as demonstrated in several chapters in this book. What is particularly insightful and instructive are the findings from some of the case studies that the provision of post-disaster housing does not necessarily reduce vulnerability; some residents become more vulnerable over time. Repeated and protracted displacement, and resettlement in communities disconnected from traditional livelihoods and social networks, are some of the factors contributing to this problem.

Problems related to vulnerability are compounded by issues related to *location, land tenure, and land-use planning,* which is another theme that is discussed in several chapters. Challenges in locating housing (whether temporary or permanent) range from finding locations that are safe from future hazards, close to livelihoods, and acceptable to beneficiary as well host communities. Chapters in Sections I, II, and IV highlight various aspects of complex historical and regulatory national policies related to land tenure, land rights, and land entitlement, and the implications for residents who seek to relocate after major disasters. Several case studies in Sections II and III make reference to various land-use planning techniques, tools, and initiatives important to post-disaster housing recovery. Pre-disaster community conditions, pre-event housing and inventory assessments, zoning codes, building and urban design codes are part of the toolkit used by local and national planners in pre-disaster planning processes and deliberations.

Other threads running through this book focus on the appropriate role that *government institutions* should play in relation to non-state actors such as *the private and nongovernmental sectors.* Post-disaster housing solutions are typically either seen as the responsibility of individuals, the primary responsibility of government, or best left to market forces to determine. Various chapters in this book show that either all or a combination of all three factors prevail. Where both the private solutions (individuals and markets) and government institutions fail, it is typically the voluntary sector that comes in to respond to unmet needs. While Sections I and IV specifically discuss these issues, the case studies in the United States and globally also deliberate on how the political, policy, and governance challenges surrounding the interaction of these players within communities impact housing recovery.

Finally, this book also discusses how the sustainability of long-term housing solutions is critically dependent on the *participation of the communities* and the *holistic recovery* of communities. The case studies and the other chapters consistently find that the speed of reconstruction or the quality of buildings erected is not sufficient to engender successful housing solutions. More inclusive and participatory community-based approaches tend to have more positive spin-offs and externalities. Coming home needs to be accompanied by community recovery. Attention needs to be paid to community norms and identities, forms of livelihood, demographic and social dimensions, as well as the role of the informal sector, social ties, and place attachment.

Alka Sapat and Ann-Margaret Esnard

REFERENCES

Arendt, L.A. and D.A. Alsek. 2015. *Long-Term Community Recovery from Natural Disasters* (1st Edition). Boca Raton, Florida: CRC Press.

Arlikatti, S., K.C. Bezboruah, and L. Long. 2012. Role of voluntary sector organizations in posttsunami relief: Compensatory or complementary? *Social Development Issues* 34(3): 64–80.

Bates, F.L. and W.G. Peacock. 1987. Disasters and social change. In *The Sociology of Disasters*, R. R. Dynes, B. Demarchi, and C. Pelanda (eds), Milan, Italy: Franco Angeli Press, 291–330.

Blaikie, P., T. Cannoon, I. Davis, and B. Wisner. 1994. *At Risk: Natural Hazards, People's Vulnerability, and Disasters.* New York: Routledge.

Bogard, W.C. 1988. Bringing social theory to hazards research: Conditions and consequences of the mitigation of environmental hazards. *Sociological Perspectives* 31(2): 147–168. doi: 10.2307/1389080.

Bohle, H.G., T.E. Downing, M.J. Watts, and R.S. Chen. 1994. Climate change and social vulnerability: Toward a sociology and geography of food insecurity. *Global Environmental Change* 4(1): 37–48.

Bolin, R. and L. Stanford. 1991. Shelter, housing and recovery: A comparison of US disasters. *Disasters* 15(1): 24–34.

Bolin, R.C. 1986. Disaster impact and recovery: A comparison of black and white victims. *International Journal of Mass Emergencies and Disasters* 4: 35–50.

Comerio, M. 1998. *Disaster Hits Home: New Policy for Urban Housing Recovery.* Berkeley, California: University of California Press.

Companion, M. ed. 2015. *Disaster's Impact on Livelihood and Cultural Survival: Losses, Opportunities, and Mitigation.* Boca Raton, Florida: CRC Press.

Crowe, S., K. Creswell, A. Robertson, G. Huby, A. Avery, and A. Sheikh. 2011. *BMC Medical Research Methodology* 11: 100. http://www.biomedcentral.com/1471-2288/11/100.

Cutter, S.L., B.J. Boruff, and W.L. Shirley. 2003. Social vulnerability to environmental hazards. *Social Science Quarterly* 84(2): 242–261.

Dow, K. 1992. Exploring differences in our common future(s): The meaning of vulnerability of global environmental change. *Geoforum* 23(3): 417.

Dow, K. and T.E. Downing. 1995. Vulnerability research: Where things stand. *Human Dimensions Quarterly* 1: 3–5.

Downing, T.E. 1991. Vulnerability to hunger and coping with climate change in Africa. *Global Environmental Change* 1: 365–380.

Eikenberry, A.M., V. Arroyave, and T. Cooper. 2007. Administrative failure and the international NGO response to Hurricane Katrina. *Public Administration Review* 67(1): 160–70.

Flatt, V.B. and J.J. Stys. 2013. Long term recovery in disaster response and the role of nonprofits. *Oñati Socio-Legal Series* 3(2): 346–62.

Internal Displacement Monitoring Centre (IDMC). 2013. *Global Estimates 2012: People Displaced by Disasters.* Geneva, Switzerland: IDMC.

International Federation of Red Cross and Red Crescent Societies (IFRC). 2012. *World Disasters Report 2012, Focus on Forced Migration and Displacement.* Geneva, Switzerland: IFRC.

Jenkins, P., T. Lambeth, K. Mosby, and B. Van Brown. 2015. Local nonprofit organizations in a post-Katrina landscape help in a context of recovery. *American Behavioral Scientist* 59(10): 1263–1277.

Laska, S. and B. Morrow. 2006. Social vulnerabilities and Hurricane Katrina: An unnatural disaster in New Orleans. *Marine Technology and Society Journal* 40(4): 16–26.

McCurry, R.A. 2009. *Dependence on Non-Profits during Major Disaster Relief: A Risky Dilemma*. Washington, DC: The George Washington University Homeland Security Policy Institute.

Miles, M.B., A.M. Huberman, and J. Saldaña. 2014. *Qualitative Data Analysis: A Methods Sourcebook*. Thousand Oaks, California: SAGE Publications, Inc.

National Research Council (NRC). 2011. *Building Disaster Resilience through Public–Private Collaboration*. Washington, DC: National Academies Press, National Research Council, Committee on Private–Public Sector Collaboration to Enhance Community Disaster Resilience.

Peacock, W.G., N. Dash, and Y. Zhang. 2007. Sheltering and housing recovery following disaster. In *Handbook of Disaster Research*, H. Rodriguez, E.L. Quarantelli, and R.R. Dynes (eds), New York: Springer, 258–274.

Peacock, W.G., S. Van Zandt, D. Henry, H. Grover, and W. Highfield. 2012. Social vulnerability and Hurricane Ike: Using social vulnerability mapping to enhance coastal community resilience in Texas. In *After Ike: Severe Storm Prediction, Impact, and Recovery on the Texas Gulf Coast*, P.B. Bedient (ed.), College Station, Texas: Texas A&M University Press, 66–81.

Peacock, W.G., S. Van Zandt, Y. Zhang, and W.E. Highfield. 2014. Inequities in long-term housing recovery after disasters. *Journal of the American Planning Association* 80(4): 356–371.

Phillips, B. 2016. *Disaster Recovery* (2nd edn). Boca Raton, Florida: CRC Press.

Quarantelli, E. 1982. General and particular observations on sheltering and housing in American disasters. *Disasters* 6: 277–281.

Sapat, A., C.M. Mitchell, Y. Li, and A.-M. Esnard. 2011. Policy learning: Katrina, Ike and post-disaster housing. *International Journal of Mass Emergencies and Disasters* 29(1): 26–56.

Simo, G. and A.L. Bies. 2007. The role of nonprofits in disaster response: An expanded model of cross-sector collaboration. *Public Administration Review* 67(s1): 125–142.

Stys, J.J. 2011. *Non-Profit Involvement in Disaster Response and Recovery*. Prepared for the Center for Law, Environment, Adaptation and Resources (CLEAR) at the University of North Carolina School of Law, Chapel Hill, North Carolina (online) URL: http://www.law.unc.edu/documents/clear/nonprofit.pdf.

Zhang, Y. and W.G. Peacock. 2009. Planning for housing recovery? Lessons learned from Hurricane Andrew. *Journal of the American Planning Association* 76(1): 5–24.

Section I

Context and Concepts

1 Disaster Recovery and Community Renewal
Housing Approaches

Mary C. Comerio

CONTENTS

1.1 INTRODUCTION

Jobs and housing are often cited as the key elements of disaster recovery. Individuals and communities struck by an earthquake, hurricane, or other calamity cannot "return to normal" unless people have means of supporting themselves and places to live. For residents and for the community as a whole, however, normalcy also requires that community services such as roads, bridges, and the utility infrastructure be functional; schools, health care, and social services be available; and banks, businesses, and governments be functioning. The way recovery is defined, the way it is financed, and the metrics used to evaluate its success or failure are critical to the kinds of assistance policies governments devise.

The concept of disaster resilience can be defined simply as the capacity to rebound from future disasters. Several efforts are under way in the United States and globally among researchers and policymakers to develop the means of measuring and monitoring community resilience. Although no single model can quantify disaster resilience, the growing consensus is that resilience is a multifaceted concept, with social, economic, institutional, infrastructural, ecological, and community dimensions (Folk 2006; Gunderson et al. 2010; National Research Council [NRC] 2010; Peacock et al. 2008). Several sets of resilience indicators or attributes can serve as baselines for measuring recovery progress and outcomes after a disaster event

(Bruneau et al. 2003; Community and Regional Resilience Institute [CARRI] 2009; Cutter et al. 2010; Miles and Chang 2006; Norris et al. 2008; SPUR 2009–2010; Twigg 2009). Community functions such as infrastructure, housing, economic viability, and social conditions are typically listed as performance indicators. This excellent work on resilience has advanced understanding of the multifaceted components of recovery and provided metrics for measurement, but there is a need to translate academic concepts into programs to help people in affected communities and local governments and to redefine policies in agencies at the national government level.

Theory, unfortunately, is way ahead of practice. Even with the Federal Emergency Management Agency's (FEMA's) development of the National Disaster Recovery Framework, several problems make implementing forward-thinking ideas on resilience and recovery problematic.

1. *Lack of preparedness for recovery.* With the exception of a few cities in Japan and California, most jurisdictions and most individuals are not prepared for any major disaster or national emergency. Not only are individuals unprepared, communities are largely uninsured and have unrealistic expectations that government will make them whole. Jaffe and Russell (2013) identified four major trends in the economics of catastrophes since World War II: (a) the number and severity of catastrophic events is increasing; (b) insurance markets that cover these risks have steadily disappeared; (c) government relief has expanded significantly; and (d) public- and private-sector actions to mitigate risks, including avoiding development in risky areas and reinforcing structures, has been limited. Although many societies invest a great deal of effort in teaching the basics of emergency preparedness (such as "duck and cover"), those same societies have invested little in serious planning for recovery from disasters.
2. *Lack of local implementation capacity.* Like individuals, local governments are pushed beyond their capacities during and after a disaster. In normal times, cities collect taxes, manage traffic, repair potholes, and balance the concerns of residents and businesses. None have financial reserves for disasters. City government agencies know how to regulate for planning and building, but most do not have the staff to think in terms of redevelopment, economic development, or new housing models—all of which are critical after a disaster. City governments often lose their tax base after major disasters, and they struggle to provide basic services while attempting to negotiate national government funding and manage a recovery process for citizens and business.
3. *Lack of funding.* In the United States, the national government supports the restoration of highways and public infrastructure, but government funding to assist with housing—which typically represents 50% of the value of any disaster loss—is very limited. Funding is also lacking to support the human effort needed to implement a truly coordinated recovery effort. In both developed and developing countries, disaster recovery aid is often narrowly targeted toward building physical facilities, particularly infrastructure, without comprehensive housing, social, and economic development efforts.

4. *Antiquated and inflexible government programs.* Most countries that have disaster aid legislation will find that it is based on historic events that do not reflect current social or economic circumstances or levels of urbanization. In the United States, for one example among many, the Stafford Act* allows only for the federal government to provide "temporary housing." As a result, an idea such as the Katrina Cottages—small starter homes designed in the wake of Hurricane Katrina in 2005 at a lower cost than temporary trailers—could not be funded under the Stafford Act. Although an Affordable Housing Pilot Program responsive to the Katrina Cottages idea was implemented in different ways in four states following Katrina, only a relatively small number were built, and the idea of cost-efficient and permanent government-funded housing would not be possible in the future without special congressional authorization.
5. *Poverty and dilapidated public institutions.* Whether in Haiti, Latin America, Africa, Asia, or parts of North America and Europe, health care, education, clean water, and other basic public services are simply not accessible for the world's poor citizens. Disasters in these settings cause what Farmer (2011) calls "acute-on-chronic" problems that humanitarian aid cannot begin to resolve.

Recognizing the problems with disaster recovery implementation is a first step to thinking about how to operationalize resilience ideas. Scholars involved with resilience in relation to complex adaptive systems increasingly avoid the use of the term "recovery" and prefer the concepts "renewal," "regeneration," and "reorganization" (Bellwood et al. 2004). If resilience is considered as an approach to disaster recovery, it can become a valuable tool for policies that support sustainable redevelopment.

1.2 HOUSING AS A CORE ELEMENT OF RECOVERY AND RENEWAL

Housing is a core element of daily life and a critical component of any disaster recovery effort. In most parts of the world, housing is privately owned and, as such, housing recovery is managed differently than recovery in the public sector (roads, schools, hospitals, and government and cultural facilities). Housing recovery, however, is critically interdependent with recovery of those public-sector facilities. Until the 1970s, no US disaster assistance policies provided any funding for housing recovery. Later, small programs were designed to assist homeowners with Small Business Administration (SBA) loans and modest FEMA grants for limited repairs, but national policies assume that private funds, insurance, or both will be used for housing repair (Comerio 1998). In the United States, limited US Department of Housing and Urban Development involvement in public housing repairs and block grants for rental housing repairs are insufficient to meet the needs in contemporary society.

* *Robert T. Stafford Disaster Relief and Emergency Assistance Act.* Public Law 93–288.

In the United States, policymakers assume that the private property market will adapt in post-disaster situations. Economic conditions since the financial crisis of 2008, however, suggest that markets alone would not be able to solve post-disaster housing reconstruction. The nation now has 10.8 million homeowners (heavily concentrated in disaster-prone regions such as California and Florida) whose home value is less than their mortgage (Zillow Real Estate Research 2013). These homeowners are not likely to have disaster insurance—only 11% of California homeowners have earthquake insurance (Jones 2014)—and, should a disaster occur, would not qualify for SBA loans. Typical FEMA individual assistance programs would not cover their repair costs. Without assistance, would homeowners abandon their homes? Where would they go?

U.S. policies furthermore assume that renters can find alternate rentals, but, in what has become a highly urbanized society, multifamily losses will leave many renters homeless while building owners make investment decisions that may not include replacement housing. In the San Francisco Bay Area, after the 1989 Loma Prieta earthquake, it took 10 years to replace 75% of the affordable housing lost. It took 4 years to rebuild middle-class apartments lost in Los Angeles after the 1994 Northridge earthquake, and it took 7–10 years to rebuild housing in Kobe, Japan, after the 1995 Hanshin-Awaji earthquake. In New Orleans, the recovery since Hurricane Katrina made landfall in 2005 has been extremely uneven, with high out-migration, limited home repairs, high vacancy rates, and very few new rental units replaced (San Francisco Planning and Urban Research [SPUR] 2012).

In San Francisco, where 75% of the city dwellers are renters, 25% of the city's housing would be rendered uninhabitable in a magnitude (M) 7.25 earthquake on the San Andreas Fault. The city does not have enough shelter capacity, much less interim-housing capacity, for that population (SPUR 2012). This shortage is not unique to San Francisco. In urban settings around the world, renters and squatters make up 30–70% of the housing market (Mukherji 2010, 2011) and have limited capacity to find alternate housing after disasters.

Everyone who loses their home in a disaster has needs greater than shelter. They need to replace their possessions—clothes, medicine, cars, bicycles, documents, and so on. They need to know if they have a job, if their children will have a school, if an injured family member can get medical care, or if health care will be available for chronic and routine needs. If they are homeowners, they depend on rulings from local government regarding the safety of their dwelling and permits for repairs, if they can finance the repairs. Legal renters have to find alternatives (with some federal assistance), but shadow renters (families who double up, those in short-term single-room occupancy rentals, squatters, immigrants, and so on) also need alternatives and have no status in government programs. They can seek help only from churches and nongovernmental organizations (NGOs).

All of them, however, need to decide whether to stay (rebuild or find alternative accommodations) or to leave the disaster area, and they all need information. What they need is an understanding of what help is available to them and what public decisions will affect their private decisions. Individuals' capacity to stay in a disaster-affected jurisdiction is as much about their jobs and the availability of services as it is about how to solve their shelter problem. Will the incentive to stay be greater if individuals and families are engaged in a community process? Will the programs enhance individual and community resilience? Examples from Chile and New Zealand, discussed in the next section, represent two different approaches. In Chile, the national effort to rebuild low- and moderate-income housing is an attempt to improve housing standards and to promote community empowerment and economic development. In New Zealand, the availability of government insurance is funding repairs at the same time that government policies are focused on regulating land use and improving building standards to inform individual decisions.

1.3 LESSONS FROM CHILE AND NEW ZEALAND

Comparing the disaster losses and recovery programs of different countries is extremely difficult when local conditions make each situation unique, but some generalizations can be made. The greatest loss of life tends to be concentrated in developing countries, whereas substantial property losses typically are a result of urban disasters in developed countries. The scale of housing loss is a combination of the disaster's intensity, the level of building code enforcement, and the quality of construction. Housing recovery (and recovery in general) is often a combination of a proactive government role in the reconstruction process, funding, community participation, and resilient improvements in infrastructure and planning.

To measure the success of recovery, it is important to look at different scales of intervention over different timeframes. Success in recovery will depend first on the scale at which that recovery is measured: at the level of the individual or household, at the level of the neighborhood or community, or at the level of the city or region. Success in recovery will also depend on the timeframe in which recovery is measured: in years or in decades. Finally, the degree of success in recovery will depend on the perspective of the evaluator: a family, a community, a government, an outside funder, or an independent evaluator (Comerio 2005).

With the caveat that comparisons are difficult and tempered by differing perspectives and timeframes, it can be useful to compare Chile's and New Zealand's housing recoveries, along with those in other countries with a strong central government role in recovery management, with housing recoveries in countries characterized by a more limited government role. Table 1.1 provides a comparison of losses in six recent disasters (see Table 1.1). Three recoveries (in Chile, China, and New Zealand) had strong national government leadership and three (Haiti, Japan, and the United States) had more limited government roles. Note that all the countries listed, except Haiti, have building codes that are similar to those in the United States, although construction practices and oversight vary.

1.4 HOUSING RECOVERY IN CHILE

On Saturday, February 27, 2010, at 3:34 a.m. local time, an M8.8 earthquake struck the south central region of Chile. The earthquake produced a tsunami that caused major damage over 630 km of coastline. The earthquake and tsunami impacted 75% of the population of Chile, which is concentrated in six central regions. Overall, some 370,000 housing units (10% of the housing in the six regions) were affected. Of those units, 220,000 (60%) were rebuilt with government assistance and 150,000 (40%)

TABLE 1.1
Comparison of Losses in Selected Recent Disasters

	Strong National Government Role in Recovery			Limited National Government Role in Recovery		
	Chile	China	New Zealand	Haiti	Japan	United States
	M8.8 Earthquake and Tsunami, 2010	M7.9 Sichuan Earthquake, 2008	M7.1 & M6.3 Canterbury/Christchurch Earthquakes, 2010–2011	M7.0 Port-au-Prince Earthquake, 2010	M9.0 Earthquake and Tsunami, 2011	Hurricane Katrina, 2005
Damage value ($ billions)	$30	$30–50	$40	$12	$300+	$80–150
Housing units lost[a] (thousands)	370	5000	17	300+	113[b]	500
Deaths	526	90,000	184	316,000	19,000	1970

Note: M = Magnitude.

[a] Housing units lost is an attempt to quantify those units that were uninhabitable after a disaster. The number of units damaged is much greater in all cases.

[b] Plus 82,000 evacuated because of nuclear radiation.

were repaired or rebuilt privately, often with insurance. Of the 220,000 units targeted for government assistance, 109,000 involved repairs of damaged homes and 113,000 required rebuilding (Ministry of Housing and Urban Development (MINVU) 2010). Within a few months after the earthquake, Chile developed a national reconstruction plan that required special legislation and funding through various business taxes and (unaffected) property tax increases. The plan covered major sectors, including infrastructure, hospitals, schools, and so on. Housing, a central element of the plan, was managed by the Ministry of Housing and Urban Development. MINVU, whose mission is to improve the quality of housing for vulnerable populations, thought the earthquake and tsunami overturned 4 years of housing program efforts to reduce the already existing housing deficit (Comerio 2013).

The reconstruction plan was aimed at low- and middle-income populations (annual incomes of <$12,000 per family per year and home values of <$88,000). The process involved coordinating more than 239 municipalities and included reconstructing temporary and permanent housing, urban planning, and reconstructing historic heritage. More than 70% of the homes to be rebuilt were on sites where the beneficiaries had a house before the disaster, which meant that, in Chile, recovery policy was focused on keeping families in their communities, limiting greenfield developments, and improving seismic and thermal rebuilding standards in rural and urban localities.

A variety of options were available to qualified families: funds to repair an existing house, to acquire a new house, to build a new house on the owners' land, to build a house on a new site, or to build units in social housing (see Table 1.2). Repair funds were dispersed in three increments (of 30%, 30%, and 40%) to ensure that funds were used for construction. Landowners needing new homes could choose from models based on presentations from several predominantly local builders, some of whom offered prefabricated homes, some of whom offered site-built homes, and all of whom MINVU pre-certified for engineering standards. After the community voted, the builder received the contract for that community—providing some advantages

TABLE 1.2
Breakdown of Number of Units by Programs

	Problem		
Approach	**Repairable House, Landowner**	**Nonrepairable House, Landowner**	**Non-Landowner**
Family led	12,000 use banks of materials for repairs	3000 acquisitions 3000 do-it-yourself buildings	16,000 acquisition subsidies
State led	32,000 social condominium building repairs	8000 social condominium demolitions/rebuildings	30,000 new developments
Third-party intermediary	84,000 repair subsidies	48,000 precertified houses	4000 urban densifications

Source: MINVU (Government of Chile, Ministry of Housing and Urban Development). 2012. *Interviews with Senior Personnel.* Santiago, Chile: Ministry of Housing and Urban Development.

of scale for builders in remote regions and encouraging competition among builders. Families could also add additional rooms or special finishes after the base unit was provided.

Families without land were accommodated in temporary camps while social condominium projects were designed and completed. These projects typically improved on previous housing quality in terms of unit size (from 38 to 50 square meters), services, and site amenities. In cities such as Talca, where 30% of the housing stock was damaged, additional subsidies enabled builders to work on inner-city sites in an attempt to counteract the rush to build on the periphery. In coastal cities, new master plans were developed for tsunami protection, infrastructure, and urban relocations.

Within 1 year after the earthquake, 60% of the government subsidies were allocated, 35% of the housing was in construction, 5% of the new housing was complete, and all insurance payouts were complete. After 2 years, all the subsidies were allocated and about 70% of the home repairs were complete, but only 10% of the new construction was complete, although 45% had started. After 3 years, 68% of the government-funded housing was complete and, at the fourth anniversary, in February 2014, nearly all 220,000 units were complete (Comerio 2013).

The Chilean government's housing program demonstrates an effort to combine new, safe building technologies with local vernacular lifestyles and to improve the welfare standards for a significant population. The program is also remarkable because it reflects a policy that kept most of the reconstruction as part of the urban fabric instead of in greenfield developments. It was conceptualized and funded at the national level, but local and regional agencies handled management and implementation—with oversight from local architects and engineers and construction competitively bid by local builders. Plans for hazard abatement were integrated into coastal redevelopment, and efforts were made to rebuild with greater density to counteract exurban development. What is important to success in the Chile case is the combination of political will, funding, strong leadership, flexibility in adapting existing programs, and professional best practices (Comerio 2013). The overall program was extraordinarily successful in terms of replacement housing, improved building standards, improved resilience for future disasters, and maintained community cohesion.

1.5 HOUSING RECOVERY IN NEW ZEALAND

In the early hours of Saturday, September 4, 2010, people in Christchurch and the surrounding Canterbury region of New Zealand were surprised by an M7.1 earthquake, the most damaging earthquake to hit the country since 1931. The epicenter was located west of the city which experienced moderate shaking levels, but the earthquake caused major damage because liquefaction and lateral spreading affected sewer and water lines and damaged home foundations. The earthquake caused significant nonstructural damage but limited structural damage to buildings throughout Christchurch. This event was followed by thousands of aftershocks (Geonet 2012). The most damaging occurred on February 22, 2011, when a shallow M6.3 earthquake devastated the central business district and caused widespread foundation movement and extensive utility loss across the city, with the heaviest liquefaction damage in the eastern suburbs.

Christchurch, a city of about 400,000 people and the largest city on the South Island, has a housing stock composed primarily of well-built, single-family, wood-frame homes, with only a smattering of condominiums and apartments. Approximately 87% of the homes in greater Christchurch were damaged. Of those, 30% had major damage and 70% sustained minor damage (Earthquake Engineering Research Institute [EERI] 2011; Earthquake Commission [EQC] 2012; Markum 2012). In most cases, liquefaction and subsidence were the predominant causes of damage and ongoing problems. In a country with a population of only four million, the national government took a proactive role in recovery. It established the Canterbury Earthquake Recovery Authority (CERA) to act as facilitator and coordinator, particularly for planning and implementing the downtown and infrastructure recovery. The government insurance program, the EQC,* managed residential claims. EQC provides earthquake and fire insurance that is required with every mortgage. Approximately 95% of New Zealand homeowners have EQC-backed earthquake insurance coverage.

At the time of the earthquakes, an EQC insurance policy cost homeowners $67.50 NZ per year and provided protection of up to $100,000 NZ for a dwelling (building) and $20,000 NZ for contents (personal belongings). If the site was destroyed (originally conceptualized for landslides, but applicable in the liquefaction zones), an amount for the land lost could also be added. When the actual damage was beyond the EQC limit, homeowners were responsible for the difference, either from savings or additional private insurance (Earthquake Engineering Research Institute [EERI] 2010).

Although the EQC was well capitalized, the courts ruled that claims from each event must be covered separately, which led to a situation in which EQC was managing more than five times the number of claims as there were damaged homes. The claims furthermore had to be apportioned over 12 different events among EQC, primary insurers, and reinsurers (King et al. 2014). At the end of May 2013, 1000 days after the first earthquake, only 45% of the residential claims were settled (Gates 2013). Although the funding for repairs will ultimately be available to homeowners, the settlement process has been incredibly complicated, not only by the number of events and the apportionment of claims, but also by government decisions to limit development in liquefaction zones and require improved building standards for foundations in large portions of the city (MBIE 2013).

Land was zoned red (no rebuilding allowed), orange (further study needed), or green (rebuilding allowed) based on geotechnical studies and assessments of where utilities could be replaced. More than 7000 homes in the red zones were offered a buyout package to leave their unsalvageable houses. The government bought their land (more than 700 ha, or 2.7 square miles), which is now subject to an increased threat of river and ocean flooding. Another 2500 homes in the orange zone were on hold for many months, pending further study. The Department of Building and Housing subdivided the green zone into three subzones. There, 10,000–15,000 homes in Technical Category (TC) 3 will require substantial foundation work to

* In 1945, the government established an insurance program to protect its residents from the financial impacts of war. Later, it repurposed this program as coverage for natural catastrophes such as earthquakes, landslides, tsunamis, volcanic eruptions, hydrothermal activities, and floods.

be considered habitable. The homeowners in TC3 homes are afraid they will not be able to afford the added cost of complex structural foundation repairs, which are not covered by insurance settlements. They are also concerned they may not be able to sell a TC3 home in the future (Markum 2012).

TC1 homeowners are free to rebuild according to the basic building code, but TC2 homeowners will have to have foundation plans reviewed. Despite homeowner anxiety, these engineering standards are critical to the city's long-term resilience. They represent a tough but important decision on the part of CERA to enact realistic standards for long-term land use given the effects on land and elevation changes resulting from liquefaction.

In the Christchurch, New Zealand case, the government acted quickly to establish CERA, recognizing the need for national government leadership in a disaster that caused losses of 20% of the national gross domestic product (GDP). Although the government was comfortable with the capacity of insurance to fund the housing recovery, no one quite realized how complex administering the staggering number of claims over multiple events with multiple payers would be. The longer timeframe and extra costs (higher repair costs for foundations, higher housing costs for those having to move) are pushing development to the outskirts of the city at the same time that civic leaders hope to entice development back into the downtown area. For residents, the 3- to 5-year wait for payment from insurance claims combined with rezoning and foundation standards are sources of considerable stress. Overall, the country has done remarkably well in organizing a recovery effort and maintaining extremely transparent processes. The Christchurch lesson, however, is that insurance should not be the sole pre-disaster recovery finance plan.

1.6 GOVERNMENT RECOVERY MANAGEMENT IN OTHER RECENT EVENTS

Other nations have had differing approaches to housing recovery. The M7.9 Sichuan earthquake of May 12, 2008, in western China caused extensive damage in a large and remote region, destroying some five million homes. As a nation, China has stringent building codes, but regulations in the Sichuan region were less vigorously enforced, resulting in a high death toll. The central government took an active role, requiring wealthier eastern provinces to contribute 1% of their local GDP for 3 years to the recovery, in a program in which damaged cities were twinned with contributors. As is common in China, planning and central management were used to develop new towns and large-scale housing construction sites. The goal of moving families out of temporary housing after two winters meant little time to review building codes, little time to consult impacted residents about their desires or needs, and little environmental review of site selection (Cui et al. 2011).

In addition, no real choice of housing type or location was available to families. China's strong emphasis on expediency may have compromised overall construction quality and limited integration with jobs and social services. Thus, whereas the central government of China focused on a massive and speedy rebuilding program, it lost opportunities for sustainable development and hazards mitigation and opportunities to reduce social vulnerability through coordinated efforts in jobs, health care, and other services. Victims furthermore had little choice in their housing options, and many families were separated because the new housing was not near jobs.

The April 6, 2009 M6.3 earthquake in the Abruzzi region of Italy devastated 49 small towns and the central city of L'Aquila, leaving more than 60,000 people homeless. Within 6 months, the national government built base-isolated housing for 15,000 people on a variety of sites in the region. Intended as long-term temporary housing, the units will be repurposed as student housing after 20 years (Calvi 2010). Although the effort was critical for many families with no housing options, larger recovery efforts have stalled for lack of funding. Families who did not receive the new housing lived in hotels and coastal towns (2 hours away) for 2–3 years, and many have relocated permanently. University students commute 2 hours from Avenzano. After 5 years, some rebuilding has begun on the outskirts of L'Aquila, but it is unclear how the university, the tourist industry, or local business will support the larger community recovery without greater housing stability.

Other examples of strong central government recovery management come from efforts after earthquakes in Turkey (e.g., the 1999 Kocaeli and Düzce earthquakes) and in India (e.g., the 1993 Maharashtra and 2001 Gujarat earthquakes). In these cases, World Bank funding was channeled through national and state governments to support rebuilding programs (Mukherji 2010, 2011). Although the finance mechanisms were different, the approaches were similar to those in China and Italy, with heavy investment in replacement units in new developments. Some limited efforts by NGOs engaged small subsets of the affected population in self-building and repair programs.

In nearly all these cases, governments used existing agencies and programs to deliver housing after disasters. Some, as in Sichuan, China, and L'Aquila, Italy, were highly centralized with few opportunities for housing choice or participation in planning by the citizenry, whereas others provided varying degrees of flexibility and housing choice to earthquake victims. For the more recent events, it will be valuable to reexamine the relationship between housing construction and community economic and social stability 10 years after the event to see how the impacted populations have fared.

1.7 LIMITED GOVERNMENT MANAGEMENT WITH PRIVATE INVESTMENT

The United States and Japan are similar in their approaches to a more limited role for government in disaster recovery, with a focus on public funding primarily for infrastructure, limited government support for housing and private-sector recovery, and limited disaster insurance for homes.

Although Hurricane Sandy (which devastated portions of New York and New Jersey in October 2012) is now considered the largest US disaster, it is too soon to assess recovery efforts, and it is more useful to review the aftermath of Hurricane Katrina, which devastated New Orleans and the Gulf Coast in August 2005. The damage was distributed over a large geographic area, but New Orleans lost 100,000 units (50% of city households) of the approximately 400,000 units damaged across the region. The city did not have enough capacity to provide temporary housing (such as mobile homes and trailers), and many families were evacuated to other cities and states (Olshansky and Johnson 2010).

Flood insurance did not cover all the storm damage for homeowners who had insurance, because storm surge was not covered, and many homeowners who were behind levee walls did not have insurance because they were not in the designated flood plain. Politics, at all levels of government, hampered government assistance programs. Housing repairs and reconstruction required substantial private investment, and relatively little low-income and multifamily housing was rebuilt. New Orleans now has about 25% fewer habitable housing units than it had before the storm. Since Hurricane Sandy came ashore, similar issues have come up in New York and New Jersey, where public investment in infrastructure will encourage private investment in high-income areas but leave lower income regions with few options for recovery finance.

Japan's March 11, 2011 M9.0 Great Eastern Japan earthquake and tsunami devastated a large coastal region, similar in scale to the region affected in the Chile earthquake. Because of the additional complexity created by damage to the Fukushima Daiichi Nuclear Power Station, housing recovery will go beyond the replacement of disaster losses to include long-term evacuation from undamaged communities affected by fallout. With limited insurance for homes, declining economies, an aging population in coastal fishing villages, and complex social adjustments for nuclear-displaced families, the recovery will be prolonged and require a combination of public and private investment. Coastal planning, similar to that undertaken in Chile to mitigate tsunami hazards, has been completed, but decision making, distribution of funding, and plan implementation are taking place at the central government, prefecture, and local municipality levels without good coordination (Maki 2012).

Past events in the United States and Japan—the 1989 M7.1 Loma Prieta (San Francisco Bay Area) earthquake, the 1994 M6.8 Northridge (Los Angeles area) earthquake, and the 1995 M7.2 Hanshin-Awaji (Kobe, Japan) earthquake—discussed subsequently—demonstrate the outcomes from a limited government approach to housing recovery.

Some 25 years after the Loma Prieta earthquake, major investments in public infrastructure have brought about the transformation of the San Francisco waterfront (resulting from the demolition of the Embarcadero freeway) and the rebuilding of the bay bridge as well as museum, cultural, and civic buildings. The Hayes Valley neighborhood was also revitalized, with the replacement of the damaged Central Freeway with a boulevard design. By contrast, only 75% of the total housing destroyed by the earthquake was replaced within 10 years after the event. High-income areas recovered quickly, but many residents of low-income, single-room occupancy hotels and apartments were left homeless after the Loma Prieta earthquake. The time-consuming repair and replacement of these units were carried out largely by nonprofit housing groups, which meant that no additional units of government-subsidized affordable housing were added in the decade after the earthquake (Association of Bay Area Governments [ABAG] 2000; Comerio 1998).

After the Northridge earthquake, nearly 300,000 owners of damaged single-family homes made claims on their earthquake insurance; repairs required 2–5 years to complete. Rebuilding multifamily housing was more difficult. Two-thirds of the 59,000 multifamily units declared uninhabitable required at least 5 years for repairs, and the remaining one-third were abandoned or torn down (Comerio 1998; Comerio and HR&A 1996). High rental vacancies in the San Fernando Valley, and in much of the City of Los Angeles at the time of the earthquake, provided families with relocation options, so people were not displaced. The rebuilt apartments typically served newcomers to the area.

In Kobe, some 400,000 housing units were damaged or destroyed. The government provided 48,300 temporary units, which were occupied for 6–8 years after the event. A complex planning process involved a variety of land use and zoning adjustments, which were effective but time consuming, to aid the rebuilding process. The government set a target of 125,000 replacement housing units, of which 38,600 were designated for low-income people. The "Phoenix Plan" stated that two-thirds of the new units were to be built by the public sector and one-third by the private sector. After 5 years, private-sector housing was being built much faster than public-sector housing, particularly in outlying areas (Olshansky et al. 2005; Preuss 1998). Although the national government ultimately met the overall housing replacement goal, many earthquake victims were displaced, and new housing in Kobe served a gentrified population. Some 10% of Kobe's population left the city, and it took 10 years for the population to return to pre-disaster levels (Maki 2012).

The United States and Japan are developed nations that make some investment in post-disaster housing, but their policies suggest that they are willing to accept a greater reliance on the private sector for disaster recovery, even if that recovery is uneven across income groups. In developing countries, a limited government role in disaster recovery can extend the hardships for disaster victims.

The devastating losses in Port-au-Prince, Haiti, from the January 12, 2010 M7.0 earthquake—in terms of the number of deaths and the physical losses in housing, schools, hospitals, and public buildings—extend to the capacity to manage the country. Haiti lost a significant portion of its weak national government in the earthquake and was already dependent on NGOs for many social services (Farmer 2011). For any developing country, the losses incurred in natural disasters are in part products of their pre-disaster conditions—poverty and lack of jobs, education, and training. After a disaster, the problems are often compounded by the unintended consequences of international aid. In Haiti, less than 1% of the aid went to the public sector; yet, long-term recovery requires a functioning public sector. An NGO can build a school or a clinic, but the building is of limited use without a public mechanism to pay teachers or nurses.

Only 3% of the donor funds were spent on permanent housing (Sontag 2012), and, as of April 2013, individual households had constructed nearly 10 times as many housing units as had international agencies. Now 4 1/2 years after the earthquake, 172,000 residents are still in tent camps (Konotchick 2013), and much remains to be done in addition to providing housing, including resolving landownership, developing public services (water, sanitation, education, and health care), providing job training, and developing the economy.

1.8 COMPARISON OF APPROACHES

When the housing recovery in a variety of countries is reviewed, two metrics stand out: (1) a strong government role in funding, management, and coordination improves housing reconstruction and (2) more individual choice in housing combined with citizen participation in larger planning processes improves citizen recovery.

The chart in Figure 1.1 provides a way to look at the balance between government roles and community participation in various recovery efforts (Comerio 2012). The placement of each country is based on the author's judgment, but the aim is to represent the variety of approaches used (see Figure 1.1). The chart shows that Chile and New Zealand have combined both "top-down" and "bottom-up" approaches, providing government leadership and funding along with community empowerment in decision making. It is important to recognize that these approaches are not mutually exclusive and can be combined effectively.

By contrast, China and Italy took strong government leadership roles in providing replacement housing but did not engage local communities in most aspects of the decision making. Turkey and India had mixed programs—with some housing developed by government in large tracts and some village programs in which NGOs worked with residents on self-help construction. The United States and Japan provided strong leadership during the emergency phase and funded some aspects of recovery, such as infrastructure and public facilities, but left most of the housing reconstruction to the private market. Haiti's weak government and high poverty levels limited recovery from both perspectives.

In the future, countries with major housing losses in a disaster can learn from the experience of others and attempt to find the "sweet spot" that provides the best of government management, for expediency and flexibility, and incorporates opportunities for citizens to take some control over their own recovery, with housing choice

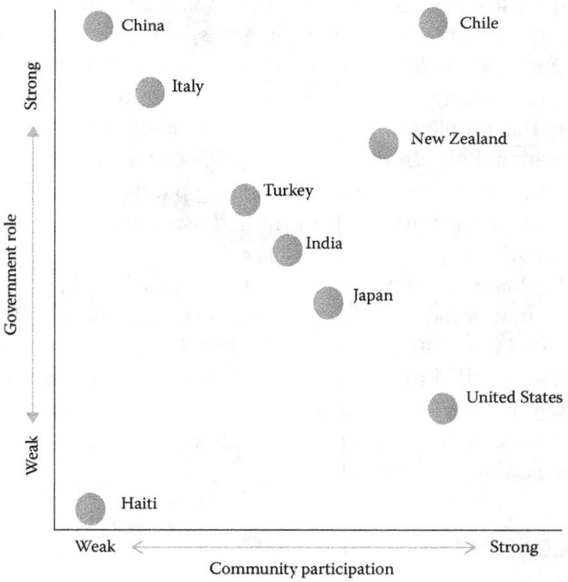

FIGURE 1.1 Comparison of recovery management approaches.

and participation in plans for the community's future. In this regard, Chile's performance stands out.

1.9 CONCLUSION

After a disaster, people who have lost homes and all semblance of normal life may be confused, disorganized, and demoralized. They grieve for what was lost. Their needs go beyond physical replacements. People-focused approaches—that is, recovery programs that engage citizens in decisions about the future—have the advantage of empowering these individuals, turning passive into active, turning lack of control into control, and promoting community engagement. Psychiatrist Craig Van Dyke (2012, p. 1, personal email communication, professor emeritus, Department of Psychiatry, San Francisco, California: University of California) wrote, "...the grief literature describes the endpoint of successful mourning as a point when the individual is capable of making new emotional investments in the future. It is not defined by happiness or even well-being. Rather it is an acknowledgment that one is forever changed, but it is time to get on with life and make new investments and not have one's personal development permanently arrested."

A community likewise cannot go back to how things were before a disaster but must adapt and move forward. A few simple lessons emerge from recent experiences that can be useful in coping with a large-scale disaster and extensive housing losses.

1. Disasters create anxiety and opportunity. It takes government leadership—at national and local levels—to manage both.
2. Housing (and funding for all types of housing) is essential to recovery.
3. Government leadership is crucial.
4. Cooperation between the national and local levels of government is important—programs need local input and cooperation to succeed.
5. Existing government programs must be flexible and adaptable to meet post-disaster needs.
6. Recovery takes time to implement. In the first year, it may be possible to fix basic infrastructure, but major urban redevelopment and new civic institutions can take 10–20 years.
7. When managing information for citizens in an ongoing effort, a long-term vision helps to explain the realities of construction times and the social and economic recovery goals.
8. Balancing government assistance and individual responsibility, government leadership, and community involvement is essential in all recovery efforts. Post-disaster assistance would likely enable citizens to recover, not create entitlements.

The US government could improve its disaster recovery programs without a major overhaul of current policies by using the National Disaster Recovery Framework to expand and structure coordination between federal agencies and local governments and to focus on unmet housing needs. A few examples of specific strategies might include case management for disaster victims, targeting recovery funds for rental and affordable housing, and advancing shelter-in-place strategies and other short-term housing solutions to keep people in their communities. The examples from various nations demonstrate the many ways to manage disaster recovery. Each nation can learn from the experiences of others, however, and develop policies and programs that focus on recovery and community renewal.

ACKNOWLEDGMENTS

The author thanks Professor Lawrence Vale for the invitation to speak at the MIT Symposium "Planning Practices that Matter: Housing for Resilient Cities." The author also thanks the Earthquake Engineering Research Institute for the 2013 Distinguished Lecture Award. The ideas presented in this paper were developed for those talks. This chapter was previously published in *Cityscape*, A Journal of Policy Development and Research, Vol. 16, No. 2, 2014, published by the US Department of Housing and Urban Development, Office of Policy Development and Research (Washington DC) as a special issue, titled Form Follows Families: Evolution of US Affordable Housing Design and Construction.

REFERENCES

Association of Bay Area Governments (ABAG). 2000. Post earthquake housing issue paper B: Time needed to repair or replace uninhabitable housing following the Loma Prieta and Northridge earthquakes. In *Preventing the Nightmare: Post-Earthquake Housing Issue Papers,* ABAG (ed),. Oakland, California: ABAG, pp. B1–B40.

Bellwood, D. R., T. P. Hughes, C. Folk, and M. Nystrom. 2004. Confronting the coral reef crisis. *Nature* 429: 827–33.

Bruneau, M., S. E. Chang, R. T. Eguchi et al. 2003. A framework to quantitatively assess and enhance the seismic resilience of communities. *Earthquake Spectra* 19(4): 733–52.

Calvi, G. M. 2010. L'Aquila earthquake 2009: Reconstruction between temporary and definitive. In *New Zealand Society for Earthquake Engineering 2010 Conference Proceedings.* Wellington, New Zealand: New Zealand Society for Earthquake Engineering.

Comerio, M. C. 1998. *Disaster Hits Home: New Policy for Urban Housing Recovery.* Berkeley, California: University of California Press.

Comerio, M. C. 2005. Key elements in a comprehensive theory of disaster recovery. In *Proceedings, First International Conference on Urban Disaster Reduction (ICDR1).* Kobe, Japan: The Japan Institute of Social Safety Science.

Comerio, M. C. 2012. Resilience, recovery and community renewal. In *Proceedings of the 15th World Conference on Earthquake Engineering (15WCEE).* Lisbon, Portugal: International Association for Earthquake Engineering.

Comerio, M. C. 2013. *Housing Recovery in Chile: A Qualitative Mid-Program Review.* PEER Report #2013/01. Berkeley, California: University of California, Pacific Earthquake Engineering Research Center.

Comerio, M. C. with Hamilton, Rabinovitz and Alschuler, Inc. 1996. *The Impact of Housing Losses in the Northridge Earthquake: Recovery and Reconstruction Issues.* Publication #CEDR14-96. Berkeley, California: University of California, Center for Environmental Design Research.

Community and Regional Resilience Institute (CARRI). 2009. *Toward a Common Framework for Community Resilience*. Oak Ridge, Tennessee: CARRI. Also available at http://www.resilientus.org.

Cui, P., X.-Q. Chen, Y.-Y. Zhu et al. 2011. The Wenchuan Earthquake (May 12, 2008) Sichuan Province, China, and resulting geohazards. *Natural Hazards* 56: 19–36.

Cutter, S. L., C. G. Burton, and C. T. Emrich. 2010. Disaster resilience indicators for benchmarking baseline conditions. *Journal of Homeland Security and Emergency Management* 7(1): 1–20.

Earthquake Commission (EQC) New Zealand. 2012. Earthquake Claims Data. http://canterbury.eqc.govt.nz/ (accessed February 25, 2016).

Earthquake Engineering Research Institute (EERI). 2010. The M 7.1 Darfield (Canterbury), New Zealand earthquake of September 4, 2010. In *Learning from Earthquakes Special Report*. Oakland, California: EERI, November, pp. 1–12.

Earthquake Engineering Research Institute (EERI). 2011. The M 6.3 Christchurch, New Zealand earthquake of February 22, 2011. In *Learning from Earthquakes Special Report*. Oakland, California: EERI, May, pp. 1–16.

Farmer, P. 2011. *Haiti after the Earthquake*. New York: The Perseus Books Group, Public Affairs.

Folk, C. 2006. Resilience: The emergence of a perspective for social-ecological systems analysis. *Global Environmental Change* 16: 253–67.

Gates, C. 2013. How Far Have We Come Since September 2010? In *The PRESS* (Christchurch, New Zealand), May 30. http://www.stuff.co.nz/the-press/business/the-rebuild/8737195/How-far-have-we-come-since-Sept-2010 (accessed February 26, 2016).

Geonet. 2012. Statistics on the CanterburyAftershocks. http://www.geonet.org.nz/canterbury-quakes/aftershocks/index.html (accessed February 26, 2016).

Gunderson, L. H., C. R. Allen, and C. S. Holling. 2010. *Foundations of Ecological Resilience*. Washington, DC: Island Press.

Jaffe, D. and T. Russell. 2013. The welfare economics of catastrophic loss. *The Geneva Papers* 38: 469–94.

Jones, D. 2014. 20 years after Northridge, are homeowners ready for a quake? *Los Angeles Times*, January 17. http://www.latimes.com/opinion/commentary/la-oe-ones-northridge-quake-insurance-20140117,0,965767.story#ixzz2rGkIxEty (accessed February 26, 2016).

King, A., D. Middleton, C. Brown, D. Johnston, and S. Johal. 2014. Insurance and its role in the recovery from the 2010–2011 Canterbury earthquake sequence. *Earthquake Spectra* 30(1): 475–92, 2010–2011 Canterbury Earthquake Sequence Special Issue.

Konotchick, A. N. 2013. *Self-Reconstruction in Haiti: A Case of Reconstructing Risk*? Thesis. Department of Architecture, University of California, Berkeley, California.

Maki, N. 2012. *Multi-Location Recovery Planning in Japan*, Research Center for Disaster Reduction Systems, Kyoto University, Japan. Presentation, November, San Francisco, California.

Markum, S. 2012. *The Christchurch Earthquakes 2010–2012: Planning and Building Impacts and Recovery Issues*. Lecture and slide presentation, April 10, University of California, Berkley, California.

Miles, S. and S. E. Chang. 2006. Modeling community recovery from earthquakes. *Earthquake Spectra* 22(2): 439–58.

Ministry of Building Innovation and Employment (MBIE). 2013. *Housing Pressures in Christchurch: A Summary of Evidence*. Wellington, New Zealand: MBIE.

MINVU (Government of Chile, Ministry of Housing and Urban Development). 2010. *Reconstruction Plan*. Santiago, Chile: Ministry of Housing and Urban Development.

MINVU (Government of Chile, Ministry of Housing and Urban Development). 2012. *Interviews with Senior Personnel*. Santiago, Chile: Ministry of Housing and Urban Development.

Mukherji, A. 2010. Post-earthquake housing recovery in Bachhau, India: The homeowner, the renter and the squatter. *Earthquake Spectra* 26(4): 1085–100.

Mukherji, A. 2011. Policies for urban housing recovery. In *Managing Disaster Recovery: Policy, Planning, Concepts and Cases*, E. Blakely et al. (eds), Berkshire: Crisis Response Publications, pp. 161–163.

National Research Council (NRC). 2010. *Building Disaster Resilience through Public-Private Collaboration*. Washington, DC: National Academies Press, NRC, Committee on Private–Public Sector Collaboration to Enhance Community Disaster Resilience.

Norris, F. H., S. P. Stevens, B. Pfefferbaum, K. F. Wyche and R. L. Pfefferbaum. 2008. Community resilience as a metaphor, theory, set of capacities, and strategy for disaster readiness. *American Journal of Community Psychology* 41(1–2): 127–50.

Olshansky, R. B. and L. A. Johnson. 2010. *Clear as Mud: Planning for the Rebuilding of New Orleans*. Chicago, Illinois: American Planners Association, Planners Press.

Olshansky, R. B., L. A. Johnson, and K. C. Topping. 2005. *Opportunity in Chaos: Rebuilding after the 1994 Northridge and 1995 Kobe Earthquakes*. Research Report. Urbana, Illinois: University of Illinois, Department of Urban and Regional Planning. http://www.urban.illinois.edu/faculty/olshansky/chaos/chaos.html (accessed February 26, 2016).

Peacock, G., H. Kunreuther, W. H. Hooke, S. L. Cutter, S. E. Chang, and P. R. Berke. 2008. *Toward a Resiliency and Vulnerability Observatory Network: RAVON*. College Station, Texas: Texas A&M University, College of Architecture, Hazard Reduction and Recovery Center. http://www.nehrp.gov/pdf/ravon.pdf (accessed February 26, 2016).

Preuss, J. 1998. *Kobe Reconstruction: Community Planning, Design and Construction Practices*. Interim Report No. 2 for National Science Foundation Grant CMS 9632508. Seattle, Washington: Urban Regional Research.

San Francisco Planning and Urban Research (SPUR). 2009–2010. *The Resilient City*. Multiple SPUR Reports. San Francisco, California: SPUR. http://www.spur.org/policy/the-resilient-city (accessed February 26, 2016).

San Francisco Planning and Urban Research (SPUR). 2012. *Safe Enough to Stay: What Will It Take for San Franciscans to Live Safely in Their Homes after an Earthquake?* SPUR Report. San Francisco, California: SPUR. http://www.spur.org/publications/spur-report/2012-02-01/safe-enough-stay (accessed February 26, 2016).

Sontag, D. 2012. Rebuilding in Haiti lags after billions in post-quake aid. *New York Times* December 23: A1, A6–A7. http://www.nytimes.com/2012/12/24/world/americas/in-aiding-quake-battered-haiti-lofty-hopes-and-hard-truths.html?_r=1 (accessed February 26, 2016).

Twigg, J. 2009. *Characteristics of a Disaster-Resilient Community: A Guidance Note*. London: Aon Benfield University College London Hazard Research Centre. http://discovery.ucl.ac.uk/1346086/ (accessed February 26, 2016).

Zillow Real Estate Research. 2013. U.S. Negative Equity Rate Falls at Fastest Pace Ever in Q3. *Zillow Blog*, November 20. http://www.zillow.com/blog/research/2013/11/20/zillow-negative-equity-q3-2013/ (accessed February 26, 2016).

2 Post-Disaster Housing Vulnerability
Getting People Back Home

Brenda D. Phillips

CONTENTS

2.1 INTRODUCTION

Social vulnerability, which "arises out of differential social relations among groups in a given society," complicates, exacerbates, and undermines the process of post-disaster housing recovery (Fordham et al. 2013, p. 4). That process, often conceptualized neatly as a series of steps and stages that people move through from emergency into temporary shelter/housing and then permanent housing (Quarantelli 1982), is in reality far from sequential or certain.

The process occurs experientially more in fits and starts as people stumble over, around, or through cumbersome barriers that undermine, thwart, and stall movement toward some semblance of pre-disaster normalcy. Ten years after 2005 hurricane Katrina, people remained displaced and dispersed across the United States as their New Orleans homes were declared abandoned and then sold (Kroll-Smith et al. 2015, see Figure 2.1). Populations, particularly in historic, racially, and ethnically diverse neighborhoods, never returned to pre-Katrina levels (Crowley 2006; Fussell et al. 2010; Kroll-Smith et al. 2015). The same situation occurs globally as well:

- *1998, Honduras.* Hurricane Mitch relentlessly poured water into impoverished areas of the nation. Street children perished—perhaps as many as half of the 19,000 people who died. Honduras struggled to rebuild in the face of staggering debt repayments (BBC 1998). Widespread displacement pushed people to migrate. Attempts to cross the border into the United

FIGURE 2.1 Homes in the Lower Ninth Ward of New Orleans: A historic African American community home to generations of families, suffered severe damage in 2005 from hurricane Katrina. (Photo by Brenda D. Phillips, with permission.)

States increased by 61% and the total number of Hondurans living in the United States doubled (Decesare 1998).

- *1998, Princeville, North Carolina.* River flooding inundated an historic community first incorporated in 1885 by African Americans. Settled on the floodplain side of the Tar River, the 1998 flood was only the latest of many such events. Populated mainly by elderly women living on fixed incomes, rebuilding would prove difficult due to the intertwined complexity of gender, income, aging, and disabilities. Offered a buyout of their homes, the community declined, preferring to save the historic locale that had been home to generations of families. Such patterns of holding on to land have been observed in other racially and ethnically diverse communities (Phillips et al. 2012; Phillips 2014).
- *2004, Indian Ocean.* A massive tsunami impacted over 13 nations, killing as many as 300,000. In Sri Lanka, a school for children with disabilities was washed away (Hope for Children 2014). Advocacy organizations reported that many people with pre-tsunami and new, post-tsunami disabilities were being overlooked. Camp directors failed to observe accessibility needs for people with disabilities in their shelters (Disability World 2005).
- *2015, Nepal.* A massive earthquake displaced hundreds of thousands. Shelters grew insecure for women and girls where privacy for sleeping and personal hygiene remained limited. In a male-dominated economy, gender influenced their ability to secure resources. Aid agencies scrambled to provide safe shelter and housing as aftershocks rumbled through encampments. The United Nations Population Fund, among others, provided reproductive health kits and "women-friendly spaces" to reduce gender-based violence (UNFPA 2015).

2.2 UNDERSTANDING SOCIAL VULNERABILITY

Clearly, disasters are not equal opportunity events where all sectors of a community share proportionately in the damage. Rather, injuries, fatalities, and exposure occur disproportionately. Furthermore, shelter and housing for the most vulnerable often fails to provide security or rapid routes to the best permanent housing options. Several theories shed insight into the conditions that initiate and perpetuate social vulnerability including vulnerability (Wisner 1998; Cutter 2006; Fordham et al. 2013), socio-political ecology (Peacock and Ragsdale 1997), and intersectionality theories (Walby et al. 2012).

The driving concept throughout each of these theories is that social inequality impedes those trying to return home. As a structural problem deeply embedded within societies, organizations, and communities, social inequality remains persistently difficult to overcome. Recovery, however, presents an opportunity to avoid replicating such patterns (Oliver-Smith 1990). To move toward such an end goal, this chapter begins by explaining social vulnerability followed by a discussion of best practices that address social vulnerability and disrupt social inequality.

To start, vulnerability theorists typically focus on the socioeconomic circumstances that place some populations at higher risk than others (Fordham et al. 2013). Recognizing this, international disaster humanitarian Fred Cuny (1983) emphasized that poverty makes people vulnerable and without tackling said poverty, we cannot increase safety or provide a meaningful recovery.

To illustrate, low-income workers live even in the wealthiest of communities to labor in retail or as landscapers, sanitation workers, cleaners, child minders, or in the hospitality industry. Marginal incomes accompany such jobs, limiting the means to deal with deferred maintenance (e.g., weakened roofs) or to purchase insurance that offsets losses (Dash et al. 2007). When disaster strikes, resources to evacuate, relocate, and repair or rebuild are meager to nonexistent. The recovery process is likely to become a lengthy journey (Hodgson 1995; Dash et al. 2007).

People surviving in developing nations face even more arduous journeys home where the combined loss of homes, possessions, and livelihoods preempts any expedited route home (Wamsler 2006). For example, Haiti's pre-disaster economy ranked as the poorest in the Western Hemisphere before the 2010 earthquake. Coupled with historic patterns of political corruption and significant amounts of external debt, Haitians faced well-known pre-disaster conditions that blocked recovery (Kreimer 1980; Pardee 2012). Indeed, political systems that institutionalize or allow segregation (such as South Africa under apartheid), perpetuate discrimination (Kurds under Syrian governmental policies), and/or operate under corrupt conditions (Haiti) further marginalize people into hazardous settings with substantial exposure to risk (Cutter 2006; Fordham et al. 2013). A lack of equity and access to resources undermines abilities to prepare for, respond to, recover from, or build resilience to disasters.

Compounded by more micro-level human interactions that rely on stereotypes and misperceptions, people with disabilities, children and elders, racial and ethnic groups, women, people who are homeless, language groups, and individuals with mental illness often experience significant impediments to acquire post-disaster housing (Phillips 1995; Fothergill 2004; Dash 2013; Davis et al. 2013; Peek 2013;

Santos-Hernández and Morrow 2013; Tobin-Gurley and Enarson 2013; Fothergill and Peek 2015; Stough and Kelman 2015). As one instance, those who report pre-disaster homelessness fall even further back in line for permanent housing, based on the erroneous assumption that they were not affected by the disaster. Such was the case after the 1989 Loma Prieta earthquake in California (Phillips 1995). Homeless persons may not even be considered for disaster recovery efforts, as observed in Japan (Wisner 1998).

Even those tasked with providing shelter and coordinating housing have failed to recognize needs related to social vulnerability (National Council on Disability 2009). For example, failing to recognize accessibility needs means that people linger in shelters, a problem that occurred after Hurricane Katrina in the United States and led to a successful lawsuit against the Federal Emergency Management Agency (Fitzmaurice 2006 and also see https://www.gpo.gov/fdsys/pkg/USCOURTS-laed-2_06-cv-00838, accessed January 5, 2016). Though progress has occurred since then, accessibility remains a significant impediment to moving through the stages of shelter, temporary housing, and permanent housing.

Problems also develop from a lack of access to resources. Socio-political ecology theorists suggest that those with less power or influence secure fewer resources in the journey home (Peacock and Ragsdale 1997). Characterized as competition over scarce resources, socio-political ecologists argue that survivors battle over food, hygiene supplies, and protection from harm among other resources. Women and children seeking a route through shelter and into permanent housing remain entrapped within gendered conditions and cultures that block forward movement (for an extensive list of examples, visit www.gdnonline.org, accessed January 8, 2015). After the 2005 earthquake in Pakistan, for example, separate units had to be established to provide nutritional support, medical care, and shelter for women and girls (Sayeed 2009). In the search for safe shelter and housing after disaster, human trafficking and gender-based violence have repeatedly prevented people from reaching safety (Jenkins and Phillips 2008; Phillips and Jenkins 2013, 2016).

On a deeper and more complex level, intersectionality theory compels analysts to look at the confluence of multiple factors or conditions. Intersectionality theory directs us to think beyond a single set of circumstances that may impede progress home, such as gender *or* disability and look at the intersection of gender *and* age (Walby et al. 2012). Focusing exclusively on gender, for example, often fails to recognize the ways in which women and men of color have experienced disaster recovery. The disproportionate loss of life among men who were elderly, African American, and low income as a consequence of Hurricane Katrina demonstrates this (Sharkey 2007). One's life chances (the probabilities that one will benefit from what society has to offer), are compounded and undermined when coupled with the entangled complexities of income, race, age, and gender. How then, might practitioners and policymakers enable progress toward post-disaster housing for socially vulnerable populations?

2.3 MODELS OF POST-DISASTER HOUSING RECOVERY

Different models demonstrate the challenges of supporting persons impacted by disasters. The redevelopment model tasks governments with the responsibility of caring for their citizens (Comerio 1997; Comerio 1998a,b; Comerio et al. 1994). To do so, governments take on the complete financing and even planning for rebuilt communities, although their commitment may vary. The 1976 Tangshan, China earthquake demonstrates a full government embracing of recovery, with funds and personnel brought in to rebuild much of the devastated area (Mitchell 2004). In contrast, the government of Myanmar failed to provide for those affected by Cyclone Nargis in 2008, and denied entry to international organizations as well.

The capital-infusion model occurs most commonly in developing nations, where outside organizations bring in assets to fuel rebuilding (Comerio 1998a,b). Recent examples of this include the significant amount of donor aid that poured into Haiti after the earthquake. Both governmental and nongovernmental organizations provided funding, volunteers, and other resources. The problem with capital infusion, as will be discussed shortly, is that donors have expectations which may not be consistent with the preferences or needs of those affected.

A third model, called limited intervention, relies on insurance and government assistance (Comerio 1998a,b; Esnard and Sapat 2014). This model is used in the United States, with the assumption that homeowners hold sufficient insurance to recover and rebuild. However, low-income families (e.g., seniors, single parents) often lack sufficient coverage. Insurance companies may also refuse to cover some hazards, such as wind or flooding. In these instances, government loans or grants may be secured. However, people may give up during the paperwork-laden process to secure such funds. This process also largely ignores renters or those in public housing. Even with government grants, funds may not cover rebuilding costs particularly those accompanied by mitigation requirements (e.g., elevations). For those lucky enough to be selected (see Boxes 2.1 and 2.2), voluntary organizations may provide help.

Finally, the market model means that displaced people are on their own, will compete with others for available housing, and will not receive other aid (Comerio 1998a,b). Even with models that provide the most generous of help, people still experience difficulty trying to return home.

2.4 DESIGNING POST-DISASTER HOUSING FOR SOCIALLY VULNERABLE POPULATIONS

Existing models neglect deeply embedded and highly resistant social inequalities as well as the preferences of those affected. Such models also allow socially vulnerable people to fall through the cracks of available aid. An alternative approach recognized in the extant literature is to empower people in their own recovery, albeit a strategy that also contains its own challenges.

2.4.1 Using Local Knowledge

As far back as 1982, the United Nations indicated (1982, p. 4), "the most effective relief and reconstruction policies result from the participation of survivors in determining and planning their own needs." The social vulnerability approach also relies on "local knowledge, networks, imagination and creativity" to address post-disaster housing (Fordham et al. 2013, p. 4) and to involve survivors in planning

BOX 2.1 SINGLE MOTHERS

Hurricane Katrina devastated the US Gulf Coast in 2005, destroying housing that even a decade of work would not fully resolve. In Pass Christian, Mississippi, massive destruction occurred. Entire neighborhoods, some home to multiple generations of families, disappeared in a massive storm surge. In the days that followed the hurricane, the National Guard cut their way down the highway, moving downed trees and debris aside to reach the small town. The coastal community, home to people dependent on the sea as well as area tourism, would face a staggering recovery. Hundreds of residents lost their homes, coupled with a lingering period of economic recovery and newly acquired distance from their kin. With many working at low-wage jobs in area industries, and lacking insurance sufficient to cover losses, a return home seemed impossible.

But the event would also provide an opportunity to increase resilience. One strategy common to areas subject to storm surge flooding is elevation. In the aftermath, governments put such codes into place, raising the required elevations of some homes as high as 19 feet. While offering protection against future flooding, the elevations also proved financially impossible. Help would be needed, and it came in a combination of local leadership coupled with outside resources. A local recovery committee formed, identifying people in need of assistance. One local leader, involved in Rotary Club service, traveled extensively to secure funding. His efforts resulted in funding for dozens of homes, many of them built by a faith-based organization using mostly volunteer labor.

The combination of local knowledge and leadership with outside resources proved valuable to one single mother. As a local tourism-based worker, her income would not cover the daily costs of living along with expenses due to elevation and reconstruction. A local recovery committee identified her needs and pledged support. Government funds covered some of the expenses, with additional donations by a Rotary Club located in Naperville, Illinois. Mennonite Disaster Service brought volunteers in, working carefully with local code officials and inspectors to insure compliance with new post-disaster codes. The new home, completed several years after Katrina, keep her in a place her family had called home for generations—where she relied on kin for child care and social relationships vital to recovery after disaster.

Phillips
2014

and decision-making (National Council on Disability 2009). Sometimes referred to as traditional ecological knowledge (TEK), local "knowledge is derived from experience and shared from person to person" (Prober et al. 2011, p. 12).

Yet decades later, people affected in the 1999 Turkey earthquake and the 2004 tsunami reported a lack of consultation about temporary housing sites, permanent housing designs, or relocation and avoided the structures built by government and

BOX 2.2 DISASTER CASE MANAGEMENT

Helping people through the challenges of returning home has, in recent years, been supported by the practice of disaster case management. Defined as "a practice used to connect individuals to needed resources and services such as housing, employment, and transportation" (Stough et al. 2010, p. 211), the effort is designed to assess needs and connect survivors with resources. Case managers perform those duties, and often advocate for their clients as well. Socially vulnerable populations are often the focus of their efforts, including connecting such clients to area organizations dedicated to recovery.

In the United States, for example, a case manager might present a client's needs to a long-term recovery committee (LTRC). The LTRC then reviews what needs might be met with available resources. Often, voluntary organizations including those from outside the affected area will make offers to assist particular clients. They may take on the entire rebuilding project, for example, of a senior citizen or person with a disability, or they may perform a portion of a task perhaps replacing a roof. The case manager then follows the client's progress through resolution of their housing recovery experience.

nongovernmental organizations (Davidson et al. 2007; Raju 2013, see Figure 2.2). Indeed, failure to involve local people may lead to unsuccessful, even miserable, recovery outcomes. To illustrate, the 2004 tsunami devastated fishing villages along the southeastern coast of India. Post-tsunami reconstruction in India relied on governmental and nongovernmental expertise (including contractors) to construct

FIGURE 2.2 Temporary housing near Nagapattinam, India after the 2004 tsunami lies within view of the ocean but several kilometers distant from livelihoods and family homes. (Photo by Brenda D. Phillips, with permission.)

permanent housing. However, pre-disaster area building practices had never involved outsiders, involving instead careful attention to local beliefs and customs. Gender also influenced local construction, with women taking on home construction and supporting local construction industries (Barenstein 2006).

Local building practices also reflected the local ecosystem. Pre-tsunami, many people had lived in small houses with a signature veranda at the front: "it is where people spend their leisure time and entertain guests during the day, and where they sleep at night" (Barenstein 2006, p. 39). Interiors typically lacked a kitchen, which may be located separately near the garden. Such traditional dwellings were not rebuilt. Instead, government, nongovernmental organizations, and contractors opted for concrete structures. They also removed trees needed to cool homes, and failed to consider prevailing winds. Returning residents found the conditions to be sweltering and did not use the dwellings, further disrupting social relationships (Barenstein 2006).

From the perspective of those trying to help, pressure to complete projects is likely to compete with local consultation, especially when seasonal weather sets in or donors want results (Davidson et al. 2007). Still, evidence suggests that owner-driven approaches are preferred over donor-driven approaches (Karunasena and Rameezdeen 2014). In post-tsunami Sri Lanka, "beneficiaries of donor-built houses complained that designs do not conform to their rural lifestyle. Kitchens were designed for use of gas cookers instead of firewood, attached toilets instead of normally used detached toilets, less semi-open spaces, no space to keep fishing gear" (Karunasena and Rameezdeen 2014, p. 183). Clearly, locals require a connected set of culturally and functionally situated housing located near sustainable livelihoods.

In reality, then, a continuum of engagement methods may need to be considered along a "ladder of community participation" (Arnstein 1969). For such an approach, the top rung involves and empowers residents in active decision making compared to the least preferable bottom rung where officials simply inform survivors of decisions (Davidson et al. 2007). As noted in Australia and the United Kingdom, "effective recovery can be achieved only where the affected community participates fully in the recovery process and where it has the capacity, skills and knowledge to make its participation meaningful" (Coles and Buckle 2004, p. 6).

The means for acquiring TEK can be daunting given disaster conditions. After the 2010 Haiti earthquake, efforts coordinated by the United Nations included surveying 1750 Haitians in 156 focus groups (Montas-Dominique 2011). Haitian survivors expressed pride in their history and people, with a deeply embedded desire to rebuild their own land. And—while rebuilding would commence—they also wanted significant transformation to sustain their recovery. Haitians very much wanted a different country, one that included education, housing, economic opportunity, health care, and civic empowerment. Rebuilding would not be enough, rather, they desired widespread transformation to address social inequalities and become more resilient to future risks (Montas-Dominique 2011).

2.4.2 Resilience and Risk Reduction for Socially Vulnerable Groups

Resilience, in some definitions, serves as the antithesis or transformation of vulnerability. Becoming more resilient involves building a more adaptive state of living.

BOX 2.3 BOTTOM-UP RESILIENCE

Recommended practices for building resilience rely on community participation. Indeed, "bottom-up interventions—the engagement of communities in increasing their resilience—are essential because local conditions vary greatly" (National Academies 2012, p. 4). Recommended strategies include (Verbatim, National Academies 2012, p. 4):

- "Engaging the whole community in disaster policymaking and planning;
- Linking public and private infrastructure performance and interests to resilience goals;
- Improving public and private infrastructure and essential services (such as health and education);
- Communicating risks, connecting community networks, and promoting a culture of resilience;
- Organizing communities, neighborhoods, and families to prepare for disasters;
- Adopting sound land-use planning practices; and
- Adopting and enforcing building codes and standards appropriate to existing hazards."

The idea of the whole community embraces individual, group, organizational, community, national, and international diversity. To fully recover, all parties must become engaged in the processes of preparing for, responding to, and recovering from a disaster. Rebuilding housing options post-disaster, in a manner that increases resilience to future events, will require a robust set of participatory strategies across all sectors.

Thus, a disaster recovery process must provide a means to increase resilience (see Box 2.3). The concept of resilience typically involves some ability to rebound from an event including: "the capacity of individuals, families, communities, systems, and institutions to anticipate, withstand and/or judiciously engage with catastrophic events and/or experiences" as a "response to adversity" (Almedom and Tumwine 2008, p. S1).

Suggestions to become more resilient have included pre-disaster recovery planning which should include mitigation efforts (Wu and Lindell 2004), although such an effort historically lacks interest or participation. After a disaster, interest may well be higher but pressures will also build to provide shelter and housing. People may not want to wait, though. The 1999 Chi-Chi earthquake in Taiwan, for example, failed to add improved mitigation as "mitigation was no longer a high enough priority to overcome political pressure from victims living in the risk area" (Wu and Lindell 2004, p. 75).

Ways to incorporate community interests must thus be rapidly consultative and integrate local knowledge of the area. These might include educational efforts, focus groups, radio or television call-in programs, internet sites, social media, planning events, visits by officials to affected areas to meet with residents, surveys, or other techniques to collect information efficiently after a disaster (Pearce 2003; Natural Hazards Research Applications and Information Center [NHRAIC] 2005; Dash et al. 2007). Participatory methods might also include hiring locally affected people to convene groups or gather information to amass into a set of recommendations (Stoecker 2005; McNiff 2013; see Box 2.4 also). One New Zealand effort involved building local leadership among interested participants. Groups and organizations then formed, enabling the affected communities to influence decision makers (Love and Vallance 2013). Practitioners may need to encourage the development of such local leadership rather than fight their appearance. When emergent groups and organizations have appeared, critical needs have been identified and met, such as when low-income women represented and advocated for themselves after hurricane Andrew in 1992 (Enarson and Morrow 1997).

Another suggestion to mitigate future risk has been relocating people out of harm's way, an effort that has been met with limited success among socially vulnerable populations. In India, relocation efforts failed among the fishing villages (Raju 2013) as they have in the United States and Australia (Handmer 1985; Phillips et al. 2012). Failure occurs because places matter to people (Hummon 1990; Levine et al. 2007; Perry and Lindell 1997). People do not want to leave familiar communities, historic and culturally relevant sites, social networks, and livelihood sources (Center for Hazards Assessment, Research, and Technology [CHART] 2005; Handmer and Nalau 2013; Raju 2013). Relocation can also present psychological stress for survivors, because they lose critical social networks that would normally provide support (Riad and Norris 1996). Relocation resistance is also often tied to work needs. A buffer zone limiting reconstruction was created in Sri Lanka after the tsunami, for example, but was rejected by area residents who needed to live closer to the sea for their livelihoods (Karunasena and Rameezdeen 2014). Residents of La Yerbabuena, near the Colima, Mexico volcano, rejected relocations as well. Fearing a loss of their land and homes and suspicious of potential outside investors, some residents chose risk over relocation (Cuevas-Muñiz and Luján 2005; Gavilanes-Ruiz et al. 2009).

A broader resilience effort called the Hyogo Framework took place between the years of 2005–2015. Among the priorities for action can be found a recommendation for community participation coupled with an emphasis on gender and cultural diversity (UNISDR 2015). Though dedicated action took place in many locations to implement the Hyogo Framework, significant social vulnerability remains. Those involved in post-disaster housing construction will need to understand that long-standing patterns of social inequality will continue to generate risk.

2.5 DISCUSSION AND CONCLUSION

Altering socially stratified systems is not within the power of most trying to help. More practical means will be necessary. The strategies presented here of inclusion and involvement will take place in a dynamic post-disaster environment

BOX 2.4 STRATEGIES TO ENGAGE

While experts recommend community participation, it also remains clear that strategies to engage the public have not always been clear or successful. Consider these ways that have demonstrated varying degrees of success in previous disasters:

- The 1999 Marmara, Turkey earthquake destroyed approximately 100,000 homes. Immediate shelter for 800,000 people came in the form of 121 tent cities. Less than a year later, nongovernmental agencies and contractors had erected 42,000 temporary housing units (Yonder et al. 2009). Criticism erupted over the temporary housing, which focused on homeowners and failed to consider gender-based needs. One nongovernmental organization chose a different route to aid women in particular. Within the tent cities, they created tents specific for women's needs. They also secured shipping containers to use for childcare. Women surviving the disaster embraced these gendered spaces where they began to design their own recovery, including creating their own toy factory to produce income. Temporary housing, though, proved isolating after life in the tent cities. Women created a means to sell their toys and then moved into other industries including making recycled paper and engaging in carpentry. A core group of women continued to meet over the ensuing months to develop ideas about housing. They mapped areas, conducted needs assessments, and met with authorities. Through "group discussions of shared-concerns," women advocated for their own needs. Within 4 years, 200 women from four provinces had established housing cooperatives and gained "confidence to act as grass-roots experts on micro-finance schemes, housing processes, information gathering and on the establishment and operation of Women and Children Centers" (Yonder et al. 2009, p. 203; see also Johnson et al. 2006).
- In Grand Bayou, Louisiana, a community of Atakapa-Ishaak Native Americans faced absolute devastation from hurricane Katrina after 2005. A first effort to design recovery came from a community meeting along the banks of the bayou. But meetings alone do not lead to successful recovery efforts. It took 3 years for an experienced case manager to establish relationships with the community and the surrounding area (including government offices) before rebuilding began. When it did, volunteers entered the bayou community in boats to pull debris out of affected areas. Rebuilding, which required donations and more volunteers, took several more years. At the 5-year mark, volunteers had rebuilt 10 homes—all of them elevated against repetitive and common flooding threats. Still, nearly 100 people had lived in the bayou before the storm compared to less than half that after the storm (Phillips 2014).

characterized by pressures from multiple sources. Nonetheless, increasing adoption of new housing and disaster resiliency must incorporate local needs and preferences, especially for socially vulnerable populations who know their circumstances and environment best. To do otherwise represents a paternalistic approach that is likely to fail.

Simultaneously, socially vulnerable populations will require significant levels of support to secure appropriate, safe, and resilient housing before or after any disaster event. Housing must be tied to cultural preferences and economic livelihoods as well as to supportive social networks, to avoid patronizing those who must live on in the choices of others. If such housing options are not provided, then vulnerable populations may feel compelled to accept places that force a choice between food, income, socially meaningful relationships, and risk.

Louisiana residents in coastal communities have struggled to keep their ecosystem intact in the face of continued disasters and environmental devastation (Laska et al. 2004). Not only do they see their environmental resources as relevant, they also often view themselves as stewards of environmental resources, cultural ties, and historic connections: "if the ecosystem is lost, this way of life will be lost, and the effects will be felt far beyond the borders of the state" (Gramlin and Hagelman 2004, p. 131). Still, those affected in Louisiana's coastal communities usually return after a disaster given "their deep-rooted belonging to the way of life … bound up in the environment in which they live" (Gramlin and Hagelman 2004, pp. 131–132). People just want to go home, to the places where they had work, to familiar environments, and among family and friends who provide meaningful relationships and a reason to go on.

REFERENCES

Almedom, A. and J. Tumwine. 2008. Resilience to disasters: A paradigm shift from vulnerability to strength. *African Health Sciences* 8(S1): S1–4.

Arnstein, S. 1969. A ladder of citizen participation. *Journal of the American Institute of Planners* 35(4): 216–24.

Barenstein, J. 2006. Challenges and risks in post-tsunami housing reconstruction in Tamil Nadu. *Humanitarian Exchange* 33: 39–40.

BBC. 1998. Hurricane Mitch. http://news.bbc.co.uk/hi/english/static/in_depth/world/2000/dealing_with_disaster/hurricane.stm (accessed December 9, 2015).

Center for Hazards Assessment, Research, and Technology (CHART). 2005. *Relocation Practices in Communities that Have Had to Move*. New Orleans, Louisiana: University of New Orleans/CHART.

Coles, E. and P. Buckle. 2004. Developing community resilience as a foundation for effective disaster recovery. *The Australian Journal of Emergency Management* 19(4): 6–15.

Comerio, M. 1997. Housing issues after disasters. *Journal of Contingencies and Crisis Management* 5: 166–78.

Comerio, M. 1998a. *Disaster Hits Home: New Policy for Urban Housing Recovery*. Berkeley, California: University of California Press.

Comerio, M. 1998b. Hazards mitigation and housing recovery—Watsonville and San Francisco one year later. In the *National Report to Congress on the Loma Prieta Earthquake*. Washington, DC: US Geological Survey, D29–34.

Comerio, M., J. Landis, and Y. Rofé. 1994. *Post-Disaster Residential Rebuilding*. Berkeley, California: Institute of Urban and Regional Development, University of California.
Crowley, S. 2006. Where is home? Housing for low-income people after the 2005 hurricanes. In *There Is No Such Thing as a Natural Disaster*, C. Hartman and G. D. Squires (eds), New York: Routledge, 121–66.
Cuevas-Muñiz, A. and J. Luján. 2005. Reubicación y desarticulación de La Yerbabuena: Entre el riesgo volcánico y la vulnerabilidad política. *Desacatos* 19: 41–70.
Cuny. F. 1983. *Disasters and Development*. Dallas, Texas: Oxford University Press.
Cutter, S. 2006. The geography of social vulnerability: Race, class, and catastrophe. http://understandingkatrina.ssrc.org/ (accessed December 14, 2015).
Dash, N. 2013. Race and ethnicity. In *Social Vulnerability to Disaster*, D. Thomas et al. (eds), Boca Raton, Florida: CRC Press, 113–38.
Dash, N., B. H. Morrow, J. Mainster, and L. Cunningham. 2007. Lasting effects of hurricane Andrew on a working class community. *Natural Hazards Review* 8(1): 13–21.
Davidson, C., C. Johnson, G. Lizarralde, N. Dikmen, and A. Sliwinski. 2007. Truth and myths about community participation in post-disaster housing projects. *Habitat International* 31(1): 100–15.
Davis, E., R. Hansen, M. Kett, J. Mincin, and J. Twigg. 2013. Disability. In *Social Vulnerability to Disaster*, D. Thomas et al. (eds), Boca Raton, Florida: CRC Press, 199–234.
Decesare, D. 1998. Hurricane Mitch devastates Honduras. http://www.destinyschildren.org/en/timeline/hurricane-mitch-devastates-honduras/ (accessed December 9, 2015).
Disability World. 2005. Disabled people's organizations working in tsunami-affected areas. http://www.disabilityworld.org/12–02_05/news/tsunaminews.shtml (accessed January 5, 2016).
Enarson, E. and B. Morrow. 1997. A gendered perspective: The voices of women. In *Hurricane Andrew: Ethnicity, Gender, and the Sociology of Disasters*, W. Peacock et al. (eds), New York: Routledge, 116–40.
Esnard, A. and A. Sapat. 2014. *Displaced by Disaster: Recovery and Resilience in a globalizing world*. New York: Routledge.
Fitzmaurice, S. 2006. Katrina disability information, FEMA lawsuit. http://www.katrinadisability.info (accessed March 3, 2008).
Fordham, M., W. Lovekamp, E. Thomas, and B. Phillips. 2013. Introduction to social vulnerability. In *Social Vulnerability to Disasters*, D.S.K. Thomas et al. (eds), 2nd edn, Boca Raton, Florida: CRC Press, 1–32.
Fothergill, A. 2004. *Heads above Water: Gender, Class and Family in the Grand Forks Flood*. Albany, New York: State University of New York Press.
Fothergill, A. and L. Peek. 2015. *Children of Katrina*. Austin, Texas: University of Texas Press.
Fussell, E., N. Sastry, and M. Vanlandingham. 2010. Race, socioeconomic status, and return migration to New Orleans after hurricane Katrina. *Population and Environment* 31(1–3): 20–42.
Gavilanes-Ruiz, J., A. Cuevas-Muñiz, N. Varley. et al. 2009. Exploring the factors that influence the perception of risk: The case of Volcán de Colima, Mexico. *Journal of Volcanology and Geothermal Research* 186: 238–52.
Gramlin, R. and R. Hagelman. 2004. A working coast: People in the Louisiana wetlands. *Journal of Coastal Research* 44: 112–33.
Handmer, J. 1985. Local reaction to acquisition: An Australian study. Working Paper #53, Centre for Resource and Environmental Studies. Canberra, Australia: Australian National University.
Handmer, J. and J. Nalau. 2013. Is relocation transformation? http://research-hub.griffith.edu.au/display/nb44819abc2abb41486d9f5b324cc5921 (accessed January 5, 2016).

Hodgson, R. 1995. Housing improvements: Disaster response or hazard mitigation? Examples from Bangladesh. *Built Environment* 21(2/3): 154–63.

Hope for Children. 2014. Sri Lanka Tsunami—10 years on. http://hope-for-children.org/sri-lanka-tsunami-10-years-on/ (accessed January 5, 2016).

Hummon, D. 1990. *Commonplaces.* Albany, New York: SUNY Press.

Jenkins, P. and B. Phillips. 2008. Battered women, catastrophe and the context of safety. *NWSA Journal* 20(3): 49–68.

Johnson, C., G. Lizarralde, and C. Davidson. 2006. A systems view of temporary housing projects in post-disaster reconstruction. *Construction Management and Economics* 24: 367–78.

Karunasena, G. and R. Rameezdeen. 2014. Post-disaster housing reconstruction: Comparative study of donor vs. owner-driven approaches. *International Journal of Disaster Resilience in the Built Environment* 1(2): 173–91.

Kreimer, A. 1980. Low-income housing under "normal" and post-disaster situations: Some basic continuities. *Habitat International* 4(3): 273–83.

Kroll-Smith, S., V. Baxter, and P. Jenkins. 2015. *Left to Chance: Hurricane Katrina and the Story of Two New Orleans Neighborhoods.* Austin, Texas: University of Texas Press.

Laska, S., G. Wooddell, R. Hagelman, R. Gramling, and M. Teets Farris. 2004. At risk: the human, community and infrastructure resources of Coastal Louisiana. *Journal of Coastal Research* SI, 44(Spring): 154–75.

Levine, J., A. Esnard, and A. Sapat. 2007. Population displacement and housing dilemmas due to catastrophic disasters. *Journal of Planning Literature* 22(1): 3–15.

Love, R. and S. Vallance. 2013. The role of communities in post-disaster recovery planning: A Diamond Harbour case study. *Lincoln Planning Review* 5(1–2): 3–9.

McNiff, J. 2013. *Action Research*, 3rd edn, New York: Oxford Press.

Mitchell, K. 2004. Reconceiving recovery. In *New Zealand Recovery Symposium Proceedings*, S. Norman (ed.), Wellington, New Zealand: Ministry of Civil Defence and Emergency Management, 47–68.

Montas-Dominique, M. 2011. Sim Pa Rele (If I don't shout). In *Haiti: After the Earthquake*, P. Farmer (ed.), New York: Public Affairs, 259–72.

National Academies. 2012. *Disaster Resilience: A National Imperative.* Washington, DC: National Academies.

National Council on Disability. 2009. *Effective Emergency Management.* Washington, DC: National Council on Disability.

Natural Hazards Research Applications and Information Center (NHRAIC). 2005. *Holistic Disaster Recovery.* Boulder, Colorado: University of Colorado/NHRAIC.

Oliver-Smith, A. 1990. Post-disaster housing reconstruction and social inequality: A challenge to policy and practice. *Disasters* 14(1): 7–19.

Pardee, J. 2012. Living through displacement: Housing insecurity among low-income evacuees. In *Displaced: Life in the Katrina Diaspora*, L. Weber and L. Peek (eds), Austin, Texas: University of Texas Press, 63–78.

Peacock, W. and A. K. Ragsdale. 1997. Social systems, ecological networks, and disasters: Toward a socio-political ecology of disasters. In *Hurricane Andrew: Ethnicity, Gender and the Sociology of Disorders*, W. G. Peacock, B. H. Morrow, and H. Gladwin (eds), London: Routledge.

Pearce, L. 2003. Disaster management and community planning, and public participation: How to achieve sustainable hazard mitigation. *Natural Hazards* 28: 211–28.

Peek, L. 2013. Age. In *Social Vulnerability to Disaster*, D. Thomas et al. (eds), Boca Raton, Florida: CRC Press, 167–98.

Perry, R. and M. Lindell. 1997. Principles for managing community relocation as a hazard mitigation measure. *Journal of Contingencies and Crisis Management* 5(1): 49–59.

Phillips, B. 1995. Creating, sustaining and losing place: Homelessness in the context of disaster. *Humanity and Society* 19: 94–101.
Phillips, B. 2014. *Mennonite Disaster Service: Building a Therapeutic Community after the Gulf Coast Storms.* Lanham, Maryland: Lexington.
Phillips, B. and P. Jenkins. 2013. Violence in disasters. In *Social Vulnerability to Disasters*, D. Thomas et al. (eds), 2nd edn, Boca Raton, Florida: CRC Press, 311–40.
Phillips, B. and P. Jenkins. 2016. Forthcoming. Gender-based violence and disasters: South Asia in comparative perspective. In *Gender, Women and Disasters: Survival, Security and Development*, L. Racioppi and S. Prajnya (eds), Boca Raton, Florida: Taylor & Francis, 225–250.
Phillips, B., P. Stukes, and P. Jenkins. 2012. Freedom Hill is not for sale and neither is the Lower Ninth Ward. *Journal of Black Studies* 43(4): 405–426.
Prober, S., M. O'Connor, and F. Walsh. 2011. Australian Aboriginal peoples' seasonal knowledge: A potential basis for shared understanding in environmental management. *Ecology and Society* 16(2): 12. http://www.ecologyandsociety.org/vol16/iss2/art12/ (accessed January 5, 2016).
Quarantelli, E. L. 1982. *Sheltering and Housing after Major Community Disasters: Case Studies and General Observations.* Newark, Delaware: Disaster Research Center, University of Delaware.
Raju, E. 2013. Housing reconstruction in disaster recovery: A study of fishing communities post-tsunami in Chennai, India. *PLOS Currents Disasters.* http://currents.plos.org/disasters/article/housing-reconstruction-in-disaster-recovery-a-study-of-fishing-communities-post-tsunami-in-chennai-india/ (accessed January 5, 2006).
Riad, J. and F. Norris. 1996. The influence of relocation on the environmental, social and psychological stress experienced by disaster victims. *Environment and Behavior* 28(2): 163–82.
Santos-Hernández, J. and B. Morrow. 2013. Language and literacy. In *Social Vulnerability to Disaster*, D. Thomas et al. (eds), Boca Raton, Florida: CRC Press, 265–80.
Sayeed, A. 2009. Victims of earthquake and patriarchy: The 2005 Pakistan earthquake. In *Women, Gender and Disaster: Global Issues and Initiatives*, E. Enarson and P. Chakrabarti (eds), Los Angeles, California: Sage, 142–51.
Sharkey, P. 2007. Survival and death in New Orleans: An empirical look at the human impact of hurricane Katrina. *Journal of Black Studies* 37(4): 482–501.
Stough, L. and I. Kelman. 2015. Exploring and exchanging (dis)ability and (dis)aster. In *Disability and Disaster: Explorations and Exchanges*, I. Kelman and L. Stough (eds), New York: Palgrave MacMillan, 175–85.
Stough, L., A. Sharp, C. Decker, and N. Wilker. 2010. Disaster case management and individuals with disabilities. *Rehabilitation Psychology* 55(3): 211–20.
Tobin-Gurley, J. and E. Enarson. 2013. Gender. In *Social Vulnerability to Disaster*, D. Thomas et al. (eds), Boca Raton, Florida: CRC Press, 139–66.
UNFPA. 2015. News on the earthquake in Nepal, overview. http://www.unfpa.org/emergencies/earthquake-nepal (accessed January 6, 2016).
UNISDR. 2015. Summary of the Hyogo Framework for Action 2005–2015: Building the resilience of nations and communities to disasters. http://www.unisdr.org/files/8720_summaryHFP20052015.pdf (accessed January 5, 2016).
United Nations. 1982. *Shelter after Disaster: Guidelines for Assistance.* Geneva, Switzerland: Office of the United Nations Disaster Relief Co-Ordinator.
Walby, S., J. Armstrong, and S. Strid. 2012. Intersectionality: Multiple inequalities in social theory. *Sociology* 48(2): 1–17.
Wamsler, C. 2006. Mainstreaming risk reduction in urban planning and housing: A challenge for international aid organizations. *Disasters* 30(2): 151–77.

Wisner, B. 1998. Marginality and vulnerability: Why the homeless of Tokyo don't 'count' in disaster preparations. *Applied Geography* 18(1): 25–33.
Wu, J. Y. and M. Lindell. 2004. Housing reconstruction after two major earthquakes: The 1994 Northridge earthquake in the United States and the 1999 Chi-Chi earthquake in Taiwan. *Disasters* 28: 63–81.
Yonder, A., S. Akcar, and P. Gopalan. 2009. Women's participation in disaster relief and recovery. In *Women, Gender and Disaster, Global Issues and Initiatives*, E. Enarson and P. Chakrabarti (eds), New Delhi, India: Sage, 189–211.

3 Displacement, Return, and Relocation
Housing and Community Recovery Considerations

Ann-Margaret Esnard

CONTENTS

3.1 INTRODUCTION

> Displacement related to disasters is becoming more widely recognized as an issue requiring specific attention, but it is still sometimes downplayed or dismissed as a temporary or marginal concern. This occurs in spite of the fact that displacement plays a central role in determining how many disasters evolve, the importance to long-term recovery of sustainable settlement and integration through return or relocation, and its disproportionate and repeated impact on highly vulnerable people (Internal Displacement Monitoring Centre [IDMC] 2014, p. 45).

Internal and transnational movement and mobility of persons affected by disasters can be characterized in myriad ways based on the severity of the event (hazard, crisis, disaster, and catastrophe), type of movement (voluntary and forced), drivers (economic, political, demographic, social, and/or environmental conditions), recovery timeframes (short- or long-term recovery), and outcomes (evacuation, displacement, return, and relocation). These drivers and outcomes overlap in multiple ways, both spatially and temporally.

Displacement from home and community as a result of fast- and slow-onset natural disasters is a global phenomenon growing in scale, frequency, and complexity (Esnard and Sapat 2014; IDMC 2014). An analysis of trends since the 1970s shows that displacement has increased more quickly with regard to weather-related and geophysical hazards (IDMC 2014, p. 9). The Philippines, Vietnam, and Bangladesh recorded the highest levels of displacement relative to population size, but it is the Philippines that suffered the two largest displacements of 2013: typhoon Trami displaced 1.7 million people in September 2013 and typhoon Haiyan displaced 4.1 million in November 2013 (IDMC 2014, p. 18). Urban development patterns and population growth in vulnerable areas have added to the exposure of homes, livelihood assets, and infrastructure, and subsequent loss and destruction. While the focus of this chapter is on natural hazards and disasters, the added threats from wars and conflicts cannot be ignored. The number of persons facing protracted and repeated displacement is also expected to increase both as a result of pre-disaster vulnerability as well as the frequency of disasters (Esnard and Sapat 2014, 2015).

With catastrophic disasters comes a range of sheltering, housing, and recovery paths, concurrent with decision-making about recovery and rebuilding in-place or recovery and relocation elsewhere. Devastating and catastrophic disasters lessen the probability that unilateral decisions can be made by individual households. As such, governments and their agencies, humanitarian and development organizations, nongovernmental organizations (NGOs), international institutions, and donors also influence household and community recovery trajectories, as well as displacement timelines and outcomes. Combined, these are real dilemmas that complicate durable solutions to post-disaster recovery of households and communities.

This chapter is an attempt to place displacement, return, and relocation outcomes in the context of this complex reality. The next section discusses overlapping forms of in situ, cultural-economic, and protracted displacement, followed by background information on various types of displacement and relocation. A section of the chapter is also devoted to discussing the impacts of sheltering and housing policies, as well as community social ties on displacement timelines and outcomes. Examples from post-disaster recovery processes around the globe are used to elucidate pathways from displacement to return and relocation.

3.2 INTANGIBLE AND OVERLAPPING FORMS OF DISPLACEMENT

Displacement can be both tangible (physical/locational) and intangible/intractable, and is largely driven by the severity of the disaster and its impacts on one's home and community (see Box 3.1). People do not have to be physically displaced at the

BOX 3.1 DEFINITION: DISPLACEMENT

Displacement: forced removal of a person from his/her home or country, often due to armed conflict or natural disasters (International Organization for Migration [IOM] 2011, p. 29).

time that disaster strikes. They can shelter-in-place or community (e.g., in family or friend's residence nearby), but later be displaced because of severe damage to their home (owned or rented) or due to threats from damages to lifeline infrastructure and critical facilities (e.g., water supply contamination). This can be characterized as micro-displacement, which occurs within or between urban neighborhoods (Carrillo 2009; International Federation of Red Cross and Red Crescent Societies [IFRC] 2012; Singh 2012). This section focuses on three overlooked forms of displacement: in situ, cultural-economic, and protracted, given their overlapping and intractable nature, ramifications for housing, and implications for second levels of vulnerability and insecurity for displaced persons.

3.2.1 In Situ Displacement

The concept of in situ displacement refers to displacement experienced by people while staying in place, where people find themselves in a new position in the social hierarchy, leading to exclusion and impediments to physical and social movement (Feldman et al. 2003, p. 9). After Hurricane Katrina, low-income and working-poor families faced unprecedented rent increases; some were evicted from undamaged units or faced rent hikes for failure to pay while evacuated, and others were evicted even when their apartment or residence suffered no damage (Pardee 2012). The experiences of the Honduran Garifuna* after Hurricane Katrina provide a different perspective. Although long-time residents of New Orleans, they were classified as new Latinos who had come to work in the cleanup and reconstruction. They faced the dilemma of negotiating their place in post-Katrina New Orleans (England 2009) to overcome marginalization, invisibility, and in situ displacement. Persons not directly impacted by disasters can also experience in situ displacement. For example, the Tata Institute of Social Sciences (2005) reported that after the 2004 tsunami, some unaffected households in Indian coastal villages were left in place and were excluded from relocation, resettlement, and compensation policies, while the surrounding affected community was relocated. This led to a lack of resources to these remaining households. Disruption to livelihood dependency chains for these remaining households essentially altered their economic and social status and roles in the coastal fishing community.

3.2.2 Cultural-Economic Displacement in Host Communities

In situ displacement can also apply to affected individuals and households that find themselves in host communities (communities that are not affected by the primary event, but to which displaced persons turn to as safe havens) and societies (especially in the case of refugees fleeing from conflict situations). There are also the intertwining effects of both culture and economics that surface in host communities.

* The Garifuna of New Orleans is described by Garza (2012) as a historically mobile and transnational community, whose members originally from Honduras first settled in New Orleans in the early nineteenth century when the Standard Fruit Company carried cargo and workers through the port city. More recently, movement from Honduras to New Orleans was prompted by Category 5 Hurricane Mitch in 1998.

Weber and Peek (2012a,b) documented economic hardships related to housing and jobs, as well as widespread marginalization, prejudices, and stigmatization faced in their new locations by persons displaced from New Orleans after Hurricane Katrina (Weber and Peek 2012a,b). Reasons underlying the "Katrina fatigue" by early 2006 (Peek 2012, p. 33) included resentment by some long-time residents of host/receiving communities that the newcomers moved ahead of them in the social service queues (Miller 2012, p. 25). Over time, the social status of displaced persons was further weakened as they were not only viewed as competitors for jobs, social services, and other amenities, but also as outsiders changing the racial, cultural, and economic composition of the receiving community (Meyer 2013). One can argue that the long-time residents of host communities seeking jobs, homes, and services faced their own share of in situ displacement as well. The decrease in the affordable housing stock, as well as increase in house rental costs are examples of impacts that can affect these long-time residents.

3.2.3 Protracted Displacement

For some, displacement tends to be for a very long duration, resulting in movement back and forth between insecure locations, thereby experiencing displacement many times in search of safety and livelihoods (IFRC 2012). Natural disasters represent a primary source of insecurity in countries such as the Philippines, where repeated disasters have led to protracted displacement, increased vulnerabilities, and a lack of access to adequate and affordable housing (Bradley 2015). Haiti has seen its fair share of disasters during the 10-year period between 2004 and 2014: Hurricane Jeanne in 2004, tropical storm Fay and Hurricanes Gustave, Hanna, and Ike in 2008, the 2010 magnitude 7 earthquake and the ensuing cholera epidemic (Esnard and Sapat 2014). Repeated disasters and crises, and protracted displacement have slowed the pace of recovery for displaced persons while exacerbating preexisting vulnerabilities and persistent challenges, such as poverty and homelessness.

Overall, these intangible forms of displacement are impediments to positive recovery trajectories of disaster survivors. As noted by Esnard and Sapat (2014), the prospect of finding a durable solution to displacement such as return or relocation stalls with such protracted displacement, as displacees remain marginalized and caught in further cycles of disaster and displacement.

3.3 RELOCATION AND RESETTLEMENT

> In all too many cases, resettlement, particularly when done at the community level, ends up becoming a secondary disaster. Therefore, when disasters, conflicts, or development damage or destroy communities, uprooting people, displacing them far from homes and jobs, the process of recovery is made doubly complex (Oliver-Smith 2013, p. 187).

What typically starts out for some as temporary evacuation or micro-displacement often evolves into permanent displacement and eventual relocation. Relocation is often voluntary, particularly in the United States where one makes the decision to move to a different home or community based on home ownership status, a variety of push–pull factors such as jobs and social service support, and compensation policies

BOX 3.2 DEFINITIONS: RELOCATION AND RESETTLEMENT

Relocation: a way to protect people or a structure from a hazard by moving them or it away from the hazard; flooding is the most common reason that structures are relocated (Coppola 2011, p. 215).

Resettlement: relocation and integration of people (e.g., refugees, Internally Displaced Persons, etc.) into another geographical area and environment, usually in a third country (IOM 2011, pp. 84–85).

such as buyouts and insurance. The terms relocation and resettlement are sometimes used interchangeably, but resettlement is just one type of relocation; one which conveys the concept of planned, physical displacement of people to a new, permanent location (Arnall et al. 2013, 468) or a managed activity, and intervention by an agency of the state (Wilmsen and Webber 2015) (See Box 3.2). Referring to displacement as a result of climate change, Wilmsen and Webber (2015, p. 78) cautioned that while on one hand, voluntary movement is preferable to forced resettlement to avoid "a high risk of maladaptation," the reality is that organized resettlement might be the only option for those without freedom of mobility.

Moving entire neighborhoods and communities due to lingering hazards is expensive and time consuming and generally easier for small towns and communities. A case in point is the small town of Grantham with a population of 370 people in Queensland, Australia which was relocated to a contiguous relocation site in the same school district after the January 2011 flash flood (Sipe and Vella 2014). In addition to the challenges of negotiating with home and land owners, securing funding for critical infrastructure and design of processes for deciding who would participate in land swaps were other challenges that arose. Mandatory relocation and resettlement, particularly in coastal communities tend to be more controversial with accusations and perceptions of land grabs for tourism and lucrative redevelopment projects. For example, after the 2004 tsunami in Tamil Nadu, relocation was not favored by local communities and villagers who made their living from fishing and related activities such as fish drying, and storage of fishing boats and nets (Tata Institute of Science 2005). After Hurricane Katrina, there were similar concerns in the cities of Gulfport and Biloxi in Mississippi about development initiatives negatively impacting poor African American neighborhoods that had already been squeezed by urban development strategies prior to the disaster (Derickson 2014).

Another nagging dilemma is the emergence of [un]planned illegal new communities and settlements. In Haiti, for example, there is ongoing discussion about land tenure, land rights, and land entitlement for residents who seek to resettle themselves after the catastrophic 2010 earthquake. The city of Canaan on the periphery of the capital city of Port-au-Prince was originally the site of the Corail-Cesselesse "model camp" created by the international community for Haiti's 2010 earthquake survivors. The population in Canaan is said to have tripled between 2011 and 2015 (UN-OCHA 2011; Zidor 2012; Haiti Grassroots Watch 2013; Welsh 2015) with major investment by residents in housing, schools, churches, and shops. This self-resettled community moved ahead despite the limited access to water, sanitation, and waste removal services, despite not being sanctioned by government (Zidor 2012), and most significantly despite being built on land that is vulnerable to landslide from heavy rains (UN-OCHA 2011). The likelihood for repeated displacement is very real for this new community.

Relocation and resettlement also needs to be addressed from the perspectives of conflict and climate change, which will continue to cause internal and transnational flight to host communities and countries. Additionally, relocation and resettlement of residents with short tenures in host countries will require adaptation to new settings, integration into new host societies, and overcoming usually higher unemployment rates, access to fewer resources, less secure housing, and linguistic issues (Marlowe 2013; Marlowe and Lou 2013). Such adaptation is further complicated in host communities and countries that may themselves face crises and disasters. For example, the Bhutanese who were relatively recent arrivals and did not have community centers, suffered more complications than their Ethiopian and Afghan counterparts in the aftermath of two major earthquakes in Christchurch* in 2010 and 2011 (Marlowe 2013).

The pathways from displacement to return or relocation while highly variable from one community to another, are also influenced by macro-level sheltering and housing policies, as well as micro-level community social ties and collaborative decision-making dynamics. Relocation is also shaped by what Iuchi (2014) referred to as the two resettlement dynamics; one between the government and the community and the second within the community itself.

3.4 HOME AND COMMUNITY RECOVERY: INFLUENCE ON DISPLACEMENT TIMELINES AND PATHWAYS

> Reconstructing/reconstituting a community means attempting to replace through administrative efforts an evolutionary process in which social, cultural, economic, and environmental interactions arrived at through trial and error, and deep experiential knowledge develop, enabling a population to achieve a mutually sustaining social coherence and material sustenance over time.... One of the best outcomes that might be imagined for resettlement projects is to work out a system in which people can materially sustain themselves while they themselves begin the process of social reconstruction (Oliver-Smith 2013, p. 206).

Emergency sheltering and temporary housing phases are critically important in the pathway from displacement to return or relocation. In the United States, formulation of national-level temporary housing strategies and guidance policies materialized after the housing problems that followed Hurricane Katrina, and included provisions for affordable temporary housing options for displaced persons and appropriate zoning and other land use regulations (Levine et al. 2007; Mitchell et al. 2012; Sapat et al. 2011; Boyd 2014). In a comparative assessment of post-disaster sheltering and housing timelines after Hurricanes Andrew, Katrina, and Ike, Mitchell et al. (2012)

* New Zealand is the third largest refugee resettlement area containing relatively large Afghan, Ethiopian, and Bhutanese communities.

highlighted the importance of recognizing the differential needs of displaced persons, as well as the importance of federal and local agencies integrating and coordinating programs and disseminating resources. In the case of Japan, pre-established temporary housing programs for displaced persons have made it possible to start the process for planning temporary housing almost immediately after the disaster. There has also been an evolution of housing policies in Japan from the "one track" government built pre-fabricated temporary housing option after the 1995 Kobe earthquake, to more options (e.g., payment of rent for the disaster survivors to live in privately owned rental apartments) after the 2011 Great East Japan earthquake (Iuchi et al. 2015). Evaluation of the success of these different approaches will require a longitudinal assessment but concerns revolve around reducing unintended effects of temporary housing locations, splintering communities and, in the case of Japan, depopulating rural communities.

Keeping communities and social networks together continues to be a goal of many community rebuilding advocates in NGOs and government entities, who coordinate and facilitate initiatives to return and rebuild. After the Chilean earthquake of 2010, the recovery effort was led by Chile's Ministry of Housing and Urban Development (MINVU), which had a track record of improving housing conditions of low-income families. According to Comerio (2014), the Ministry focused on both temporary housing and rebuilding on-site. Specifically, subsidies were provided for housing construction on owner sites in order to keep communities intact, to allow access to their jobs and family networks, to facilitate monitoring of construction, and to support local builders and the local economy. Families without land were put up in temporary housing camps while "social condominiums*" were designed on sites selected for pre-organized groups of families by community leaders (Comerio 2014, p. 343).

Storr and Haeffele-Balch (2012, p. 295) characterize post-disaster community rebound as "a collective action problem" where every individual's decision to rebuild is impacted by the likelihood that others in the community will rebuild," also noting that "the longer return is delayed while displaced residents wait to see what other displaced residents will return and rebuild, the greater the chance that individuals will settle down in new locations, abandoning all hopes of returning to their previous communities" (Storr and Haeffele-Balch 2012, p. 296). Community leaders play similarly important roles in community cohesion. They keep their neighbors informed about recovery, rebuilding, and reconstruction timelines and, in some instances, organize and rally them when communities are in jeopardy of elimination.

However, displacement of community members to the same temporary housing sites is no guarantee of decisions to return or relocate jointly, as documented by Iuchi (2014) for two neighboring districts that faced decisions to either relocate or return after the 2004 Chuetsu earthquake. That same study by Iuchi (2014) also highlighted the importance of context in understanding decisions of households and communities—socioeconomic conditions, geographic location (urban/rural), demographics, population growth and decline trends, and culture of community

* Social condominiums are similar to public housing in the United States, except that residents own the units in Chile (Comerio 2014, p. 345).

gatherings and decision making. On the flip side, dispersed host communities and decentralized community-based efforts have led to successful return and community redevelopment. The case of the Vietnamese-American community in the Mary Queen of Vietnam Catholic parish in New Orleans East is one example. The tight-knit community facilitated the return of their fellow residents and parishioners. The displacement to far-flung cities across the United States with other poorer populations, and eventual return to New Orleans is well documented (Leong et al. 2007; Chamlee-Wright and Storr 2009; Storr and Haeffele-Balch 2012). Similar ethnic diaspora social ties are instrumental even in instances where community cohesion might be less apparent in highly dispersed ethnic households throughout cities. For example, the Honduran Garifuna, while very dispersed in New Orleans before Hurricane Katrina, all lived in the same host community of Houston after the hurricane (Garza 2012). The group, according to Garza (2012), became a more cohesive community linked by their migration to and evacuation from New Orleans. Pastor Erik, a Houston resident also of Garifuna descent facilitated acquisition of temporary housing, assisted with FEMA and insurance paperwork, and conducted therapy sessions and Garifuna-language church services thus enabling and fostering this Garifuna community cohesion in the host community of Houston (Garza 2012). Overall, the strength of ethnic diaspora networks in host communities was important for community cohesion and joint return decisions.

What rings true in the examples and communities featured in this section is that reconstructing and reconstituting cohesive communities are fundamental to household and community recovery and vice versa, and that population displacement pathways, processes, players, and outcomes are key determinants of return, relocation, and resettlement dynamics.

3.5 CONCLUDING THOUGHTS

As a society, we have made progress in acknowledging the long-term recovery implications of devastating disasters. That it takes years if not decades to recover, particularly for vulnerable households and communities, is increasingly evident in both developed and developing countries. Displacement adds to the multifaceted and complex nature of post-disaster housing recovery, but drivers of displacement and decision-making processes underlying how return and relocation decisions are made remain highly nuanced and variable between places and societies. The domino effects of conflicts, as well migration and displacement from slow-onset hazards such as climate change on top of increasing weather disasters will present a whole host of other challenges as well, including socio-legal and additional human rights issues. A broad range of community practitioners who interface with displaced persons—social workers, school administrators, social service providers, health care providers, planners, policy makers, lawyers, human rights advocates, and government entities—must acknowledge and address the complexities of displacement to facilitate and enable appropriate outcomes for both internal and transnational displacees. Housing and community considerations need to remain front and center in such research and practice initiatives.

ACKNOWLEDGMENTS

The ideas presented in this chapter were formed based on research supported by the US National Science Foundation (NSF) Grant Nos. CMMI-0726808, CMMI-1034667, and CMMI-1162438. Any opinions, findings, and conclusions or recommendations expressed in this chapter are those of the author.

REFERENCES

Arnall, A., D. S. G. Thomas, C. Twyman, and D. Liverman. 2013. Flooding, resettlement, and change in livelihoods: Evidence from rural Mozambique. *Disasters* 37(3): 468–88.

Boyd, A. 2014. Long-term recovery planning: Goals and policies. In *Planning for Post-Disaster Recovery: Next Generation*, J. C. Schwab (ed.), Washington, DC: American Planning Association, 72–91.

Bradley, M. 2015. Resolving post-Typhoon Haiyan displacement in the Philippines. Brookings Institution. http://www.brookings.edu/blogs/order-from-chaos/posts/2015/06/15-philippines-typhoon-recovery-strategies-bradley (accessed June 15, 2015).

Carrillo, A. C. 2009. Internal displacement in Colombia: Humanitarian, economic, and social consequences in urban settings and current challenges. *International Review of the Red Cross* 91(875) (September): 527–46.

Chamlee-Wright, E. and V. H. Storr. 2009. Club goods and post-disaster community return. *Rationality and Society* 21(4): 429–58.

Comerio, M. C. 2014. Housing recovery lessons from Chile. *Journal of the American Planning Association* 80(4): 340–50.

Coppola, D. P. 2011. *Introduction to International Disaster Management*, 2nd edn, Burlington, Massachusetts: Elsevier Inc.

Derickson, K. 2014. After Hurricane Katrina, devastated black neighborhoods created an "opportunity" for redevelopment that focused on gentrification. *LSE US Centre* blog on *American Politics and Policy*. http://blogs.lse.ac.uk/usappblog/2014/07/07/after-hurricane-katrina-devastated-black-neighborhoods-created-an-opportunity-for-redevelopment-that-focused-on-gentrification/ (accessed February 26, 2016).

England, S. 2009. Afro-Hondurans in the chocolate city: Garifuna, Katrina, and the advantages of racial invisibility in the nuevo New Orleans. *Journal of Latino/Latin American Studies* 3(4): 31–55.

Esnard, A. M. and A. Sapat. 2014. *Displaced by Disasters: Recovery and Resilience in a Globalizing World*. Boca Raton, Florida: Routledge Press, Taylor & Francis.

Esnard, A. M. and A. Sapat. 2015. Vulnerabilities magnified: A closer look at disasters and displacement. In *Cities and Disasters*, D. Downey (ed.), Boca Raton, Florida: CRC Press, 201–16.

Feldman, S., C. Geisler, and L. Siberling. 2003. Moving targets: Displacement, impoverishment, and development. *International Social Science Journal* 55(175): 7–13.

Garza, C. M. 2012. Twice removed: New Orleans Garifuna in the wake of Hurricane Katrina. In *Displaced: Life in the Katrina Diaspora*, L. Weber and L. Peek (eds), Austin, Texas: University of Texas Press, 198–217.

Haiti Grassroots Watch. 2013. Reconstruction of Haiti slum to cost hundreds of millions of dollars. http://www.ipsnews.net/2013/06/reconstruction-of-haiti-slum-to-cost-hundreds-of-millions-of-dollars/ (accessed February 26, 2016).

Internal Displacement Monitoring Centre (IDMC). 2014. *Global Estimates 2014: People Displaced by Disasters*. Geneva, Switzerland: IDMC. http://www.internal-displacement.org/assets/publications/2014/201409-global-estimates2.pdf (accessed February 26, 2016).

International Federation of Red Cross and Red Crescent Societies (IFRC). 2012. *World Disasters Report 2012, Focus on Forced Migration and Displacement.* Geneva, Switzerland: IFRC.

International Organization for Migration (IOM). 2011. *International Migration Law: Glossary on Migration*, 2nd edn, Geneva, Switzerland: IOM.

Iuchi, K. 2014. Planning resettlement after disasters. *Journal of the American Planning Association* 80(4): 413–25.

Iuchi, K., E. Maly, and L. A. Johnson. 2015. Three years after a mega-disaster: Recovery policies, programs, and implementation after the Great East Japan earthquake. In *Post-Tsunami Hazard Reconstruction and Restoration*, V. Santiago-Gandino, Y. A. Kontar, and Y. Kaneda (eds), London: Springer, 29–46.

Leong, K. J., C. A. Airriess, W. Li, A. C. C. Chen, and V. Keith. 2007. Resilient history and the rebuilding of a community: The Vietnamese American community in New Orleans East. *The Journal of American History* 94(3): 79–88.

Levine, J., A. M. Esnard, and A. Sapat. 2007. Population displacement and housing dilemmas due to catastrophic hurricanes. *Journal of Planning Literature* 22(1): 3–15.

Marlowe, J. 2013. Resettled refugee community perspectives to the Canterbury earthquakes; Implications for organizational response. *Disaster Prevention and Management* 22(5): 434–44.

Marlowe, J. and L. Lou. 2013. The Canterbury earthquakes and refugee communities. *Aotearoa New Zealand Social Work* 25(2): 58–68.

Meyer, M. A. 2013. Internal environmental displacement: A growing challenge to the United States welfare state. *Oñãti Socio-Legal Series* 3(2): 326–45.

Miller, L. M. 2012. Receiving communities. In *Displaced: Life in the Katrina Diaspora*, L. Weber and L. Peek (eds), Austin, Texas: University of Texas Press, 25–30.

Mitchell, C. M., A. M. Esnard, and A. Sapat. 2012. Hurricane events and the displacement process in the United States. *Natural Hazards Review* 13: 150–61.

Oliver-Smith, A. 2013. Catastrophes, mass displacement, and population resettlement. In *Preparedness and Response for Catastrophic Disasters*, R. Bissell (ed.), Boca Raton, Florida: CRC Press, 185–224.

Pardee, J. W. 2012. Living through displacement: Housing insecurity among low-income evacuees. In *Displaced: Life in the Katrina Diaspora*, L. Weber and L. Peek (eds), Austin, Texas: University of Texas Press, 63–78.

Peek, L. 2012. They call it "Katrina fatigue": Displaced families and discrimination in Colorado. In *Displaced: Life in the Katrina Diaspora*, L. Weber and L. Peek (eds), Austin, Texas: University of Texas Press, 31–46.

Sapat, A., C. M. Mitchell, Y. Li, and A. M. Esnard. 2011. Policy learning: Katrina, Ike and post-disaster housing. *International Journal of Mass Emergencies and Disasters* 29(1): 26–56.

Singh, D. 2012. *Disaster Prevention Key to Stopping Climate Displacement.* Geneva, Switzerland: UN International Strategy for Disaster Reduction. https://www.unisdr.org/archive/24725 (accessed February 26, 2016).

Sipe, N. and K. Vella. 2014. Relocating a flood-affected community: Good planning or good politics? *Journal of the American Planning Association* 80(4): 400–12.

Storr, V. H. and S. Haeffele-Balch. 2012. Post-disaster community recovery in heterogeneous, loosely connected communities. *Review of Social Economy* LXX 70(3): 295–314.

Tata Institute of Social Science. 2005. *The State of Civil Society in Disaster Response: An Analysis of the Tamil Nadu Tsunami.* Bombay, India: Tata Institute of Social Science.

UN-OCHA. 2011. First assessment of Canaan settlement highlights urban structural issues. In: OCHA *Haiti Humanitarian Bulletin* (February 18 to March 9, 2011). http://reliefweb.int/sites/reliefweb.int/files/resources/0866C8247EBA6D784925785000 06D934-Full_report.pdf (accessed April 2015).

Weber, L. and L. Peek (eds). 2012a. *Displaced: Life in the Katrina Diaspora*. Austin, Texas: University of Texas Press.

Weber, L. and L. Peek. 2012b. Documenting displacement: An introduction. In *Displaced: Life in the Katrina Diaspora*, L. Weber and L. Peek (eds), Austin, Texas: University of Texas Press, 1–20.

Welsh, T. 2015. The promised land: 5 years later, Haitians find hope in Canaan. *U.S. News and World Report*. http://www.usnews.com/news/articles/2015/01/12/5-years-later-haitians-find-hope-in-canaan-after-the-2010-earthquake (accessed February 26, 2016).

Wilmsen, B. and M. Webber. 2015. What can we learn from the practice of development-forced displacement and resettlement for organised resettlements in response to climate change? *Geoforum* 58: 76–85.

Zidor, K. 2012. In Haiti's Land of Canaan, a promised land empty of promise. *Caribbean Journal*. http://www.caribjournal.com/2012/08/17/in-haitis-land-of-canaan-a-promised-land-empty-of-promise/ (accessed March 2015).

4 Financing Housing Recovery through Hazard Insurance

The Case of the National Flood Insurance Program

Michael K. Lindell, Samuel D. Brody, and Wesley E. Highfield

CONTENTS

4.1 INTRODUCTION

Disasters damage critical assets such as buildings, contents, and vehicles, which create losses in asset values that can be measured by the cost of repair or replacement (Lindell and Prater 2003). Such reconstruction is relatively straightforward when there are only a few affected households, but problems increase with the number of victims. In the aftermath of Hurricane Katrina, for example, there was $200 billion in damage (Scales 2006). Some financial losses are absorbed by disaster victims, resulting in reduced consumption of shelter, food, clothing, medical care, entertainment, and other goods and services. This decrease is often temporary, lasting only until the household can replace its critical assets by drawing on personal savings. However, a significant portion of financial loss is redistributed through peer relief, government relief, or hazard insurance. In the case of peer relief, money comes from relatives—as well as friends, neighbors, and coworkers or from nongovernmental organizations. Peer relief is uncertain, as the amount of money from relatives, for example, depends on the physical proximity of other nuclear families in the kin network, the closeness of the psychological ties within the network, the assets of the other families and, of course, the extent to which those families also suffered losses.

In the case of government relief, disaster victims can obtain tax deductions or deferrals, unemployment benefits, Small Business Administration loans (paying back the principal at low- or no-interest), and grants (requiring no return of principal). This institutional recovery depends on whether victims meet the qualification standards, usually consisting of documented residence in the impact area and proof of loss.

In the case of hazard insurance, widespread destruction creates massive demand for insurance adjusters and, thus, substantial delays. The approximately 10,000 adjusters dispatched to resolve 1,000,000 claims from Hurricane Katrina were delayed by the number of claims as well as the inaccessibility of some of the homes in the disaster area (Hooks and Miller 2006). Claims settlements can be further complicated by the causal complexity of disaster impact (e.g., the number and timing/sequence of hazard agents such as wind, surge, and inland flooding from hurricanes). In addition, there are problems of underinsurance, insurer bankruptcy (Peacock and Girard 1997), and insurer under-compensation (Scales 2006).

In practice, most households rely on multiple sources of post-disaster financial assistance. Morrow (1997) reported that the primary source of Hurricane Andrew reconstruction funds was private insurance (81% of households reported no other sources) but 60% thought insurance payments alone would be insufficient to rebuild. Indeed, Browne and Hoyt (2000) concluded that insurance covered less than 10% of flood losses—an estimate consistent with Kunreuther's (1996) report that most risk area residents expect to finance recovery through their own resources.

Households suffer from the current system of disaster recovery financing because they experience decreases in living standards when inadequate redistribution leaves them with uncompensated losses. In turn, their communities suffer because households decrease their spending in local businesses—reducing income to merchants and sales taxes to local government. Moreover, damaged or destroyed houses experience decreased property values that depress the values of surrounding properties and decrease the property taxes their owners pay.

The United States federal government also suffers from the status quo because it is the primary source of disaster relief. These expenditures are well-intentioned but problematic because they transfer disaster losses from disaster victims (in proportion to their losses) to the taxpayers (in proportion to their tax burden). The most basic way to reduce the cost of federal disaster relief is to reduce hazard exposure (land use practices) and structural vulnerability (building construction practices), but the federal government has no direct authority over land use regulations and building codes. Local governments do have this authority but are often motivated to avoid stringent development regulations that might hinder local growth. Another way to reduce disaster relief is to increase the rate of hazard insurance purchase. Indeed, the US federal government has attempted to link recovery financing with disaster risk reduction through the National Flood Insurance Program (NFIP) by offering reduced flood insurance premiums to households in communities that adopt disaster-resilient land use practices and building construction practices.

The rest of this chapter will focus on the issues that affect the share of disaster recovery financing that is generated by hazard insurance. The next section describes the basic structure of hazard insurance, especially the way in which it differs from more familiar forms of insurance—life, health, and automobile. In particular, it addresses important issues—such as adverse selection, moral hazard, charity hazard, and concurrent hazards—that affect an insurance program's viability. Section 3 describes the NFIP and the Section 4 examines the factors that influence hazard insurance purchase. The final section addresses some of the NFIP's limitations and identifies recommendations for future research and policy.

4.2 HAZARD INSURANCE BASICS

Insurance is a contractual relationship in which an insurer accepts a premium in exchange for a commitment to pay for losses incurred due to a covered event (Kunreuther 1998). In some respects, insurance for environmental hazards is similar to more familiar forms of insurance by redistributing financial losses over time (policyholders usually file claims in only a few of their many years of premium payments) and people (multiple policyholders without losses are also paying for any year's claims). Policyholders pay their insurance premiums each year to obtain specified levels of coverage for defined categories of hazard. If a covered event causes a loss (e.g., a falling tree branch damages a policyholder's car), the insurance company provides funds for repair or replacement. Insurers are most likely to maintain a viable business if policyholders' losses are generated by a large number of relatively small, independently distributed losses that produce relatively constant levels of total claims each year. Indeed, some environmental hazards such as tornadoes and other wind hazards are included within homeowners' insurance policies because an insurer's total annual claims are produced by events meeting these conditions.

Other environmental hazards such as floods and earthquakes (EQs) require special additional coverage and landslides are not covered (Gall et al. 2009) because they produce claims for compensation that are extremely variable over time. There are many years in which few policyholders file claims but an occasional bad year in which a single extreme event affects a large percentage of the insurer's policyholders and causes it major losses. This large variance in total claims over time compounds the insurer's problems if the probability of the events that cause these claims is uncertain (Scales 2006). For example, the historical record is too short to precisely determine the probability of an extremely rare event such as a Category 5 hurricane striking Galveston Texas. Consequently, insurers are reluctant to offer coverage for catastrophic risks because the probability of occurrence and the consequent loss are ambiguous so it is difficult to determine the appropriate premium structure and an extreme event might bankrupt them if their financial reserves are inadequate (Kunreuther et al. 1993).

Insurers can only remain in business if policyholder premiums can cover the costs of claim settlements plus administrative costs. Consequently, insurance companies avoid excessive administrative costs from numerous small claims using deductibles (a fixed amount of the loss that the policyholder must bear). *Adverse selection* is a threat to an insurer's viability if its premium pricing structure does not adequately account for each purchaser's actual risk of loss—for example, when its policyholders are concentrated in the high hazard area for a single extreme event (e.g., the floodplain of a single river basin). In principle, insurers can avoid this problem by using accurate hazard maps to calculate a property's expected losses for different environmental extremes, pricing insurance policies appropriately, establishing coverage caps (a maximum amount of the loss that the insurer will cover), and maintaining a diverse set of policyholders that will not all be affected by the same extreme environmental event.

4.2.1 Moral Hazard

Moral hazard is a potential threat if policyholders relax their efforts to avoid losses once they have obtained insurance—for example, failing to maintain sump pumps or backflow preventer valves to avoid flood damage. In principle, insurers can avoid this problem by conducting periodic inspections to verify that the policyholders are maintaining their properties to the extent specified in the insurance contract but individual inspections would be prohibitively expensive for residential coverage. Instead, insurers maintain policyholders' protection motivation through deductibles (requiring policyholders to pay for the first portion of a loss), coinsurance (requiring them to pay for a fixed percentage of the remaining loss), and coverage caps (limiting the insurer's liability).

The need to control their financial liability also leads insurers to restrict the list of *covered losses*. If a term such as flooding is to have any meaning other than its common dictionary meaning, it must be defined within the policy. For example, NFIP (2011, p. 2) defines flood to include not only the inundation from adjacent water bodies, but also surface ponding from intense rainfall, mudflows, and land subsidence or collapse due to flooding. There are other definitions that have evolved through case law, which might (or might not) overlap with government agency and private insurer definitions. Unfortunately, courts in different states have differed in their interpretation of a wide range of terms and principles relevant to hazard insurance (Scales 2006).

4.2.2 Charity Hazard

Charity hazard is assumed to result from households' decisions to forego hazard insurance in an expectation of obtaining compensation from others—especially government but also nongovernmental organizations and peers. As Raschky and Weck-Hannemann (2007, p. 324) note, "[p]rivate charity and governmental financial relief are premium-free insurance against disasters." Thus, an expectation of adequate governmental disaster relief would make it rational for households to underinsure. However, they also observe that this is an advantage to households that forego market insurance only if they receive benefits that are as large as those received by those who purchase insurance (Raschky et al. 2013). Prettenthaler et al. (2004, cited in Raschky et al. 2013) argue that charity hazard arises from social legitimization and governmental institutionalization. In turn, social legitimization is attributable to beliefs that government, not the individual household, is responsible for protection from natural hazards. Governmental institutionalization is defined by the establishment of special agencies, laws and regulations, and procedures for distributing governmental funds to disaster victims.

4.2.3 Concurrent Hazards

Concurrent hazards are distinctly different environmental phenomena that damage property at, or near, the same time. For example, hurricanes cause damage by straight-line wind, tornadoes, storm surge, and inland flooding. Determining which specific agent caused a loss can be difficult but is very important because most homeowner insurance policies have *anti-concurrent causation* (ACC) clauses that allow compensation only for wind damage. ACC clauses frequently cause legal disputes about whether it was wind or water that acted first, with insurers claiming in a number of Hurricane Katrina cases that the damage was caused by water and they owed the policyholder nothing. A decision by the US Court of Appeals ruled that losses from mixed-cause events should be compensated in proportion to the damage attributable to each cause (Scales 2006). ACC clauses have been upheld in most courts but not in states that have statutes adopting the principle of *efficient proximate cause*, which states that an insurer must compensate a policyholder for a loss caused by a named peril even if excluded perils were contributing causes (Taylor et al. 2013).

As this discussion indicates, ACC clauses and other coverage issues can produce an adversarial relationship between insurers and policyholders after a loss is incurred (Viaene and Dedene 2004). After some disasters, policyholders have sued their insurers because they believed the compensation offered by the insurer was substantially less than the cost of repair. Plaintiffs have contended that claims adjusters systematically offer unreasonably low settlements in the knowledge that local courts have long backlogs. Consequently, policyholders are forced to accept inadequate settlements immediately rather than wait years—with no assurance that they will get a better outcome. On the other hand, insurers are concerned about catastrophe fraud, which is a material misrepresentation intended to deceive the insurer into paying compensation for which the policyholder would not otherwise be eligible (Viaene and Dedene 2004). This includes claims for damage caused by non-covered causes, claims for business losses under the business owner's homeowner's policy, collusion with contractors to inflate repair costs, moving other people's damaged building contents into a policyholder's house and claiming it as their damage, and claiming relocation expenses but not actually moving (Kerstein 2005). One possible reason for such fraudulent claims is that policyholders expect insurance companies to offer settlements that are less than the cost of repair.

4.3 THE NFIP

The NFIP was established in 1968 as a way for those at risk to pre-fund their losses (Scales 2006). One important feature of the NFIP is the Community Rating System (CRS), which rewards communities for flood mitigation activities that exceed the NFIP's minimum floodplain management standards with flood insurance premium discounts that range from 0% to 45% (Zahran et al. 2009). The CRS rewards 18 flood mitigation activities in four categories of flood management: (i) public information, (ii) mapping and regulations, (iii) flood damage reduction, and (iv) flood preparedness. Series 300 (public information activities) involve local government actions that inform local populations about flood hazards, insurance, and protection measures. Series 400 activities (maps and regulation) involve regulatory enactment and enforcement actions that exceed the NFIP minimum standards. Series 500 activities (damage reduction) involve measures such as acquiring, relocating, or retrofitting existing buildings and maintaining drainage and retention basins. Series 600 activities (flood preparedness) coordinate local managerial efforts to minimize the effects of a flood on people, buildings, and contents. Up to 4500 points are awarded for these activities, with the total number of points in all activities earning flood insurance premium discounts. For example, activity 420 (open space preservation) awards up to 900 points for restriction of development in flood-prone areas—such as protection or restoration of natural areas such as wetlands (Brody et al. 2007; Costanza et al. 2008). The CRS point total corresponds to a class rating that ranges from 10 to 1 (where 10 is the lowest class and 1 is the highest class).

The NFIP has been an important technique for financing disaster recovery. In 2015, there were over 5.2 million policies in force insuring almost $1.3 trillion in property (www.fema.gov/statistics-calendar-year). From 1978 through 2015, the NFIP has paid over $52.5 billion to cover approximately 2.1 million individual losses (bsa.nfipstat.fema.gov/reports/1040.htm). Thus, flood insurance is reducing the burden of federal disaster relief by substituting insurance claims for disaster grants and also by tying insurance subsidies to hazard mitigation measures (Sarmiento and Miller 2006; Wetmore et al. 2006, cited in Kousky 2011). Arguably, any level of insurance purchase reduces the burden on federal taxpayers as long as the NFIP does not induce growth in hazard-prone areas due to the illusion of protection or continue to pay indefinitely for repetitive losses. Repetitive losses have been a major problem until recently because these comprised 2% of all policies but 30% of all claims. For many years, the only mechanism for reducing the program's risk was to require that the property owners elevate the property if the damage has reduced its value by at least 50%. Only in 2004 did the Flood Insurance Reform Act allow the program to refuse insurance to repetitive loss properties (Bagstad et al. 2007).

4.4 HOUSEHOLD INSURANCE PURCHASE, COVERAGE, AND RETENTION

Some basic assumptions about hazard insurance are that prospective policyholders accurately assess their risks, know that hazard insurance is available, know how much it costs, and are able to assess whether to purchase it. In the simplest case, they should judge the probability (p) of an extreme environmental event and the likely amount of damage that event would cause them (L). They should purchase insurance if the premium is less than the product of the probability (p) times their expected loss (L). For example, any premium less than \$3000 should be attractive if $p = 0.01$ and $L = \$300{,}000$. A more realistic formulation would consider the cumulative probability of a loss during the entire time the household occupies the structure which, in turn, requires consideration of the prospective policyholder's discount rate (Kunreuther 1996). Conversely, households should be motivated to avoid insurance if they think (a) the probability/amount of a loss is low—especially if these are within their ability to self-insure, (b) insurance premiums exceed their risk assessment, or (c) if their assessment of the probability/amount of a successful claim is low (MacDonald et al. 1987).

This model is problematic for a number of reasons. First, it oversimplifies the problem by ignoring policyholders' ability to choose their level of insurance coverage; a household might decide to limit the coverage for a \$300,000 house to \$150,000 to make the premiums more affordable. For example, Kousky (2011) found that, of the households required to purchase hazard insurance, some insured their homes for less than full replacement value because that kept their premiums more affordable. Second, it assumes that insurance is a one-time purchase but, in fact, policies are renewed annually, so insurance retention is a potential problem. Indeed, Kunreuther (1996) reported that approximately 20% of NFIP policyholders cancel each year. Michel-Kerjan and Kousky (2010) reported that only 38% of the policies initially purchased were still in force 5 years later and Kousky (2011) found that only 72% of homeowners still in the same dwelling had insurance 6 years later. Browne and Hoyt (2000) found that flood insurance purchase was correlated with the level of flood losses the previous year but retention decayed substantially over a 5-year period if there were no subsequent losses. Third, people do have confidence in insurers (Palm 1998; Petrolia et al. 2013) but confidence that insurers will pay does not necessarily imply confidence that the payments will be prompt and complete (Petrolia et al. 2013).

Fourth, households are likely to forego insurance purchase if their perceived probability of loss is lower than the true probability or their discount rate is high because hazard insurance has a high initial cost but an uncertain "payoff date" when a loss is actually incurred. The role of risk perception in hazard insurance purchase and other *hazard adjustments* (pre-impact disaster loss reduction actions such as hazard mitigation, emergency preparedness, and recovery preparedness—Lindell and Perry 2000) has generated a substantial amount of research. According to the model in Figure 4.1, adapted from Lindell and Hwang (2008), hazard adjustments are most directly determined by people's core perceptions (threat perceptions, protective action perceptions, and stakeholder perceptions, Lindell and Perry 2012), as well as their income and assets (see Figure 4.1). Lindell and Hwang (2008) found that hazard proximity and hazard experience had indirect effects on hazard adjustment adoption via their effects on risk perception. In addition, these variables also had direct effects that were probably due to unmeasured aspects of the core perceptions (that study measured risk perception, but not stakeholder perceptions and protective action perceptions). Gender, ethnicity, income, and hazard information also had

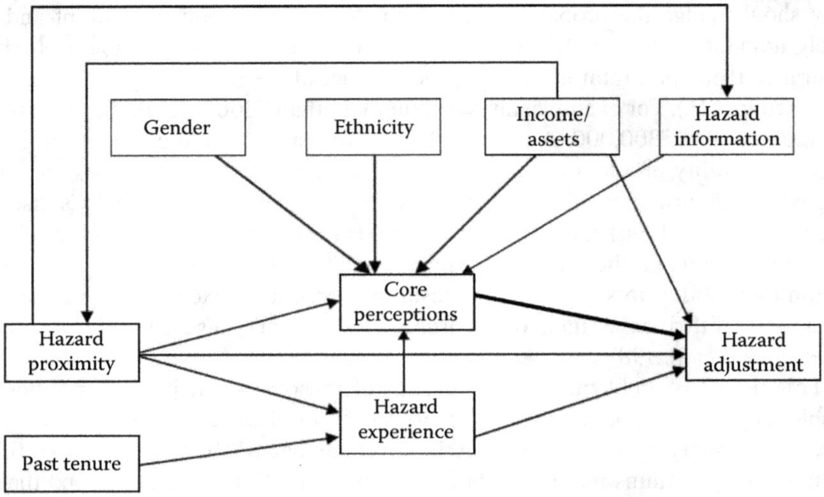

FIGURE 4.1 Revised model of hazard adjustment adoption. (Adapted from Lindell, M.K. and S.N. Hwang. 2008. *Risk Analysis*, 28: 539–556; Lindell and Perry 2012.)

direct effects on risk perception; income had a direct effect on hazard proximity (wealthier people lived closer to the water); hazard proximity had a direct effect on hazard information; and past tenure had a direct effect on hazard experience. Research from the hazard insurance literature on the effects of these and other variables is addressed below.

4.4.1 Risk Perception

An extensive body of research on hazard insurance purchase has found that perceived risk deviates from scientifically estimated risk (e.g., Petrolia et al. 2013). In some cases, the perceived risk is implicitly zero because of a complete lack of hazard awareness, a belief that "it can't happen to me" (Kunreuther 2001), or that a 100-year flood occurs at 100-year intervals—a delay far beyond the individual's myopic time horizon (Palm 1998). In other cases, legally mandated hazard disclosures have been provided but were either not heeded, not recalled, or misunderstood (Palm 1998). Moreover, people often have overconfidence in engineered protection works such as dams and levees (Harding and Parker 1974; Kousky 2011; Pynn and Ljung 1999), although Kriesel and Landry (2004) reported artificial protection proximity had a modest positive relation with insurance purchase. Finally, people underestimate hazard probabilities because they believe environmental systems are more stable than they actually are; in fact, flood risks often increase over time due to upstream development and, in areas behind levees, due to inadequate design and maintenance of protection works. Nonetheless, there are cases where people overestimate risks as, for example, Petrolia et al.'s (2013) finding that respondents expected a Category 3 hurricane every 7.4 years (which is more frequent than the historical average but had a nonsignificant effect on insurance purchase), with each storm causing a loss of 34% of structure value (which had a significant but small effect on insurance purchase). In general, risk perception—often measured as the probability of personal consequences such as the likelihood that one's house will be destroyed, home equity is the household's asset, and damage will be greater than the deductible (Palm 1998) and at other times as affective responses such as fear, worry, or concern—is often the most important determinant of flood insurance purchase (Blanchard-Boehm et al. 2001; Pynn and Ljung 1999; Seifert et al. 2013).

4.4.2 Hazard Experience

Most studies report a correlation of flood hazard experience with insurance purchase (Baumann and Sims 1978; Laska 1990; Lindell and Hwang 2008; Petrolia et al. 2013; Seifert et al. 2013; Zahran et al. 2009), but Pynn and Ljung (1999) did not. Some researchers have examined respondents' *recency* of hazard experience rather than whether they had *any* hazard experience and found a slight positive relation with flood insurance purchase (Kriesel and Landry 2004). Consistent with the other studies, flood insurance purchases increased about 6% after the 2004 Florida hurricanes (Michel-Kerjan 2010). Blanchard-Boehm et al. (2001) reported increased insurance purchases after a flood, with the percentage of households with flood insurance increasing from 52% at the time of the flood to 62% at the time of a survey 6 months later. Atreya et al. (2015) found that flood damage significantly increased flood insurance purchases for 3 years but then became nonsignificant. However, the relationship between hazard experience and insurance purchase might vary by hazard. Palm and Hodgson (1992) found the Loma Prieta EQ had negligible effects of experience on insurance purchase.

4.4.2.1 Hazard Proximity

A number of studies have reported significant correlations of hazard proximity with flood hazard insurance purchase (Kousky 2011; Kriesel and Landry 2004; Lindell and Hwang 2008; Montz 1982; Petrolia et al. 2013; Pynn and Ljung 1999; Zahran et al. 2009). Similar results were reported by Gares (2002), who found that a majority (52%) of those in the 100-year floodplain had flood insurance, whereas only a small minority (5%) of those outside the floodplain did. More recently, Petrolia et al. (2013) found that insurance purchase was very high inside Special Flood Hazard Area zones (78%) but smaller outside (28%). Moreover, policyholders purchased greater coverage if they were in coastal high velocity zones than if they were in the standard 100-year flood zone, and greater coverage in the latter than in the 500-year flood zone (Landry and Jahan-Parvar 2011).

The positive association between flood hazard proximity and flood insurance purchases is partially explained by the NFIP mandate requiring all homes and commercial buildings in the 100-year floodplain to purchase federal flood insurance. Accordingly, Zahran et al. (2009) and Petrolia et al. (2013) found that insurance purchase rates were correlated with NFIP ratings. The finding that insurance purchase rates are also high in the 500-year floodplain and outside the 500-year floodplain suggests adverse selection is not as significant a problem as economic theory suggests (Kousky 2011). The unanswered question is whether these voluntary purchases are due to risk aversion, misperception of risk, mistrust of floodplain maps, or some other reason (Kousky 2011).

4.4.3 Demographic Characteristics and Other Variables

There is some research showing that household income/wealth (Eisenman et al. 2009; Kunreuther et al. 1978; Laska 1990; May 1992; Mileti 1999), education (Atreya et al. 2015; Bauman and Sims 1978; Kunreuther et al. 1978), and age (Atreya et al. 2015; Bauman and Sims 1978; Kunreuther et al. 1978)—which tend to be correlated with each other—influence household flood insurance purchase and other hazard adjustments. Wealthy households have more expensive property at risk and therefore have a greater likelihood of insurance purchase (Petrolia et al. 2013; Zahran et al. 2009). Household income has been positively (Baumann and Sims 1978; Browne and Hoyt 2000), but sometimes nonsignificantly (Kousky 2011), related to purchase rates and coverage levels. Kriesel and Landry (2004) found the effect of household income to be curvilinear, with the highest coverage levels in the $75,000–$149,999 range, next highest in the $30,000–$49,999, $200,000–$249,999, and greater than $250,000 ranges, and lowest in the less than $30,000 range. Assessed valuation had a nonlinear relation with insurance purchase in one study, with the lowest and highest valuations having the highest purchase rates (Pynn and Ljung 1999). Atreya et al. (2015) also found that African Americans were more likely to purchase flood insurance. More generally, however, systematic literature reviews have found that demographic variables tend to have weak and inconsistent correlations with hazard adjustments such as insurance purchase (Lindell 2013; Lindell and Perry 2000).

4.4.3.1 Moral Hazard

Botzen et al. (2009) found that people were willing to engage in hazard mitigation measures in exchange for insurance premium reductions but other studies have reported a willingness to invest in hazard mitigation measures even without subsidies. For example, Blanchard-Boehm et al. (2001) found no significant difference between insured and uninsured residents regarding post-flood mitigation. Similarly, Yamori et al. (2009) found nonsignificant differences in the rates of hazard mitigation by those who had EQ insurance (28.8%), those covered by fire insurance only (24.3%), and those who were uninsured (23.7%). Atreya et al. (2015) found a nonsignificant relationship between flood insurance purchase and mitigation assistance—where a negative relationship would be expected if these were substitutes. Lindell and Hwang (2008), Lindell et al. (2009), and Hudson et al. (2015) all found significant positive correlations between hazard insurance purchase and adoption of other hazard adjustments, although the latter study found this result in their US sample but not their German sample.

4.4.3.2 Charity Hazard

Concern about charity hazard is unsupported by empirical research (Browne and Hoyt 2000; Kunreuther et al. 1978). People consider themselves to have greater responsibility than government agencies for their protection from natural hazards

(Arlikatti et al. 2007; Lindell and Perry 2000; Lindell and Whitney 2000) and do not expect federal disaster relief (Raschky and Weck-Hannemann 2007; Schwarze and Wagner 2004). Indeed, Palm (1998) found that people expect government loans/grants will be insufficient and others have found that concern about inadequate federal/state disaster relief was an important predictor of insurance purchase (Blanchard-Boehm et al. 2001; Petrolia et al. 2013; Pynn and Ljung 1999). These findings are consistent with those of Raschky et al. (2013), who found that expected governmental disaster relief decreased insurance demand, especially when the perceived likelihood of loss was greater—rather than when the maximum loss was greater. In addition, a laboratory experiment by Brunette et al. (2008, cited in Raschky et al. 2013) found that the provision of disaster relief decreased demand for hazard insurance but, unlike the experience in actual disasters, there was no uncertainty about the likelihood and amount of compensation. Moreover, in another experimental study, Seifert et al. (2013) found that willingness to pay for insurance was related to expectations of government disaster assistance in the Netherlands but not in Germany. This might be due to the absence of insurance for catastrophic flooding in the Netherlands.

4.4.4 Awareness and Perceptions of Hazard Insurance

Kunreuther et al. (1978) found that many residents of hazard-prone areas were unaware that their homeowner's insurance did not cover flood losses or that a separate flood hazard policy existed, let alone what the premium would be for that policy (see also Chivers and Flores 2002). More recent research has produced mixed results on the effects of price on hazard insurance purchase—substantial negative (Kriesel and Landry 2004), slight negative (Browne and Hoyt 2000; Dixon et al. 2006), and nonsignificant (Atreya et al. 2015; Kousky 2011) effects. In addition, Pynn and Ljung (1999) reported that their respondents rated policy affordability as important.

In addition to premium costs, other attributes such as transaction costs are potential impediments to household hazard insurance purchase because this involves searching for insurers, examination of information about contract conditions, comparison of alternative policies, and filing claims after experiencing a loss (Raschky et al. 2013). Bubeck et al. (2013) found that individual perceptions about the availability and effectiveness of insurance have a large influence on flood insurance purchases in Germany. Other studies have examined people's perceptions of the attributes of hazard insurance in comparison to household hazard mitigation and emergency preparedness actions (Lindell and Prater 2002; Lindell and Whitney 2000; Lindell et al. 2009). Figure 4.2 shows that EQ hazard insurance is less likely to be adopted than a first aid kit (the most popular hazard adjustment) because it has lower scores on the hazard-related attributes (protect persons, protect property, and other uses) and a higher score on cost, but is roughly equivalent on the other resource-related attributes (required knowledge/skill, time/effort, and social cooperation). Indeed, EQ insurance is less likely to be adopted than the average of all 16 hazard adjustments studied because of its lower scores on protecting persons and other uses, as well as its much higher cost (see Figure 4.2). Terpstra and Lindell (2013) found similar results for flood hazard in the Netherlands.

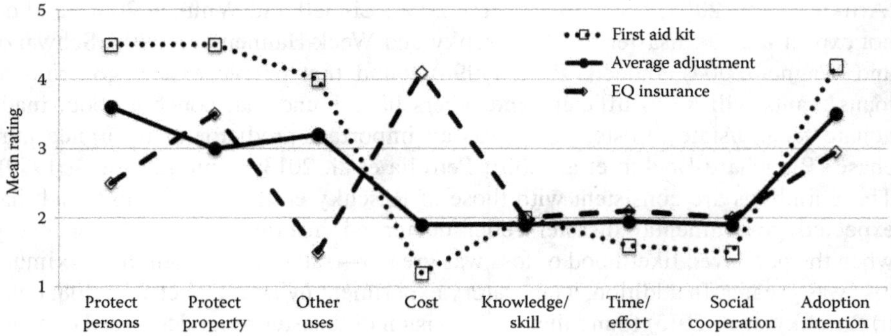

FIGURE 4.2 Perceived attributes of hazard adjustments. (Adapted from Lindell, M.K., S. Arlikatti, and C.S. Prater. 2009. *Risk Analysis*, 29: 1072–1088.)

Finally, there is also evidence that "myopic" planning horizons affect insurance purchase and adoption of other hazard adjustments (Kunreuther 2006). A decision maker's planning horizon is considered myopic when it focuses on a hazard adjustment's immediate benefits and ignores the protection that it would provide in the more distant future.

4.4.5 Mandatory Insurance Requirement

One might assume that, since all properties purchased in the 100-year flood plain are required to purchase flood insurance in order to qualify for federally backed mortgages, the vast majority of flood-prone properties would be covered. Indeed, Kriesel and Landry (2004) found that 78% of flood insurance purchasers did so because it was required. However, Kunreuther (2006) found that almost half of flood victims who lacked insurance should have been required to have it. One reason for this incomplete coverage is that some jurisdictions have many homes that are not financed by federally backed mortgages (39% in those studied by Landry and Jahan-Parvar 2011). Thus, the effect of a mandatory purchase requirement on insurance purchase is significant in some studies (Blanchard-Boehm et al. 2001; Kriesel and Landry 2004) but not in others (Kousky 2011).

4.5 CONCLUSIONS AND RECOMMENDATIONS

Unless households can obtain the money needed to rebuild their homes, they will experience decreases in living standards that affect other households in their communities through reduced income to merchants and sales taxes to local government, as well as decreased property values that depress the values of surrounding properties and decrease property taxes. Unfortunately, current solutions for financing housing reconstruction after disasters are problematic. Personal savings, peer relief, and government relief are generally insufficient and insurance programs such as the NFIP need significant revisions because of the problems arising from conflicting goals. As noted above, the NFIP seeks to limit flood zone occupancy by regulating wetlands and development in coastal zones through CRS ratings that provide insurance rate reductions. However, the program has had limited effectiveness in preventing developers from increasing disaster losses by purchasing undeveloped flood-prone land at a discount and selling the developed property at a profit (Holway and Burby 1990). There is no market mechanism to discourage this practice because developers have minimal risk while they own the raw land (there are no structures or infrastructure to damage) and can sell the property within a very short time. Consequently, they are able to pass the risk of financial loss from flooding to other stakeholders—homeowners, mortgage holders, and the federal government (Bagstad et al. 2007). In addition, flood insurance rates were subsidized to avoid penalizing those who already owned property in floodplains. The amount of the subsidy is the difference between the average residential premium of $585 and the $2000 charge that would be necessary to protect the NFIP against catastrophic losses (Bagstad et al. 2007). Unfortunately, these subsidized rates reinforce the effect of flood control projects in promoting rather than inhibiting development of flood-prone areas.

Despite the incentives provided by the CRS, the NFIP has not yet achieved adequate purchase rates and coverage levels in 100-year floodplains. In addition, too many policies are allowed to lapse in later years because neither the government nor the banks holding mortgages verify that the policies are continued. To address these limitations, a number of researchers have identified ways in which the NFIP could be changed (e.g., Burby 2001; Kunreuther and Pauly 2006). One way to overcome incomplete coverage is to require comprehensive (all-hazards) disaster insurance, which would diversify losses over multiple geographical regions and eliminate the conflicts associated with ACC clauses. The NFIP could continue to rely on private insurance companies to serve as its agents in marketing all-hazards insurance policies, which could overcome the current problem of flood insurance policy unfamiliarity and complexity (Scales 2006). In addition, charging risk-based premiums would signal to communities to avoid locating anything other than the most essential structures in hazard-prone areas and to encourage such structures to use the best hazard-resistant construction technologies. Any adverse impact of risk-based premiums on low-income residents could be alleviated by providing means-tested subsidies that decrease progressively with household income—just as with income taxes. In addition, the NFIP could also be changed to require that houses be inspected, at least initially, to ensure that they meet hazard-resistant building standards (Kunreuther 1996). After the initial inspection, NFIP could provide a seal of approval so the future homebuyers would know that the structure was a reasonably safe investment. The NFIP could also offer premium discounts to policyholders who invest in hazard mitigation measures.

Of course, a modified NFIP would also need to enlist the collaboration of banks and other mortgage holders to ensure that hazard insurance provided an adequate level of coverage for reconstruction and that the policy would not be allowed to lapse. Additional provisions would also be required for houses that did not have federally insured mortgages (cf. Landry and Jahan-Parvar 2011). In some cases, these structures might be owned by households that are self-insuring but, in other cases, more effective risk communication may be needed to convince households to purchase hazard insurance (Botzen and van den Bergh 2012; Botzen et al. 2013; Lindell and Perry 2004; Lindell et al. 1997).

More generally, empirical research indicates that concerns about moral hazard and charity hazard are largely unsubstantiated. Figure 4.2 suggests that moral hazard is not a major issue because hazard insurance only protects the value of a structure; it does not protect the structure from damage—let alone protect the occupants from injury or death. Thus, hazard insurance is part of a portfolio of hazard adjustments rather than a substitute for other protective measures. One aspect of charity hazard, reliance on government relief, is a default option rather than a deliberate strategy because it is (accurately) perceived as providing insufficient funds for complete recovery. Another aspect of "charity hazard," reliance on peers, also seems to be a default option rather than a deliberate strategy but can alternatively be viewed as a form of self-insurance in which "self" is defined as an extended family or community. It is only "premium-free insurance" if a household accepts assistance from others but does not reciprocate when those others are in need. This disparity between what seems to be economically rational and what people actually do underscores the need for policy makers to design insurance programs based on thorough consideration of the research on behavioral economics (Kunreuther et al. 2013) and behavioral decision theory (Lindell 2014).

ACKNOWLEDGMENTS

This work was supported by the National Science Foundation under Grants CMMI-1129998 and IIS-1540469. We thank W.J.W. Botzen and the editors for helpful comments. None of the conclusions express here necessarily reflects views other than those of the authors.

REFERENCES

Arlikatti, S., M. K. Lindell, and C. S. Prater. 2007. Perceived stakeholder role relationships and adoption of seismic hazard adjustments. *International Journal of Mass Emergencies and Disasters* 25: 218–56.

Atreya, A., S. Ferreira, and E. Michel-Kerjan. 2015. What drives households to buy flood insurance? New evidence from Georgia. *Ecological Economics* 117: 153–61.

Bagstad, K. J., K. Stapleton, and J. R. D'Agostino. 2007. Taxes, subsidies, and insurance as drivers of United States coastal development. *Ecological Economics* 63: 285–98.

Baumann, D. D. and J. H. Sims. 1978. Flood insurance: Some determinants of adoption. *Economic Geography* 55: 189–96.

Blanchard-Boehm, R. D., K. A. Berry, and P. S. Showalter. 2001. Should flood insurance be mandatory? Insights in the wake of the 1997 New Year's Day flood in Reno–Sparks, Nevada. *Applied Geography* 21: 199–221.

Botzen, W. J. W., J. C. J. H. Aerts, and J. C. J. M. van den Bergh. 2009. Willingness of homeowners to mitigate climate risk through insurance. *Ecological Economics* 68: 2265–77.

Botzen, W. J. W., J. de Boer, and T. Terpstra. 2013. Framing of risk and preferences for annual and multi-year flood insurance. *Journal of Economic Psychology* 39: 357–75.

Botzen, W. J. W. and J. C. van den Bergh. 2012. Risk attitudes to low-probability climate change risks: WTP for flood insurance. *Journal of Economic Behavior and Organization* 82: 151–66.

Brody, S. D., S. Zahran, P. Maghelal, H. Grover, and W. E. Highfield 2007. The rising costs of floods: Examining the impact of planning and development decisions on property damage in Florida. *Journal of the American Planning Association* 73: 330–45.

Browne, M. J. and R. E. Hoyt. 2000. The demand for flood insurance: Empirical evidence. *Journal of Risk and Uncertainty* 20: 291–306.

Brunette, M., L. Cabantous, S. Couture, and A. Stenger. 2008. *Insurance Demand for Disaster-Type Risks and the Separation of Attitudes toward Risk and Ambiguity: An Experimental Study*. No. 2008-05. Laboratoire d'Economie Forestiere, AgroParisTech-INRA, Nancy, France.

Bubeck, P., W. J. W. Botzen, H. Kreibich, and J. C. J. H. Aerts. 2013. Detailed insights into the influence of flood-coping appraisals on mitigation behaviour. *Global Environmental Change* 23(5): 1327–38.

Burby, R. J. 2001. Flood insurance and floodplain management: The US experience. *Global Environmental Change Part B: Environmental Hazards* 3: 111–22.

Chivers, J. and N. E. Flores. 2002. Market failure in information: The National Flood Insurance Program. *Land Economics* 78: 515–21.

Costanza, R., O. Pérez-Maqueo, M. Luisa Martinez, P. Sutton, S. J. Anderson, and K. Mulder. 2008. The value of coastal wetlands for hurricane protection. *Ambio* 37: 241–48.

Dixon, L., N. Clancy, S. A Seabury, and A. Overton. 2006. *The National Flood Insurance Program's Market Penetration Rate: Estimates and Policy Implications*. Santa Monica, California: RAND.

Eisenman, D. P., D. Glik, R. Maranon, L. Gonzales, and S. Asch. 2009. Developing a disaster preparedness campaign targeting low-income Latino immigrants: Focus group results for project PREP. *Journal of Health Care for the Poor and Underserved* 20: 330–45.

Gall, M., K. A. Borden, and S. L. Cutter. 2009. When do losses count? Six fallacies of natural hazards loss data. *Bulletin of the American Meteorological Society* 90: 799–809.

Gares, P. 2002. Adoption of insurance coverage and modes of information transfer: Case study of Eastern North Carolina floodplain residents. *Natural Hazards Review* 3: 126–33.

Harding, D. M. and D. J. Parker. 1974. Flood hazard at Shrewsbury, United Kingdom. In *Natural Hazards: Local, National and Global*, G. F. White (ed.), New York: Oxford University Press, 43–52.

Holway, J. M. and R. J. Burby. 1990. The effects of floodplain development controls on residential land values. *Land Economics* 66: 259–71.

Hooks, J. P. and T. B. Miller. 2006. The continuing storm: How disaster recovery excludes those most in need. *California Western Law Review* 43: 21–73.

Hudson, P., W. W. Botzen, J. Czajkowski, and H. Kreibich. 2015. Adverse selection and moral hazard in natural disaster insurance markets: Empirical evidence from Germany and the United States. Available at http://www.aria.org/.

Kerstein, F. A. 2005. An overview of post-disaster fraud. *St. Thomas Law Review* 18: 791–802.

Kousky, C. 2011. Understanding the demand for flood insurance. *Natural Hazards Review* 12: 96–110.

Kriesel, W. and C. E. Landry. 2004. Participation in the National Flood Insurance Program: An empirical analysis for coastal properties. *Journal of Risk and Insurance* 71: 405–20.

Kunreuther, H. C. 1996. Mitigating disaster losses through insurance. *Journal of Risk and Uncertainty* 12: 171–87.

Kunreuther, H. C. 1998. Insurability conditions and the supply of coverage. In *Paying the Price*, H. Kunreuther and R. J. Roth (eds), Washington, DC: Joseph Henry Press, 17–49.

Kunreuther, H. 2001. Incentives for mitigation investment and more effective risk management: The need for public–private partnerships. *Journal of Hazardous Materials* 86: 171–185.

Kunreuther, H. C. 2006. Disaster mitigation and insurance: Learning from Katrina. *The Annals of the American Academy of Political and Social Science* 604: 208–27.

Kunreuther, H. C., R. Ginsberg, L. Miller, P. Slovic, B. Borkan, and N. Katz. 1978. *Disaster Insurance Protection: Pubic Policy Lessons*. New York: Wiley.

Kunreuther, H. C., R. Hogarth and J. Meszaros. 1993. Insurer ambiguity and market failure. *Journal of Risk and Uncertainty* 7: 71–87.

Kunreuther, H. C. and M. V. Pauly. 2006. Rules rather than discretion: Lessons from Hurricane Katrina. *Journal of Risk and Uncertainty* 33: 101–16.

Kunreuther, H. C., M. V. Pauly, and S. McMorrow. 2013. *Insurance and Behavioral Economics: Improving Decisions in the Most Misunderstood Industry*. New York: Cambridge University Press.

Landry, C. E. and M. R. Jahan-Parvar. 2011. Flood insurance coverage in the coastal zone. *Journal of Risk and Insurance* 78: 361–88.

Laska, S. B. 1990. Homeowner adaptation to flooding: An application of the general hazards coping theory. *Environment and Behavior* 22: 320–57.

Lindell, M. K. 2014. Judgment and decision making. In *Laboratory Experiments in the Social Sciences*, M. Webster and J. Sell (eds), 2nd edn, San Diego, California: Academic Press, 403–31.

Lindell, M. K., with D. Alesch, P. A. Bolton et al. 1997. Adoption and implementation of hazard adjustments. *International Journal of Mass Emergencies and Disasters Special Issue* 15: 327–453.

Lindell, M. K., S. Arlikatti, and C. S. Prater. 2009. Why people do what they do to protect against earthquake risk: Perceptions of hazard adjustment attributes. *Risk Analysis* 29: 1072–88.

Lindell, M. K. and S. N. Hwang. 2008. Households' perceived personal risk and responses in a multihazard environment. *Risk Analysis* 28: 539–56.

Lindell, M. K. and R. W. Perry. 2000. Household adjustment to earthquake hazard: A review of research. *Environment and Behavior* 32: 590–630.

Lindell, M. K. and R. W. Perry. 2004. *Communicating Environmental Risk in Multiethnic Communities*. Thousand Oaks, California: Sage.

Lindell, M. K. and R. W. Perry. 2012. The protective action decision model: Theoretical modifications and additional evidence. *Risk Analysis* 32: 616–632.

Lindell, M. K. and C. S. Prater. 2002. Risk area residents' perceptions and adoption of seismic hazard adjustments. *Journal of Applied Social Psychology* 32: 2377–92.

Lindell, M. K. and C. S. Prater. 2003. Assessing community impacts of natural disasters. *Natural Hazards Review* 4: 176–85.

Lindell, M. K. and D. J. Whitney. 2000. Correlates of seismic hazard adjustment adoption. *Risk Analysis* 20: 13–25.

MacDonald, D. N., J. C. Murdoch, and H. L. White. 1987. Uncertain hazards, insurance, and consumer choice: Evidence from housing markets. *Land Economics* 63: 361–71.

May, P. J. 1992. Policy learning and failure. *Journal of Public Policy* 12: 331–54.

Michel-Kerjan, E. O. and C. Kousky. 2010. Come rain or shine: Evidence on flood insurance purchases in Florida. *Journal of Risk and Insurance* 77: 369–97.

Mileti, D. S. 1999. *Disasters by Design: A Reassessment of Natural Hazards in the United States*. Washington, DC: Joseph Henry Press.

Montz, B. E. 1982. The effect of location on the adoption of hazard mitigation measures. *The Professional Geographer* 34: 416–23.

Morrow, B. H. 1997. Stretching the bonds: The families of Andrew. In *Hurricane Andrew: Ethnicity, Gender and the Sociology of Disasters*, W. G. Peacock, B. H. Morrow, and H. Gladwin (eds), New York: Routledge, 141–70.

NFIP—National Flood Insurance Program. 2011. *Answers to Questions about the NFIP*. FEMA F-084. Washington, DC: Federal Emergency Management Agency.

Palm, R. 1998. Demand for disaster insurance: Residential coverage. In *Paying the Price*, H. C. Kunreuther and R. J. Roth (eds), Washington, DC: Joseph Henry Press, 51–66.

Palm, R. and M. Hodgson. 1992. *After a California Earthquake: Attitude and Behavior Change*. Chicago: University of Chicago Press.

Peacock, W. G. and C. Girard. 1997. Ethnic and racial inequalities in hurricane damage and insurance settlements. In *Hurricane Andrew: Ethnicity, Gender and the Sociology of Disasters*, W. G. Peacock, B. H. Morrow, and H. Gladwin (eds), New York: Rutledge, 171–90.

Petrolia, D. R., C. E. Landry, and K. H. Coble. 2013. Risk preferences, risk perceptions, and flood insurance. *Land Economics* 89: 227–45.

Prettenthaler, F., W. Hyll, and N. Vetters. 2004. *Nationale risikotransfermechanismen für naturgefahren: Analyse der problemlagen für individuen, Versicherer und Staat*. Intereg working paper nr. 19–2004. Graz, Austria: Joanneum Research Forschungsgesellschaft mbH.

Pynn, R. and G. M. Ljung. 1999. Flood insurance: A survey of Grand Forks, North Dakota, homeowners. *Applied Behavioral Science Review* 7: 171–80.

Raschky, P. A., R. Schwarze, M. Schwindt, and F. Zahn. 2013. Uncertainty of governmental relief and the crowding out of flood insurance. *Environmental and Resource Economics* 54: 179–200.

Raschky, P. A. and H. Weck-Hannemann. 2007. Charity hazard—A real hazard to natural disaster insurance? *Environmental Hazards* 7: 321–29.

Sarmiento, C. and T. R. Miller. 2006. *Costs and Consequences of Flooding and the Impact of the National Flood Insurance Program*. Calverton, Maryland: Pacific Institute for Research and Evaluation.

Scales, A. F. 2006. A nation of policyholders: Governmental and market failure in flood insurance. *Mississippi College Law Review* 26: 7–15.

Schwarze, R. and G. G. Wagner. 2004. In the aftermath of Dresden: New directions in German flood insurance. *The Geneva Papers on Risk and Insurance* 29:164–168.

Seifert, I., W. J. W. Botzen, H. Kreibich, and J. C. J. H. Aerts. 2013. Influence of flood risk characteristics on flood insurance demand: A comparison between Germany and the Netherlands. *Natural Hazards and Earth Systems Sciences* 13: 1691–705.

Taylor, W. D., A. J. Park, and S. O'Brien. 2013. Unique coverage issues in flood losses. *Tort Trial and Insurance Practice Law Journal* 48: 619–50.

Terpstra, T. and M. K. Lindell. 2013. Citizens' perceptions of flood hazard adjustments: An application of the protective action decision model. *Environment and Behavior* 45: 993–1018.

Viaene, S. and G. Dedene. 2004. Insurance fraud: Issues and challenges. *The Geneva Papers on Risk and Insurance—Issues and Practice* 29: 313–33.

Wetmore, F., G. Bernstein, D. Conrad et al. 2006. *An Evaluation of the National Flood Insurance Program: Final Report*. Washington, DC: American Institutes for Research.

Yamori, N., T. Okada, and T. Kobayashi. 2009. *Preparing for Large Natural Catastrophes: The Current State and Challenges of Earthquake Insurance in Japan*. MPRA Paper No. 8851. Available at mpra.ub.uni-muenchen.de/8851/.

Zahran, S., S. Weiler, S. D. Brody, M. K. Lindell, and W. E. Highfield. 2009. Modeling national flood insurance policy holding at the county scale in Florida, 1999–2005. *Ecological Economics* 68: 2627–36.

5 Politics of Disaster Recovery

Policy and Governance Challenges in Post-Disaster Housing

Alka Sapat

CONTENTS

5.1 INTRODUCTION

> In the immediate aftermath of any disaster, sheltering the victims is one of the great challenges posed to government officials. In the long term, planning, design, and the redevelopment of damaged areas, poses other challenges for governments and financial institutions (Comerio 2004, unpaginated).

Housing recovery is both a keystone of overall community recovery and one of the hardest to address as it is a complex and multifaceted phenomenon. While market and civil society forces affect various aspects of housing recovery, disaster management policies by governments play a critically important role in all aspects of post-disaster housing from reducing pre-disaster risks, addressing social and physical vulnerabilities of communities, evacuation, temporary shelter and housing, and rebuilding shattered lives. Public policies and regulations either reduce hazard risks and increase community resilience or perpetuate mistakes and increase vulnerabilities.

Adopting more effective policies and planning for post-disaster housing requires, however, a better understanding of institutional, political, and policy environments, their interaction with markets and civil society, and the challenges inherent within these environments. Political environments may vary and can be unique to communities and jurisdictions. However, there are several political and policy considerations common to housing recovery, albeit with variations across communities, that are often overlooked or misunderstood by those undertaking policy interventions.

This chapter is an attempt to elucidate some of these overarching policy challenges and analyze their impact on housing recovery. The next sections of this chapter discuss specific policy concerns endemic to housing recovery that include: (i) coordination and fragmented disaster governance; (ii) the politics of recovery planning; (iii) policy gaps with respect to renters; (iv) time compression; (v) accountability; and (vi) location and land issues. Examples of these crosscutting concerns and challenges are drawn from the United States and other countries to illuminate their importance in understanding post-disaster housing policies and governance.

5.2 CRITICAL CHALLENGES AND CONSIDERATIONS IN DISASTER HOUSING POLICY

Many challenges exist with regard to disaster housing and the discussion in this section is not intended to enumerate all potential policy challenges. Rather, the objective is to illustrate a few critical and overarching obstacles, particularly those that are politically motivated, and the linkages between various impediments as they affect housing recovery.

5.2.1 Coordination and Fragmented Disaster Governance

Disaster recovery processes typically involve a large constellation of agencies and organizations, which can lead to fragmentation both horizontally and vertically. When there are strong and coordinated relationships across organizations in a given area, there is horizontal integration (Smith 2012; Smith et al. 2013; Sandler and Smith 2013). Vertical integration refers to connectivity along jurisdictional hierarchies, such as between local, state, and federal stakeholders. The lack of integration between numerous stakeholders with different priorities, processes, operating procedures, goals, and objectives in disaster recovery processes renders horizontal and vertical coordination among various stakeholders problematic, resulting in fragmented governance and decision making in silos.

Housing recovery in countries with weak governance frameworks may be even more fragmented, where deficiencies in disaster governance might occur (Tierney 2012; Comerio 2014). Typically fragile and economically weaker countries that experience disaster have to rely on a range of international institutions, aid agencies, and other organizations, who are often there for relatively short periods of time, often answer to external donor priorities, and who compete for post-disaster resources. The lack of coordination among various stakeholders can lead to duplication of effort or hinder the effective use of scarce resources. For instance, in a study of post-disaster settlement and shelter across Africa, Asia, and Latin America,

Esteban et al. (2009, p. 261) point out that shelters were often not built in coordination with organizations providing other services, rendering those shelters unusable. Similarly, during the reconstruction process in Nias, Indonesia, there were several local, national, and international nongovernmental organizations (NGOs) in the area following the December 2005 tsunami and the March 2005 earthquake. Even though a reconstruction commission, Badan Rehabilitasi dan Rekonstruksi (BRR), was established to coordinate the work of these organizations, several stakeholders/organizations still failed to inform the others about ongoing work, particularly while targeting eligible beneficiaries for houses. As a result, some households received two or three houses from different organizations, while other households were not considered eligible (Guarnacci 2012, p. 79). This also led to competition among the various stakeholders (the BRR, and local and international NGOs) for funding and other resources. The resulting lack of policy coordination exacerbated inequities in the provision of housing, and eroded trust and the legitimacy of both national authorities and the international donor community.

5.2.2 The Politics of Recovery Planning

> ...a strong case can be made that it is such matters as lack of preimpact housing inventories; failure to recognize preimpact conflicts and differences in community power; inadequate use of surviving community resources; erratic organizational mobilization; poor inter-organizational co-ordination; difficulties in intergroup information flow; and other organizational and community-level factors which make the problems in preparing for and providing sheltering and housing (Quarantelli 1995, p. 46).

Within the United States and other nations, provision of temporary shelter and temporary housing generally receives attention, due in part to the resources expended by governments, politicians, the humanitarian aid community, and others to provide emergency relief and assistance to disaster survivors. However, long-term planning for community and housing recovery needs remains a challenge.

Studies of recovery after Hurricane Katrina of devastated US Gulf Coast communities, noted that the lack of a policy framework addressing recovery led to problems in provisions for long-term housing (Hooks and Miller 2006; Duhart and Rodriguez-Dod 2007; Nelson et al. 2007; McCarthy 2009). Preferred recovery scenarios and project prioritizations with community input could have enabled New Orleans to procure federal reconstruction funds more quickly and would have offset the intense post-disaster pressure to rebuild (Sard and Rice 2005; Olshansky 2006; Olshansky et al. 2008; Olshansky and Johnson 2012). Lessons learned after Katrina did lead to the adoption of the National Disaster Housing Strategy (NDHS) and the National Disaster Recovery Framework (NDRF) by FEMA in 2011 (FEMA 2011). However, the NDRF and NDHS are yet to lead to more effective local and state recovery planning. A recent analysis by Berke et al. (2014) of local disaster recovery planning in eight southeastern US states found that recovery planning lacks a public constituency to support it, that unfunded state mandated plans led to weaker local plans than those prepared voluntarily, and that less than one-third of vulnerable local jurisdictions had recovery plans, and they were of low quality. The lack of recovery planning has also been detrimental to recovery in other areas. Joakim and Doberstein

(2014) document that while there were some successes noted in housing reconstruction following the 2006 Yogyakarta earthquake in Indonesia, clearly articulated pre-disaster recovery plans delineating the types of housing solutions could have reduced delays in the rebuilding program and led to more efficient recovery.

The failure to engage in recovery planning can be attributed in part to the reliance on market ideologies with respect to housing policy, which leads to the assumption that private household insurance and other market forces will play a role in the restoration and recovery of permanent housing (Sapat et al. 2011; Esnard and Sapat 2014). However, political factors are also critical in understanding the neglect of pre-disaster planning. Engaging in mitigation measures such as pre-disaster recovery planning is likely to yield few political dividends and receives little media attention. Moreover, with the "CNNization" (Comerio 1998, p. 19) of disasters and the "camcorder policy process" (National Academy of Public Administration [NAPA] 1993, p. 18; Schroeder et al. 2001), political careers may be broken or bureaucrats may lose their jobs if disaster response is seen as being inadequate (Sapat et al. 2011). The media sensationalizes disasters presenting opportunities for politicians to showcase their "leadership" and adopt the crusading role of "disaster heroes." The politicization of disaster aid, fueled by media exposure and the relatively low salience of mitigation measures, reduces incentives to engage in disaster recovery planning. When political incentives are layered over other complexities such as diminished administrative capacity and conflict over land, adopting effective recovery planning particularly in the pre-disaster phase becomes even more challenging.

5.2.3 Policy Gaps: Renters, Income, and Housing Recovery

> There does appear to be a consistent problem in finding rental housing for households with low incomes (Quarantelli 1995, p. 49).

In her seminal book on housing, Comerio (1998) noted that housing recovery policy in the United States targets owner-occupied single-family housing, neglecting rentals. This observation has been echoed in numerous studies that have consistently shown that housing recovery policies have structurally favored middle-class homeowners at the expense of low-income renters and homeowners (Fothergill and Peek 2004; Kamel and Loukaitou-Sideris 2004; Levine et al. 2007; Mueller et al. 2011; Sapat et al. 2011; Esnard and Sapat 2014; Peacock et al. 2014, p. 357). The policy focus on homeowners raises serious concerns given the growth in the number of rental properties. Within the United States, the renter share of all US households grew to about 35% in 2012. By early 2013, the total number of households renting in the United States grew to 43 million and rental housing was particularly common in low-income neighborhoods (Joint Center for Housing Studies [JCHS] 2013). Nearly, half (46%) of all unassisted housing with rents under $400 were built before 1960 (JCHS 2013, p. 6), putting these rentals at greater risk of damage during disasters. After disaster, affordable rentals are even harder to find and redevelopment in the form of gentrification exacerbates the problem. For instance, after Katrina, rents rose by approximately 36% in the first year; but wages did not keep pace with these spikes in rental rates (Brookings Institution and Greater New Orleans Community

Data Center [GNOCDC] 2008). Similar problems arose after hurricane Ike; as noted in Sapat et al. (2011) rents had risen from $500 before Ike to $1200–$1500 after the storm (Stanton 2009). Housing in lower income areas suffers greater damage and generally experiences slower recovery rates. In addition, recovery rates for multi-family housing that are typically associated with rental housing are also much slower than single-family housing (Peacock et al. 2014). With fewer personal resources of their own to deal with higher rents or to repair their existing homes (Van Zandt and Rohe 2011; Peacock et al. 2014), and the lack of an advocacy base (Sapat et al. 2011), low-income renters and homeowners are at greater risk for temporary or permanent displacement (Burby et al. 2003) and rarely return to their units after disaster (Levine et al. 2007).

Policy deficiencies in recovery assistance programs for renters also continue to persist. Rental property owners find it more difficult to access recovery programs due to more complicated ownership structures (Wu and Lindell 2004; Gould 2009). In countries where informal modes of renting are prevalent, housing recovery assistance programs tend to favor homeowners, who have legal titles to their residential properties, as compared to renters. In Bhachau, one of the towns affected by the 2001 earthquake in Gujarat, Mukherji (2010) documents that compensation for rebuilding was provided to landlords and was contingent upon the landlord's willingness to rebuild the housing for their renters. Rather than rebuilding and receiving joint compensation with their tenants, the landlords viewed the earthquake as an opportunity to get rid of their rent-controlled tenants and to sell or redevelop their land for more profit. As a result, many renters, particularly those with no connections to those with resources or without any resources of their own, became squatters on public land (Mukherji 2010, p. 1094).

5.2.4 Time Compression and Housing Recovery Policies

> In normal times, the quantities of capital services (e.g., housing, bridges, paving, schools) reaching the end of their life cycle and being replaced vary only slightly over long periods of time.... When a disaster occurs, however, it causes an unusually large and immediate loss of capital services. In other words, it is an extreme, time-compressed case of the normal process of capital depletion and replacement as, for example, for water infrastructure disruptions.... This loss, in turn, triggers a compression in time of the normal demand for rates of capital replacement and thus capital expenditures (Olshansky et al. 2012, p. 170).

Time compression (Haas et al. 1977; Quarantelli 1999; Olshansky and Chang 2009) after disaster, leads to variations in different aspects of recovery such as physical construction, financial transactions, information flows, social capital formation, and institution building. These varying recovery processes that compress differently over time cause distortions in the disaster recovery process (Olshansky et al. 2012, p. 170).

Post-disaster housing processes are affected by time compression in a number of ways. First, time compression can affect critical flows of funds needed to repair, rebuild, or resettle. As Olshansky et al. (2012, p. 174) note, after Hurricane Katrina in New Orleans, government sources of funding for rebuilding, private insurance, and funds from the Road Home Program in Louisiana all came at vastly different rates and times. For instance, funds for mitigation came after funds for rebuilding, leading a homeowner to remark that "he was being paid to rebuild the second floor before building the first floor" (Olshansky et al. 2012, p. 175). At the same time, information about state and federal programs and those from insurance were unclear and inconsistent. The differences in timing and the lack of synchronization prolonged the rebuilding process. Second, given the compression of time, deliberation is often compromised in favor of speed (Olshansky et al. 2006). The pressure to act quickly is often exerted by residents and property owners themselves to have their homes rebuilt to pre-disaster forms and conditions (Schwab et al. 1998, p. 48) or by politicians, or national or international agencies anxious to prove their capabilities to their electorate, auditors, or donors. This can lead to problems of synchronization between public participation and housing reconstruction (Ganapati and Mukherji 2013). Finally, the pressure to speedily rebuild can attenuate goals of sustainability and risk reduction. For example, urgent demands for housing can often lead decision makers to follow the path of least resistance—construction on vacant and often cheaper land at the urban fringe, exacerbating urban sprawl.

5.2.5 Accountability and Related Tensions

Administrative accountability has always been an important principle for policy implementers, who are seen as stewards of the public purse and implicitly of the public trust. To avoid fraud and corruption, particularly in recovery assistance programs, bureaucracies often face pressure from auditing agencies and legislatures to ensure that public funds are being spent appropriately. For instance, the United States Government Accountability Office (US GAO) found that there were an estimated $600 million to $1.4 billion in potentially fraudulent or improper payments made by FEMA after hurricanes Katrina and Rita (US GAO 2006a–d, 2007). While FEMA's verification process improved, monitoring eligibility was still a difficult task as indicated by GAO investigations (US GAO 2014, 2015a–c) of FEMA disaster assistance after Hurricane Sandy.

The focus on accountability is critical given that public taxpayer money funds recovery activities. Achieving administrative accountability during and after disasters remains, however, extremely challenging for a number of reasons. Money remains a powerful incentive for poorly paid bureaucrats in some countries. In other cases, physical damage to government buildings, records, and archives may greatly reduce an already thin layer of government capacity and can further break down fragile capacity to monitor non-state actors. For instance, the 2010 Haiti earthquake destroyed 15 out of 17 ministry buildings, devastated a large percentage of Haiti's civil service and obliterated major state archives (Zanotti 2010). Similarly, the 2004 tsunami severely damaged local and provincial government capacity in Aceh, Indonesia. As Podger (2015, p. 5) points out, "public accountability itself is devastated by disaster."

Accountability is also difficult to achieve given horizontal and vertical fragmentation across jurisdictions and state and non-state actors. For instance, following Hurricane Sandy, FEMA did not have any mechanism to verify whether individuals had homeowners insurance that would limit Individual Household Program payments for damages also covered by private insurance (US GAO 2015c, p. 32). Similarly, FEMA and the states faced challenges in obtaining and sharing information needed to prevent payments from potentially overlapping sources. Implementation by a greater number of networked players increases the complexity of decision making, potentially altering power relations, and worsens the ability to maintain accountability (Behn 2001; Posner 2002; O'Toole and Meier 2004; Scott 2006; Mathur and Skelcher 2007; Koliba et al. 2010). Sharing accountability among many players presents logistical difficulties and makes it easier to finger point, free ride, and avoid blame (Depoorter 2006).

Tensions between different forms of accountability may also arise. For instance, vertical accountability toward government authorities, donors, and auditing agencies is often accompanied by extensive paperwork, reporting protocols, and detailed accounting mechanisms to improve aid effectiveness. However, organizations that lack the time or capacity in disaster situations find it hard to comply with protocols and completion of formal reports (Podger 2015). Excessively stringent reporting requirements can also lead to increased bureaucratization (Lewis and Kanji 2009) or distractions from the core mission (Edwards and Hulme 1996) for NGOs. Downward accountability to disaster survivors (Davis et al. 2015) gets lost at times in trade-offs with upward accountability.

5.2.6 Location and Land

> Success in reconstruction is closely linked to the question of land tenure, government land policy, and all aspects of land-use and infrastructure planning (Davis et al. 2015, p. 143).

While the etymology of the real estate aphorism "Location, location, location" is unclear (Safire 2009), it continues to be a central issue and a global problem in post-disaster housing recovery. Finding appropriate locations for disaster housing that are safe from hazards but that do not negatively impact relocated and displaced survivors is a challenge that emerges in numerous cases. Often the lack of affordable, vacant, or suitable land may lead to the relocation of communities to urban peripheries (Lizarralde 2014) and distant sites leading to the loss of access to livelihoods, networks, and markets. At times, post-disaster housing locations may lack critical infrastructure such as water, sanitation, electricity, and other social services. A case in point is the relocation of families from temporary shelters in Tegucigalpa, Honduras, after Hurricane Mitch, who were assisted with vouchers and housing provided by NGOs to relocate sites in the Amarateca Valley. The housing was 35 km away from the center of Tegucigalpa and lacked access to solid waste services, electricity, and water. This relocation led "to sanitation and health hazards, defaults on house payments, loss of livelihood opportunities, disruption of social networks, and even social unrest and insecurity in the new settlements" (Jha et al. 2010, p. 83).

Similar problems arose following the 2004 Indian Ocean tsunami, when buffer zones implemented in coastal communities led to the relocation of survivors in sites often more than 5 km from the boats which the inhabitants used for their fishing livelihoods (Kennedy et al. 2008, p. 32); other coastal communities were relocated to areas that led to disruptions in economic and social ties, endangering social cohesion and power relations (Tata Institute of Social Sciences 2005). The economic and social impacts on fishing communities were further exacerbated by concerns that repurposed coastal buffer zones were being used to unfairly benefit commercial tourism and recreation (Bristol 2010).

Other challenges to locating post-disaster housing for evacuees and displaced populations stem from opposition by host communities. Not in My Backyardism (NIMBYism) is steeped in social constructions about displaced survivors and temporary housing and presents challenges for local, state, and federal officials in relocating survivors. After Katrina, 32 of 64 parishes in Louisiana banned new group trailer sites that were heavily stigmatized as representing blight. One in four FEMA trailer parks initially proposed for previously undeveloped sites were rejected by the potential host community and residents often formed human and vehicular barrier chains to block construction by federal workers who intended to begin siting new temporary housing developments (Aldrich and Crook 2008, p. 2).

Protecting vulnerable land areas from hazards to mitigate potential housing damage is also a critical challenge for policy makers. Powerful economic interests in developed and developing countries alike can stymie efforts to control risky development in vulnerable areas. In some cases, the role of the state in creating and legitimizing land rights is frequently compromised by the lack of state capacity or the role played by powerful elites, who block legal and regulatory reforms to develop a more equitable distribution of land. For instance, the lack of a cadastral system in Haiti has long been a major obstacle in Haiti and continued to present a challenge in rebuilding efforts made after the 2010 earthquake (Castor 2012). Understanding power equations and economic stakes impeding land distribution reform is thus critical to adopting more effective housing recovery policies.

5.3 LOOKING AHEAD

The key concerns discussed above stem from the myriad complexities of housing recovery and underlying power and resource dynamics. These policy challenges will likely be exacerbated further by a number of interrelated factors. Increased urbanization, higher exposure to disaster risks, climate change effects, demographic changes, rising income inequalities, and population growth are likely to intensify and worsen the impact of disasters and add to housing reconstruction needs. At the same time, however, societal expectations of government actors are likely to grow (Comerio 2004), fueled by the politicization of disaster response and media coverage. Expectations of government assistance after disaster are unlikely to diminish even by those who call for reductions in government size and power.

To increase the effectiveness of housing recovery, pre-disaster housing recovery policies and planning could:

- Focus public attention and debate on mitigation and leverage community assets in ways to counterbalance social inequities and accelerate disaster recovery times (Berke et al. 1993; Burby 1998; Schwab et al. 1998)

- Build awareness of disaster risks and ways to reduce such risks (Berke and Campanella 2006)
- Help address pre-disaster conflicts among groups
- Improve inter-organizational coordination; develop mechanisms to improve accountability, including downward accountability to survivors (Davis et al. 2015)
- Focus on building potential post-disaster temporary and transitional housing inventories and options using disaster housing task forces and agencies
- Manage burgeoning expectations of assistance after disaster

The frequency and intensity of disasters is expected to increase and developing effective disaster governance systems to address these policy challenges and their drivers will be critical to achieving successful housing and community recovery outcomes.

ACKNOWLEDGMENTS

The concepts and ideas presented in this chapter were formed from research supported by the US National Science Foundation Grants Nos. CMS-9813611, CMMI-0726808, CMMI-1034667, and CMMI-1162438. The findings are not necessarily endorsed by the NSF. Any opinions, findings, and conclusions or recommendations expressed in this material are those of the author and do not necessarily reflect the views of the National Science Foundation.

REFERENCES

Aldrich, D. P. and K. Crook. 2008. Strong civil society as a double-edged sword: Siting trailers in post-Katrina New Orleans. *Political Research Quarterly* 61: 379–89.

Behn, R. 2001. *Rethinking Democratic Accountability.* Washington, DC: Brookings Institution Press.

Berke, P. R. and T. J. Campanella. 2006. Planning for post-disaster resiliency. *The Annals of the American Academy of Political and Social Science* 604(1): 192–207.

Berke, P. R., J. Kartez, and D. E. Wenger. 1993. Recovery after disaster: Achieving sustainable development, mitigation and equity. *Disasters* 17(2): 93–109.

Berke, P. R., W. Lyles, and G. Smith. 2014. Impacts of federal and state hazard mitigation policies on local land use policy. *Journal of Planning Education and Research* 34(1): 60–76.

Bristol, G. 2010. Surviving the second tsunami: Land rights in the face of buffer zones, land grabs and development. In *Rebuilding after Disasters: From Emergency to Sustainability*, G. Lizarralde, C. Johnson, and C. Davidson (eds), New York: Taylor & Francis, 133–48.

Brookings Institution and Greater New Orleans Community Data Center (GNOCDC). 2008. *Anniversary Edition: Three Years after Katrina.* New Orleans, Louisiana: GNOCDC. http://www.gnocdc.org (accessed September 1, 2015).

Burby, R. J. (ed.). 1998. *Cooperating with Nature: Confronting Natural Hazards with Land-Use Planning for Sustainable Communities.* Washington, DC: Joseph Henry Press.

Burby, R. J., L. J. Steinberg, and V. Basolo. 2003. The tenure trap: The vulnerability of renters to joint natural and technological disasters. *Urban Affairs Review* 39(1): 32–58.

Castor, A. 2012. The Haitian cadastral system: The case of the commune of Aquin: Revealing the opportunities and challenges. *Conference Proceedings*, Aquin, Haiti (Aldy Hotel, December 14, 2012, Opening remarks and welcome). http://www.hrdf.org/files/rapport-conference-cadastre-aquin-dec-14-2912-english.pdf (accessed September 1, 2015).

Comerio, M. C. 1998. *Disasters Hits Home: New Policy for Urban Housing Recovery*. Berkeley, California: University of California Press.

Comerio, M. C. 2004. Housing issues in future U.S. disasters. Paper No. 2634. *13th World Conference on Earthquake Engineering*, Vancouver, Canada, August 1–6.

Comerio, M. C. 2014. Housing recovery lessons from Chile. *Journal of the American Planning Association* 80(4): 340–50.

Davis, I., P. Thompson, and F. Krimgold (eds). 2015. *Shelter after Disaster, Guidelines for Assistance*, 2nd edn, Geneva, Switzerland: United Nations.

Depoorter, B. 2006. Horizontal political externalities: The supply and demand of disaster management. *Duke Law Journal* 56(1): 101–25. http://scholarship.law.duke.edu/dlj/vol56/iss1/3 (accessed September 1, 2015).

Duhart, O. and E. C. Rodriguez-Dod. 2007. Evaluating Katrina: A snapshot of renters' rights following disasters. *Nova Law Review* 31: 467–85.

Edwards, M. and D. Hulme. 1996. Too close for comfort? The impact of official aid on non-governmental organizations. *World Development* 24(6): 961–73.

Esnard, A.-M. and A. Sapat. 2014. *Displaced by Disaster: Recovery and Resilience in a Globalizing World*. New York: Routledge Press.

Esteban, L., I. Kelman, J. Kennedy, and J. Ashmore. 2009. Capacity building lessons from a decade of transitional settlement and shelter. *International Journal of Strategic Property Management* 13(3): 247–65.

Fothergill, A. and L. A. Peek. 2004. Poverty and disasters in the United States: A review of recent sociological findings. *Natural Hazards* 32(1): 89–110.

Ganapati, E. N. and A. Mukherji. 2013. Out of sync: World Bank funding for housing recovery, post-disaster planning, and participation. *Natural Hazards Review* 15(1): 58–73.

Gould, C. W. 2009. The right to housing recovery after natural disasters. *Harvard Human Rights Journal* 22: 169–204.

Guarnacci, U. 2012. Governance for sustainable reconstruction after disasters: Lessons from Nias, Indonesia. *Environmental Development* 2: 73–85, April. http://dx.doi.org/doi:10.1016/j.env.dev.2012.03.010 (accessed September 1, 2015).

Haas, E. J., R. W. Kates, and M. J. Bowden (eds). 1977. *Reconstruction Following Disaster*. Cambridge, Massachusetts: Massachusetts Institute of Technology.

Hooks, J. P. and T. B. Miller. 2006. The continuing storm: How disaster recovery excludes those most in need. *California Western Law Review* 43(1) (Article 4): 21–54.

Jha, A. K., J. E. Duyne Barenstein, P. M. Phelps, D. Pittet, and S. Sena. 2010. *Safer Homes, Stronger Communities: A Handbook for Reconstructing after Natural Disasters*. Washington, DC: The International Bank for Reconstruction and Development/World Bank.

Joakim, E. and B. Doberstein. 2014. Planning for long-term housing reconstruction following a major disaster: A case study of the 2006 Yogyakarta (Indonesia) earthquake. *Journal of the American Planning Association* 80(4): 352–53.

Joint Center for Housing Studies (JCHS). 2013. *America's Rental Housing: Evolving Markets and Needs*. Boston, Massachusetts: Harvard University.

Kamel, N. M. and A. Loukaitou-Sideris. 2004. Residential assistance and recovery following the Northridge earthquake. *Urban Studies* 41(3): 533–62.

Kennedy, J., J. Ashmore, E. Babister, and I. Kelman. 2008. The meaning of 'build back better': Evidence from post-tsunami Aceh and Sri Lanka. *Journal of Contingencies and Crisis Management* 16(1): 24–36.

Koliba, C., J. W. Meek, and A. Zia. 2010. *Governance Networks in Public Administration and Public Policy*. Boca Raton, Florida: CRC Press.

Levine, J. N., A.-M. Esnard, and A. Sapat. 2007. Population displacement and housing dilemmas due to catastrophic disasters. *Journal of Planning Literature* 22(1): 3–15.
Lewis, D. and N. Kanji. 2009. *Non-Governmental Organizations and Development.* New York: Routledge.
Lizarralde, G. 2014. *Invisible Houses: Rethinking and Designing Low-Cost Housing in Developing Countries.* Florence, Italy: Routledge.
Mathur, N. and C. Skelcher. 2007. Evaluating democratic performance: Methodologies for assessing the relationship between network governance and citizens. *Public Administration Review* 67(2): 228–37.
McCarthy, F. X. 2009. *FEMA Disaster Housing: From Sheltering to Permanent Housing.* Washington, DC: Congressional Research Service.
Mueller, E. J., H. Bell, B. Brunsma Chang, and J. Hansberger. 2011. Looking for home after Katrina postdisaster housing policy and low-income survivors. *Journal of Planning Education and Research* 31(3): 291–307.
Mukherji, A. 2010. Post-earthquake housing recovery in Bachhau, India: The homeowner, the renter, and the squatter. *Earthquake Spectra* 26(4): 1085–100.
National Academy of Public Administration (NAPA). 1993. *Coping with Catastrophe: Building an Emergency Management System to Meet People's Needs in Natural and Manmade Disasters.* Washington, DC: NAPA.
Nelson, M., R. Ehrenfeucht, and S. Laska. 2007. Planning, plans, and people: Professional expertise, local knowledge, and governmental action in post-Hurricane Katrina New Orleans. *Cityscape: A Journal of Policy Development and Research* 9(3): 23–52.
Olshansky, R. B. 2006. Planning after Hurricane Katrina. *Journal of the American Planning Association* 72(2): 147–53.
Olshansky, R. B. and S. Chang. 2009. Planning for disaster recovery: Emerging research needs and challenges. *Progress in Planning* 72(4): 200–09.
Olshansky, R. B., L. D. Hopkins, and L. A. Johnson. 2012. Disaster and recovery: Processes compressed in time. *Natural Hazards Review* 13(3): 173–78.
Olshansky, R. B. and L. A. Johnson. 2012. *Clear as Mud: Planning for the Rebuilding of New Orleans.* Chicago, Illinois: American Planning Association Press.
Olshansky, R. B., L. A. Johnson, J. Horne, and B. Nee. 2008. Longer view: Planning for the rebuilding of New Orleans. *Journal of the American Planning Association* 74(3): 273–87.
Olshansky, R. B., L. A. Johnson, and K. C. Topping. 2006. Rebuilding communities following disaster: Lessons from Kobe and Los Angeles. *Built Environment* 32(4): 354–74.
O'Toole, L. J. and K. J. Meier. 2004. Public management in intergovernmental networks: Matching structural networks and managerial networking. *Journal of Public Administration Research and Theory* 14(4): 469–94.
Peacock, W. G., S. Van Zandt, Y. Zhang, and W. Highfield. 2014. Inequities in long-term housing recovery after disasters. *Journal of the American Planning Association* 80(4): 356–71.
Podger, O. M. 2015. Reconstructing accountability after major disasters. *The Governance Brief* 22: 1–7.
Posner, P. L. 2002. Accountability challenges of third-party government. In *The Tools of Government: A Guide to the New Governance*, L. M. Salamon (ed.), New York: Oxford University Press, 523–51.
Quarantelli, E. L. 1995. Patterns of sheltering and housing in US disasters. *Disaster Prevention and Management: An International Journal* 4(3): 43–53.
Quarantelli, E. L. 1999. Implications for programmes and policies from future disaster trends. *Risk Management* 1(1): 9–19.
Safire, W. 2009. Location, location, location. *New York Times Magazine*, June 26. http://www.nytimes.com/2009/06/28/magazine/28FOB-onlanguage-t.html?_r=0 (accessed September 1, 2015).

Sandler, D. and G. Smith. 2013. Assessing the quality of state disaster recovery plans: Implications for policy and practice. *Journal of Emergency Management* 11(4): 281–91.

Sapat, A., Y. Li, C. Mitchell, and A.-M. Esnard. 2011. Policy learning and policy change: Katrina, Ike and post-disaster housing. *International Journal of Mass Emergencies and Disasters* 29(1): 26–56.

Sard, B. and D. Rice. 2005. *Changes Needed in Katrina Transitional Housing Plan to Meet Families' Needs.* Washington, DC: Center on Budget and Policy Priorities.

Schroeder, A. D., G. Wamsley, and R. Ward. 2001. The evolution of emergency management in America: From a painful past to a promising but uncertain future. In *Handbook of Crisis and Emergency Management*, A. Farazmand (ed.), New York: Marcel Dekker, Inc., 357–420.

Schwab, J. C., K. C. Topping, C. C. Eadie, R. E. Deyle, and R. A. Smith, 1998. *Planning for Post-Disaster Recovery and Reconstruction, PAS Report 483/484.* Chicago, IL: American Planning Association.

Scott, C. 2006. Spontaneous accountability. In *Public Accountability: Designs, Dilemmas and Experiences*, M. W. Dowdle (ed.), Cambridge: Cambridge University Press, 174–94.

Smith, G. 2012. *Planning for Post-Disaster Recovery: A Review of the United States Disaster Assistance Framework.* Washington, DC: Island Press.

Smith, G., D. Sandler, and M. Goralnik. 2013. Assessing state policy linking disaster recovery, smart growth, and resilience in Vermont following Tropical Storm Irene. *Vermont Journal of Environmental Law* 15: 66–102.

Stanton, R. 2009. Galveston after Ike: Hurricane Ike disaster assistance deadline is January 12. *Houston Chronicle* Blog. January 7. http://blog.chron.com/galveston/2009/01/hurricane-ike-disaster-assistance-deadline-is-jan-12/ (accessed September 1, 2015).

Tierney, K. 2012. Disaster governance: Social, political and economic dimensions. *Annual Review of Environment and Resources* 37: 341–63.

US Federal Emergency Management Agency (FEMA). 2011. *National Disaster Recovery Framework: Strengthening Disaster Recovery for the Nation.* Washington, DC: US FEMA, September.

US Government Accountability Office (GAO). 2006a. *Expedited Assistance for Victims of Hurricanes Katrina and Rita: FEMA's Control Weaknesses Exposed the Government to Significant Fraud and Abuse.* GAO-06-655. Washington, DC: US GAO, June.

US Government Accountability Office (GAO). 2006b. *Hurricanes Katrina and Rita: Coordination between FEMA and Red Cross Should Be Improved for 2006 Season.* GAO-06-712. Washington, DC: US GAO, June 8.

US Government Accountability Office (GAO). 2006c. *Hurricanes Katrina and Rita Disaster Relief: Improper and Potentially Fraudulent Individual Assistance Payments Estimated to be between $600 Million and $1.4 Billion: Reports to Congressional Committees.* GAO-06–844 T. Washington DC: US GAO, June 14.

US Government Accountability Office (GAO). 2006d. *Hurricanes Katrina and Rita: Unprecedented Challenges Exposed the Individuals and Household Program to Fraud and Abuse: Actions Needed to Reduce Such Problems in Future: Report to Congressional Committees.* GAO-06-1013. Washington, DC: US GAO, September.

US Government Accountability Office (GAO). 2007. *Hurricanes Katrina and Rita Disaster Relief: Continued Findings of Fraud, Waste and Abuse: Report to the Committee on Homeland Security and Governmental Affairs, U.S. Senate.* GAO-07-300. Washington, DC: US GAO, March.

US Government Accountability Office (GAO). 2014. *Hurricane Sandy Relief: Improved Guidance on Designing Internal Control Plans Could Enhance Oversight of Disaster Funding.* GAO-14-58. Washington, DC: US GAO, November 2013.

US Government Accountability Office (GAO). 2015a. *Budgeting for Disasters: Approaches to Budgeting for Disasters in Selected States*. GAO-15-424. Washington, DC: US GAO, March.

US Government Accountability Office (GAO). 2015b. *Hurricane Sandy: An Investment Strategy Could Help the Federal Government Enhance National Resilience for Future Disasters*. GAO-15-515. Washington, DC: US GAO, July.

US Government Accountability Office (GAO). 2015c. *Hurricane Sandy: FEMA Has Improved Disaster Aid Verification but Could Act to Further Limit Improper Assistance*. GAO-15-15. Washington, DC: US GAO, December 2014.

Van Zandt, S. and W. Rohe. 2011. The sustainability of low-income homeownership: The incidence of unexpected costs and needed repairs among low-income home buyers. *Housing Policy Debate* 21(2): 317–41.

Wu, J. Y. and M. K. Lindell. 2004. Housing reconstruction after two major earthquakes: The 1994 Northridge earthquake in the United States and the 1999 Chi-Chi earthquake in Taiwan. *Disasters* 28(1): 63–81.

Zanotti, L. 2010. Cacophonies of aid, failed state building and NGOs in Haiti: Setting the stage for disaster, envisioning the future. *Third World Quarterly* 31(5): 755–71.

Section II

Understanding Housing Recovery in the United States

6 The Texas Experience with 2008's Hurricanes Dolly and Ike

Shannon Van Zandt and Madison Sloan

CONTENTS

6.1 INTRODUCTION

Disasters occur when hazards interact with the built and social environment (Mileti 1999). Texas is one of the most at-risk states in the United States, experiencing higher than average levels of almost every type of disaster—hurricanes, tornadoes, flooding, drought, wildfire, and technological disasters from hazardous materials (Masterson et al. 2014). Further, the population continues to expand rapidly along the Texas coast, placing increasing numbers of both people and goods in harm's way. For example, although the Texas coastal counties account for only about 6% of Texas' land mass, they are home to one-quarter of the state's population—more than six million residents (US Census 2010).

In the fall of 2008, Texas' Gulf Coast was struck by two hurricanes. Dolly struck the southernmost tip of Texas on July 23, 2008, home to one of the most impoverished regions in the United States, Texas' Lower Rio Grande Valley. Approximately 2 months later on September 13, 2008, Ike made a direct hit on Galveston Island, one of the most urbanized barrier islands in the nation. These storms followed the 2005 hurricane season that included Katrina and Rita, both of which also impacted Texas. Together, these four storms caused more than $38 billion in damage in the state (Texas Department of Housing and Community Affairs [TDHCA] 2011).

The process of recovery from Dolly and Ike has highlighted what many other states have recognized in the aftermath of record storms: that natural disasters expose pre-existing inequalities within the affected communities. Poor and minority households often live in areas most at risk of being impacted by natural disasters, and have the least ability to withstand the impact (Highfield et al. 2014). These same communities are often excluded from the recovery process, despite having received the highest levels of damage. While disparities based on race and income in the immediate aftermath of natural disasters have been extensively examined, much less attention has been paid to inequities in long-term disaster recovery—the process of rebuilding homes, infrastructure, and whole communities. Inequities may be related to household characteristics, housing type, housing tenure, and/or housing value (Peacock et al. 2015). Federal, state, and local systems for recovery tend to reinforce these inequalities in the rebuilding and recovery process.

This chapter first lays out social factors that mitigate or exacerbate vulnerability to disasters. Using the two cases, we then illustrate how these factors mattered during the experience of Hurricanes Dolly and Ike. Tracing the recovery process, we identify specific obstacles to recovery for vulnerable populations and offer recommendations for overcoming them.

6.1.1 Housing for Vulnerable Populations

Impacts from disasters are due to interactions between *hazard exposure*, *physical vulnerability*, and *social vulnerability*. Hazard exposure is the probability that extreme events (e.g., flooding, wind, surge, etc.) will occur, while physical vulnerability refers to the potential damage to the built environment, especially housing (NRC 2006). More recent perspectives have expanded vulnerability to consider social vulnerability, which refers to characteristics of a subpopulation that create variability in vulnerability to disasters* (Van Zandt and Peacock 2012). Social vulnerability factors include income or poverty, race/ethnicity, gender, household composition, age, housing tenure, and education levels, among others. Frequently, these

* For a review, see Van Zandt (2012).

factors exist in combinations (both poor and black, for example), which may compound vulnerability (Morrow 1999).

Socially vulnerable populations are not randomly distributed throughout communities. They are spatially distributed based on the availability and location of appropriate housing that they can afford. Consequently, these populations become concentrated in predictable patterns characterized by concentrated poverty and segregation. Housing markets, for example, are characterized by a sequential process of "filtering" in which successively lower-income households inhabit single-family homes and neighborhoods as they deteriorate physically (Grigsby 1963; Myers 1975). Poor and minority households dwell in older and poorer quality homes in less desirable and potentially more risky neighborhoods (Foley 1980; Bolin 1986; Bolin and Bolton 1986; Logan and Molotch 1987; Phillips and Ephraim 1992; Massey and Denton 1993; Phillips 1993; Peacock and Girard 1997; Charles 2003; Peacock et al. 2006; Van Zandt 2007). Older homes are typically built to less rigorous standards, use lower quality construction materials, and are less well maintained (Bolin and Bolton 1983; Bolin 1994; Girard and Peacock 1997; Bolin and Stanford 1998).

In addition, lower-income households may find homeownership out of reach completely and instead are constrained to renting more affordable housing types, such as condominiums, townhomes, or apartments. These housing types are often regulated out of more desirable areas through large-lot or low-density zoning and building permit caps that limit the availability of affordable housing options (Pendall 2000). What affordable housing is available is typically isolated in areas where large proportions of low-income and minority populations are already located. Evidence suggests that these practices exacerbate income and racial segregation (Pendall 2000; Pendall and Carruthers 2003; Dawkins 2005; Talen 2005). Further, these housing types may be more likely to be located in low-lying or flood-prone areas.

Renting itself introduces an additional source of vulnerability. Renters, particularly those that are low income, have lower levels of housing security, personal efficacy, and privacy (Rohe et al. 2001) and have fewer resources (lower incomes, less job stability, and less savings) with which to address maintenance, repair, and recovery (McCarthy et al. 2001; Van Zandt and Rohe 2011). Further, renters have almost no control over the decision to rebuild, and are at much greater risk of temporary and permanent displacement (Burby et al. 2003).

The interactions between household characteristics, housing type, housing tenure, and housing location means that socially vulnerable populations have increased hazard exposure AND increased physical vulnerability. Further, they have fewer resources—social, economic, and political—with which to repair and rebuild, leading to longer recovery trajectories which may not achieve restoration to pre-storm conditions at all. In the next section, we examine how these factors played out in the cases of Hurricanes Dolly and Ike.

6.1.2 Cases

The *Lower Rio Grande Valley* is located at the southernmost tip of the state (see Figure 6.1). It is comprised of three of the poorest counties in the United States: Cameron, Willacy, and Hidalgo. With economies based on seasonal agriculture and

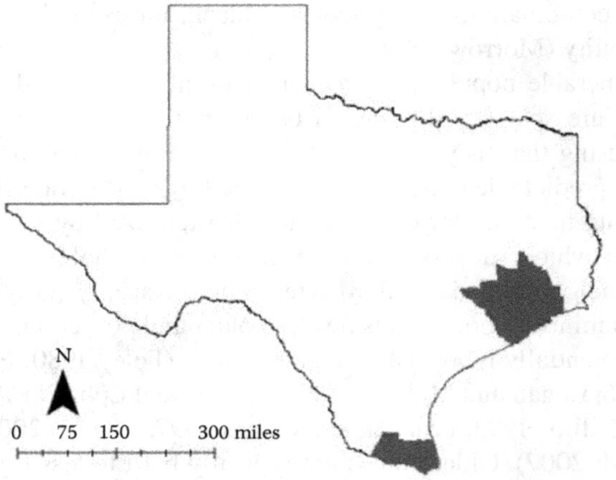

FIGURE 6.1 Location of the Houston–Galveston and Lower Rio Grande Valley regions of Texas. (With permission from Michelle Meyer, unpublished.)

to a lesser extent, manufacturing, these counties are also heavily Hispanic, with low levels of education and low levels of civic capacity, as seen in Table 6.1. Much of the housing stock in these counties is of poor quality, and is inadequately served by public services, including storm water management (Henneberger et al. 2010). When Hurricane Dolly struck, it was primarily a rain event, dropping up to 16 inches of rain, and leaving standing water in many areas—mostly the low-income, underserved *colonias**—for more than a month, due to the impermeability of soils and the

TABLE 6.1
Demographic Characteristics of Study Counties (Year 2010)

County	Population	Median Age	Race and Ethnicity	Below Poverty	Median Home Value	Education Completed
Galveston	291,309	37.2 years	13.8% black 22.4% Hispanic	13.3%	$148,600	87.1% high school 28.5% college
Cameron	406,220	30.6 years	0.5% black 88.1% Hispanic	34.8%	$78,300	63.7% high school 15.4% college
Hidalgo	744,769	28.3 years	0.6% black 90.6% Hispanic	34.8%	$78,100	61.8% high school 15.9% college
Willacy	22,134	32.1 years	2.1% black 87.2% Hispanic	40.0%	$48,800	62.2% high school 8.8% college

Source: US Census Bureau. 2010. Year 2010 US Decennial Census. http://www.census.gov/2010census/data/ (accessed February 29, 2016).

* The *colonias* are substandard subdivisions that are outside of city limits. They typically have nonexistent or poor drainage, road conditions, and other public services. It is estimated that more than 500,000 Texas residents live in *colonias* along the Texas–Mexico border.

inadequacy of drainage solutions. The standing water caused widespread moderate damage in addition to disruption of normal routines for these households.

Galveston Island, just south of the Houston metropolitan area, is the site of the historic 1900 storm that killed more than 6000 people; it is still the most devastating natural disaster in US history. Hurricane Ike took a very similar path to the 1900 storm, and stands as the third most costly storm in US history behind Katrina and Sandy. Ike struck Galveston as a Category 2 storm based on wind speeds, but maintained a Category 4 surge. This discrepancy between wind speeds and surge levels has resulted in a revision of the Saffir–Simpson scale to better reflect the relationship between these two factors.

Galveston has a tourism-based economy, with additional significant segments of the economy also stemming from its port, and a large medical facility on the island. Galveston's full-time population has been declining for the past three decades due to the relative strength of Houston's economy, the risk associated with its exposure to the Gulf of Mexico, and limited economic opportunities on the island. While summertime daily populations can swell to 250,000 or more, the year-round population of the island was at 50,000 prior to Hurricane Ike, but dropped below that due to population loss from the storm. The permanent residents are largely low-wage, tourism workers who cannot afford to live on the mainland and drive to the island daily. More than a third of residents are minority community.

6.1.2.1 Approach

We have followed closely the recovery of both Galveston and the Lower Rio Grande Valley. Our work in Galveston is based on a 3-year longitudinal study funded by the National Science Foundation, including data collection and empirical analysis of primary surveys and damage assessments of over 1500 properties, along with analysis of secondary data on all residential parcels on Galveston Island and advocacy for low-income residents with state and federal agencies. Our work in the Lower Rio Grande Valley is based on observation and analysis of administrative data, and the involvement of the authors in advocacy for low-income residents to state lawmakers.* Our Galveston analyses highlight the factors associated with different trajectories of housing recovery, while our Lower Rio Grande Valley analyses offer insight into the policy responses and failures in addressing the unevenness of recovery trajectories. We integrate these to show long-term recovery serves to exacerbate inequalities within communities.

6.1.3 Inequities in Long-Term Housing Recovery

When segments of the population recover at different rates, it can undermine economic recovery of the community as a whole. For example, if workers are unable to return to their homes, then some businesses will not be able to reopen or recover

* Author Sloan is an attorney for Texas Appleseed, a nonprofit civil rights firm that advocates for the rights of low-income and disenfranchised Texans. Author Van Zandt has served as a third-party evaluator of a disaster recovery housing demonstration program and is a member of the board of the Texas Low-Income Housing Information Service, an advocacy group that addresses the housing needs of low-income Texans.

(Xiao and Van Zandt 2012). Further, because the segments of the population that are likely to be delayed in their recovery are concentrated in particular areas, these areas can become vulnerable to vacancy, abandonment, and further deterioration. Over the long term, these land uses may be converted from residential to other uses, many of which may be undesirable or inconsistent with community goals (Zhang and Peacock 2009). Consequently, public programs to support recovery of lower-income, minority, elderly, and more rural residents provide important resources for the recovery of communities as a whole. In this section, we examine evidence from Ike and Dolly that illustrate the inequities in long-term housing recovery.

6.1.3.1 Lower-Value Homes Receive More Damage, and the Effects of Damage are Long Lasting

While it may seem obvious, homes which receive more damage will take longer to recover. But because lower-value homes are more likely to receive greater damage (Highfield et al. 2014), this leads to disproportionately longer recoveries. In Galveston, lower-value homes received heavier damage, and as a result, took much longer to recover; in many cases, the homes had not reached restoration values even after 4 years, while higher-value homes typically recovered after 2 years (Peacock et al. 2015). In the Lower Rio Grande Valley, similar impacts are seen. Although Hurricane Dolly struck the Lower Rio Grande in 2008, at the end of 2015 not all of the disaster recovery money targeted for lower-income households had been spent, and many *colonia* families were still waiting for new homes.

Federal disaster recovery assistance is administered by multiple federal agencies and through multiple programs, from the Federal Emergency Management Agency (FEMA) to the Department of Agriculture and the Small Business Administration (SBA).* FEMA is primarily responsible for emergency response and short-term assistance, but much of the longer term rebuilding assistance, particularly for housing recovery, comes through supplemental appropriations of funding through the Community Development Block Grant (CDBG) Program which is administered by the Department of Housing and Urban Development (HUD n.d.), and are not a formal part of the disaster recovery system (Stafford Act 42 U.S.C. §5174; HUD CPD). This structure itself places low-income households and communities at a disadvantage. FEMA's short-term financial assistance is limited to an annually adjusted amount under the Stafford Act, and FEMA repair assistance is intended to "return the home to a safe and sanitary living or functioning condition" and "FEMA will not

* Following Hurricanes Katrina and Rita, for example, Congress appropriated $116 billion for recovery efforts along the Gulf Coast—$94.8 billion of which was emergency supplemental spending covering recovery activities such as flood control mitigation, Small Business Administration loans, federal highway funds, Social Services Block Grants, and other health care and antipoverty programs. Over half of the emergency supplemental funds went to two agencies: $45.3 billion to the Federal Emergency Management Agency (FEMA) and $16.7 billion to the Department of Housing and Urban Development (HUD). Testimony of Donald E. Powell, Federal Coordinator for Gulf Coast Rebuilding Before the H. Comm. on the Budget (August 2, 2007) (statement of Donald E. Powell, Federal Coordinator, Gulf Coast Rebuilding), available at http://www.dhs.gov/files/programs/gc_1187965134242.shtm; Congressional Budget Office (CBO), *The Federal Government's Spending and Tax Actions in Response to the 2005 Gulf Coast Hurricanes* at 2 (August 1, 2007), available at www.cbo.gov/doc.cfm?index=8514.

pay to return a home to its condition before the disaster" (FEMA 2015). This leaves homeowners with fewer resources (like savings and adequate insurance) dependent on an uncertain future allocation of CDBG-disaster recovery (DR) funding, on an allocation timeline that can range from several months to a year, and on state and local decisions about the distribution of those funds.

Compounding these structural issues, following Hurricanes Dolly and Ike, one of the biggest obstacles to accessing FEMA funds in low-income neighborhoods was repeated denials of applications for housing assistance, including assistance with repairs. Following Hurricane Ike, FEMA denied at least 85% of the more than 578,000 applications for housing assistance. The most common denial code used by FEMA (in over 100,000 cases) was "insufficient damage" (FEMA 2009). Many low-income applicants were told informally by FEMA that their "insufficient damage" denials were actually based on "deferred maintenance."* FEMA alleged that the homes had been in poor condition before the storm and therefore, damage could not be attributed to the hurricane. Because the houses of low-income households are more likely to be in poor condition these denials had a disproportionate impact on low-income households, particularly in minority neighborhoods (Snyder 2009). FEMA similarly denied half of all applications for housing assistance following Hurricane Dolly.† This type of discrimination is not only illegal under the Stafford Act and other civil rights laws, it delays recovery and increases costs; not only by allowing homes to deteriorate until they require complete reconstruction, but because the costs of temporary housing for disaster victims often exceed the cost of repairing their homes (General Accounting Office [GAO] 2007). Application of the "deferred maintenance" policy also significantly undercounted damage in low-income and minority neighborhoods.

Congress appropriated CDBG-DR funds for the 2008 hurricanes at the end of September 2008, and those funds were allocated to the affected states in two rounds. HUD allocated $3 billion in CDBG-DR funds to Texas for Hurricanes Dolly and Ike; $1.3 billion November 26, 2008 (Round One) and $1.7 billion August 14, 2009 (Round Two) (HUD 2008, 2009a,b; Appropriations Act 2009) For the allocation of Round 2 funds, HUD created a new formula for allocating CDBG-DR funds between states. The formula compensated for some of the problems with FEMA data—particularly the underrepresentation of unmet needs in low-income minority families and communities (HUD 2009a,b). However, because there are no standard regulations for the CDBG-DR program, there is no guarantee that this formula, or any standard formula, will be used for future disasters.

6.1.3.2 Renter-Occupied Single-Family Housing and Housing Types More Likely to be Occupied by Renters are Even Slower to Recover

Housing recovery policy in the United States has long overlooked rental housing (Comerio 1998). Although some improvements in this policy approach were made during the recovery from Katrina, such as the Road Home Small Rental Property program, these improvements have not been institutionalized in federal recovery

* Email from FEMA External Affairs to the Houston Chronicle, June 26, 2009.

† See, *LUPE* v. *FEMA*, Case: 1-08-cv-00487 (S. D. Texas, 2008).

policy. In Galveston, rental properties suffered significantly more damage, and the gap between valuations of owner- and renter-occupied housing grew over time, indicating that efforts to help rental housing recover fell well short of those targeted toward owner-occupied housing (Peacock et al. 2015).

Multifamily housing shows similar patterns of recovery, although a more volatile trajectory. Multifamily housing suffers higher damage, makes an initial recovery, but then falls back as abandoned properties are demolished or partially torn down (Peacock et al. 2015). Differences in recovery for rental housing, and housing types most often occupied by renters have the potential to contribute to turnover of the population. In many states, disasters are grounds for terminating leases. Rarely do original renters return to their units after a disaster (Levine 2007; Hori and Schafer 2010). Thus, renters are perhaps most at risk of permanent displacement. They are difficult to track after a disaster, and almost nothing is known about their long-term outcomes.

Even when rental recovery programs are available, the eligibility process for small rental landlords is time consuming and confusing. Further, individual assistance for many low-income owners or renters is only available for 18 months after the President makes a disaster declaration, with the expectation that individuals will be able to return home or have secured other permanent housing in that time period. While this may be a realistic expectation for higher income families with resources that allow them to find permanent housing or rebuild more quickly, it is not realistic for lower-income homeowners or renters that need federal funds to help them rebuild, or are dependent on third-party decisions about the rebuilding of rental housing.*

6.1.3.3 Socially Vulnerable Residents, Including Those Who are Lower-Income and Minority, have More Difficulty Accessing Benefits

Literature suggests that minorities, low-income household, and female-headed households can be at disadvantage when it comes to qualifying for and negotiating the process of obtaining recovery assistance from FEMA and the SBA (SBA loans) (Bolin 1985; Bolin and Stanford 1991; Phillips 1993; Morrow and Enarson 1996; Morrow 1997). In Galveston, we found that households in low-income and minority neighborhoods were less likely to have private homeowners or flood insurance, and those with insurance were less likely to have received a settlement (Van Zandt et al. 2012). We also found that neighborhoods with high levels of social vulnerability were more likely to have applied for individual assistance from FEMA, but were less likely to have received it (Van Zandt et al. 2012). Further, they were less likely to have applied for loans from the SBA, perhaps because of the loan qualifications requirements and expectation of repayment for this type of assistance (Van Zandt et al. 2012).

In post Dolly and Ike recovery, a number of issues had disproportionate impacts on socially vulnerable residents, particularly those who are low-income and/or

* The President may extend housing assistance beyond 18 months for "extraordinary circumstances." Following Hurricanes Katrina, Rita, and Ike, housing assistance was extended multiple times. The Disaster Housing Assistance Program for Hurricane Ike, for example, ended on January 31, 2012, some 40 months after the disaster. Stafford Act, Title IV, §408(c)(1)(B)(1)(iii).

minority. First is the *inability to establish clear title to real property.* Heir property (divided ownership of property inherited by multiple heirs, often over multiple generations) and other real property ownership issues are particularly prevalent in low-income communities, and disproportionately affect African-American and elderly populations. In 2009, the Texas Legislature passed HB 2450, which allowed TDHCA to accept alternative proof of ownership, including an Affidavit of Heirship, for purposes of disaster recovery programs only. This alternative process was only possible because Texas administered a reconstruction program, in which the state itself rebuilt homes, rather than a compensation program.

The second concern is the *duplication of benefits.* Federal statutes require that applicants for homeowner assistance, who received money for home repair or replacement from FEMA or the SBA, either verify that those funds were used for allowable activities or have that amount deducted from their grant award. Many low-income recipients spent these funds on subsistence needs following the storm or, given the delayed implementation of recovery efforts, did not have receipts for the initial emergency repairs when later housing programs were rolled out. In Texas, the deduction often resulted in a financing gap that had to be bridged by the homeowner before construction could begin, disqualifying the very low-income homeowners most reliant on the program to rebuild their homes. This is unlike the compensation programs run after Hurricane Katrina in Louisiana and Mississippi that allowed recipients to simply deduct the amount of the duplication of benefits from their check. HUD issued new guidance on duplication of benefits in November 2011 that clarified requirements under the Stafford Act, which dramatically reduced duplication of benefits issues in the Ike and Dolly Round Two housing programs.

When different segments of the population recover at different rates, leaving some behind while others return to pre-storm conditions or even leap ahead, it can undermine the resilience of a community. Our work across Texas and beyond shows strong potential for redevelopment and population change; slower recovery times for minorities; permanent displacement of minorities, low-income households, and renters; and a loss of affordable housing stock (Peacock et al. 2015). Since these outcomes disproportionately impact lower-income, minority, or otherwise socially vulnerable residents and neighborhoods, they have the long-term outcome of exacerbating pre-existing inequalities.

6.1.4 Failures of Recovery Policy

The inequities seen in Texas result from a systematic lack of attention and resources based on both household type and housing type, both prior to and subsequent to a disaster. In the paragraphs that follow, we highlight the ways in which both federal and state policies have undermined the ability of local governments, nonprofits, and individual residents to respond to disasters and address their own recovery needs.

6.1.4.1 The National Statutory Disaster Recovery Scheme is Not Set Up to Handle Catastrophic Regional Disasters

One of the core principles of disaster recovery is deference to state and local governments in the planning and management of recovery. FEMA's National Disaster

Recovery Framework (2011) places the burden of disaster recovery on local, state, and tribal governments. The Stafford Act requires a governor to certify that combined state and local resources are insufficient when seeking a presidential disaster declaration. While the stated philosophy of disaster recovery emphasizes placing state and local governments in a primary position, the reality of large-scale disasters is that the bulk of resources needed for recovery will come from the federal government, and that the jurisdictions most affected by a disaster may not have the capacity to administer large amounts of funding through a complex and often unfamiliar federal program.

6.1.4.2 Lack of Federal Guidelines, Poor Data Availability, and Waivers of Federal Program Requirements Increase the Probability that Aid will be Misallocated at the Federal, State, and Local Levels

When natural disasters like Hurricanes Katrina, Ike, and Sandy strike, the federal government uses special allocations of CDBG funds to address housing recovery and rebuilding. Yet, CDBG funding is not a formal part of the federal statutory disaster recovery framework, and so HUD deals with a new set of rules for each appropriation. The informal nature of these appropriations creates confusion, leads to multiple disaster recovery programs operating simultaneously under different rules, and leaves the process vulnerable to political and media pressure, as seen in the disparities in federal appropriations to Mississippi, Louisiana, and Texas after Hurricanes Katrina and Rita (Norris 2008).

Congress can grant HUD the authority to waive certain program requirements when funds are appropriated for a natural disaster. Congress granted broad waiver authority in the 2005 and 2008 CDBG-DR appropriations, and HUD readily exercised that authority, especially with respect to the requirements relating to the amount of funding targeted to low- to moderate-income recipients. Disaster recovery housing projects tend to be targeted at specific households in the low- and moderate-income population. On the other hand, infrastructure projects tend to serve a broader segment of the local population, diluting the targeting of the funds to poorer neighborhoods. Nevertheless, because they spread the money more widely, infrastructure projects may have broader local political support, increasing pressure to divert funds from low- and moderate-income communities to jurisdiction-wide projects.

For example, among the projects proposed by Texas communities for Round Two Ike and Dolly funding were construction of a conference center and a traffic light coordination study—both questionably linked to disaster-related needs at all, let alone the unmet needs of low- and moderate-income residents and neighborhoods. As we have shown, low-income communities, which should be priority recipients of CDBG funds, are more likely to be located in disaster-vulnerable areas, and to suffer more severe housing and infrastructure damage in a disaster.

6.1.4.3 Multiple Administrative Layers at the Different Levels of Government Could Hamper Efficient, Effective, and Timely Use of Disaster Recovery Funds

After Hurricanes Dolly and Ike, the state of Texas submitted its action plan for disaster recovery, required before CDBG-DR funds can be released to a state. The plan effectively funneled all $3 billion of the awarded aid to local councils of government (COGs), but did not specify how the money would be distributed to units of local government served by the COGs. It also relied on flawed data, and resulted in a low percentage of funds designated for activities benefitting low- and moderate-income households (Texas Appleseed Comment, January 5, 2009). Following an administrative complaint filed by a civil rights and fair housing nonprofit, HUD took the unprecedented step of rejecting both the original plan as well as its first amendment (Letter from Asst. Secretary Mercedes Marquez to Gov. Rick Perry, November 10, 2009). Another complaint filed in 2010 alleged that the state permitted subrecipients to steer CDBG-DR funds away from the housing needs of very low-, low-, and moderate-income households specifically to avoid the integrative effect such housing would have on overwhelmingly white communities (TxLIHIS 2009). In May 2010, HUD signed a Conciliation Agreement requiring that a minimum of 55% of the $3 billion in CDBG disaster relief funds would be targeted to rebuild housing and benefit low-income people (Editorial *New York Times* 2010, unpaginated).

6.1.5 The Future of Housing Recovery

Communities (cities and counties) should make mitigation and recovery planning part of regular and ongoing comprehensive planning and capital investment planning, so that priorities and important decisions are made prior to a disaster. Land-use planning (the identification of what can be built where and how) is one of the most powerful tools that cities have to mitigate against disaster impacts. It allows cities to restrict development in areas that are likely to be impacted by hazards, and can require that structures built in vulnerable areas be built (or upgraded) to standards which make them more resistant to disaster impacts. Capital investment planning permits investment in structural mitigation projects that can protect vulnerable areas from disaster impacts. While most jurisdictions in Texas have tools for both structural and nonstructural mitigation at their disposal, few use them to anywhere near their full potential, according to a recent study of Texas jurisdictions conducted for the General Land Office (Peacock et al. 2011).

Further, the implementation of these tools should be prioritized by demonstrated need as determined by an assessment of both physical and social vulnerability. Neighborhoods that are home to socially vulnerable populations are likely to experience the greatest needs in post-disaster recovery. Thus, prioritizing them for pre-storm capital investments to strengthen infrastructure and mitigate against disasters is likely to reduce damage and losses, requiring less public investment in recovery. Further, prioritizing them for post-disaster recovery funding is likely to result in more targeted use of public funds to locations with need, hastening the recovery process for the entire community and enhancing future resilience.

When done poorly, the disaster recovery process shortchanges actual recovery needs and results in delay, waste of funds, inequities, a lack of accountability, and protracted displacement and hardship for families whose lives have been disrupted by natural disasters. When done properly, it emphasizes the needs of populations most affected by the disaster, resulting in recovery and enhanced resilience for the whole community.

ACKNOWLEDGMENTS

Our research on Galveston's recovery was sponsored by the National Science Foundation. We would also like to acknowledge the Ford Foundation, the Texas Low-Income Housing Information Service, the Community Development Corporation of Brownsville, and Building Community Workshop for their support of our research in the Lower Rio Grande Valley.

REFERENCES

Bolin, R. 1985. Disasters and long-term recovery policy: A focus on housing and families. *Policy Studies Review* 4: 709–15.

Bolin, R. 1986. Disaster impact and recovery: A comparison of black and white victims. *International Journal of Mass Emergencies and Disasters (IJMED)* 4: 35–50.

Bolin, R. 1994. *Household and Community Recovery after Earthquakes*. Boulder, Colorado: University of Colorado, Institute of Behavioral Science, Program on Environment and Behavior.

Bolin, R. C. and P. Bolton. 1983. Recovery in Nicaragua and the USA. *International Journal of Mass Emergencies and Disasters* 1(1): 125–144.

Bolin, R. C. and P. A. Bolton. 1986. Race, religion, and ethnicity in disaster recovery. In *Program on Environment and Behavior* (No. 42). US University of Colorado. Institute of Behavioral Science.

Bolin, R. and L. Stanford. 1991. Shelter, housing and recovery: A comparison of U.S. disaster. *Disasters* 15: 24–34.

Bolin, R. and L. Stanford. 1998. *The Northridge Earthquake: Vulnerability and Disaster.* New York: Routledge.

Burby, R. J., L. J. Steinberg, and V. Basolo. 2003. The tenure trap the vulnerability of renters to joint natural and technological disasters. *Urban Affairs Review* 39(1): 32–58.

Charles, C. Z. 2003. The dynamics of racial residential segregation. *Annual Review of Sociology* 29: 167–207.

Comerio, M. C. 1998. *Disaster Hits Home: New Policy for Urban Housing Recovery.* Berkeley, California: University of California Press.

Consolidated Security, Disaster Assistance, and Continuing Appropriations Act. 2009. Pub. L. 110-329.

Dawkins, C. J. 2005. Tiebout choice and residential segregation by race in US metropolitan areas, 1980–2000. *Regional Science and Urban Economics* 35(6): 734–755.

Department of Housing and Urban Development (HUD). 2008. Preston announces $2.1 billion in disaster assistance to 13 states and Puerto Rico impacted by 2008 storms. *HUD Press Release*, November 26. http://archives.hud.gov/news/2008/pr08-179.cfm (accessed February 28, 2016).

Department of Housing and Urban Development (HUD). 2009a. Additional allocations and waivers granted to and alternative requirements for 2008 Community Development Block Grant (CDBG) disaster recovery grantees. *Federal Register* 74(156): Docket No. FR-5337-N-01. https://www.federalregister.gov/articles/2009/08/14/E9-19488/additional-allocations-and-waivers-granted-to-and-alternative-requirements-for-2008-community (accessed February 26, 2016).

Department of Housing and Urban Development (HUD). 2009b. Donovan announces $3.7 billion in disaster assistance to 11 states impacted by 2008 natural disasters. *Clarksville Online Blog*, June. http://www.clarksvilleonline.com/2009/06/11/donovan-announces-3-7-billion-in-disaster-assistance-to-11-states-impacted-by-2008-natural-disasters/ (accessed February 28, 2016).

Federal Emergency Management Agency (FEMA). 2015. *Assistance to Individuals and Households*. Washington, DC: FEMA. https://www.fema.gov/recovery-directorate/assistance-individuals-and-households (accessed February 28, 2016).

FEMA External Affairs to the Houston Chronicle, June 26, 2009. *FEMA Top Five Reasons for FEMA Ineligibility for Housing*. http://www.fema.gov/hazard/hurricane/2008/ike/factsheets/housing.shtm (accessed June 4, 2009).

Foley, D. L. 1980. The sociology of housing. *Annual Review of Sociology* 6: 457–78.

General Accounting Office (GAO). 2007. *Ineffective FEMA Oversight of Housing Maintenance Contracts in Mississippi Resulted in Millions of Dollars of Waste and Potential Fraud*. GAO 08–106, Washington, DC: GAO. http://www.gao.gov/products/GAO-08-106 (accessed February 26, 2016).

Girard, C. and W. G. Peacock. 1997. Ethnicity and segregation: Post-hurricane relocation. *Hurricane Andrew: Ethnicity, gender and the sociology of disasters*, London; New York: Routledge, pp. 191–205.

Grigsby, W. 1963. *Housing Markets and Public Policy*. Philadelphia, Pennsylvania: University of Pennsylvania Press.

Henneberger, J., K. Carlisle, and K. Paup. 2010. Housing in the Texas colonias. In *The Colonias Reader: Economy, Housing, and Public Health in US–Mexico Border Colonias*, A. J. Donelson and A. X. Esparza (eds), Tucson, Arizona: University of Arizona Press, 101–14.

Highfield, W., W. G. Peacock, and S. Van Zandt. 2014. Mitigation planning: Why hazard exposure, structural vulnerability, and social vulnerability matter. *Journal of Planning Education & Research*, p. 0739456X14531828.

Hori, M. and M. J. Schafer. 2010. Social costs of displacement in Louisiana after Hurricanes Katrina and Rita. *Population and Environment* 31(1–3): 64–86.

Editorial. 2010. HUD steps up in Texas. *New York Times*, June 13. http://www.nytimes.com/2010/06/14/opinion/14mon3.html?_r=0 (accessed February 26, 2016).

Levine, J. C. 2005. Equity in infrastructure finance: When are impact fees justified? *Land Economics* 70(2): 210–222.

Logan, J. and H. Molotch. 1987. Urban fortunes. *The Political Economy of Place*. Berkeley: University of California.

Marquez, M. 2009. Letter to Governor Rick Perry, November 10. http://www.texasappleseed.net/index.php?option=com_docman&task=doc_download&gid=226&Itemid (accessed February 27, 2016).

Massey, D. S. and N. A. Denton. 1993. *American Apartheid: Segregation and the Making of the Underclass*. Cambridge, MA: Harvard University Press.

McCarthy, G., S. Van Zandt, and W. M. Rohe. 2001. *The Economic Benefits and Costs of Homeownership: A Critical Assessment of the Research*. Working Paper 01-02, Washington, DC: Research Institute for Housing America.

Mileti, D. 1999. *Disasters by Design: A Reassessment of Natural Hazards in the United States*. Washington, DC: Joseph Henry Press, National Academy Press.

Morrow, B. H. 1997. Stretching the bonds: The families of Andrew. *Hurricane Andrew: Ethnicity, Gender and the Sociology of Disasters*. New York, NY: Routledge, pp. 14–170.

Morrow, B. H. 1999. Identifying and mapping community vulnerability. *Disasters* 23(1): 1–18.

Morrow, B. H. and E. Enarson 1996. Hurricane Andrew through women's eye: Issues and recommendations. *International Journal of Mass Emergencies and Disasters* 14(1): 5–22.

Myers, D. 1975. Housing allowances, submarket relationships and the filtering process. *Urban Affairs Quarterly* 11: 215–40.
Peacock, W. G. and C. Girard. 1997. Ethnic and racial inequalities in hurricane damage and insurance settlements. *Hurricane Andrew: Ethnicity, Gender and the Sociology of Disasters*. London: Routledge, pp. 171–190.
Peacock, W. G., N. Dash, and Y. Zhang. 2006. Shelter and housing recovery following disaster. In *The Handbook of Disaster Research*, H. Rodriguez, E. L. Quarantelli, and R. Dynes (eds), New York: Springer, 258–74.
Peacock, W. G., H. Grover, J. Mayunga, S. Van Zandt, S. D. Brody, H. J. Kim, and R. Center. 2011. *The Status and Trends of Population Social Vulnerabilities Along the Texas Coast with Special Attention to the Coastal Management Zone and Hurricane Ike: The Coastal Planning Atlas and Social Vulnerability Mapping Tools*. College Station, TX: Hazard Reduction & Recovery Center, pp.1–56.
Peacock, W. G., S. Van Zandt, Y. Zhang, and W. Highfield. 2015. Inequities in long-term housing after disaster. *Journal of the American Planning Association* 80(4): 356–71. doi:10.1080/01944363.2014.980440.
Pendall, R. 2000. Local land use regulation and the chain of exclusion. *Journal of the American Planning Association* 66(2): 125–42.
Pendall, R. and J. I. Carruthers. 2003. Does density exacerbate income segregation? Evidence from US metropolitan areas, 1980 to 2000. *Housing Policy Debate* 14(4): 541–589.
Phillips, B. D. 1993. Cultural diversity in disasters: Sheltering, housing, and long-term recovery. *International Journal of Mass Emergencies and Disasters* 11(1): 99–110.
Phillips, B. and M. Ephraim. 1992. *Living in the Aftermath: Blaming Processes in the Loma Prieta Earthquake* No. 80, Boulder, Colorado: University of Colorado, Institute of Behavioral Science, Natural Hazards Research Applications Information Center.
Rohe, W. M., S. Van Zandt, and G. McCarthy. 2001. *The Social Benefits and Costs of Homeownership: A Critical Assessment of the Research*. Working Paper 00-01, Washington, DC: Research Institute for Housing America.
Snyder, M. 2009. Pre-Ike damage restricts funding/homes were in bad shape already, FEMA tells many. *Houston Chronicle* Section B (January 25): 1.
Talen, E. 2005. Land use zoning and human diversity: Exploring the connection. *Journal of Urban Planning and Development* 131(4): 214–232.
Testimony of Donald E. Powell, Federal Coordinator for Gulf Coast Rebuilding. 2009. The Robert T. Stafford Disaster Relief and Emergency Assistance Act, 42 U.S.C. §5174. Hearing before the US House Committee on the Budget. Washington, DC: US House of Representatives, August 2. http://www.c-span.org/video/?200268-1/gulf-coast-hurricanes-federal-budget&start=NaN (accessed February 29, 2016).
Testimony of Jack Norris, Executive Director Mississippi's Office of Recovery and Renewal. 2008. *Emergency CDBG Funds in the Gulf Coast: Uses, Challenges, and Lessons for the Future*. Hearing before the US House Financial Services Committee. Washington, DC: US House of Representatives, May 8. http://archives.financialservices.house.gov/hearing110/hr050808.shtml (accessed February 29, 2016).
Texas Appleseed Comment. 2009. January 5. http://www.texasappleseed.net/index.php?option=com_docman&task=doc_view&gid=65&Itemid= (accessed May 2013).
Texas Department of Housing and Community Affairs (TDHCA). 2011. Internal Audit of the Disaster Recovery Program. https://www.gpo.gov/fdsys/pkg/CHRG-110hhrg38256/pdf/CHRG-110hhrg38256.pdf (accessed October 6, 2016).
US Census Bureau. 2010. Year 2010 US Decennial Census. http://www.census.gov/2010census/data/ (accessed February 29, 2016).
Van Zandt, S. 2007. Racial/ethnic differences in housing outcomes for first-time, low-income home buyers. *Housing Policy Debate* 18(2): 431–74.

Van Zandt, S., W. G. Peacock, D. Henry, H. Grover, W. Highfield, and S. Brody. 2012. Mapping social vulnerability to enhance housing and neighborhood resilience. *Housing Policy Debate* 22(1): 29–55.
Van Zandt, S. and W. M. Rohe. 2011. The sustainability of low-income homeownership: The Incidence of unexpected costs and needed repairs among low-income home buyers. *Housing Policy Debate* 21(2): 317–41.
Xiao, Y. and S. Van Zandt. 2012. Building community resiliency: Spatial links between household and business post-disaster return. *Urban Studies* 49(11): 2523–2542.
Zhang, Y. and W. G. Peacock. 2009. Planning for housing recovery? Lessons learned from Hurricane Andrew. *Journal of the American Planning Association* 76(1): 5–24.

7 Affordable Housing and Disaster Recovery

A Case Study of the 2013 Colorado Floods

Andrew Rumbach and Carrie Makarewicz

CONTENTS

7.1 INTRODUCTION: DISASTERS, AFFORDABLE HOUSING, AND RECOVERY

Affordable housing* is an essential part of healthy and sustainable communities, creating health, education, and economic benefits to households (Mueller and Tighe 2007; Housing Colorado 2014). It is also a central issue in disaster recovery. When affordable housing is damaged or destroyed, communities must decide whether to

* Housing is considered affordable when occupant(s) pay 30% or less of their gross income, including utilities (HUD 2015). Households are considered "housing burdened" if they pay more than 30% of their gross income for housing. Subsidized housing is generally restricted to households earning less than the area median income (AMI), though in some high cost regions, eligibility may exceed 120% of the AMI.

rebuild it, and if so, where and when. Such decisions shape the long-term character of the community, as well as the recovery of households who rely upon affordable housing. These households are often more exposed to hazards, and after a disaster, they often are at the mercy of landlords and local governments to repair or rebuild housing they can access and afford. In this chapter, we explore key variables that guide decisions about affordable housing post-disaster, based on the 2013 floods in Colorado. The floods destroyed a significant amount of affordable housing in a region where housing affordability is a major and ongoing challenge.

We seek to answer what drives some communities to rebuild, or attempt to rebuild, affordable housing post-disaster, and not others? First, we discuss research on disaster recovery and affordable housing that forms the theoretical and regulatory context for our case. Next, we describe the 2013 flood in Colorado and its effect on affordable housing in the Front Range region.* We then present brief case studies of three flooded communities that lost a significant amount of affordable housing during the floods: the town of Lyons, in Boulder County, and the city of Evans and town of Milliken in Weld County. We conclude with key findings from Colorado and general lessons for post-disaster affordable housing.

7.2 DISASTER RECOVERY AND AFFORDABLE HOUSING

In contrast to earlier studies that theorized disaster recovery as "ordered, knowable, and predictable" (see e.g., Haas et al. 1977; Kates and Pijawka 1977), contemporary research shows that disaster recovery is an uneven process with some households and groups recovering more quickly and completely than others (Mileti 1999; Cutter et al. 2003; Wisner et al. 2003; Daniels et al. 2006; NRC 2006; Olshansky et al. 2012). Others also find that the terrain of recovery is quite varied (Rubin 1985, 2009; Olshanskys et al. 2006; Ganapati and Ganapati 2009; Smith 2012). Smith and Wenger (2007, p. 238) argue that recovery is largely a social, not technical, process, and unequal recovery reflects larger social, economic, and institutional processes that reproduce inequality outside of disasters (see also Benner and Pastor 2012). Housing is a key component of sustainable disaster recovery (Bolin 1985; Berke et al. 1993; Smith and Wenger 2007; Olshansky 2009; Smith 2012). Although affordable housing is just one element of recovery, it is a fundamental and often controversial issue, particularly around issues of equity and sustainability (Bolin and Stanford 1991; Kamel and Loukaitou-Sideris 2004; Green et al. 2007).

Disasters can impact affordable housing directly through damage or destruction of homes (the focus of this chapter) or indirectly through housing price increases due to the sudden drop in supply. Rebuilding affordable housing post-disaster confronts the same constraints faced under normal conditions, including location and land availability, the will and capacity of local actors, and the availability of external resources, among others. Affordable housing tends to be disproportionately located in hazard-prone areas, where land is often cheapest, causing disproportionately

* The Colorado Front Range is an urban corridor east of the Rocky Mountains housing more than 80% of Colorado's population. It stretches from Pueblo to Fort Collins, including the cities of Colorado Springs, Denver, Boulder, and Greeley, and surrounding communities.

higher levels of damage during disasters to lower income households (Peacock et al. 2007, p. 265; Lee and Jung 2014). After a disaster, rebuilding in hazard-prone areas often triggers new regulatory and insurance burdens, making recovery more costly and difficult (Green et al. 2007) when redevelopment on these sites is restricted by contemporary floodplain development rules and regulations.*

Thus, local actors and institutions are critical to affordable housing recovery. Although research has shown that permanent housing replacement is "primarily a market driven process" (Peacock et al. 2007, p. 264; Zhang and Peacock 2009), housing is highly regulated and dependent upon appropriate zoning and infrastructure, and hazard and mortgage insurance is regulated at the state and federal levels. Public sector actions are especially critical for affordable housing, which is rarely provided without incentives, write-downs, special financing, and other tools (Nelson and Khadduri 1992; Mueller and Schwartz 2008). While household resources and market mechanisms are important, municipal decisions regarding land, allocation of public resources (e.g., fee waivers), communications, recovery plans, pursuance of grants and partnerships, and public involvement are also essential. Local government capacity also dictates recovery since housing reconstruction can be overwhelming, including permitting, inspection, zoning, financing, negotiating with larger governments, and identifying new housing models and more sustainable designs (Comerio 2014).

Like other aspects of recovery, external resources drive the reconstruction of affordable housing. Traditionally, housing reconstruction has relied upon private funds like personal savings, loans, and insurance, with government programs filling the gaps (Zhang and Peacock 2010, p. 6; referencing Comerio 1998). It follows that recovery for households with few resources and reliance upon affordable housing lags behind other groups. But the Department of Housing and Urban Development (HUD) is attempting to address this disparity. Eligible communities can request an advance on their existing HUD funds† to repair public housing and construct rental housing (Zhang and Peacock 2009; Comerio 2014) and HUD and Federal Emergency Management Agency (FEMA) have created the CDBG-Disaster Recovery (CDBG-DR) block grant. When used for housing, 50% of the CDBG-DR funds must benefit low and moderate income households.

Despite its importance, the topic of affordable housing recovery remains understudied (Tierney et al. 2006, p. 100; quoted in Peacock et al. 2007, p. 260). There are exceptions, of course, namely the post-Katrina literature (e.g., Green et al. 2007; Quigley 2007), as well as recent national publications that provide guidance for

---

* In the United States, communities participating in the National Flood Insurance Program (NFIP) are required to regulate development within mapped floodplains. In many communities, development that existed prior to the creation of the NFIP program is not built to contemporary codes and standards. After a disaster, owners of those developments must rebuild them to the most current codes (e.g., by elevating above the base flood elevation), which can be cost prohibitive. In some cases, redevelopment is not allowed at all, because the damaged properties are located in high hazard areas like floodways.

† These HUD funds include Community Development Block Grants (CDBG) and the HOME Investment Partnership Program.

housing reconstruction.* Nevertheless, there is a dearth of research on local level post-disaster decision making for affordable housing. This chapter aims to fill those gaps in prior research.

7.3 THE 2013 COLORADO FLOODS

The September 2013 floods were one of the costliest disasters in state history (Colorado Resiliency and Recovery Office [CRRO] 2014, 2015), affecting dozens of communities across the Front Range.† Eighteen counties were in the federal disaster declaration, with much of the damage concentrated in Boulder, Larimer, and Weld counties (see Figure 7.1).

Affordable housing was a major challenge for the Front Range before the disaster. Typical of many regions in the western United States, the Front Range is experiencing rapid population growth with an accompanying rise in housing prices and decline in the availability of affordable housing (Lindenstein 2014). Regionally, average rents and median home prices have increased 10%–16% each year since the flood, and rental vacancy rates continue to drop (Svaldi 2013; Housing Colorado 2014; S&P Dow Jones Indices LLC 2015).

7.4 METHODS

To understand the decision-making process for affordable housing recovery, we followed the recovery process in three selected communities for 2 years (2013–2015)

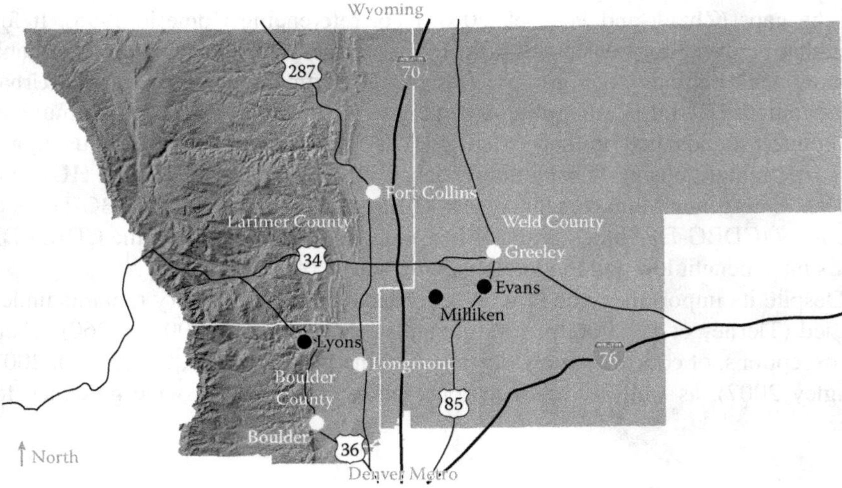

FIGURE 7.1 Location of case study communities.

* See for instance, FEMA's *National Disaster Housing Strategy* (2009), HUD's *Pre-Disaster Housing for Permanent Housing Recovery* (2012), and the American Planning Association's *Planning for Post-Disaster Recovery: Next Generation* (2014).

† The historic flood event destroyed 1500 homes and resulted in nearly $4 billion in economic loss (CRRO 2015).

using a case study research design. Our data include surveys with 97 households, 45 interviews with local, county, and state officials involved in recovery, and direct observation of over 50 recovery meetings and events. We analyzed the household surveys to compare household recovery trajectories across communities (Rumbach et al. 2016). We summarized notes from the meetings and transcribed the interviews in order to identify themes, processes, stakeholders, and other influences. Throughout the research, we sought clarification and confirmation of our findings from individuals directly involved in the recovery.

7.5 LOSS OF AFFORDABLE HOUSING: EVANS, LYONS, AND MILLIKEN

In this section, we present brief case studies of each community, describing the flood's impacts on affordable housing and subsequent actions (or inactions) taken locally during the recovery.

7.5.1 Evans, Colorado

Evans is a fast-growing city located along the South Platte River in the plains east of the Rocky Mountains. Over the past decade, Weld County has had strong economic growth from the oil and gas, agriculture, and meatpacking industries. From 1990 to 2013, the population of Evans tripled, from 6150 to an estimated 19,994 (US Census 2014; Weld County 2014), creating significant housing pressures in Evans and nearby communities. At the time of the flood, the city's rental housing vacancy rate was below 2%, a historic low, while rental prices had reached an all-time high (Greeley-Weld Housing Authority, personal communication 2015).

The flooding of the South Platte River (see Figure 7.1) significantly damaged or destroyed over 300 housing units in Evans, including 208 mobile homes and several dozen market-rate affordable rentals. The mobile homes were located in two adjacent communities near the river, outside the regulatory (100-year) floodplain. As a consequence, the vast majority of residents did not have flood insurance. After the flood, Evans quickly condemned the destroyed trailers, citing the potential public health impacts of the flooded homes. In January 2014, Evans revised and updated their floodplain maps, designating large portions of the two mobile housing parks as within the regulatory floodplain. City leadership argued the pre-flood maps were outdated and their primary charge was to protect public safety moving forward. The updated maps made reconstruction of the mobile home parks cost prohibitive. The owner of the largest park sued the city for impeding his business,* but both mobile home parks remain closed.

As of 2015, most of the site-built affordable rental housing had been repaired and reoccupied, but anecdotal conversations with former tenants suggest that some owners are now charging significantly higher (20% or more) rents.

Though the floods permanently destroyed 208 mobile homes, and rental prices have risen, Evans has not pursued federal recovery grants or committed public

* As of 2015, the lawsuit was rejected by the Weld County courts, and is under appeal.

resources to rebuilding affordable housing. Based on interviews with public officials, the city and elected officials believe the market will supply lower cost units if there is a demand, and that the local government's primary responsibility in disaster recovery is to protect public safety and ensure that infrastructure and critical facilities are repaired and protected. Since the flood, more than 800 permanent housing units have been built or planned, but very few (<10%) will be affordable to households earning less than 80% of the area median income (AMI), and none will be government regulated (permanently) affordable (Greeley-Weld Housing Authority, personal communication 2015).

7.5.2 Lyons, Colorado

Lyons is an historic small town in Boulder County at the foothills of the Rocky Mountains and the confluence of the St. Vrain and South St. Vrain rivers (see Figure 7.1). Originally a mining and railroad town, Lyons is now known for its arts, culture, and summertime music festivals. Lyons has grown in recent years from 1287 residents in 1990 to 2035 in 2013 (US Census 2014). Growth has been spurred by the population and economic growth in the region, and the increasingly expensive and growth-controlled housing market in the nearby city of Boulder.

Lyons also faced significant affordable housing shortages prior to the flood. From 2000 to 2010, the median home value rose by 71% to over $340,000, while the number of available rentals fell by half (Town of Lyons 2015). At the time of the flood, rental vacancy in Lyons and Boulder County was at a 12-year low (APA 2014). Of the renters in Lyons who earned less than 80% of the AMI, more than half (52%) were cost-burdened (Town of Lyons 2015).

The floods significantly damaged or destroyed roughly 20% of the Lyon's housing stock, including 172 site-built homes and 43 mobile homes, approximately 90% of the town's low income housing (Town of Lyons 2014, 2015). The town recognized that the loss of affordable housing would be a major recovery challenge and a citizens' housing recovery group formed immediately. Three months later, the town undertook an intensive 8-week recovery planning process with hundreds of local participants, resulting in the LRAP. The LRAP has a dedicated chapter on housing recovery, including a goal to increase opportunities for affordable housing. The Board of Trustees (BOT) designated the citizens' group as an official task force on housing recovery and charged them with studying the issue and generating proposals. Their actions were regularly reported in the town's local newspapers and at BOT meetings.

Despite political and popular support, 2 years after the flood the town has been unable to replace but a handful of the affordable units. As a result, the population has shrunk to 1865, with 185 households still displaced (Colorado Public Radio 2015). Of those, 72% (133) were low income (80% of the AMI), and 39% (72) were very low income (30% of the AMI) (Town of Lyons 2015).

Two related factors led to the long-term loss of affordable housing in Lyons. First, many of the damaged or destroyed homes were in the designated 100-year floodplain or floodway, introducing significant regulatory and financial barriers to rebuilding. Both mobile home parks, which included 43 affordable units, were located in the floodway and have permanently closed. A substantial number of homeowners (over 30) in the Confluence neighborhood, a flood-damaged area with many affordable homes, are voluntarily participating in two property buyout programs funded by FEMA and HUD. Second, Lyons has a severe shortage of developable land within its planning boundaries but outside of the floodplain, due to the steep terrain surrounding the town and Boulder County's Open Space program, which has purchased land near Lyons since the 1970s. The few available parcels are unsuitable for replacement housing for a variety of reasons, particularly conservation easements, unsuitable terrain, and high valuations.

After more than a year of intensive debate and planning, the town proposed a new 66-unit affordable housing development that would give preference to flood-displaced households. The proposed site was an approximately 6-acre parcel within a 30-acre park near downtown and existing infrastructure. Possible funding included disaster recovery grants and affordable housing tax credits totaling $27 million (Town of Lyons 2015). Colorado state law requires that the sale or disposal of municipal parkland be subject to a popular vote (Colorado Revised Statutes 31-15-713). The election, held in March 2015, rejected the proposal by a count of 614-498. Full analysis of the vote is beyond this chapter's scope, but opposition centered on concerns over lost park space, distrust by some local residents of the county's housing authority and federal recovery programs, and the proximity to nearby schools and neighborhoods, as well as the floodplain.

7.5.3 Milliken, Colorado

Milliken is a small historic agricultural town near the confluence of the Big Thompson and Little Thompson rivers, in Weld County. It has grown rapidly in the past two decades, from a population of 1605 in 1990 to 5610 in 2010 (US Census). It is mostly a bedroom community; less than 3% of the population works locally (US Census). Milliken also faced significant housing pressure prior to the flood—the vacancy rate for rent or purchase was less than 2% and the town had very little affordable housing (Town of Milliken 2014). Besides two mobile home parks, Milliken had a 28-unit market-rate apartment complex with affordable rents and a 20-unit permanently affordable senior housing facility. Over 90% of the housing in Milliken is single-family detached homes.

The floodwaters from the Big and Little Thompson destroyed 35 mobile homes and substantially damaged eight more, much of Milliken's affordable housing. Immediately after the flood, the town authorized the reopening of the mobile home parks to prevent displaced residents from becoming homeless (Draper 2013). The residents were required to sign an affidavit, however, that stated the mobile home park might be included in the floodplain of an updated flood map and "...in such instance, I may be required to relocate my mobile home in the future at my own cost...I understand that this relocation might be outside Milliken" (Brown and Crummy 2013).

By 2015, approximately 28 of the 43 mobile homes have been repaired or replaced on a temporary basis, while the owner of one of the two parks continues the process of obtaining floodplain development permits. In March of 2014, the town adopted temporary floodplain maps, which expanded the flood hazard area to include the mobile home parks, beyond what is officially regulated by FEMA. As such, the parks' owners and residents will need to clear a series of costly regulatory hurdles in order to rebuild, and residents will need to carry flood insurance. They have also been required to rebuild the parks, lots, and homes to current development codes. Milliken officials argue the new regulations are necessary to ensure the health and safety of the parks' residents and anticipate the official floodplain map revisions will likely expand the special flood hazard area to reflect the temporary maps. Residents and owners have publicly questioned whether the town is trying to rid itself of mobile homes (Peif 2014; Romano 2014).

The town is also actively attempting to purchase both mobile home parks (along with other nearby properties) for the purpose of flood mitigation using federal hazard mitigation and recovery grants (Town of Milliken 2015). These funds require the voluntary sale of the parks by the landowners and necessitate that the land be used for open space or passive recreation, and never again be used for residential or commercial development. In the event the purchase occurs, the households would need to be relocated, almost certainly outside of Milliken. Since the flood, there has been no new affordable housing built outside of the repaired mobile home parks. Town officials acknowledge that the free market is not producing new affordable housing, and that it is problematic for recovery since they expect 86% of the future housing demand will come from households earning less than $35,000 (Town of Milliken 2014, p. 55). However, the town argues it does not have the capacity to develop and manage affordable housing projects.

7.6 AFFORDABLE HOUSING AND RECOVERY IN COLORADO: KEY INSIGHTS

The loss of at least 300 units of low-cost housing in the three cases offers important insights into the dynamics of affordable housing in post-disaster recovery.

7.6.1 Affordable Housing as Pre-Existing Problem

Which households were most affected, and which have recovered, reflect the area's broader social, political, and economic context, similar to other disasters. Despite the region's growth and economic prosperity, neither the market nor the public sector have produced sufficient amounts of affordable housing before, or since, the flood. What relatively little affordable housing existed before the disaster was often affordable, because it was older, in poor condition, in undesirable locations, or was a mobile home and not because it had been subsidized. Replacement subsidies for these market-affordable units are not available. As a result, some displaced residents have referred to the *disaster gentrification* phenomenon—that the flood has accelerated the replacement of older housing with more costly and less diverse neighborhoods.

7.6.2 Vulnerability of Lower Income Households

Affordable housing was disproportionately affected because of its physical location on flood-prone, less expensive land, and households living in mobile home parks were especially vulnerable. The flood caused 13 mobile home parks to close, displacing at least 400 households. In addition to their location, mobile home residents were uniquely affected because of their lack of legal protections, the inability to relocate damaged trailers, and community ambivalence toward rebuilding the parks (Lyons Emergency Assistance Fund 2015). This mirrors experiences in other disasters (e.g., Baker et al. 2014).

7.6.3 Role of Local Government and Residents

The varying experiences of the three cases show post-disaster affordable housing decisions are made primarily by local actors, despite communities recovering under the same federal and state regime with significant external support for rebuilding subsidized affordable housing. In Evans, the local government closed the mobile home parks immediately, and has left recovery to the private market. In Milliken, the local government recognized the need for affordable housing, but did little to facilitate its replacement, and proactively made the rebuilding of mobile home parks more expensive and difficult in anticipation of updated floodplain maps. In Lyons, the town government and a large share of residents made a strong commitment to rebuild affordable housing and were backed by significant external resources, but a slight majority of residents voted to stop their efforts. In all three cases, the local government's decision framed the issue: was affordable housing a priority, and if so, under what conditions? For example, CDBG-DR grants are a major source of funding but because they have significant "strings attached," only Lyons was willing to pursue the funds. Resident demand also mattered. Evans did not perceive strong demand from residents to replace the affordable housing, in part because of their beliefs about the role of government, but also because the most affected households were displaced and no longer had a voice in local affairs. Although Milliken's mobile home park residents could return, their voices were limited in comparison to voices desiring recovery of local recreation and infrastructure. Without a critical mass of voices, or a strong culture of community engaged planning, a local government is unlikely to prioritize affordable housing during recovery. While the Lyons case perhaps illustrates the limitations of local government power, it confirms that the decision to rebuild affordable housing hinges on local community dynamics.

7.6.4 Other Actors and Specialized Agencies

Other agencies and organizations are vital for affordable housing recovery, particularly public housing authorities and local nonprofits. In Lyons, the affordable housing proposal was based on $250,000 in pre-application studies funded by the Boulder County Housing Authority (BCHA). The BCHA won the proposal to lead the development team, and committed substantial resources to the design and public engagement processes. In Evans and Milliken, the housing authority is much more limited in its budget and mission. It is unclear if either community considered applying for federal funds, but they likely would not have been able to fund the pre-application studies. The strength of local organizations also varied. In Lyons, several nonprofits contacted and organized displaced residents, and advocated for their needs, giving voice to the displaced. Local officials credited these organizations with helping to justify their actions for the affordable housing proposal. In Evans and Milliken, no such advocacy organizations exist. Outside nonprofits assisted with flood relief, but no local organizations existed or emerged to address housing. We cannot say whether local advocacy would have created more public demand for affordable housing in Evans and Milliken, but it is true that the disaster-affected households in Lyons had a more active role in recovery (Rumbach et al. 2016), and that Lyons is working with the households and organizations to identify other affordable housing options.

7.7 CONCLUSIONS: LESSONS AND IMPLICATIONS

Through this chapter we have begun to understand why some communities rebuild, or attempt to rebuild, affordable housing post-disaster, and others do not. Local conditions, including land availability, the housing market, government priorities and capabilities, resident support of affordable housing, and the resources, reputations, and commitments of local agencies, all play a role. These findings suggest at least two strategies for improving the recovery of affordable housing. Cities and towns, the local housing authority, and nonprofits should work with the community prior to disasters to plan for the potential loss of affordable housing (HUD 2012). This would identify the level of risk and the potential for mitigation, engage with those who are most vulnerable, and gauge public support for recovery options. They should also evaluate the major external programs for housing recovery like the CDBG-DR and Hazard Mitigation Grant Program, to determine whether they have the resources, capacity, and political will to pursue such resources in the event of a major disaster.

ACKNOWLEDGMENTS

This work was supported by the National Science Foundation (grant number CMMI #1446031) and the Natural Hazards Center (Quick Response Grant #250).

REFERENCES

American Planning Association. 2014. *Living with the Saint Vrain*. Chicago, Illinois: American Planning Association. https://planning-org-uploaded-media.s3.amazonaws.com/legacy_resources/communityassistance/teams/lyons/pdf/finallyonsreport.pdf (accessed June 18, 2015).

Baker, D., S. D. Hamshaw, and K. A. Hamshaw. 2014. Rapid flood exposure assessment of Vermont mobile home parks following tropical Storm Irene. *Natural Hazards Review* 15(1): 27–37.

Benner, C. and M. Pastor. 2012. *Just Growth: Inclusion and Prosperity in America's Metropolitan Regions*. New York: Taylor and Francis.

Berke P., J. Karetez, and D. Wenger. 1993. Recovery after disaster: Achieving sustainable development, mitigation and equity. *Disasters* 17(2): 93–109.

Bolin, R. 1985. Disasters and long-term recovery policy: A focus on housing and families. *Review of Policy Research* 4(4): 709–15.

Bolin, R. and L. Stanford. 1991. Shelter, housing and recovery: A comparison of U.S. disasters. *Disasters* 15(1): 24–34.

Brown, J. and K. E. Crummy. 2013. State hurries to update maps; Many damaged homes not in floodplain. *The Denver Post*, December 29. http://www.denverpost.com/news/ci_24809765/state-update-maps-many-damaged-homes-not-floodplain (accessed February 29, 2016).

Colorado Public Radio. 2015. Two years after Colorado's floods, affordable housing still tough to find. *CPR News*, September 9. https://www.cpr.org/news/story/2-years-after-colorados-floods-affordable-housing-still-tough-find (accessed February 29, 2016).

Colorado Resiliency and Recovery Office (CRRO). 2014. One Year Report. https://docs.google.com/a/state.co.us/viewer?a=v&pid=sites&srcid=c3RhdGUuY28udXN8Y29sb3JhZG91bml0ZWR8Z3g6Mjk1MGY0NWJmOGIyZjM0MQ (accessed August 10, 2016).

Colorado Resiliency and Recovery Office (CRRO). 2015. *Two-Year Report*. Denver, Colorado: CRRO. https://www.colorado.gov/pacific/sites/default/files/CRRO%20Two-Year%20Report%2010-23-15.pdf (accessed February 17, 2016).

Comerio, M. 1998. *Disaster Hits Home: New Policy for Urban Housing Recovery*. Berkeley, California: University of California Press.

Comerio, M. 2014. Disaster recovery and community renewal: Housing approaches. *Cityscape: A Journal of Policy Development and Research* 16(2): 51–64.

Cutter, S. L., B. J. Boruff, and W. L. Shirley. 2003. Social vulnerability to environmental hazards. *Social Science Quarterly* 84(2): 242–61.

Daniels, R. J., D. F. Kettl, and H. Kunreuther. (eds). 2006. *On Risk and Disaster: Lessons from Hurricane Katrina*. Philadelphia: University of Pennsylvania Press.

Department of Housing and Urban Development (HUD). 2012. *Pre-Disaster Planning for Permanent Housing Recovery*. Washington, DC: HUD. http://www.huduser.gov/portal/publications/Pre_DisasterPlanningVol1.pdf (accessed June 18, 2015).

Draper, E. 2013. Road home has been bumpy, impassable for flooded mobile-home residents. *The Denver Post*, November 27. http://www.denverpost.com/news/ci_24608652/road-home-has-been-bumpy-impassable-flooded-mobile (accessed February 29, 2016).

Federal Emergency Management Agency (FEMA). 2009. *National Disaster Housing Strategy*. Washington, DC: US Department of Homeland Security. http://www.fema.gov/pdf/emergency/disasterhousing/NDHS-core.pdf (accessed May 6, 2015).

Ganapati, N. E. and S. Ganapati. 2009. Enabling participatory planning in post-disaster contexts. *Journal of the American Planning Association* 75(1): 41–59.

Green, R., L. K. Bates, and A. Smyth. 2007. Impediments to recovery in New Orleans' Upper and Lower Ninth Ward: One year after Hurricane Katrina. *Disasters* 31(4): 311–35.

Haas, J. E., P. B. Trainer, M. J. Bowden, and R. Bolin, eds. 1977. *Reconstruction Following Disaster*. Cambridge, Massachusetts: The MIT Press.

Housing Colorado. 2014. *Driving a Vibrant Economy: Housing's Role in Colorado's Economic Success*. Denver, Colorado: The Piton Foundation, Housing Colorado, and Colorado Futures Center. http://www.piton.org/sites/default/files/Economic%20Impacts%20Study_%20Online%20Version.docx_.pdf (accessed June 1, 2015).

Kamel, N. M. O. and A. Loukaitou-Sideris. 2004. Residential assistance and recovery following the Northridge earthquake. *Urban Studies* 41(3): 533–62.

Kates, R. W. and D. Pijawka. 1977. From rubble to monument: The pace of reconstruction. In: *Reconstruction Following Disaster*, J. E. Haas, R. W. Kates, and M. J. Bowden (eds). Cambridge: MIT Press, 1–23.

Lee, D. and J. Jung. 2014. The growth of low-income population in floodplains: A case study of Austin, TX. *KSCE Journal of Civil Engineering* 18(2): 683–93.

Lindenstein, J. 2014. Inventory of homes on market remains low. *BizWest*, January 17. http://bizwest.com/inventory-of-homes-on-market-remains-low/ (accessed February 29, 2016).

Lyons Emergency Assistance Fund. 2015. Manufactured Housing and Flood Recovery in Lyons, Colorado. http://www.leaflyons.org/uploads/5/0/9/0/50909033/leaf_mhc_report_final__04-15-2015.pdf (accessed June 15, 2015).

Mileti, D. 1999. *Disasters by Design: A Reassessment of Natural Hazards in the United States*. Washington: Joseph Henry Press.

Mueller, E. J. and A. Schwartz. 2008. Reversing the tide: Will state and local governments house the poor as federal direct subsidies decline? *Journal of the American Planning Association* 74(1): 122–35.

Mueller, E. J. and J. R. Tighe. 2007. Making the case for affordable housing: Connecting housing with health and education outcomes. *Journal of Planning Literature* 21(4): 371–85.

National Research Council of the American Academies. 2006. *Facing Hazards and Disasters: Understanding Human Dimensions*. Washington: The National Academies Press.

Nelson, K. P. and J. Khadduri. 1992. To whom should limited housing resources be directed? *Housing Policy Debate* 3(1): 67–75.

Olshansky, R. 2009. The challenges of planning for post-disaster recovery. In: *Building Safer Settlements: Governance, Planning, and Responses to Natural Hazards*, U. F. Paleo (ed.), NATO Science for Peace and Security Series—E: Human and Societal Dynamics, Vol. 58, Amsterdam: IOS Press, 175–81.

Olshansky, R., L. D. Hopkins, and L. A. Johnson. 2012. Disaster and recovery: Processes compressed in time. *Natural Hazards Review* 13: 173–178.

Olshanksy, R. B., L. A. Johnson, and K. C. Topping. 2006. Rebuilding communities following disaster: Lessons from Kobe and Los Angeles. *Built Environment* 32(4): 354–74.

Peacock, W. G., N. Dash, and Y. Zhang. 2007. Sheltering and housing recovery following disaster. In *Handbook of Disaster Research*, R. Dynes, H. Rodriguez, and E. Quarantelli (eds), New York: Springer, 258–74.

Peif, S. 2014. Milliken residents still unsure of future nearly one year after the flood. *The Tribune*, August 1. http://www.greeleytribune.com/news/12438733-113/town-solomon-flood-park# (accessed February 29, 2016).

Quigley, W. 2007. Obstacle to opportunity: Housing that working and poor people can afford in New Orleans since Katrina. *Wake Forest Law Review* 42: 393–419, Summer.

Romano, A. 2014. Milliken, Evans mobile home parks say new floodplain rules too costly. *The Tribune*, March 21. http://www.greeleytribune.com/news/10701554-113/milliken-mobile-floodplain-flood (accessed February 29, 2016).

Rubin, C. 1985. *Community Recovery from a Major Natural Disaster*. Boulder, Colorado: University of Colorado.

Rubin, C. 2009. Long term recovery from disasters—The neglected component of emergency management. *Journal of Homeland Security and Emergency Management* 6(1): 1–17.

Rumbach, A., C. Makarewicz, and J. Németh. 2016. The importance of place in early disaster recovery: A case study of the 2013 Colorado Floods. *Journal of Environmental Planning and Management*. doi: 10.1080/09640568.2015.1116981

Smith, G. 2012. *Planning for Post-Disaster Recovery: A Review of the United States Disaster Assistance Framework*. Chicago, Illinois: Island Press.

Smith, G. and D. Wenger. 2007. Sustainable disaster recovery: Operationalizing an existing Agenda. In *Handbook of Disaster Research,* R. Dynes, H. Rodriguez, and E. Quarantelli (eds), New York: Springer, 234–57.

S&P Dow Jones Indices LLC. 2015. S&P/Case-Shiller Denver Home Price Index. McGraw Hill Financial. http://us.spindices.com/indices/real-estate/sp-case-shiller-co-denver-home-price-index/ (accessed August 18, 2015).

Svaldi, A. 2013. Colorado flood victims face a tight rental market. *The Denver Post*, September 17. http://www.denverpost.com/breakingnews/ci_24116858/flood-victims-face-tight-rental-market (accessed February 29, 2016).

Tierney, K. 2006. Social inequality, hazards and disasters. In *On Risk and Disaster: Lessons from Hurricane Katrina*, R. J. Daniels, D. F. Kettl, and H. Kunreuther (eds), Philadelphia, Pennsylvania: University of Pennsylvania Press, 109–28.

Town of Lyons. 2014. *Lyons Recovery Action Plan.* http://co-lyons.civicplus.com/DocumentCenter/View/388 (accessed October 2, 2016).

Town of Lyons. 2015. 2015 Affordable Housing Recovery Project, Design/Build, Tax Credit, & CDBG-DR Applications Request for Proposals. https://www.rockymountainbidsystem.com/xfer/PublicSolicitation_Docs/SDIR~125864/0-2015%20Lyons%20Affordable%20Housing%20Recovery%20Project%20RFP.pdf (accessed June 15, 2015).

Town of Milliken. 2014. *Town of Milliken Housing Needs Assessment.* Colorado: Town of Milliken.

Town of Milliken. 2015. Issues and Opportunities Summary. Colorado: Town of Milliken. http://www.millikenco.gov/document_center/CommunityDevelopment/2015_Comprehensive_Plan___Issues_and_Opportunities_Summary.pdf (accessed June 21, 2015).

United States Census 2014. QuickFacts: Weld County, Colorado. http://www.census.gov/quickfacts/table/PST045215/08123 (accessed August 10, 2016).

U.S. Department of Housing and Urban Development (HUD). 2015. Glossary of Terms. Online at https://www.huduser.gov/portal/glossary/glossary_a.html. (Accessed October 2, 2016)

Weld County. 2014. Economic and Demographic Profile 2013–2014. https://www.co.weld.co.us/assets/c88682A241c8B23c0837.pdf (accessed August 10, 2016).

Wisner, B., P. Blaikie, T. Cannon, and I. Davis. 2003. *At Risk: Natural Hazards, People's Vulnerability and Disasters.* New York: Routledge.

Zhang, Y. and W. G. Peacock. 2009. Planning for housing recovery? Lessons from Hurricane Andrew. *Journal of the American Planning Association* 76(1): 5–24.

Zhang, Y. and W. G. Peacock. 2010. Planning for housing recovery? Lessons learned from Hurricane Andrew. *Journal of the American Planning Association* 76(1): 5–24.

8 Tornado Housing Recovery

Brenda D. Phillips and Susamma Seeley

CONTENTS

8.1 INTRODUCTION

On May 22, 2011, a devastating tornado raked large portions of Joplin, Missouri in the United States (see Figure 8.1). The tornado path reached 1 mile wide in some locations, and stretched over 22 miles. One hundred and sixty-one people died and 1000 sustained injuries (National Weather Service [NWS] 2011; Kuligowski et al. 2014). As a measure of impact, the number of deaths were "almost twice the national average of 91.6 tornado fatalities per year" (Kuligowski et al. 2014, p. xiii), creating the highest number of fatalities from a single tornado in US history (Prevatt et al. 2012; Simmons and Sutter 2012).

This chapter describes the process of tornado housing recovery, with illustrations from Joplin. Building damage is assessed using the Enhanced Fujita (EF) scale (see Table 8.1). The EF-scale measures wind speed and considers the type of damage that might affect various residential buildings using damage indicators. Twenty-eight damage indicators provide insights into a range of buildings from small residences and mobile homes to motels, apartments, and institutional buildings including hospitals or university settings. Each of the damage indicators can have several degrees of damage, with increasing wind speed tied to increasing degrees of damage. A damage indicator is matched to the building structure that is being assessed for damage.

FIGURE 8.1 Joplin housing damage (FEMA by Jace Andersen).

Destruction to that structure should then match the degree of damage—the combination then leads to identification of an EF rating (Wind Science and Engineering Center 2006). Ratings, though, can be controversial as evaluators review challenging debris paths with varying wind speeds and tornado intensity. Joplin's event ranged from EF4 to EF5, the strongest and most devastating levels possible.

The EF-scale reveals that challenges associated with tornado damage can vary considerably. The magnitude, scope, and impacts often depend on the location. An EF5 tornado in a rural area may damage trees or fields but not homes or other buildings. Conversely, an EF2 that moves through a mobile home community can be catastrophic for people's homes.

A tornado can also impact a focused area and then dissipate or, like Joplin, create a wide path through neighborhood and business sectors. For example, only one or a few neighborhoods in a large urban area may be directly impacted with the surrounding area able to provide materials and aid. The Brooklyn and Queens

TABLE 8.1
Operational EF Scale for Tornado

EF Number	3 Second Gust (MPH)
0	65–85
1	86–110
2	111–135
3	136–165
4	166–200
5	Over 200

Source: http://www.spc.noaa.gov/faq/tornado/ef-scale.html, last accessed July 21, 2015.

neighborhoods in New York City experienced an EF1 tornado in 2010 resulting in damage to homes, power lines, and highways, but surrounding areas proved able to supply needed resources.

A tornado can also damage entire communities. Geography and location of impact can, therefore, make a difference. A small, rural area may be harder hit if the tornado damages most of the businesses or homes, leaving the area with fewer resources to recover. This happened in Mulhall, Oklahoma in 1999 when the small town of 250 people sustained major damage from an EF4. A few weeks before Joplin, an EF4-5 tornado devastated Tuscaloosa County, Alabama. Sixty four people died and over 1500 became injured. Though major portions of the city remained undamaged, key locations were considerably damaged. Multiple vortices damaged the city of Tuscaloosa including homes, businesses, the police station, and the emergency operations center.

8.2 CONCEPTUALIZING RECOVERY

Picking up the pieces begins immediately, although recovery in an area like that impacted by Joplin takes years. The post-tornado housing recovery timeframe is best conceptualized as a process, meaning that people move through a series of steps or stages. The short- and long-term recovery periods characterize two such stages. Short-term recovery periods include the transition from debris removal and utility restoration into the initial efforts to repair or rebuild affected homes. Government officials will enact emergency measures, redesign building codes, establish building permitting processes, and create contracts for debris removal and disposal. The short-term time period usually also encapsulates the meetings and relationship building that voluntary organizations engage in. Voluntary organizations and local leaders will begin to establish Long-Term Recovery Committees (LTRCs), train case managers, search for funds, identify clients, and design a process for moving volunteers in to help with rebuilding. Meanwhile, homeowners with insurance will be awaiting funds to commence repairs or rebuilding (Comerio 1997, 1998). They will also be trying to secure contractors who will be searching for subcontractors. Short-term recovery is a time of preparation and positioning (Phillips 2016).

Long-term recovery can extend from weeks to months to years. Funding helps expedite recovery. Still, delays may occur because insurance policies lacked "high wind" clauses leading to insufficient insurance payouts. Many insurance policies also do not include removing debris removal, slabs, or basements. Homeowners, especially those lacking sufficient insurance coverage, may need to wait for assistance. Homeowners without any insurance will likely require a combination of governmental funding and voluntary help. People living on fixed incomes are at particular risk for an elongated recovery. Renters may also face a lengthy return to permanent housing if the landlord cannot rebuild quickly or if area real estate provides limited or affordable rental options. In Joplin, a number of families were in lease-to-own contracts. As a result of tornado damage, they often lost the money they had spent toward ownership when the homeowner did not or could not rebuild (Novogradac 2012). It was a double blow.

8.3 SHORT-TERM RECOVERY TASKS, ACTIONS, AND CONSIDERATIONS

The short-term recovery phase includes a range of tasks such as estimation of damage and removal of debris. These tasks would be daunting in Joplin given the tornado path, and would take several months to complete.

8.3.1 Damage Assessment

The process of post-tornado housing recovery begins with preliminary damage assessment (PDA) (Fleming 2014). For housing, an initial "windshield" survey may be conducted by driving through an affected area. These data, which usually describe the type and number of homes with minor, major, and total damage then form the PDA used to request federal aid.

Given that 64% of Joplin's residences were built over 30 years ago, the tornado would seriously damage these older dwellings. To illustrate, older construction techniques (not built to current codes), aging, and deferred maintenance led to significant failures such as complete building collapses with debris strewn for considerable distances (Roueche and Prevatt 2013). With winds estimated at 200 mph, approximately 7500 homes sustained damage with about 4000 completely destroyed. The event displaced an estimated 9200 people (Roueche and Prevatt 2013).

There was also notable damage to the only hospital, a nursing home, half of the local schools, dozens of faith-based settings, numerous businesses, and two fire stations (NWS 2011; Kuligowski et al. 2014). The tornado affected lifeline systems, including electricity, water, and gas. By the numbers, damage close to $3 billion locates the Joplin tornado as the costliest tornado on record (Kuligowski et al. 2014). In a community of just over 50,000 people, about 41% experienced direct effects to their lives (NWS 2011).

8.3.2 Debris Generation, Estimation, and Removal

Tornadoes may leave part of a home relatively untouched while another section shears away. Powerful winds will carry items aloft in debris balls, to be strewn dozens of miles from the original impact site. According to FEMA (2010), a typical single-wide mobile home will generate 290 cubic yards of debris. Larger homes, apartment buildings, and congregate facilities will further increase the amount of debris, especially with this magnitude of tornado. The Joplin tornado generated approximately 3 million cubic yards of debris or enough to fill a football field to a height of 120 stories (Kuligowski et al. 2014; City of Joplin 2015).

Typically, communities focus first on clearing roadways for emergency response vehicles as debris can include nails, glass, and other projectiles that will impale tires and cause personal injuries. If a Presidential Disaster Declaration has been issued, then federal guidelines will need to be monitored for removal, measurement, contracting, oversight, and disposal. Communities will need to provide guidance to residents on how to dispose properly of their debris, which cannot just be pushed to curbside for pick up. Instead, residents will need to sort through debris that can be composted, incinerated, or taken to the landfill.

Hidden within tornado debris piles will be hazardous materials, sharp objects, and chemicals that cause injuries. Those piles of muddy, splintered matter also contain memories—people's wedding photos, their children's baby shoes, essential work items such as tools and clothing, and personal records like military papers or university degrees. Damaged homes may also include pets awaiting rescue. Care must be taken to retrieve what can be salvaged because the debris, as splintered as it looks, contains the remnants of people's lives and livelihoods. In Joplin, a Facebook page posted photos and other items hoping to reunite people with their mementoes.

Other challenges develop as well. Not everyone has the ability to deal with debris. Parents must care for children after a tornado, and single parents in particular will experience significant demands on their time. Senior citizens may not be able to sort or carry debris to curbside or may have health conditions that limit their abilities. Some people with disabilities may require assistance too. Moving damaged furniture is difficult from a wheelchair as is sorting debris for those with visual challenges. Volunteers often arrive to help with debris, usually unsolicited. While they represent potentially valuable resources, they also require coordination, supervision, and effective deployment. Volunteers, unless arriving self-contained, will also require food, hydration, bathrooms, and instructions on how to safely sort and move debris. Leveraging their energy, while worthwhile, takes local effort and resources.

In Joplin, FEMA established an area named the expedited debris removal (EDR) initiative (City of Joplin 2015). By working together, FEMA coordinated EDR with the US Army Corps of Engineers and the Missouri National Guard. In addition, property owners removed debris through volunteer efforts or contractors. Clearing the EDR took several months with operations ceasing on August 7, 2011 (City of Joplin 2015). By its conclusion, the EDR effort transferred 1.2 million cubic yards of debris from over 2700 lots to disposal sites. In excess of 249,000 volunteer hours and 25,000 Missouri National Guard hours supported the initiative (Office of Missouri Governor 2012). The state governor used the Missouri Disaster Recovery Jobs program to hire local residents for debris removal to supplement this initiative. The EDR also required special handling of over 100,000 pieces of "household hazardous waste, appliances, electronics & motorized equipment" (Office of Missouri Governor 2012, p. 22).

8.4 LONG-TERM RECOVERY TASKS, ACTIONS, AND CONSIDERATIONS

Although people begin repairs and reconstruction during debris removal, the path to recovery can accelerate when debris removal ends. Post-tornado housing recovery, though, is more than repairs and reconstruction (Phillips 2014).

8.4.1 The Range of People's Needs

At the most basic level, people require that physical needs be met (food, water, clothing, and shelter) as well as their personal safety (i.e., "Maslow's Hierarchy," see Maslow 1954) in emergency sheltering, temporary shelters, and during the transition from temporary housing to permanent housing.

In Joplin, the American Red Cross sent over 800 staff and volunteers and 21 emergency response vehicles to help. The first shelter opened at Missouri Southern State University, which had hosted the Joplin High School graduation just before the disaster (American Red Cross 2011). Joplin opened a total of five shelters with a peak population of 500 (Office of the Missouri Governor 2012). To aid those suffering losses, volunteers and officials established sites to handle donations of clean up kits, clothing, food, and water. Missouri Southern State University offered donations space, later supplemented by a 22,000 square foot warehouse at the local airport (Office of the Missouri Governor 2012). The city of Joplin further responded to safety needs by providing 4000 NOAA weather radios to residents (City of Joplin 2015).

Higher-level needs must be met as well, including emotional and psychological needs and a feeling of belonging to social networks. Erikson (1978) wrote of "collective trauma" when the 1972 Buffalo Creek, West Virginia flood devastated an entire community, undermining families and their social networks. Survivors lamented the loss of their "social arrangements" as the "larger collectivity around you becomes an extension of your own personality, an extension of your own flesh" (Erikson 1978). To illustrate, one could compare the loss of the community to the loss of limbs in a tragic accident. People do not expect to lose the limb(s). The logical step would be to secure a prosthetic limb. However, amputees often still feel pain in their "ghost" limbs and attaching a prosthetic limb does not automatically replace any lost function. The individual who has lost his or her limb must learn how to function with this new limb, just like the individual who has lost a community must learn how to fit into a new social network. Keeping a community's social fabric intact represents one of the most crucial resources necessary for recovery, and also one of the greatest challenges (Erikson 1978; Norris et al. 2002a,b). With the loss of over 4000 homes, Joplin residents would face disruption to their social networks for some time.

Renewal of one's dignity or esteem through returning to a path of self-actualization represents another crucial higher-level need, such as being able to parent (Maslow 1954). Temporary housing can facilitate this journey from basic needs to self-actualization, where families can live together and establish routines (Quarantelli 1982). Temporary housing in Joplin included Community Group Sites funded by FEMA with development supported by the US Army Corps of Engineers (USACE 2011). As examples, Hope Haven included 152 units and Officer Jeff Taylor Memorial Acres offered 194 units. To establish a household routine and enable self-actualization, 170 units became available to families with school-age children prior to the start of the next school year (USACE 2011). In an effort to address needs for personal safety, the sites included 20 storm shelters (see Figure 8.2). To further meet a range of needs, government funded 52 accessible units. Amenities also included school bus and trolley stops (USACE 2011).

Reaching permanent housing means people can rebuild social networks (love and belonging) and function as employees or parents (self-actualization). Yet, reaching permanent housing can prove challenging depending on the local real estate market and availability of rentals. In Joplin at the time of the tornado, about 56% of the local housing stock was owner-occupied single-family homes

FIGURE 8.2 Joplin safe room (FEMA by Elissa Jun).

(Arthur et al. 2015). Prior to the disaster, renters could have secured such units for a median price of $623 (Arthur et al. 2015). The tornado increased home sales, with a median price in July 2011 of $108,000, which was a 22% increase (Arthur et al. 2015). One of the challenges faced by displaced residents was finding rentals for both temporary and permanent housing. A few months after the tornado, vacancy rates ranged from zero to 12.5% with most properties using a wait list (Arthur et al. 2015).

Donahue et al. (2012) encourage those involved in disaster human services to consider that both people's needs and the activities that enable reaching the said needs will overlap and change. For emergency managers and Voluntary Organizations Active in Disaster partners who specialize in disaster human services, the goal is to empower the family to achieve their own recovery in a manner that enables individuals and family units to meet their needs. Enabling them to do so emanates most effectively from a case management process which usually links to or arises out of an LTRC.

8.4.2 The Roles of LTRC

As they have evolved over the past few decades, the LTRC first becomes established as a group of local leaders and agencies to help their community to rebuild. Though an LTRC may take many forms and directions, the most common is to serve as a means through which planning, fundraising, leadership, and advocacy will occur. One typical feature of an LTRC is to identify and address unmet needs. For individuals and families struggling to return home, the LTRC can link them to resources.

To do so, a case manager will present their client's needs to the LTRC, which then discusses the client with their partners. Examples of partners might include local agencies (furniture and clothing), faith-based disaster organizations (rebuilding teams), or donors (roofing supplies and funds). By matching needs with available resources, the LTRC works with the case manager to enable progress for their clients. After Joplin, clients often needed to replace large appliances like refrigerators, stoves, washers, and dryers. Fortunately, some LTRC partners warehoused items from public, private, and nonprofit donors. Case managers then accessed appliances, furniture, and kitchen tools to support clients.

The Jasper County COAD (a form of a LTRC or Community Organizations Active in Disaster) began in June 2011 and wrapped up in October 2013 (Cage 2013). Their experience resulted in a series of recommendations beginning with learning how LTRCs function. They coordinated efforts to avoid duplication of benefits and leveraged resources and established subcommittees with set protocols. The Joplin LTRC also recognized "there is an urgency to act and organize and yet, it will take time to find rhythm and routine while developing a community-wide coordinating committee" (Cage 2013, p. 106). Joplin's LTRC advised "be patient with allowing the chaos to settle and the rhythm to surface" (Cage 2013, p. 106). The LTRC realized that compassion fatigue could set in and provided food, diversions, motivational speakers, and celebrations of success (Boscarino et al. 2004; Pulido 2007; Cage 2013). Joplin kept LTRC leadership in place for at least a year to facilitate client assistance. Recovery chairs would hold office for at least 1 year in order to provide continuity of leadership. The Joplin LTRC included over 50 voluntary agencies that assisted over 1500 cases (City of Joplin 2015).

8.4.3 The Case Management Process

Disaster case management occurs when a case manager helps a client to identify needs and find resources such as housing, employment, emotional or spiritual care, child care, clothing, transportation resources, and more (Bell 2010; Stough et al. 2010; National Voluntary Organizations Active in Disaster [NVOAD] 2012a,b).

Case managers rely on local experts and the process of collaboration to enable them to assist clients. As one example from Joplin illustrates, local people's ties to the community matter. One elderly Joplin couple, referred to the Joplin Independent Living Center (ILC), expressed fear that they would become institutionalized if they left their unsafe housing. Through a collaborative effort between the ILC, FEMA, AmeriCorps, and the faith-based community, the couple moved into a temporary housing unit and then into a permanent apartment. They maintained their independence because local people listened and outside agencies worked together (Cage 2013). The couple's situation represents what happens to many people living in circumstances marginalized by income, discrimination, disability, or other situations. The ILC supported over 750 families including building 15 new ramps for clients with wheelchairs.

Case managers, in concert with others, address such circumstances in an effort to ensure that everyone has a chance to return home. Without the assistance of an LTRC or case manager, the inequitable effects of a disaster would elongate recovery for many—and would likely institutionalize that inequity for future disasters. In short, recovery offers an opportunity to address the needs of historically marginalized and underserved populations. The recovery process may even improve their circumstances and increase their future safety and resiliency.

8.4.4 Addressing Unmet Needs

One of the tasks of case managers and an LTRC is to identify people or groups with underserved needs. Such households usually face a longer road home because they lack funds to rebuild or require volunteer assistance. Historically, those at risk for a longer recovery include seniors, people with disabilities, single parents, low income families, or immigrants, essentially those lacking access to recovery resources. For example, an individual or household might face specific needs such as caring for a frail senior or a dependent child with a cognitive disability. They may need recovery assistance to build a ramp, install accessible bathrooms, or pay for a chair lift. Ideally, a case manager will present their circumstances to the LTRC with available organizations offering their resources. With proper advocacy, those organizations can leverage their resources to address specific needs.

Data from the Joplin tornado showed that higher numbers of those aged 60 or more were either killed or injured (Kuligowski et al. 2014), a pattern consistent in other disasters (Sharkey 2007). Deaths included those living in congregate care, with 16 fatalities in one facility. Reconstruction must consider the needs of those most at risk in a tornado by incorporating features such as a safe room. Rebuilding efforts should address these requirements. For example, basements and other shelters or safe rooms with entrances that utilize stairs or steps may impede protective actions (Crawford, W. 2015, personal communication). Even if there is a safe room in the basement, getting there may require negotiating narrow staircases and doorways. Assistive devices may not fit (Crawford, W. 2015, personal communication, see Box 8.1). In previous disasters, addressing such needs has required significant levels of collaboration from an array of partners.

8.4.5 The Roles of Partners

In most disasters, local communities need help. Massive numbers of volunteers typically respond, and with direction from experienced organizations, can provide significant amounts of aid (Phillips 2014). State and national government assistance will be needed as well. While numbers vary, the turnout of volunteers into 2012 provided hours "equivalent to a full-time workforce of 330 people working for a year with no vacations or holidays" (Office of the Missouri Governor 2012, p. 36).

A wide array of local and outside agencies and organizations, particularly faith-based ones, sent volunteers and resources. Their services ranged from prayer to fundraising to counseling and long-term reconstruction. Many of them expanded or adapted their normal activities. The local Humane Society cared for over 1000 displaced animals, reunited about half with their families, and arranged adoptions. The local shelter for domestic violence witnessed increased violence about 6 months after the tornado as well as an increase in sexual assaults from the first week to 3 months after the disaster happened. With limited opportunities for safe area housing, families stayed in the shelter for longer times than in previous disasters (Cage 2013). The Joplin Habitat for Humanity (in the area since 1989) expanded their building model from three to five houses per year to have completed 71 homes by the second anniversary of the storm (Cage 2013, see Figure 8.3).

BOX 8.1 REBUILDING ACCESSIBLY

Rebuilding provides an opportunity to enhance the physical environment for all residents. For example, basements and other shelters or safe rooms with entrances that utilize stairs or steps may impede protective actions for elderly or for some people with disabilities (Crawford, W. 2015, personal communication). Disaster thus provides a construction opportunity to improve both accessibility and safety.

The principle of Universal Design (UD), a broadly accepted approach to enhance accessibility, can improve a home not only for people now but also as they age (National Council on Disability 2009). Indeed, "Universal Design is not about a disability. It is about meeting the needs of all [people] throughout their lifetimes" (Crawford, W. 2015, personal communication).

Seven principles apply to the implementation of UD (Universal Design 2015). The first principle, equitable use, requires designs that benefit a range of people's abilities. Second, flexibility in use adapts designs to a broad scope of personal preferences and capabilities. Third, simple and intuitive use means that a design can be easily understood, despite a user's capabilities, comprehension, language skills, or attention level. Fourth, perceptible information designs provide information efficiently to the user, regardless of surrounding conditions or the user's sensory abilities. Designs with a tolerance for error (fifth) reduce risks and the unfavorable consequences of inadvertent actions. Individuals can competently and easily use a design with minimum fatigue under the principle of low physical effort (sixth). The seventh principle of size and space for approach and use enables "approach, reach, manipulation, and use regardless of user's body size, posture, or mobility" (Universal Design 2015). Post-tornado construction that features UD would mean, at a minimum:

> 36″ wide doors, five-foot diameter clearance in kitchens and bathrooms, adjustable closet and pantry shelving, side by side refrigerator/freezer, adjustable countertops, hardwood floors and low pile carpet that allows ease of access, no more than a 1/2″ threshold between flooring surfaces, no step entrances, sloped walkways … with consistent access to a safe room (Universal Design 2015).

In Joplin, the Missouri Inclusive Housing Development Corporation (MO Housing) assisted survivors with existing or newly acquired access and functional needs. MO Housing worked to find inclusive housing or to incorporate adjustments in line with UD principles without additional costs (Crawford, W. 2015, personal communication).

Sources: The authors relied on extant academic literature (particularly those enriched by case studies), practical experience derived from professional work, and first-hand research conducted during the past 15 years. Personal communications with professional colleagues also provided valuable insights that were used with their permission.

FIGURE 8.3 Habitat for Humanity funded homes in Joplin (FEMA by Steve Zumwalt).

Local agencies and organizations needed outside aid, particularly funds to rebuild. Habitat's efforts relied on partnerships with the faith-based community, the state of Missouri, and sports teams that provided funding. Joplin's Habitat for Humanity unit was joined by others from across the United States as well as focused attention from a popular television show, "Extreme Makeover" (Rohr 2012).

FEMA provided temporary housing to 586 households on 15 sites in Joplin, which transitioned formally into other temporary housing or into permanent housing by June 2013 (City of Joplin 2015). To facilitate the transition, case managers from Catholic Charities, the American Red Cross, Salvation Army, Lutheran Social Services, and other partners benefited from a FEMA Disaster Case Management grant of $5.3 million to the Missouri Department of Economic Development (City of Joplin 2015). An additional $4.8 million in crisis counseling services came from FEMA to help survivors. Low interest loans came from the US Small Business Administration to homeowners, businesses, and nonprofits totaling $43.4 million (City of Joplin 2015).

The Missouri governor created "Jumpstart Joplin" which focused on single-family homes as an immediate priority as well as longer-term reconstruction of both single- and multifamily units (Office of the Missouri Governor 2012). To support the initiative, the Missouri Housing Development Commission "authorized $94 million in tax credits for housing construction" (Office of the Missouri Governor 2012, p. 32). The governor later sent $4 million from Community Development Block Grant funds to clear structures, deal with foundations and slabs, and push forward rebuilding efforts. As mentioned earlier, insurance can be challenging in what it covers. The Missouri Department of Insurance helped over 1000 consumers with coverage problems and expedited complaints (Office of the Missouri Governor 2012).

8.5 RECOMMENDATIONS

The most important post-tornado housing recovery recommendation that can be made is to mitigate future risks. Safe rooms provide the chance to survive an event and must be integrated into all repaired or rebuilt dwellings, schools, and congregate settings (FEMA 2015). They must also be accessible, particularly for seniors and people with disabilities, pets, and service animals. Reconstruction must also incorporate the best building codes and engineering designs (Prevatt et al. 2012), while ensuring that funding enables those at lowest incomes to benefit from such safety precautions. Given that Joplin's housing stock included older construction, it may be advisable to establish structural inspections to inform homeowners of risks (Prevatt et al. 2012). Insurance companies could offer incentives to strengthen homes against wind damage.

In lieu of individual safe rooms, congregate shelters can be put into place. As of 2015, Joplin had significantly increased its storm shelters by creating multipurpose safe rooms. During the day, the safe rooms are used as gymnasiums in schools and can provide shelter for hundreds in the event of a tornado (Younker 2015). Such congregate locations are especially important for people in higher-risk housing including manufactured housing. Facilities for medical care, seniors, and people with disabilities also benefit from sturdier construction and rapidly accessible safe rooms. The loss of life at one Joplin nursing home alone compels us to increase safety for all.

Clearly, Joplin's recovery experience shows that funding and an array of partnerships facilitate rebuilding, especially for those with unmet needs. Post-tornado efforts, like those of other disasters, require creative and flexible ways to secure and leverage funds. Knowing where the funds exist takes knowledge of disaster-focused funders and programs. Much of that knowledge is learned as the recovery unfolds, but knowing how recovery works beforehand could inform and facilitate efforts. Training and education on disaster recovery should be a part of any community facing a common hazard like tornadoes. The good news is that many voluntary agencies arrive in the aftermath, experienced, and ready to assist. Among them, the FEMA Voluntary Agency Liaison serves as a link between those newly affected by disaster and those with significant experience and resources.

Leadership from a broad spectrum of agencies, organizations, and government partners will also be needed, coupled with inter-organizational collaboration and cooperation. Their leadership must be informed by stakeholders, as their homes and communities are what people want to return to. The Joplin Citizens' Advisory Recovery Team serves as an example of how local input influenced the recovery. By incorporating the perspectives of residents, the final products of housing in any disaster will be improved and will meet more needs.

Tornado housing recovery efforts, especially in an event the magnitude and scope of Joplin, will require coordination among people from many places to bring people back home. It may take years and extensive effort, but it is worth it. Everyone deserves a chance to go home again.

ACKNOWLEDGMENTS

Brenda Phillips thanks Mary Jane Phillips and Dave Neal. Susamma Seeley wants to thank Jono Anzalone, Debi Meeds, Wayne Crawford, and Steve Irwin.

REFERENCES

American Red Cross. 2011. One Month after Deadly Joplin Tornado, Red Cross Continues to Help. http: //www.redcross.org/news/article/One-Month-After-Deadly-Joplin-Tornado-Red-Cross-Continues-to-Help- (accessed October 6, 2015).

Arthur, R. S., J. E. Fairchild, and B. A. Meinzer. 2015. *Updated comprehensive housing market analysis, Joplin, Missouri.* Overland Park, Kansas: Novogradac & Company LLP. http://joplinmo.org/DocumentCenter/View/1265 (accessed October 6, 2015).

Bell, H. 2010. Case management with displaced survivors of Hurricane Katrina. *Journal of Social Service Research* 34(3): 15–27.

Boscarino, J. A., C. R. Figley, and R. E. Adams. 2004. Compassion fatigue following the September 11 terrorist attack: A study of secondary trauma among New York City social workers. *International Journal of Emergency Mental Health* 6(2): 57–66. http://www.ncbi.nlm.nih.gov/pmc/articles/PMC2713725/ (accessed February 29, 2016).

Cage, J. 2013. *Joplin Pays It Forward: Community Leaders Share Our Recovery Lessons.* Missouri: City of Joplin. http://www.joplinmo.org/joplinpaysitforward (accessed October 6, 2015).

City of Joplin. 2015. Fact sheet—City of Joplin, Missouri. Joplin, Missouri: Public Information Office. http://joplintornadoanniversary.com/factsheet.php (accessed February 29, 2016).

Comerio, M. 1998. *Disaster Hits Home: New Policy for Urban Housing Recovery.* Berkeley, California: University of California Press.

Comerio, M. 1997. Housing issues after disasters. *Journal of Contingencies and Crisis Management* 5: 166–78.

Donahue, D., S. Cunnion, C. Balaban, and K. Sochats. 2012. The all needs approach to emergency response. *Homeland Security Affairs* 8(1): 1–17. https://www.hsaj.org/articles/204 (accessed October 6, 2015).

Erikson, K. T. 1978. *Everything in Its Path: Destruction of Community in the Buffalo Creek Flood.* New York: Simon & Shuster.

FEMA. 2010. *Debris Estimating Field Guide.* FEMA 329, Washington, DC: Author. https://www.fema.gov/pdf/government/grant/pa/fema_329_debris_estimating.pdf (accessed February 29, 2016).

FEMA. 2015. *Safe Rooms for Tornadoes and Hurricanes: Guidance for Community and Residential Safe Rooms.* 3rd edn, FEMA P-361, Washington, DC: Author. https://www.fema.gov/media-library/assets/documents/3140 (accessed October 6, 2015).

Fleming, M. 2014. *An Exploratory Study of Preliminary Damage Assessments in Northern Illinois.* Master's Thesis. Stillwater, Oklahoma: University of Oklahoma.

Kuligowski, E., F. T. Lombardo, L. T. Phan, and M. L. Levitan. 2014. Final Report National Institute of Standards and Technology (NIST): Technical Investigation of the May 22, 2011, Tornado in Joplin, Missouri. Washington, DC: National Institute of Standards and Technology. http://nvlpubs.nist.gov/nistpubs/NCSTAR/NIST.NCSTAR.3.pdf (accessed January 4, 2016).

Maslow, A. 1954. *Motivation and Personality.* New York: Harper.

National Council on Disability. 2009. *Effective Emergency Management.* Washington, DC: National Council on Disability.

National Voluntary Organizations Active in Disaster (NVOAD). 2012a. *Long Term Recovery Guide.* Washington, DC: NVOAD.

National Voluntary Organizations Active in Disaster (NVOAD). 2012b. No date. Points of consensus. http://www.nvoad.org/ (accessed October 6, 2015).

National Weather Service (NWS). 2011. *NWS Central Region Service Assessment: Joplin, Missouri, Tornado (May 22).* Kansas City, Missouri: NWS, Central Region Headquarters.

Norris, F. H., M. J. Friedman, and P. J. Watson. 2002a. 60,000 disaster victims speak: Part II. Summary and implications of the disaster mental health research. *Psychiatry* 65(3): 240–60.

Norris, F. H., M. J. Friedman, P. J. Watson, C. M. Byrne, E. Diaz, and K. Kaniasty. 2002b. 60,000 disaster victims speak: Part I. An empirical review of the empirical literature, 1981–2001. *Psychiatry* 65(3): 207–39.

Novogradac & Company. 2012. *Updated Comprehensive Housing Market Analysis*. Overland Park, Kansas: Novogradac & Company, LLP.

Office of the Missouri Governor. 2012. *After the Storm: Missouri's Commitment to Joplin*. St. Louis, Missouri: Office of Missouri Governor.

Phillips, B. 2014. *Mennonite Disaster Service: Building a Therapeutic Community after the Gulf Coast Storms*. Lanham, Maryland: Lexington Books.

Phillips, B. 2016. *Disaster Recovery*, 2nd edn, Boca Raton, Florida: CRC Press.

Phillips, B., T. Wikle, A. Hakim, and L. Pike. 2012. Establishing and operating shelters after Hurricane Katrina. *International Journal of Emergency Management* 8(2): 153–67.

Pulido, M. L. 2007. In their words: Secondary traumatic stress in social workers responding to the 9/11 terrorist attacks in New York City. *Social Work* 52(3): 279–81.

Quarantelli, E. L. 1982. *Sheltering and Housing after Major Community Disasters: Case Studies and General Observations*. Newark, Delaware: Disaster Research Center, University of Delaware.

Rohr, M. 2012. *Joplin: The Miracle of the Human Spirit*. Mustang, Oklahoma: Tate Publishing.

Roueche, D. and D. Prevatt. 2013. Residential damage patterns following the 2011 Tuscaloosa, AL and Joplin, MO Tornadoes. *Journal of Disaster Research* 8(6): 1061–67.

Sharkey, P. 2007. Survival and death in New Orleans. *Journal of Black Studies* 37(4): 482–501.

Simmons, K. and D. Sutter. 2012. The 2011 tornadoes and the future of tornado research. *American Meteorological Society* 93: 959–61.

Stough, L., A. Sharp, C. Decker, and N. Wilker. 2010. Disaster case management and individuals with disabilities. *Rehabilitation Psychology* 55(3): 211–20.

Universal Design. 2015. The 7 principles. http://universaldesign.ie/What-is-Universal-Design/The-7-Principles/ (accessed October 6, 2015).

US Army Corps of Engineers (USACE). 2011. USACE Joplin Area Tornado Recovery Mission/Commander's Final Report. http://silverjackets.nfrmp.us/Portals/0/doc/Missouri/Joplin_RFO_Presentation_to_SilverJackets_MO.pdf?ver=2015-07-09-175137-897 (accessed October 6, 2015).

Wind Science and Engineering Center. 2006. *A Recommendation for an Enhanced Fujita Scale (EF-Scale)*. Lubbock Texas: Texas Tech University.

Younker, E. 2015. Joplin, MO., Tornado Spurs Explosion of School Safe Room Projects. http://www.emergencymgmt.com/disaster/Joplin-Tornado-Spurs-School-Safe-Room-Projects.html (accessed October 6, 2015).

9 Housing Recovery after Hurricane Sandy
A Vignette Study

Ali Nejat, Souparno Ghosh, Zhen Cong, and Daan Liang

CONTENTS

9.1 INTRODUCTION

Effective post-disaster planning is essential to enable communities to recover from natural catastrophes, such as hurricanes, earthquakes, and tsunamis, as well as human-induced events such as acts of terrorism or accidents. In anticipation of these high-impact low-probability events, at-risk communities need policies, contingency plans, procedures, guidelines, and budgets that can enable them implement recovery actions. However, recent major disasters in the United States (e.g., Hurricanes Sandy, Katrina, Rita, and the Joplin Tornado) reveal the inability of existing policies and practices to promptly restore infrastructure, residential properties, and commercial activities in affected communities. The exponential increase in future extreme events (Bournay and UNEP/GRID-Arendal 2007) coupled with the growing population in disaster-prone regions has created an urgent need for a better understanding of the process of disaster recovery and more effective strategies to enhance it. These enhancements can in turn lead to fewer casualties, and saving of federal resources, which according to US Department of Housing and Urban Development (US HUD) (2011) amounted to $19.7 billion for grants used in Louisiana, Mississippi, and Texas in 2005 alone.

This chapter reports on results from a collaborative research effort to use face-to-face surveys to collect data on the determinants of post-disaster housing recovery and compares the results with a vignette design to assess how affected households perceive the importance of various factors on reconstruction decisions under several hypothetical and scarce scenarios. Vignettes, simulations of real events portraying hypothetical scenarios (Wilks 2004), have a long history of application in studying norms, perceptions, and beliefs (Finch 1987). In other words, vignettes used in video material and cartoons (Ouslander et al. 1993; Cohen and Strayer 1996) are elicitation tools intended to facilitate the investigation of responses to hypothetical scenarios. Vignette studies help with counterbalancing the weaknesses associated with classical experiments and survey methodology by combining the ideas from both (Atzmüller and Steiner 2015). This combination provides high internal validity by using features of classical experiments and active modes of measurement and high external validity through characteristics of traditional surveys and their multivalent measurements. In the field of designing public opinion surveys, vignettes are regarded by Sniderman and Grob (1996) as innovative breakthroughs. Vignettes also have the flexibility of being used both in quantitative and qualitative designs. In quantitative design, a series of predetermined responses are made available to the respondents (Wilks 2004). Quantitative vignette studies have been used in various fields of application including psychology (Thurman et al. 1988; Hunter and McClelland 1991; Barrera and Buskens 2007), sociology (Alves and Rossi 1978; Jasso and Webster Jr 1999; Wallander 2009), and other fields (Atzmüller and Steiner 2015). However, to the best of our knowledge there are no similar designs and studies within the context of post-disaster housing recovery.

Apart from the vignette design and study, several factors that were deemed to be influential on housing recovery decisions were included in the face-to-face survey. These factors encompassed internal attributes such as family structure, location bonds, and socioeconomic status, as well as external factors such as reconstruction of neighboring households. The case study area for this research was Staten Island, New York, which was chosen because it was severely impacted by hurricane Sandy and due to the variations in demographic and socioeconomic attributes of its population. The face-to-face survey was designed to elicit the factors that directly affect a household's decision to rebuild/repair, wait, or relocate, while the vignette study was used to gather recommendations from respondents about hypothetical scenarios. This chapter begins with a discussion of social networks, social capital, and place attachment as factors that affect household recovery. Next, we provide information on the impact of Hurricane Sandy on the study area of Staten Island, New York, followed by a description of the methodologies used in this study. We conclude with key findings from the face-to face surveys and vignette studies to inform recommendations, which are offered in the final section of the chapter.

9.2 FACTORS AFFECTING HOUSEHOLD RECOVERY

There is ample literature on the determinants of post-disaster housing recovery each highlighting a specific aspect of the process (Nejat and Ghosh 2016). For example, demographic, socioeconomic, and psychosocial control variables such as age, gender, ethnicity, income, employment, assets, and familial links/social networks are internal factors that affect household recovery (Kutak 1938; Moore 1958; Stoddard 1961; Bolin 1976, 1982, 1993, 1994; Bates 1982; Bolin and Bolton 1983; Peacock et al. 1987). The existence of private insurance, a restored economy, and spatial externalities are seen as being crucial external control factors (Tierney and Dahlhamer 1997; Alesch and Holly 1998; Chang 2001; Peacock et al. 2007). Peacock et al. (2014) highlighted the long-term aspect of housing recovery through a longitudinal study in Miami-Dade and Galveston after Hurricane Andrew and Hurricane Ike. In this study income, race, and ethnicity were shown to be the critical determinants of losses and recovery in Miami versus income in Galveston. Functionality of businesses, transportation and utility infrastructure as well as the recovery of schools, healthcare, and social services are other factors needed to achieve normalcy after disasters (Comerio 2014). Henry (2013) performed an inductive analysis of recovery decisions in the aftermath of Hurricanes Katrina and Rita in August and September 2005 and found that for those who planned to return to damaged areas, housing circumstances and to a lesser degree family and work played a significant role in their decision. In addition for those who chose to relocate, the decision was based on three equally weighted and interconnected parameters of family, risk, and work. Finally for those who remained undecided, housing and work seemed to be the main decision-making drivers. Social networks and place attachments are two other important factors that affect recovery decisions and are briefly discussed below.

9.2.1 Social Networks and Social Capital

Recovery is not only the act of individuals but also a collective action based largely on extensive interactions within the members of households and their social networks (Nejat and Ghosh 2016). The collective aspect of recovery decisions surfaced in the aftermath of Katrina when a significant portion of the affected population eventually relocated for multiple reasons (Frey 2005; Morin and Rein 2005; Dewan et al. 2006; McCarthy et al. 2006; Alfred 2007). Social networks influence such collective decisions in two ways: (1) they greatly influence the psychological well-being of the affected families (Bolin 1976), helping them reduce the effects of the traumatic event and prevent families from abandoning their residences and (2) they promote housing recovery of the families as studies have highlighted the tendency of families to relocate or to go back to their own homes (Bates et al. 1963; Barton 1969) accompanied by family or friends (Bolin 1976). The role of social capital as a facilitator of post-disaster recovery was also reflected in the work of Aldrich (2011) as the strongest predictor of recovery in the aftermath of 1995 Kobe earthquake in Japan. In addition, Aldrich (2010, 2012) pointed out the importance of social capital as the engine for recovery and the reason behind the display of resilience in some neighborhoods and stagnation in others. Nakagawa and Shaw (2004) describe social capital in terms of three actions, namely recognize, preserve/conserve, and invest; in the context of disaster recovery, these actions lead to collective actions by members in communities. Chamlee-Wright and Storr (2009) also highlight the collective narrative associated with social capital and its impact on post-disaster recovery. Others such as Yandong (2007) studied the role of social capital in the context of post-disaster recovery in 11 provinces in Western China and found that trust had a positive role and that the dependence of socially vulnerable groups on their strong ties network might have negative impacts on their overall recovery. More specifically, Rust and Killinger (2006) noted that the reconstruction decisions of the affected households were significantly linked to the decisions of their neighbors.

9.2.2 Place Attachment

The role of place attachment as a potential factor in influencing recovery decisions has been highlighted by several research studies (Binder et al. 2015; Henry 2013; Kick et al. 2011; Sanders et al. 2004). Based on the existing research studies, two major components have been associated with place attachment. The first is place identity which refers to how residents perceive their identity relative to their surrounding physical environment and the second is place dependence which refers to how residents perceive their community's potential to address their needs (Kick et al. 2011; Shriver and Kennedy 2005; Williams and Vaske 2003). According to Jamali and Nejat (2016), determinants of place attachment can be categorized into four major categories including: demographic, socioeconomic, spatial, and psychosocial. In the context of post-disaster recovery, understanding the determinants of place attachment is important as it can assist policymakers make informed decisions regarding the enhancement of survivors' recovery. Under the demographic category and based on Hidalgo and Hernandez (2001), Jack (2010), and Rollero and De Piccoli (2010) research studies, age and gender were shown to be important in causing distinctive place attachment behavior by individuals. More specifically in (Hidalgo and Hernandez 2001) women were shown to have greater place attachment than men while the exact opposite was reported in (Magalhaes and Calheiros 2015). From the socioeconomic standpoint, inequalities in access to economic resources and diversity in social bonds together with race were concluded to be influential on place attachment (Elliot and Pais 2006; Oh 2004). Furthermore according to Oh (2004), African-American individuals generally tend to have a lower level of interactions with their neighborhood compared to Caucasians. This behavior was concluded to originate from a lower economic status and sense of instability, which act as a burden towards building positive relationships within their neighborhood. Additionally, according to Mazumdar and Mazumdar (2004), religion was shown to be an influential parameter in driving individuals' attachment to their place of living. On the other hand, job opportunities within the living area were shown to drastically affect the level of place attachment (Anton and Lawrence 2014). Also level of education can lead to variation in level of place attachment (Anton and Lawrence 2014).

Under the spatial category, availability of natural features such as water elements and green spaces was reported to be significant in increasing rootedness in certain age groups (Shabak et al. 2015; Jack 2010). It is also important to know that according to Brown et al. (2003) homeowners display a totally different attachment behavior than do renters as they are more concerned about their living areas. The definition of "place" in "place attachment" was investigated in the work of Lewicka (2010). According to Anton and Lawrence (2014), living in areas with higher exposure to risks and coastal zones can lead to diverse levels of attachment. These diverse levels of attachment can also result from living in various community settings such as living in urban and rural areas. This is deemed to happen due to the variations in economic and social conditions of these two types of areas (Turcotte 2005). Finally, mental health and community involvement can be categorized under psychosocial category. Mental health (Cope et al. 2013) is an important parameter in determining an individual's perception of disaster recovery and is influenced by place of living. Community involvement (Ritchie and Gill 2007) on the other hand relates to a sense of being involved within one's community.

While the existing literature covers a wide range of parameters affecting housing recovery, there are still gaps in fully understanding the recovery decisions of households in the aftermath of a disaster and how these decisions affect the overall recovery of the community. This is partially due to the lack of a more comprehensive data collection approach capable of integrating scenarios that are hard to collect in the aftermath of a disaster. We report on our research effort to bridge the existing gap by combining a face-to-face survey with a vignette study in which scarce scenarios can be included in the analysis. The findings can ultimately inform our understanding of households' recovery decisions.

9.3 HURRICANE SANDY AND ITS IMPACTS ON STATEN ISLAND, NEW YORK

Staten Island, New York was one of the major areas which was severely impacted by Hurricane Sandy in October 2012. The total deaths associated with Hurricane Sandy was 43, among which 23 occurred in Staten Island including 10 deaths in the neighborhood of Midland Beach (CityNY 2013), one of the two case study targeted neighborhoods in this research. The damage caused by Sandy to economy, homes, and businesses was estimated to be more than $19 billion (CityNY 2013, p. 5). Among the hundreds of homes destroyed by Sandy or determined to be structurally compromised, 30% were located in Staten Island (CityNY 2013, p. 21). The storm surge in Sandy devastated southern beach neighborhoods including Midland Beach and New Dorp Beach, the two study areas for this research. Overall, Staten Island had higher rates of yellow (significant nonstructural damage) and red tagged (structural damage) and lower rates of damaged buildings compared to citywide rates. Results of a thorough assessment of building damage by New York City Department of Buildings found that 23% of yellow and red tagged buildings were located in the east and south shores (CityNY 2013), including the neighborhoods of South Beach, Midland Beach, New Dorp Beach, and Oakwood Beach. In addition, around 120,000 customers lost power due to the impact of Sandy on Staten Island's utilities. In the aftermath of Hurricane Sandy, several initiatives were developed under the city's five-borough building resiliency plan in order to protect structures on the eastern and southern shores against several risks including climate risks such as flooding, high winds, and other extreme events. These initiatives include measures to: (1) improve flood resiliency regulations, (2) rebuild/repair the affected housing units, (3) implement zoning changes, (4) launch a competition to encourage cost-effective housing types, (5) identify eligible communities for home buyout programs, (6) amend building code, (7) encourage adoption of flood resiliency, (8) help owners with design solution for retrofitting, and etc. According to CityNY (2015), the NYC Mayor's Build it Back overhaul was able to reimburse homeowners with over $100 million dollars making 1837 construction projects viable. More specifically, the building of 9.8 miles of dunes across the Rockaway Peninsula was among the short-term measures that were put in place to ensure the safety of the five boroughs. In addition, in Staten Island, 68 acres of degraded wetlands are being restored.

9.4 METHODOLOGY AND DATA COLLECTION

9.4.1 Face-to-Face Survey

A face-to-face survey was administered to the residents of highly affected areas in Staten Island, New York in December, 2012, approximately 35 days after Hurricane Sandy. Two faculty members and three trained students from an interdisciplinary research team at Texas Tech University were deployed in the area and conducted recruitment and face-to-face surveys. Participants were recruited through two sampling methods. The first was door-to-door survey which targeted the heavily damaged coastal areas namely New Dorp Beach and Midland Beach. The second was a survey at designated shelters for those whose residences were inhabitable. The door-to-door survey followed the succeeding process: a single address was selected randomly by each of the members of the data collection group within the targeted locations. Using this address as the benchmark, other houses neighboring this address were approached and asked to participate in the survey if the house was approachable and if the person answering the door was over 18 years old. If a home was not approachable, the adjacent home was approached and the same pattern was repeated by each of the data collection group members. If a home was not approachable at the time of surveying, the address was tagged for a follow-up on the following day and was removed from the sample after two subsequent follow-ups. Procedures similar to this have been previously employed for data collection purposes in the aftermath of disasters in which the starting point of door-to-door surveys was randomly selected and the rest of the addresses were selected using the randomly selected address as the starting point (Binder et al. 2015).

As mentioned above, our study was focused on the residents of highly affected areas in Staten Island. In particular, our goal was to study the decision-making behavior of the households that were most significantly affected by hurricane Sandy. Due to the greater emphasis that was placed on severely affected households, standard random sampling strategy would not have been suitable in our context. Instead, we targeted the worst affected neighborhoods, assuming that the subjects in these neighborhoods would be more relevant for the purpose of our investigation.

We divided the worst affected neighborhoods, Midland Beach and New Dorp Beach, into multiple clusters. Each of these clusters was centered around the foregoing randomly chosen benchmark addresses. A cluster consisted of all the houses that were on the same street and adjoining streets of the benchmark. Despite multiple attempts that were made to survey each cluster member, a large proportion of households remained unsampled due to the inhabitability of houses caused by Sandy. To supplement this shortcoming, we used a snowball sampling (Goodman 1961; Berg 1988) to integrate the experience of: (1) other survivors who lost their homes in the area and were residing in a major shelter (Bayley Seton Hospital) and (2) the people who were applying for assistance from Federal Emergency Management Agency (FEMA) in their temporary centers throughout the city and other food banks. More specifically, these centers were: (1) the FEMA disaster recovery center on Hylan Blvd. (Manfredi Auto) and (2) FEMA state disaster recovery center at New Dorp High School together with the food bank at the intersection of Midland Avenue and Patterson Avenue.

The rationale behind selecting these sampling methods was the limited availability of households in the area and consequently, a relatively small sample size, due the catastrophic nature of the event. Such small sample sizes are associated with a large margin of error which affect the generalizability of the results (Lincoln and Guba 1985). Admittedly, a greater focus on a small cross section of the population will also affect the generalizability of the results. However, we argue that since we have sampled the worst affected households as extensively as possible, our results are at least generalizable to population who have experienced moderate to severe property damages due to natural calamity. Survey participants were compensated for their participation through on-site cash payments.

Altogether, 126 surveys were completed after 5 days of data collection including 150 hours of face-to-face surveys. The survey focused on post-hurricane experience and household decision making concerning relocating and reconstructing. The face-to-face survey aimed to collect data from the affected households and was comprised of five parts. The first part included questions on the households' demographic, socioeconomic, and personal attributes (age, race, education, employment, annual income, and religion). The second part encompassed questions on residence status before hurricane (ownership, type, tenure, insurance, and residence value before impact). The third, and main part of the survey, focused on residence status after the hurricane. It incorporated questions such as level of damage and household's housing recovery decisions in the aftermath of Sandy. The housing recovery decision had three alternatives presented as the choices for response: (1) rebuild or repair, (2) wait and stay in temporary housing, and (3) relocate. Each of these alternatives was associated with follow up questions on parameters believed to influence the decision. For example, the decision of rebuild/repair was associated with the following influencing parameters: the restoration of affected infrastructure, reconstruction efforts by neighbors, availability of mental health services, reimbursement from insurance, availability of grants, loans, and temporary housing, and accessibility to family and relatives. The decision to wait was associated with the same parameters to explore which factors influenced rebuild/repair decisions among those who decided to wait and seek temporary housing. Finally, for those who decided to relocate, the location of the new residence was included in the questions. The final part was to collect information on the amount of losses and compensation received through different entities such as federal, state, and local governments, and charities. Power analysis with STATA©

indicated that this sample size would provide adequate power for multiple regression, assuming a medium effect size (Cohen 1992). The proportion of Caucasians in the selected sample was fairly similar to those obtained from census data from the area (Census 2012). However, there was a gap between the values recorded under income and gender distribution. On average, the sample population was younger, had a lower income, and had more males than the census data for those neighborhoods.

9.5 VIGNETTE SURVEY

For the purpose of this research's vignette study, the following scenarios were developed to examine factors that would possibly influence households' recovery decisions after disasters. The texts in italics highlight the parts with changing values each creating a separate scenario.

> A *(a) single-mother family with two kids/(b) family with two-parents and two kids* has been living in the area for (a) *around 10 years/(b) less than 1 year*; they own their own houses with mortgage. Hurricane Sandy severely damaged their house, and they have to make a decision about whether to "relocate" or reconstruct the house. *(a) The insurance the family has is enough to reconstruct the house/(b) not enough to build the house. (a) Most neighbors have started reconstructing/(b) most neighbors choose to relocate.*

After presenting the scenarios, the respondents were asked the following question: "What do you think the family should do?" The respondents had three choices to choose from: (a) reconstruct or repair, (b) wait and see in temporary housing, and finally (c) relocate. As the vignette had four factors each with two factor levels, it resulted in 16 ($2 \times 2 \times 2 \times 2$) combinations. Each respondent was randomly assigned a unique combination. Assigning random combinations of the dimensions to the respondents provide the ability to establish internal validity and argue for the causality of each dimension's influences on the outcome of interest. In other words, as the vignette is in essence an experimental design we can establish internal validity or causal inference by actively manipulating levels (dimensions) of independent variables and choose a randomly selected version of the vignette story for each respondent keeping almost everything the same and varying the key elements. When combined with a survey with a carefully designed sampling strategy, the vignette design also exhibits external validity of generalizability (Rossi and Rossi 1990; Ganong and Coleman 2006; Cong and Silverstein 2012). This approach is particularly useful for situations that are rare or hard to measure in reality. The vignette was approved by Texas Tech Office of Human Research Protection Program in early December 2012 following the completion of design and prior to performing the data collection. In this vignette study, the dependent variable was set to the households' preferred choice among the following options: (1) "reconstruct/repair," (2) "wait," and (3) "relocate." There were four factors associated with this vignette. The first was to examine the influence of family structure by including single-mother or two-parent family (*SM*). The second was to account for the role of place attachment through housing tenure years of 1 or 10 years (*TY*). The third was to capture the influence of having or lacking insurance (*EI*), and finally the fourth was to incorporate the impact of neighboring activities through its presence or absence (*NR*).

The completed surveys were used to build a housing recovery decision-making model. To form the model, logistic regression was used as the statistical modeling technique. Logistic regression is a form of statistical modeling which relates a set of explanatory variables to a categorical response variable. Response variables can either have two or more categories and dichotomous or polytomous, respectively. In this research, the response variable had three categories and was polytomous, entailing the use of a generalized logit (multinomial logistic regression) model (McCullagh 1980). Generalized logit models are an extended form of binary logit models in which instead of having a single-logit model, multiple logits are modeled.

9.6 MAIN FINDINGS

As previously mentioned, the face-to-face survey was designed to elicit the importance of factors that directly affected a households' decision to rebuild/repair, wait, and relocate as opposed to the vignette study where the respondents were asked to provide their recommendations given a scenario, that is, a particular combination of the foregoing four factors. For each of these surveys (face-to-face and vignette), separate statistical analysis was performed in which the reference category was set to "reconstruct/repair" for both of the analyses as it was the most frequent option selected by the respondents. The idea was to find the odds of selecting the other two categories namely "wait" and "relocate" over "reconstruct/repair" given certain internal/external attributes. This section is divided into two subsections each summarizing the outcomes of both surveys.

9.6.1 Vignette Survey

In the vignette survey, regression results (Table 9.1) denote that having sufficient insurance (*EI*) is statistically significant in both "wait" and "relocate" models. On the other hand, two-parent versus single-mother family (*SM*) while significant in

TABLE 9.1
Parameter Estimates for the Main Effect Model (Reference Category: "Reconstruct/Repair")

Category		*B*	Std. Error	Wald	df	Sig.	Exp (*B*)
Wait	Intercept	−0.195	0.599	0.107	1	0.744	
	SM	−1.252	0.597	4.406	1	0.036	0.286
	TY	0.857	0.554	2.392	1	0.122	2.356
	EI	−1.472	0.557	6.984	1	0.008	0.230
	NR	−0.350	0.539	0.423	1	0.516	0.704
Relocate	Intercept	0.683	0.458	2.225	1	0.136	
	SM	−0.327	0.411	0.632	1	0.427	0.721
	TY	−0.007	0.409	0.000	1	0.986	0.993
	EI	−1.021	0.412	6.150	1	0.013	0.360
	NR	−0.616	0.409	2.269	1	0.132	0.540

the "wait" model, is not significant in the "relocate" model in the presence of other parameters. Based on the results, it can be concluded that the odds of choosing "*wait*" over "*reconstruct/repair*" is almost 71% less (odds ratio (OR) = 0.286, $p < 0.05$) for a two-parent family scenario than for the single-mother family scenario. Also, the results denote that the odds of preferring "*wait*" to "*reconstruct/repair*" is 77% less (OR = 0.230, $p < 0.05$) for households without sufficient insurance than for those with sufficient insurance. In addition, the odds of selecting "*relocate*" strategy over "*reconstruct/repair*" decreases by 64% for scenarios about families without sufficient insurance to those who have sufficient insurance. In other words, these results imply: (1) availability of insurance will significantly increase the probability of choosing "*wait*" or "*relocate*" and (2) responses indicated a higher probability of choosing "*reconstruct/repair*" for a two-parent family has instead of a "*wait*" response for a single-mother family (see Table 9.1).

9.6.2 Face-to-Face Survey

For this survey, the regression results (Table 9.2) reveal a very different association between the predictors and the decision that the households make for themselves as compared to the aforementioned vignette study. For both decisions "wait" and "relocate," the only predictor that turns out to be significant (at 5% level of significance) is the level of place attachment (TY). Odds for households, with less than 1 year of residence in their current house, to wait before deciding on reconstruction are 13 times more than those for households who have resided in their current location for 10 years or more (OR = 13.53, $p < 0.05$). More significantly, odds for the former type households to relocate are overwhelmingly 55 times more than the households of the latter type (OR = 55.42, $p < 0.01$). Evidently, place attachment is the key driving

TABLE 9.2
Parameter Estimates for Main Effect Model (Reference Category: "Reconstruct/Repair")

Category		*B*	Std. Err	Wald	Sig.	Exp (*B*)
Wait	Intercept	−4.924	1.593	9.549	0.002	
	SM	−0.736	0.885	0.6915	0.406	0.479
	TY	2.605	1.086	5.758	**0.016**	13.531
	EI	0.929	0.827	1.263	0.261	2.532
	NR	1.486	1.12	1.768	0.184	4.435
Relocate	Intercept	−3.532	1.181	8.95	0.003	
	SM	0.269	0.635	0.179	0.672	1.309
	TY	4.015	1.0471	14.704	**0.0001**	55.428
	EI	0.1551	0.507	0.094	0.758	1.167
	NR	−0.767	0.499	2.353	0.125	0.465

Note: Bold denotes high significance.

factor in the households' decision-making processes. More established households are significantly more likely to initiate reconstruction of their residence as compared to newly established households. Contrasting this finding with the vignette study, we conjecture that the households' recommendations given hypothetical scenarios on the decision to reconstruct is primarily driven by financial considerations (sufficient insurance availability). However, their own decision-making process is heavily reliant on more emotional aspects associated with the length of their residence. Although insurance availability does not play a significant role in the households' own decision-making process, the reversal of sign associated with this predictor for the face-to-face survey is quite compelling. In the vignette study, given the availability of sufficient insurance, the households' recommendation to choose "wait" or "relocate" is significantly higher as compared to "reconstruction/repair." But in the households' own decision-making process, odds of preferring "wait" to "reconstruct/repair" is 2.5 more (OR = 2.530, $p > 0.05$) for households without sufficient insurance than for those with sufficient insurance and similarly, the odds of selecting "relocate" strategy over "reconstruct/repair" is 1.2 times more (OR = 1.167) for families without sufficient insurance to those with sufficient insurance. Clearly, households are more likely to decide in favor of reconstruction if they have sufficient insurance available to them (see Table 9.2). McFadden's pseudo-R squared statistic is 0.253 indicating an acceptable fit for the main effects model.

We can interpret the main effects in both the vignette and the face-to-face surveys because the interaction effects in both these situations turn out to be statistically insignificant. Furthermore, the Akaike information criterion (AIC) selects the main effects model when compared with intercept-only and interaction models, thereby providing further credibility to the results obtained in Tables 9.1 and 9.2. Results obtained from the interaction models are included in the Appendix.

9.7 LESSONS LEARNED AND REMAINING GAPS IN KNOWLEDGE

The results of this research provide invaluable insights on behavioral patterns of people in the aftermath of disasters. The availability of sufficient insurance, two-parent households, and place attachment were statistically significant predictors influencing household decisions to reconstruct, wait, or to relocate. However, the key finding of this research is that the households' own decision-making process is very different from their impersonal analyses of hypothetical scenarios. The vignette study was designed to understand the households' decision-making process when they were put in a simulated scenario. We believed that the impersonal nature of the scenario will induce a more logical, non-emotional analysis of the situation by the respondents. The analysis of their responses to hypothetical situations indicated that the availability of sufficient insurance was the key factor, which empirically confirms the predominance of financial considerations guiding housing decisions. However, in responding to questions about personal recovery decisions, place attachment turned out to be the principle factor guiding households; households with 10 or more years of residence were overwhelmingly more likely to reconstruct/repair their current dwelling compared to households residing there for less than 1 year. We did not find any significant impact of insurance availability in personal recovery decisions of the households.

Although our findings from the vignette survey and the main survey may seem contradictory, the main theme that emerges is that personal recovery decisions for households have a strong emotional component, which needs to be accounted for when devising recovery strategies for post-disaster housing and community recovery. An impersonal recovery strategy pivoted only on the financial structure of the community may not be a very effective one.

Due to our sampling constraints, the results are applicable to the Staten Island area. Care should be taken in generalizing these results to other geographic areas that experience different types of disasters. To increase external validity and generalizability of studies investigating the patterns of recovery decisions of households, one should survey different geographic areas suffering from similar types of disasters and examine the commonalities of the households' decision-making processes. While the results of this research cannot be readily extended to similar events and scenarios, understanding how individuals behave in different roles both when faced with making personal decisions and as an outsider making decisions for others can offer useful insight to disaster recovery professionals and scholars.

ACKNOWLEDGMENT

This research was supported by National Science Foundation (NSF) RAPID award number 1313946. The data presented, the statements made, and the views expressed are solely the responsibility of the authors.

APPENDIX 9A

Vignette Survey

To assess the interpretability of the main effects model, we proceeded to fit the interaction model to check for the significance of interactions among covariates (Table 9A.1). To avoid the complexity of interpretation, we consider only two-way interactions. None of the interactions were significant at the 5% level. Minimum p-value for the regression coefficient associated with an interaction term was 0.053 for wait and relocate categories (see Table 9A.1). The absence of significant interactions among the covariates renders the interaction model redundant in our analysis. AIC values of 263.88 for the intercept-only model, 259.56 for the main effect model, and 263.88 for the two-way interaction model confirm the results.

Face-to-Face Survey

We fit a two-way interaction model to the data obtained from the face-to-face surveys to assess the significance of all two-way interactions. The p-values associated with the regression parameters (Table 9A.2) suggest none of the two-way interactions are significant. The minimum p-value for the regression coefficient associated with an interaction terms was 0.419 for the wait category and 0.190 for the relocate category (see Table 9A.2). To assess whether this interaction model is better than the

TABLE 9A.1
Parameter Estimates for Interaction Models (Reference Category: "Reconstruct/Repair")

Category		B	Sig.	Category		B	Sig.
Wait	Intercept	0.466	0.566	Relocate	Intercept	0.486	0.514
	SM	−2.420	0.077		NR	0.086	0.917
	TY	0.447	0.670		TY	0.631	0.476
	EI	−1.831	*0.099*		SM	−0.661	0.427
	NR	−2.296	*0.081*		EI	−1.113	0.208
	TY*EI	0.390	0.762		TY*EI	−0.519	0.551
	TY*SM	−1.95	0.199		TY*SM	−1.686	0.053
	SM*EI	1.208	0.381		SM*EI	−0.121	0.888
	EI*NR	−0.771	0.561		EI*NR	−0.283	0.741
	SM*NR	3.062	*0.053*		SM*NR	0.657	0.445
	TY*NR	2.272	0.113		TY*NR	0.784	0.360

Note: Italics indicates marginal significance.

TABLE 9A.2
Parameter Estimates for Interaction Models (Reference Category: "Reconstruct/Repair")

Category		B	Sig.	Category		B	Sig.
Wait	Intercept	−24.783	0.506	Relocate	Intercept	−28.376	0.509
	SM	−0.882	0.5		NR	0.319	0.5
	TY	−1.6299	0.5		TY	28.567	0.491
	EI	10.245	0.497		SM	12.267	0.493
	NR	23.684	0.494		EI	13.334	0.494
	TY*EI	2.0931	0.499		TY*EI	−12.65	0.507
	TY*SM	13.679	0.491		TY*SM	0.1962	0.499
	SM*EI	0.42048	0.419		SM*EI	1.1838	0.190
	EI*NR	−11.671	0.508		EI*NR	−0.6032	0.704
	SM*NR	−24.783	0.506		SM*NR	−0.8972	0.750
	TY*NR	−0.882	0.5		TY*NR	−13.286	0.506

main effect model, we compute the AIC for three candidate models. AIC values of 233 for the intercept only model, 191.28 for the main effect model, and 204.98 for the two-way interaction model confirm the results. The main effect model, once again, is the best among the competing models. Thus, we assess the significance of each predictor and interpret the main effects from the foregoing main effect model only. The interaction model once again turns out to be unviable for this dataset.

REFERENCES

Aldrich, D. P. 2010. Fixing recovery: social capital in post-crisis resilience. *Journal of Homeland Security* 6: 1–10.

Aldrich, D. P. 2011. The power of people: Social capital's role in recovery from the 1995 Kobe earthquake. *Natural Hazards* 56(3): 595–611.

Aldrich, D. P. 2012. *Building Resilience: Social Capital in Post-Disaster Recovery.* Chicago, Illinois: University of Chicago Press.

Alesch, D. J., and J. N. Holly. 1998. Small business failure, survival and recovery: Lessons from the January 1994 Northridge earthquake. *NEHRP Conference and Workshop on Research on the Northridge, California Earthquake of January,* Los Angeles. Vol. 17.

Alfred, D. 2007. *Displaced Louisianans: Where Did They Go and Are They Coming Back.* New Orleans, Louisiana: Louisiana Family Recovery Corps.

Alves, W. M., and P. H. Rossi. 1978. Who should get what? Fairness judgments of the distribution of earnings. *American Journal of Sociology* 84(3): 541–64.

Anton, C. E., and C. Lawrence. 2014. Home is where the heart is: The effect of place of residence on place attachment and community participation. *Environmental Psychology* 40: 451–61.

Atzmüller, C., and P. M. Steiner. 2015. Experimental vignette studies in survey research. *Methodology: Research Methods for the Behavioral and Social Sciences* 6(3): 128–38.

Barrera, D., and V. Buskens. 2007. Imitation and learning under uncertainty: A vignette experiment. *International Sociology* 22(3): 367–96.

Barton, A. H. 1969. *Communities in Disaster: A Sociological Analysis of Collective Stress Situations.* Garden City, New York: Doubleday.

Bates, F. L. 1982. *Recovery, Change and Development: A Longitudinal Study of the 1976 Guatemalan Earthquake.* Atlanta, Georgia: University of Georgia.

Bates, F. L., C. W. Fogleman, V. J. Parenton, and R. H. Pittman. 1963. *The Social and Psychological Consequences of a Natural Disaster: A Longitudinal Study of Hurricane Audrey.* Washington, DC: Disaster Research Group, Division of Anthropology and Psychology.

Berg, S. 1988. Snowball sampling. In *Encyclopedia of Statistical Sciences*, S. Kotz and N. L. Johnson (eds), 8th edn, New York: Wiley, 528–32.

Binder, S. B., C. K. Baker, and J. P. Barile. 2015. Rebuild or relocate? Resilience and post-disaster decision-making after Hurricane Sandy. *American Journal of Community Psychology* 56(1–2): 180–96.

Bolin, R. C. 1976. Family recovery from natural disaster: A preliminary model. *Mass Emergencies* 1(4): 267–77.

Bolin, R. C. 1982. *Long-Term Family Recovery from Disaster.* Boulder, Colorado: University of Colorado.

Bolin, R. C. 1994. *Household and Community Recovery after Earthquakes.* Boulder, Colorado: University of Colorado, Institute of Behavioral Science.

Bolin, R. C., and P. A. Bolton. 1983. Recovery in Nicaragua and the USA. *International Journal of Mass Emergencies and Disasters* 1(1): 125–44.

Bolin, R. C., and US Central United States Earthquake Consortium (CUSEC). 1993. Post-earthquake shelter and housing: Research findings and policy implications. In *Monograph 5: Socioeconomic Impacts*, Washington, DC: US CUSEC, 107–31.

Bournay, E., and UNEP/GRID-Arendal. 2007. Trends in natural disasters. *Grid Arendal.* http://www.grida.no/graphicslib/detail/trends-in-natural-disasters_a899 (accessed March 2, 2016).

Brown, B., D. D. Perkins, and G. Brown. 2003. Place attachment in a revitalizing neighborhood: Individual and block levels of analysis. *Journal of Environmental Psychology* 23(3): 259–71.

Chamlee-Wright, E., and V. H. Storr. 2009. There's no place like New Orleans: Sense of place and community recovery in the Ninth Ward after Hurricane Katrina. *Journal of Urban Affairs* 31(5): 615–34.

Chang, S. E. 2001. Structural change in urban economies: Recovery and long-term impacts in the 1995 Kobe earthquake. *Journal of Economics and Business Administration* 183(1): 47–66.

Cohen, D., and J. Strayer. 1996. Empathy in conduct-disordered and comparison youth. *Developmental Psychology* 32(6): 988.

Cohen, J. 1992. Methods in psychology: A power primer. *Psychological Bulletin* 112(1): 155–59.

Comerio, M. C. 2014. Disaster recovery and community renewal: Housing approaches. *Cityscape: A Journal of Policy Development and Research* 16(2): 51–64.

Cong, Z., and M. Silverstein. 2012. A vignette study on elders' gendered filial expectations in rural China: Children's migration, child care responsibilities, and actual support provided. *Journal of Marriage and Family* 74(3): 510–25.

Cope, M. R., T. Slack, T. C. Blanchard, and M. R. Lee. 2013. Does time heal all wounds? Community attachment, natural resource employment, and health impacts in the wake of the BP Deepwater Horizon disaster. *Social Science Research* 42(3): 872–81.

Dewan, S., M. Connelly, and A. Lehren. 2006. Evacuees' lives still upended seven months after hurricane. *New York Times*. http://www.nytimes.com/2006/03/22/national/nationalspecial/22katrina.html?fta=y&_r=0 (accessed March 22, 2006).

Elliott, J. R., and J. Pais. 2006. Race, class, and Hurricane Katrina: Social differences in human responses to disaster. *Social Science Research* 35(2): 295–321.

Finch, J. 1987. The vignette technique in survey research. *Sociology* 21(1): 105–14.

Frey, W. H. 2005. City can lure back its reluctant migrants. *The Times-Picayune*. http://www.brookings.edu/research/opinions/2005/11/30demographics-frey (accessed March 2, 2016).

Ganong, L., and M. Coleman. 2006. Multiple segment factorial vignette designs. *Journal of Marriage and Family* 68(2): 455–68.

Goodman, L. A. 1961. Snowball sampling. *The Annals of Mathematical Statistics* 32(1): 148–70.

Henry, J. 2013. Return or relocate? An inductive analysis of decision-making in a disaster. *Disasters* 37(2): 293–316.

Hidalgo, M. C., and B. Hernandez. 2001. Place attachment: Conceptual and empirical questions. *Journal of Environmental Psychology* 21(3): 273–81.

Hunter, C., and K. McClelland. 1991. Honoring accounts for sexual harassment: A factorial survey analysis. *Sex Roles* 24(11–12): 725–52.

Jack, G. 2010. Place matters: The significance of place attachments for children's well-being. *British Journal of Social Work* 40(3): 755–71.

Jamali, M. and A. Nejat. 2016. Place attachment and disasters: Knowns and unknowns. *Journal of Emergency Management* (forthcoming).

Jasso, G., and M. Webster. 1999. Assessing the gender gap in just earnings and its underlying mechanisms. *Social Psychology Quarterly* 62(4): 367–80.

Kick, E. L., J. C. Fraser, G. M. Fulkerson, L. A. McKinney, and D. H. De Vries. 2011. Repetitive flood victims and acceptance of FEMA mitigation offers: An analysis with community-system policy implications. *Disasters* 35(3): 510–39.

Kutak, R. I. 1938. The sociology of crises: The Louisville flood of 1937. *Social Forces* 17(1): 66–72.

Lewicka, M. 2010. What makes neighborhood different from home and city? Effects of place scale on place attachment. *Journal of Environmental Psychology* 30(1): 35–51.

Lincoln, Y. S., and E. G. Guba. 1985. *Naturalistic Inquiry*. Newbury Park, California: Sage Publications, Inc.

Magalhães, E., and M. M. Calheiros. 2015. Psychometric properties of the Portuguese version of place attachment scale for youth in residential care. *Psicothema* 27(1): 65–73.

Mazumdar, S., and S. Mazumdar. 2004. Religion and place attachment: A study of sacred places. *Journal of Environmental Psychology* 24(3): 385–97.

McCarthy, K. F., D. J. Peterson, N. Sastry, and M. Pollard. 2006. *The Repopulation of New Orleans after Hurricane Katrina*. Santa Monica, California: RAND Corporation. http://www.rand.org/pubs/technical_reports/TR369.html (accessed March 2, 2016).

McCullagh, P. 1980. Regression models for ordinal data. *Journal of the Royal Statistical Society, Series B (Methodological)* 42(2): 109–42. http://www.stat.uchicago.edu/~pmcc/pubs/paper2.pdf (accessed March 2, 2016).

Moore, H. E. 1958. *Tornadoes Over Texas: A Study of Waco and San Angelo in Disaster*. Austin, Texas: University of Texas Press.

Morin, R., and L. Rein. 2005. Some of the uprooted won't go home again. *Washington Post*, September 16. http://www.washingtonpost.com/wp-dyn/content/article/2005/09/15/AR2005091502010.html (accessed March 2, 2016).

Nakagawa, Y., and R. Shaw. 2004. Social capital: A missing link to disaster recovery. *International Journal of Mass Emergencies and Disasters* 22(1): 5–34.

Nejat, A. and S. Ghosh. 2016. LASSO model of postdisaster housing recovery: Case study of Hurricane Sandy. *Natural Hazards Review* 17(3): 04016007.

New York City, Office of the Mayor. 2013. *A Stronger, More Resilient New York*. New York: Office of the Mayor. http://www.nyc.gov/html/sirr/html/report/report.shtml (accessed March 2, 2016).

New York City, Office of the Mayor. 2015. *De Blasio Administration Releases Progress Report on Sandy Recovery and Resiliency*. New York: Office of the Mayor. http://www1.nyc.gov/office-of-the-mayor/news/749-15/de-blasio-administration-releases-progress-report-sandy-recovery-resiliency (accessed March 2, 2016).

Oh, J. 2004. Race/ethnicity, homeownership, and neighborhood attachment. *Race and Society* 7(2): 63–77.

Ouslander, J. G., A. J. Tymchuk, and M. D. Krynski. 1993. Decisions about enteral tube feeding among the elderly. *Journal of the American Geriatrics Society* 41(1): 70–7.

Peacock, W. G., N. Dash, and Y. Zhang. 2007. Sheltering and housing recovery following disaster. In *Handbook of Disaster Research*, H. Kaplan (ed.), New York: Springer, 258–74.

Peacock, W. G., C. D. Killian, and F. L. Bates. 1987. The effects of disaster damage and housing aid on household recovery following the 1976 Guatemalan earthquake. *International Journal of Mass Emergencies and Disasters* 5(1): 63–88.

Peacock, W. G., S. Van Zandt, Y. Zhang, and W. E. Highfield. 2014. Inequities in long-term housing recovery after disasters. *Journal of the American Planning Association* 80(4): 356–71.

Ritchie, L. A., and D. A. Gill. 2007. Social capital theory as an integrating theoretical framework in technological disaster research. *Sociological Spectrum* 27(1): 103–29.

Rollero, C., and N. D. Piccoli. 2010. Does place attachment affect social well-being? *Revue Européenne de Psychologie Appliquée/European Review of Applied Psychology* 60(4): 233–38.

Rossi, A. S., and P. H. Rossi. 1990. *Of Human Bonding: Parent-Child Relations across the Life Course*. New York: Gruyter, Walter de, & Co.

Rust, E. B., and K. Killinger. 2006. *The Financial Services Roundtable Blue Ribbon Commission on Mega-Catastrophes: A Call to Action*. Washington, DC: Financial Services Roundtable. http://fsroundtable.org/category/risk-management/ (accessed December 5, 2010).

Sanders, S., S. L. Bowie, and Y. D. Bowie. 2004. Chapter 2 lessons learned on forced relocation of older adults: The impact of hurricane Andrew on health, mental health, and social support of public housing residents. *Journal of Gerontological Social Work* 40(4): 23–35.

Shabak, M., N. Norouzi, A. M. Abdullah, and T. H. Khan. 2015. Children's sense of attachment to the residential common open space. *Procedia—Social and Behavioral Sciences* 201: 39–48, August 22.

Shriver, T. E., and D. K. Kennedy. 2005. Contested environmental hazards and community conflict over relocation. *Rural Sociology* 70(4): 491–513.

Sniderman, P. M., and D. B. Grob. 1996. Innovations in experimental design in attitude surveys. *Annual review of Sociology* 22: 377–99.

Stoddard, E. R. 1961. *Catastrophe and Crisis in a Flooded Border Community: An Analytical Approach to Disaster Emergence.* PhD dissertation, Michigan State University, East Lansing, Michigan.

Thurman, Q. C., J. A. Lam, and P. H. Rossi. 1988. Sorting out the cuckoo's nest: A factorial survey approach to the study of popular conceptions of mental illness. *The Sociological Quarterly* 29(4): 565–88.

Tierney, K. J., and J. M. Dahlhamer. 1997. *Business Disruption, Preparedness and Recovery: Lessons from the Northridge Earthquake.* Newark, Delaware: University of Delaware, Disaster Research Center. http://udspace.udel.edu/handle/19716/657#files-area (accessed March 2, 2016).

Turcotte, M. 2005. Social engagement and civic participation: Are rural and small town populations really at an advantage? *Rural and Small Town Canada Bulletin* 6(4): 1–24. http://www.statcan.gc.ca/pub/21-006-x/21-006-x2005004-eng.pdf (accessed March 2, 2016).

US Census. 2012. *Staten Island's General Demographics.* http://quickfacts.census.gov/qfd/states/36/36085.html (accessed March 2, 2016).

US Department of Housing and Urban Development (HUD). 2011. *Housing Recovery on the Gulf Coast—Summary Report.* Washington, DC: US HUD, Office of Policy Development and Research. https://www.huduser.gov/portal/publications/HUDHsRecGulfCoastPhase2summary_1024_v2.pdf (accessed March 2, 2016).

Wallander, L. 2009. 25 years of factorial surveys in sociology: A review. *Social Science Research* 38(3): 505–20.

Wilks, T. 2004. The use of vignettes in qualitative research into social work values. *Qualitative Social Work* 3(1): 78–87.

Williams, D. R., and J. J. Vaske. 2003. The measurement of place attachment: Validity and generalizability of a psychometric approach. *Forest Science* 49(6): 830–40.

Yandong, Zhao. 2007. Social capital and post-disaster recovery: A sociological study of natural disaster [J]. *Sociological Studies* 5: 164–187.

10 Emergency Sheltering and Temporary Housing Issues

Assessing the Disaster Experiences and Preparedness Actions of People with Disabilities to Inform Inclusive Emergency Planning in the United States

Brian J. Gerber

CONTENTS

10.1 INTRODUCTION

Disasters are typically associated with large-scale dislocations of community residents as damage to public and residential infrastructure forces evacuations (planned or spontaneous). If critical infrastructure is damaged significantly and disaster-related evacuations do occur, then emergency sheltering, temporary housing, and permanent housing repair and replacement become central challenges for communities.

The logistics of establishing effective sheltering and temporary housing practices are managerially and administratively complex (Brodie et al. 2006; Nigg et al. 2006) and competing interests and other political considerations in rebuilding communities frequently make long-term recovery processes difficult and conflictual (Olshansky and Johnson 2010; Smith 2012).

Scholarship examining sheltering and housing as an element of disaster management often takes as a starting point a rubric on functional distinctions offered by Quarantelli (1982). The rubric outlines four basic forms of sheltering and housing in a disaster setting: emergency sheltering (seeking immediate protection for a very short period, such as less than a day), temporary sheltering (a stay at a private facility or a congregate public shelter site for several days or so), temporary housing (establishing normal housing routines at a fixed location until permanent housing is available), and permanent housing (returning to a repaired home or to a newly constructed home). These are not hard and fast distinctions exactly. For example, emergency and temporary sheltering dynamics can change because the conditions of a severe weather event might change rapidly (Bolin 1994; Tierney et al. 2001). But regardless of how precisely one might seek to define the particular categories, it is reasonable to identify short-term needs and processes for emergency sheltering, medium-term needs and processes for temporary housing, and longer-term needs and processes associated with permanent housing (see United States Federal Emergency Management Agency [US FEMA] 2009).

As Peacock et al. (2007) point out, a great deal of prior research makes clear that reestablishing housing after disaster is an essential element of the recovery process across its physical, economic, and psychological dimensions. Recognizing the importance of the relationship of effective sheltering and housing to safety and recovery is also germane to the critical concept of community resilience. There are various ways resilience can be defined (Burby et al. 2000; Mileti 1999), but whatever the disciplinary nuance, the concept at its core refers generally to some system's ability to absorb a disturbance and return to its prior condition (Holling 1973). However, Cutter et al. (2008, p. 599) note that resilience involves not only inherent characteristics permitting communities to absorb and cope with a disaster, but also "post-event adaptive processes that facilitate the ability of the social system to re-organize, change, and learn in response to a threat."

In that context, it is useful to note that in 2011, the US FEMA released a strategy document elaborating the principles of a "whole community" approach to emergency management that stress the particular needs of all members of a community be recognized in order to promote greater resilience. Governmental and nongovernmental leaders alike need to "understand how to work with the diversity of groups and organizations and the policies and practices that emerge from them in an effort to improve the ability of local residents to prevent, protect against, mitigate, respond to, and recover from any type of threat or hazard effectively" (US FEMA 2011, p. 3).

One key area where empirical evidence supporting the development of community resilience capacity and serving a truly whole community approach is somewhat limited is the study of those with disabilities or other access and functional needs. Persons can be characterized as part of a vulnerable population in the sense that they are among a subgroup of the general population that is relatively more likely to suffer harm in the face of hazards (see Bricout and Baker 2010; Peek and Stough 2010). In 2009, a report from the National Council on Disability (NCD) argued that there is a "clear lack of research validating best practices" along with a more general lack of evidenced-based effort in the areas of preparedness, response, and recovery as related to people with disabilities (NCD 2009, p. 14). While there are research and evaluation exceptions to this general assertion (see e.g., Byzek and Gilmer 2001; Dosa et al. 2007; Fischer et al. 1995; Juillet 1993; White et al. 2007), broad and generalizable studies of these issues are limited.

This limitation of extensively available evidence matters in three important ways to the subject of better integrating vulnerable populations in improved sheltering and disaster housing practices. As scholars have noted (Cutter et al. 2008; Gall et al. 2015), governance around hazards has generally not reduced risk or social vulnerability to natural hazards; indeed, risk levels are generally greater overall today compared to a half century ago. FEMA's premise of a more effective whole community approach is designed to ameliorate such shortcomings but it is dependent on quality information and comprehensive assessments of all elements of community needs—precisely what is required in the subject area of vulnerable populations. Second, it was commonplace practice in emergency response efforts to advise shelter-in-place and "wait-for-help" for people with disabilities during emergency or disaster situations. However, the two terrorist attacks on the World Trade Center in 1993 and 2001, along with the Hurricane Katrina disaster underscored the ineffectiveness of such an approach precisely because it tended to increase, rather than decrease, actual vulnerability during certain types of incidents (Juillet 1993; National Organization on Disability 2005, 2009; White et al. 2007). Likewise, a disaster evacuation safety model premised on the notion of well-resourced individuals has proved inadequate. Litman (2006) points out that City of New Orleans emergency guidance for residents with disabilities in place at the time of Katrina stated that if they needed help to leave the city during an impending hurricane, they should simply get a car ride from a neighbor, friend, or relative. Improving on these deficient practices in part requires better evidence defining the nature and scope of assistance needs and actual behavior by individuals with disabilities and their households.

Third, as a practical matter, emergency sheltering and temporary housing presents certain unique considerations for people with disabilities. Appropriate accommodation in public emergency shelters has been a common problem. Assessment of emergency sheltering issues has called attention to the need for making shelters universally accessible for persons with disabilities (Cameron 2008; Kailes 2002). Likewise, the need for emergency shelter management processes should include needed service accessibility such as permitting service animals at the site and ensuring family member cohesion. Similarly, common siting practices for temporary housing have been problematic. Alesch et al. (2009) note that temporary housing plans (e.g., a temporary trailer park of mobile homes provided by FEMA) are often located in remote or relatively inaccessible areas outside of or apart from community, commercial, and residential development areas—exacerbating accessibility and mobility challenges for those with disabilities.

Together, these considerations all point to the need for a better understanding of vulnerable populations in general, including people with disabilities as a particular focus, with respect to disaster sheltering and housing. In the remainder of this chapter, I offer a brief discussion of how the United States federal government has responded, over the past decade or so, to the intersecting issues of disaster preparedness, disaster-related housing issues, and a greater recognition of the potential additional response assistance needs of vulnerable populations. I present evidence from a study of people with disabilities in the United States, with several simple relationships illustrating how household preparedness and disaster evacuation experience are relevant to emergency sheltering and temporary housing considerations. The chapter closes with a discussion of current challenges in this area.

10.2 FEDERAL ACTIONS TOWARD IMPROVING INCLUSIVE EMERGENCY PREPAREDNESS

Following the 9/11 terror attacks, fundamental changes were made to the basic policy and administrative architecture for dealing with emergencies and disasters in the United States. Not only was a Federal Department of Homeland Security created, substantive guidance on incident management, on preparedness, and on development of standards for local capabilities were developed—mostly through a series of presidential decision directives. Similarly, following the Hurricane Katrina disaster, additional changes pertained to the relationship of federal agency resources to state requests for disaster assistance, certain federal guidelines on disaster recovery assistance, and a greater recognition for attention to unique emergency assistance needs for different subgroups of the overall general population. Such changes were codified by the Post-Katrina Emergency Management Reform Act (PKEMRA) of 2006 (Public Law 109–295); the creation of the Office of Disability Integration and Coordination within FEMA, several years later (in 2010) can also be seen as part of this broader policy adjustment effort.

In this context of significant policy and practice changes after 9/11 and Katrina, there are three federal strategy and guidance documents especially relevant to emergency sheltering and temporary housing in disaster situations. These documents underscore the federal effort toward developing a more integrated and inclusive community disaster preparedness and more effective emergency management practices generally. A key part of those efforts also includes developing more consistent disaster housing and shelter access practices across the United States. These efforts were the direct consequence of identifying certain system deficiencies and service gaps after two national catastrophes in 2001 and 2005, and yielded several major strategy and guidance statements.

In 2009, FEMA published its National Disaster Housing Strategy (NDHS) document, which identifies and assesses current disaster sheltering and housing practices (US FEMA 2009). It also outlines a focused plan on how to adapt the current disaster housing system to meet future needs. The NDHS is explicit that the Hurricane Katrina disaster prompted federal efforts to more effectively address gaps and challenges associated with disaster sheltering, interim housing, and permanent housing. The document enunciates a set of national goals pertaining to making practices more effective, improving capabilities and capacities in this domain, improving recovery through improved integration of housing concerns, and better meeting the needs of disaster victims and communities.

A year later, FEMA produced a document on functional needs support services (FNSS) for general population emergency shelters (US FEMA 2010). Historically, the more general and often ambiguous term, "special needs" has been used to identify especially vulnerable subgroups of the population. Changing terminology to functional needs offers the benefit of greater specificity with which to guide actions. This is clear when one sees the language of the FNSS document: "Children and adults requiring FNSS may have physical, sensory, mental health, and cognitive and/or intellectual disabilities affecting their ability to function independently without assistance. Others that may benefit from FNSS include women in late stages of pregnancy, elders, and people needing bariatric equipment" (US FEMA 2010, p. 8).

Robinson et al. (2013) point out that while the FNSS planning document might appear as applicable to only emergency shelters, instead its greater utility might lie in the basic model it creates for more effective integration practices when it comes to people with disabilities and emergency preparedness and response. Those authors note that the FNSS is a "bellwether" model for inclusive practices: "there is nothing inherent to a 'functional needs' approach to shelter management that limits its application to matters of shelter management or, even, emergency management as a whole. Rather, social service administration from a variety of domains may see in the FNSS an example of what an inclusiveness strategy may look like" (2013, p. 318).

In this respect, FEMA has also produced a third key document stating principles on the need for true community integration from a "whole community" perspective (US FEMA 2011). Whole community is defined as "a means by which residents, emergency management practitioners, organizational and community leaders, and government officials can collectively understand and assess the needs of their respective communities and determine the best ways to organize and strengthen their assets, capacities, and interests" (US FEMA 2011, p. 3). This "philosophical" approach enunciated by FEMA is entirely geared toward reducing community risk and enhancing resilience through greater inclusion and integration of community members.

As all three strategy and guidance documents note in some form, it is essential to understand community characteristics in sufficient detail to inform planning and operational management. This is a complex domain for action and federal actors have moved to make improvements in disaster-related housing practices and greater inclusiveness. Such efforts, if they are to be successful, require empirical evidence to help inform understanding of the underlying character for management and assistance challenges associated with emergency or temporary disaster housing—and continual practice improvements over time.

To connect the planning principles of greater inclusiveness and engagement of whole communities contained in these strategic documents, here we focus on two very fundamental empirical questions which can serve to inform planning and related efforts to improve performance in this area. First, in what manner does the presence of disability in a household affect the capacity to deal with emergency or disaster dislocations? Second, what do past disaster experiences indicate for resource and management needs for emergency sheltering or temporary housing for future disaster incidents? Addressing these two questions provides information relevant to understanding what management needs might be more or less likely to occur in emergency sheltering and temporary housing for disaster incidents.

10.3 ASSESSING DISASTER SHELTERING AND HOUSING ISSUES RELATED TO PEOPLE WITH DISABILITIES

10.3.1 Data and Analysis

To address these two basic questions, I use individual-level data from a project funded by United States Department of Education, National Institute for Disability and Rehabilitation Research (Award # H133A070005; Gerber, Principal Investigator, Zakour and Norwood, Co-Principal Investigators). A sample of 1162 completed surveys from older persons and households of persons with disabilities were collected in December, 2008. About half of the sample data were collected through mail or telephone survey of households of people with disabilities who reside in private residences, but were identified through Centers for Independent Living (CIL), the Arc, and various deaf and hard of hearing organizations. Likewise, households where individuals receive services through 1915 (c) Home- and Community-Based Services (HCBS) Medicaid waivers were also contacted to participate via state agency offices. For the remainder of the sample, the project researchers also conducted a random digit dial telephone survey of the aging public—those 55 years old and over; screening techniques were used to identify individuals' age. Those survey respondents were asked several questions to identify disability status.

Sampling occurred across several strata. First, a purposive selection of counties was made in seven states where large-scale disaster incidents—along with major levels of resident evacuations—had occurred within 3 years of the data collection process. Those locations were matched with other demographically and geographically similar counties with at least some degree of vulnerability to future events that could precipitate a disaster evacuation, but where one had not occurred in the recent past (at least 10 years, approximately). Study locations included San Bernardino and San Diego Counties in California (with wildfire being the hazard of interest), St. Louis, St. Charles, and Lincoln Counties in Missouri and Logan County and several other parts of southern West Virginia (with flooding being the hazard of interest), the area in or near Apex, North Carolina (a location with a major industrial disaster), Collier and Jackson Counties in Florida, New Orleans and Terrebonne Parishes in Louisiana, and Jefferson and Tarrant Counties in Texas (each of which had hurricanes and storm-related flooding as the hazard of interest).

Thus, the project considered multiple hazards, different types of evacuation incidents, different levels of hazards vulnerability at a county level, and different residential situations (totally independent living, HCBS waiver status, CILs clients, etc.). Perhaps, even more important, the sample also reflects respondents who vary significantly across level of disability as measured by effects on activities of daily living (ADL). In this way, the research design differs from the more common single shot case study approach of examining issues faced by people with disabilities after a major disaster. The random sampling of individual respondents, combined with intentional selection variation across hazard type, level of hazard vulnerability, differences in evacuation scale or incidence, and general geographic variation make those data presented here uniquely strong in terms of external validity considerations.

10.3.2 Preparedness and Coping Capacity for Evacuations

Our first assessment question is to consider the capacity of a household to deal with a disaster-related dislocation. This generally means temporary sheltering if parts of a community are forced to evacuate, but if the disaster incident produces enough damage, temporary sheltering can also become a matter of temporary housing. Tables 10.1 through 10.3 provide three dimensions of household capacity to cope with dislocation through evacuation. Respondents were asked a battery of questions about preparedness for disaster evacuation in terms of plans for sheltering or related housing options, about planning for maintaining supplies of medicines and related personal health protective actions, and knowledge of public shelters in their area.

TABLE 10.1
Evacuation Capacity by Presence of Disability in Household

Evacuation Capacity	Presence of Disability in Household		
Assessment	No Disability Present	Disability Present	Total
Not prepared at all	3.2 (11)	18.8 (149)	14.1 (160)
Not very well prepared	5.8 (20)	13.0 (103)	10.8 (123)
Somewhat prepared	18.4 (64)	31.4 (248)	27.4 (312)
Well prepared	72.6 (252)	36.8 (291)	47.7 (543)
Total	100.0% (347)	100.0% (791)	100.0% (1138)

Note: Pearson Chi-Sq = 133.43, d.f. = 3, $p < 0.000$, Phi = 0.342, odds ratio for collapsed 2 × 2—disability group: 0.2098.

TABLE 10.2
Evacuation Capacity by Limitation in ADL

Evacuation Capacity	Limitation in Activities per ADL				
Assessment	No Disability	Minimal	Moderate	Significant	Total
Not prepared at all	3.2 (11)	12.2 (28)	17.9 (40)	23.7 (69)	13.6 (148)
Not very well prepared	5.8 (20)	11.4 (26)	14.7 (33)	13.7 (40)	10.9 (119)
Somewhat prepared	18.4 (64)	30.6 (70)	31.3 (70)	32.3 (94)	27.3 (298)
Well prepared	72.6 (252)	45.9 (105)	36.2 (81)	30.2 (88)	48.2 (526)
Total	100.0% (347)	100.0% (229)	100.0% (224)	100.0% (291)	100.0% (1091)

Note: Pearson Chi-Sq = 133.43, d.f. = 3, $p < 0.000$, Phi = 0.342.

TABLE 10.3
Evacuation Capacity by Social Support

Evacuation Capacity Assessment	Family/Friends Support during Crises: Strongly Agree	Agree	Disagree	Strongly Disagree	Total
Not prepared at all	6.4 (33)	14.0 (65)	33.3 (24)	63.6 (28)	13.7 (150)
Not very well prepared	9.4 (48)	10.8 (50)	15.3 (11)	11.4 (5)	10.4 (114)
Somewhat prepared	25.8 (132)	30.2 (140)	31.9 (23)	9.1 (4)	27.4 (299)
Well prepared	58.4 (299)	45.0 (209)	19.4 (14)	15.9 (7)	48.4 (529)
Total	100.0%	100.0%	100.0%	100.0%	100.0%
	(512)	(464)	(72)	(44)	(1092)

Note: Pearson Chi-Sq = 163.40, d.f. = 9, $p < 0.000$, Phi = 0.387.

Because of space constraints, that information is not presented here in table form. The reader should recall that about half the sample was a random selection of individuals approaching an age level where physical disabilities begin to present themselves more frequently in the general population (55 and older). A little more than half of that subset of respondents did not indicate any disability at all—so they serve as a comparison group for households where a person with at least one disability is present. Speaking in general terms, those households with disabilities have less clear plans for where they would go for shelter or short-term housing and slightly less familiarity with locations of existing public emergency shelters in their area. However, at the same time, they report slightly greater readiness in terms of stockpiling supplies of medicine in the event of an emergency disruption.

With the general characteristics of the sample in mind, the tables below present very simple contingency table distributions for the results when respondents were asked to provide a self-assessment of their capacity to leave their home because of a disaster evacuation and deal with the associated challenges of emergency or temporary sheltering or housing. Specifically, respondents were asked the following: "In terms of personal resources, how prepared are you to take care of yourself if you had to leave your home for several days because of a disaster? Are you…not at all prepared, you don't have the resources to stay away from home; not very well prepared, you couldn't make it more than a day or two away from home; somewhat prepared, you could make it a few days away from home, but not much longer; or well prepared, you could make it for a week or more away from home without major problems?" Figure 10.1 shows the overall frequency distribution for all respondents in the sample. This suggests a fairly high level of capacity for longer-term sheltering or temporary housing (see Figure 10.1). However, the situation is a bit more complex when other considerations are assessed.

Table 10.1 draws a comparison between those respondents with or without a disability present in the household. Those without a disability show about double the proportion in reporting the highest level of capacity to cope with dislocation (see

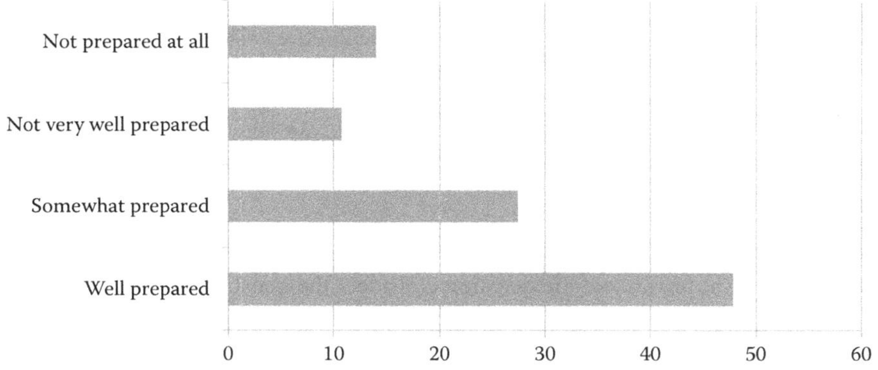

FIGURE 10.1 Prepared to leave home in case of disaster: all respondents.

Table 10.1). This distribution is statistically significant ($p < 0.000$) and collapsing categories into a 2 by 2 comparison (not well and not at all compared to somewhat and well prepared), the odds ratio reported at the bottom of the table shows that those with disabilities are far less likely to be somewhat or well prepared: 4.77 times less likely, in fact (1/0.2098). While this is a very simple contingency table analysis, it shows rather clearly that capacity to cope with challenges associated with emergency sheltering (or temporary housing) is adversely affected by the presence of a disability in a household.

Table 10.2 reconsiders this question in terms of distinctions not just between disabilities present or not present, but by the level of impact a disability has in terms of limitations on ADL. Respondents with a disability were asked to rate whether their disability (or disabilities) created limited, moderate, or significant limitations on their ADL. Table 10.2 shows that as ADL limitations increase, this has a significant negative effect on capacity to cope with disaster dislocations (again, statistically significant, $p < 0.000$, with a fairly large effect size, $Phi = 0.342$). While perhaps intuitive, this suggests it is critical that whole community planning for emergencies and disasters should be cognizant of distributions of people with disabilities in their community as it is highly relevant to understanding the potential service assistance needs of community members—both during response and early recovery phases of incident management (see Table 10.2).

Table 10.3 shows the last means of considering household coping capacity for disaster dislocation by offering a third dimension of evacuation coping capacity: level of personal social network support for dealing with disaster dislocation. In this case, the contingency table does not make comparisons based on disability, but instead on overall personal social network support, which is measured by the level of support respondents reported in dealing with a personal crisis, such as an illness or accident (see Table 10.3). Again, in the interest of space, no table is shown—but households with disabilities present report lower levels of efficacious personal networks (about 12% more respondents with disabilities disagreed with the "I have support of family and friends" statement—and that difference was statistically significant, $p < 0.000$).

Table 10.3 shows clearly that as personal networks are stronger, capacity to cope with dislocation is much stronger ($p < 0.000$, with effect size, *Phi* = 0.387). Given those households with disabilities are less likely to report strong personal networks for coping, the evidence again suggest community assistance needs are likely to be greater for emergency sheltering and temporary housing options in direct relation to the proportion of the community who experiences disabilities.

10.3.3 Evacuation Decisions and Experiences

Next, our second broad analytic question considers the question of what evacuation experiences might mean for planning emergency sheltering and temporary housing. As explained above, a little bit more than half the sample was drawn from areas with disasters that occurred fairly recently prior to the data collection process. Respondents were asked to report whether they and their household made the decision to evacuate. Overall, about 70% of those living in disaster areas did in fact decide to evacuate. Table 10.4 presents not simply the comparison in evacuation choice between disability present or not, but it considers how limitations on ADL might factor into that decision. The table is interesting because the distribution (which is statistically significant at a 95% level of confidence) shows that as limitations on ADL increase, the likelihood of evacuating increases. This suggests those households use evacuation as a protective measure. But this behavior should be understood in the context of the preceding tables: those individuals also have lower capacity to cope effectively with such dislocations (see Table 10.4).

Table 10.5 continues the potential significance of that question by presenting the results of a question on how well individuals and households fared when they did evacuate. The table shows that most respondents overall reported that their evacuation experience was either smooth or went okay. However, when one considers the effect of ADL limitations, the reporting of some or major problems increases: 19% of those with significant limitations indicated as much, as compared to 3.4% of those with no disability reported. The table also shows that if you collapse the table into a 2 by 2 comparison (things went "smoothly" and "went okay" vs. "not well" and "had major problems"), people with disabilities are nearly three times as likely to report a negative experience (see Table 10.5).

TABLE 10.4
Evacuation Decision by Limitation in ADL

Choice to Evacuate	Limitation in Activities per ADL: No Disability Reported	Minimal Impact on ADL	Moderate Impact on ADL	Significant Impact on ADL	Total
Yes	62.0 (116)	68.9 (91)	72.6 (98)	76.2 (144)	69.8 (449)
No	38.0 (71)	31.1 (41)	27.4 (37)	23.8 (45)	30.2 (194)
Total	100.0% (187)	100.0% (132)	100.0% (135)	100.0% (189)	100.0% (643)

Note: Pearson Chi-Sq = 8.66, d.f. = 3, $p < 0.034$, Eta = 0.115.

TABLE 10.5
Evacuation Experience by Limitation in ADL

Evacuation Experience	Limitation in Activities per ADL				
	No Disability	Minimal	Moderate	Significant	Total
Smooth	59.5 (69)	46.0 (40)	32.6 (30)	24.8 (34)	40.0 (173)
Okay, had necessities	31.9 (37)	41.4 (36)	47.8 (44)	48.2 (66)	42.4 (183)
Not very well	5.2 (6)	4.6 (4)	4.3 (4)	8.0 (11)	5.8 (25)
Major problems	3.4 (4)	8.0 (7)	15.2 (14)	19.0 (26)	11.8 (51)
Total	100.0% (116)	100.0% (87)	100.0% (92)	100.0% (137)	100.0% (432)

Note: Pearson Chi-Sq = 42.26, d.f. = 9, $p < 0.000$, Eta = 0.288, odds ratio for collapsed 2 × 2—disability group: 2.85.

TABLE 10.6
Evacuation Experience by Social Support

Evacuation Experience	Family/Friends Support during Crises				
	Strongly Agree	Agree	Disagree	Strongly Disagree	Total
Smooth	48.9 (111)	33.5 (55)	17.9 (5)	11.8 (2)	39.7 (173)
Okay, had necessities	41.4 (94)	47.0 (77)	53.6 (15)	5.9 (1)	42.9 (187)
Not very well	3.1 (7)	7.3 (12)	7.1 (2)	23.5 (4)	5.7 (25)
Major problems	6.6 (15)	12.2 (20)	21.4 (6)	58.8 (10)	11.7 (51)
Total	100.0% (227)	100.0% (164)	100.0% (28)	100.0% (17)	100.0% (436)

Note: Pearson Chi-Sq = 72.63, d.f. = 9, $p < 0.000$, Eta = 0.357.

The question of evacuation experience, which has a direct bearing on understanding the potential nature of sheltering or temporary housing performance in future disaster incidents, can also be explored by examining the same dimension of personal networks, as discussed in Table 10.3. For the evacuation experience question, Table 10.6 similarly shows that there is a strong relationship between social support and personal coping networks; it seems clear that individuals can cope with disaster situations better when their personal support networks are stronger. This is another important piece of assessment information the whole community planning should take into account on disaster sheltering and housing issues (see Table 10.6).

10.4 INSIGHTS AND CONCLUSION

The analysis presented here provides a description of several basic relationships that illustrate how the presence of disability in a household, ADL limitations, and personal support networks might affect household readiness to deal with sheltering or temporary housing demands during a disaster. Likewise, those same factors and their relationship to evacuation experience also shed light on potential performance of community systems in assisting disaster survivors. For instance, as ADL limitations increase, dislocation coping capacity decreases and direct evacuation experiences become more negative in practice. This points to the need for greater examination of the kinds of assistance requirements likely to be present in evacuation situations, given community members' profile of access and functional needs. This is consistent with other recent studies (such as Brittingham and Wachtendorf 2013) that have found similar differential impacts of disaster on people with disabilities—underscoring the need for continual examination of community member vulnerability if that vulnerability is to be properly mitigated.

The analysis presented here is simple and straightforward and the results generally intuitive; a comprehensive report on these and other relationships from those gathered data is offered by Gerber et al. (2010). The strength of the findings lies in the fact that those data are rather unique as they are not derived from a single case nor from a selection process oriented only toward those with disabilities. Instead, the survey data collected reflects variation in hazard vulnerability, community experience, hazard type, type of disabilities, and variation in ADL limitations. As such, we can be confident in the strength of external validity inferences precisely because of the broad-based, random selection processes across different hazards and variable levels of hazard vulnerability where respondents were located. Overall, these findings represent a useful, generalizable characterization of several key characteristics relevant to planning and preparedness in this domain.

The results complement, and offer additional insights, to prior work in this area. Among other things, Twigg et al. (2011) found it common that public sector organizations had misguided understanding or limited information about the nature of the capabilities of people with disabilities in disaster situations. In the view of those authors, this leads to weakness in overall emergency management efficacy. Priestley and Hemingway (2007) make a related point when examining how organizations rooted in communities of people with disability have an important role to play in improving disaster recovery practices. The focus here complements such observations by providing a specific empirical basis for understanding how coping capacities vary during disaster dislocation and how observations on experiences with evacuation can shape emergency sheltering and/or temporary housing practice improvements.

That is, the substance of the relationships examined is important because it is directly relevant to FEMA's still relatively new philosophical emphasis on whole community planning. It helps to provide a more complete picture of the kinds of distinctions in the overall population that exist for management of temporary housing and emergency sheltering. As several scholars cited above note, improving community resilience is at least in part dependent on a better understanding of community needs. Awareness of preparedness behavior, household capacities, and disaster-related experiences across all members of a community is an essential element of building resilience capacity.

ACKNOWLEDGMENTS

The data presented in this paper were gathered through a project funded by the United States Department of Education, National Institute for Disability and Rehabilitation

Research (Award # H133A070005; Brian J. Gerber, Principal Investigator, Frances Norwood, and Michael Zakour, Co-Principal Investigators). The analysis and interpretation presented here is solely the responsibility of the author.

REFERENCES

Alesch, D. J., L. A. Arendt, and J. N. Holly. 2009. *Managing for Long-Term Community Recovery in the Aftermath of Disaster.* Washington, DC: Public Entity Risk Institute.

Bolin, R. C. 1994. *Household and Community Recovery after Earthquakes.* Monograph No. 56, Boulder, Colorado: University of Colorado.

Bricout, J. and P. Baker. 2010. Online social networks in emergency communications and recovery: An inclusive model for people with disabilities. *Journal of Emergency Management* 7(1): 59–74.

Brittingham, R. and T. Wachtendorf. 2013. The effect of situated access on people with disabilities: An examination of sheltering and temporary housing after the 2011 Japan earthquake and tsunami. *Earthquake Spectra* 29(s1): S433–55.

Brodie, M., E. Weltzien, D. Altman, R. J. Blendon, and J. M. Benson. 2006. Experiences of Hurricane Katrina evacuees in Houston shelters: Implications for future planning. *American Journal of Public Health* 96(8): 1402–8.

Burby, R. J., R. E. Deyle, D. R. Godschalk, and R. B. Olshansky. 2000. Creating hazard resilient communities through land-use planning. *Natural Hazards Review* 1(2): 99–106.

Byzek, J. and T. Gilmer. 2001. Unsafe refuge: Why did so many wheelchair users die on Sept. 11? *New Mobility Magazine*, December. http://www.newmobility.com/2001/12/unsafe-refuge-why-did-so-many-wheelchair-users-die-on-sept-11/ (accessed February 29, 2016).

Cameron, C. T. 2008. *Emergency Preparedness for People with Disabilities and Other Special Needs: Another Look after Katrina.* Washington, DC: Inclusion Research Institute, Center for Disability and Special Needs Preparedness.

Cutter, S. L., L. Barnes, M. Berry et al. 2008. A place-based model for understanding community resilience to natural disasters. *Global Environmental Change* 18(4): 598–606.

Dosa, D. M., N. Grossman, T. Wetle, and V. Mor. 2007. To evacuate or not to evacuate: Lessons learned from Louisiana nursing home administrators following Hurricanes Katrina and Rita. *Journal of the American Medical Directors Association* 8(3): 142–49.

Fischer, H. W., G. F. Stine, B. L. Stoker, M. L. Trowbridge, and E. M. Drain. 1995. Evacuation behaviour: Why do some evacuate, while others do not? A case study of the Ephrata, Pennsylvania (USA) evacuation. *Disaster Prevention and Management: An International Journal* 4(4): 30–6.

Gall, M., K. H. Nguyen, and S. L. Cutter. 2015. Integrated research on disaster risk: Is it really integrated? *International Journal of Disaster Risk Reduction* 12: 255–67.

Gerber, B. J., F. Norwood, and M. Zakour. 2010. Disasters, evacuations and persons with disabilities: An assessment of key issues facing individuals and households. *Evacuation Study for People with Disabilities, National Institute on Disability and Rehabilitation Research, United States Department of Education* 28.

Holling, C. S. 1973. Resilience and stability of ecological systems. *Annual Review of Ecology and Systematics* 4: 1–23. http://www.annualreviews.org/doi/abs/10.1146/annurev.es.04.110173.000245?journalCode=ecolsys.1 (accessed February 29, 2016).

Juillet, E. 1993. Evacuating people with disabilities. In *The World Trade Center Bombing: Report and Analysis*, W. A. Manning (ed.), USFA-TR-076, Washington, DC: US Fire Administration, 103–5. https://www.usfa.fema.gov/downloads/pdf/publications/tr-076.pdf (accessed February 29, 2016).

Kailes, J. I. 2002. *Emergency Evacuation Preparedness: Taking Responsibility for Your Safety: A Guide for People with Disabilities and Other Activity Limitations*. Pomona, California: Center for Disability Issues and the Health Professions.

Litman, T. 2006. Lessons from Katrina and Rita: What major disasters can teach transportation planners? *Journal of Transportation Engineering* 132(1): 11–18.

Mileti, D. 1999. *Disasters by Design: A Reassessment of Natural Hazards in the United States*. Washington, DC: Joseph Henry Press.

National Council on Disability (NCD). 2009. *Effective Emergency Management: Making Improvements for Communities and People with Disabilities*. Washington, DC: NCD.

National Organization on Disability. 2005. *Report on Special Needs Assessment for Katrina Evacuees (SNAKE) Project*. Washington, DC: National Organization on Disability.

National Organization on Disability. 2009. *Disaster Mobilization Initiative: Response to September 11th*. Washington, DC: National Organization on Disability.

Nigg, J. M., J. Barnshaw, and M. R. Torres. 2006. Hurricane Katrina and the flooding of New Orleans: Emergent issues in sheltering and temporary housing. *The Annals of the American Academy of Political and Social Science* 604(1): 113–28.

Olshansky, R. B. and L. Johnson. 2010. *Clear as Mud: Planning for the Rebuilding of New Orleans*. Washington, DC: American Planning Association.

Peacock, W. G., N. Dash, and Y. Zhang. 2007. Sheltering and housing recovery following disaster. In *Handbook of Disaster Research*, H. Rodriguez, E. L. Quarantelli, and R. Dynes (eds), New York: Springer, 258–74.

Peek, L. and L. M. Stough. 2010. Children with disabilities in the context of disaster: A social vulnerability perspective. *Child Development* 81(4): 1260–70.

Priestley, M. and L. Hemingway. 2007. Disability and disaster recovery: A tale of two cities? *Journal of Social Work in Disability & Rehabilitation* 5(3–4): 23–42.

Quarantelli, E. L. 1982. General and particular observations on sheltering and housing in American disasters. *Disasters* 6(4): 277–81.

Robinson, S. E., B. J. Gerber, W. Eller, and M. Gall. 2013. Emergency planning and disabled populations: Assessing the FNSS approach. *International Journal of Mass Emergencies and Disasters* 13(2): 315–329.

Smith, G. 2012. *Planning for Post-Disaster Recovery: A Review of the United States Disaster Assistance Framework*. Washington, DC: Island Press.

Tierney, K. J., M. K. Lindell, and R. W. Perry. 2001. *Facing the Unexpected: Disaster Preparedness and Response in the United States*. Washington, DC: Joseph Henry Press.

Twigg, J., M. Kett, H. Bottomley, L. Tze Tan, and H. Nasreddin. 2011. Disability and public shelter in emergencies. *Environmental Hazards* 10(3–4): 248–61.

United States Federal Emergency Management Agency (US FEMA). 2009. *National Disaster Housing Strategy*. Washington, DC: US Department of Homeland Security.

United States Federal Emergency Management Agency (US FEMA). 2010. *Guidance on Planning for Integration of Functional Needs Support Services General Populations Shelters*. Washington, DC: US Department of Homeland Security.

United States Federal Emergency Management Agency (US FEMA). 2011. *A Whole Community Approach to Emergency Management: Principles, Themes and Pathways for Action*. Washington, DC: US Department of Homeland Security.

White, G. W., M. H. Fox, C. Rooney, and A. Cahill. 2007. *Assessing the Impact of Hurricane Katrina on Persons with Disabilities*. Lawrence, Kansas: The University of Kansas, The Research and Training Center on Independent Living. http://rtcil.org/sites/rtcil.drupal.ku.edu/files/images/galleries/NIDRR_FinalKatrinaReport.pdf (accessed February 29, 2016).

Section III

Housing Recovery in a Global Context

11 Early Post-Disaster Shelter Recovery after the 12 January 2010 Haiti Earthquake

N. Emel Ganapati and Guitele J. Rahill

CONTENTS

11.1 INTRODUCTION

In January 2010, the Haiti earthquake, measuring 7.0 on the Richter scale, claimed 222,570 lives and affected over a third (EM-DAT 2015) of Haiti's 10.4 million people (The World Bank 2015). Economic damages were estimated at about $7.8 billion (The World Bank 2011a). The ensuing cholera epidemic claimed 8346 additional lives (World Health Organization [WHO] 2015), introducing new challenges for those who strove to recover from the earthquake.

Even prior to the earthquake and the cholera epidemic, Haitians confronted challenges ranging from low incomes to lack of access to basic needs. According to the World Bank (2011a, 2015), Haiti is the poorest country in the Americas and among the poorest in the world; approximately 78% of its population survives on less than $2 US per day, 76% lack access to adequate sanitation (piped sewer system and septic tank), and 38% lack access to acceptable water sources (piped water, public taps, and protected dug wells). Life expectancy of Haitians is 63 years, below the global mean of 71 (WHO 2015). Haiti ranks the 168th of 187 countries in the 2013 United Nations Human Development Index, the lowest rank of any nation in the Western Hemisphere (UNDP 2014).

Haiti's earthquake recovery challenges are unprecedented because of its ongoing developmental challenges and because of the state of its government. Haiti became the first black republic in the western hemisphere, obtaining independence from France in the early nineteenth century. Today's international and academic community, however, often refers to Haiti as a "failed" or "fragile" state based on its limited institutional capability to perform even basic state functions such as the provision of core services, regulation, and security (Collier 2007; Pritchett et al. 2013; The World Bank 2011b). Haiti relies heavily on foreign donors to carry out its own functions (Zanotti 2010).

What are the unique challenges disaster faced by survivors in fragile states like Haiti during early shelter recovery, which involves provision and restoration of shelter? What mechanisms do they use to overcome them? Who do they rely on when their own government neglects them after a disaster? In this chapter, we address these questions, which are important for several reasons. *First*, shelter is more than just the structure in which people live. Having adequate shelter is, like the need for food, one of the basic needs (Streeten et al. 1981) and a central human capability (Nussbaum 2000). Therefore, ensuring access to shelter is essential for treating each person as worthy of regard. *Second*, housing recovery is an important component of the multifaceted post-disaster recovery process in impacted communities. Previous studies indicate a close link between housing recovery and business (Xiao and Van Zandt 2012) and psycho-social recovery (Kilmer et al. 2010). Accordingly, a better understanding of housing recovery processes could aid in recovery in other sectors. *Third*, post-disaster shelter recovery is an under-researched area, especially in fragile states. Enhanced understanding of the Haitian post-disaster context could offer useful lessons on shelter recovery for governments of other fragile nations and for international aid agencies that are poised to provide shelter aid in these contexts.

Based on fieldwork conducted in three socio-economically diverse communities (Pétion-ville, Delmas, and Canapé Vertin in Port-au-Prince) following the 2010 Haiti earthquake, we suggest that the most significant shelter-related challenges faced in Haiti after the earthquake were related to access to shelter, security in camps, and the process of recovery. We highlight the importance of leadership, social capital, faith, and adaptive flexibility in helping Haitians overcome their shelter-related challenges.

In the following section, we introduce the theoretical perspectives on shelter recovery. Next, we describe the research context and explain our data collection methods. Then, we present shelter-related challenges in Haiti and the strategies survivors used to manage such challenges. We conclude with policy recommendations and directions for future research.

11.2 TEMPORARY SHELTERING IN POST-DISASTER CONTEXTS

Post-disaster recovery is a multifaceted and complex process, a critical component of which involves rebuilding of the housing sector. Quarantelli (1982) offers four stages of post-disaster housing recovery: *Emergency sheltering* comprises temporarily housing at-risk individuals in safe locations prior to or during disaster events (e.g., schools in case of hurricanes). *Temporary sheltering* "refers to peoples' temporary displacement into other quarters, with an expected short stay" (Quarantelli 1995, p. 45) (e.g., homes of friends/relatives, tents, motels, or mass shelters); and it typically includes provision of food or emergency medical services. *Temporary housing* allows for "the reestablishment of household routines but with the understanding that more permanent quarters will be eventually obtained" (e.g., mobile homes to house disaster survivors) (Quarantelli 1982, p. 279). *Permanent housing* involves repair of existing buildings or reconstruction of new homes for those who were displaced by a disaster (e.g., in newer areas that are considered to be safer).

The four phases of sheltering and housing do not progress "in a neat linear fashion" (Quarantelli 1982, p. 280). They may coexist simultaneously. While progressing from one phase to another, socially vulnerable populations (economically disadvantaged populations, the poor, female-headed households, and children) and their communities face greater challenges than other groups and communities due to their limited access to resources (e.g., Fothergill et al. 1999; Peacock et al. 1997; Rahill et al. 2014; Andrew et al. 2013).

Our specific focus in this chapter is on the temporary sheltering phase of post-disaster shelter recovery. The US-based literature on this phase mainly deals with individual/household preferences for different types of shelters and factors that affect these preferences (e.g., Mileti et al. 1992; Paul and Che 2011). Some studies discuss the challenges of providing and managing temporary housing, including the equitable provision of shelter options for all (e.g., sex offenders), low priority given by local authorities to temporary shelters in comparison to other forms of sheltering and housing, fragmentation and limited coordination among agencies involved in temporary shelter provision, and inefficient use of resources in mass shelters (Arlikatti et al. 2012; Quarantelli 1982, 1995). Other studies note that social conflict can emerge over recovery policies and priorities during the temporary sheltering phase in communities which have had pre-disaster ethnic and class divisions (Bolin and Stanford 1991).

The term "temporary shelter" is not used consistently in the international literature on disasters, that is, some studies refer to temporary housing as temporary shelter (e.g., Omidvar et al. 2011). However, the international literature covers a wide range of issues with respect to the temporary sheltering phase, ranging from estimating the capacity of temporary shelters (Chou et al. 2013), determining the location of temporary shelters (Kılcı et al. 2015), and evacuation behavior associated with different types of temporary shelters (Andrew et al. 2013) to public participation experiences of residents of temporary shelters (Chandrasekhar et al. 2014) and the role of social capital in shelter recovery (Rahill et al. 2014). There is also a significant amount of work on the public health conditions of those who reside in temporary shelters (e.g., Kun et al. 2010).

Despite the growing international literature on the temporary sheltering phase, our understanding of the challenges disaster survivors face during this phase remains limited. Studying these challenges is especially important in the context of fragile states like Haiti where there is a lack of resources to rebuild and inadequate governmental capacity to provide temporary shelters and to coordinate aid between different actors involved in shelter provision (e.g., international aid agencies) in the aftermath of a disaster. Although studies have examined different aspects of shelter and housing recovery after the Haiti earthquake (e.g., Abrahams 2014; Hooper 2015; Rahill et al. 2014), none have focused exclusively on the challenges faced by disaster survivors in acquiring temporary shelters and the mechanisms they used to overcome these challenges. These are the issues we will highlight in this chapter.

11.3 RESEARCH METHODS

We conducted a case study of shelter recovery processes that took place in Port-au-Prince after the 2010 Haiti earthquake in the communities of Pétion-ville, Delmas, and Canapé Vert (see Figure 1 in Rahill et al. 2014 for a map of these communities) in May and October–November of 2010, followed by a data verification phase in June 2011.

Our main data collection methods for the study included interviews and focus groups. We conducted face-to-face and semi-structured interviews in Haitian Kreyòl, French, or English with two different groups ($n = 54$): (a) community leaders ($n = 38$) and (b) international (e.g., representatives from multilateral or bilateral aid agencies) ($n = 8$) as well as national (e.g., ministers) ($n = 7$) and local level (e.g., mayors) ($n = 1$) Haitian policy makers involved in recovery processes. Our sampling was targeted and purposeful since we were interested in finding study participants that would best enable us to answer our research questions as opposed to finding study participants that are representative of the population.

We identified the initial sample of interviewees with help from our local research partner, an independent research center in Pétion-ville entitled the Haitian Institute of Community Health (*Institut Haitien de Santé Communautaire*). We then expanded the sample through snowball sampling, and concluded the interviews upon reaching our theoretical saturation (Agar 1980; Strauss and Corbin 1990).

We conducted a total of 12 focus groups with those who were affected by the earthquake in the Pétion-ville, Delmas, and Canapé Vert communities. The focus groups were held in Haitian Kreyòl in places that were convenient to our study participants (e.g., schools, churches, and office of our local research partner). In each community, we conducted two focus groups initially in May 2010 (one with men and one with women), followed up by two additional focus groups 6 months later in October–November 2010. A total of 63 individuals were recruited through our local research partner to participate in our focus groups.

In order to better understand the daily routines and experiences of those affected by the disaster and of policy makers, we also engaged in participant observation in international agencies (cluster meetings), in camps of displaced Haitians, and in protests and community events (e.g., church meetings and Vodou ceremonies) during our data collection field trips. We selected these venues for participant observation based on our research interests on shelter recovery in Haiti in general and in our select communities in particular. We further reviewed secondary sources (e.g., newspaper articles, minutes of cluster meetings).

We transcribed and coded all data from the interviews and focus groups using ATLAS.ti 6.0®, a computer-assisted qualitative data analysis software. Upon completion of data collection and analysis, we facilitated two town hall meetings (organized by gender) in June 2011 to discuss and corroborate our research findings. Approximately 50–60 earthquake survivors participated in these meetings. A majority of these survivors had participated in our study earlier either as interviewees or focus group participants.

Further details on our methodology, including the strengths and limitations of our research design, are available in Rahill et al. (2014).

11.4 SHELTER-RELATED CHALLENGES

In this section, we detail the shelter-related challenges faced by displaced Haitians in Pétion-ville, Delmas, and Canapé Vert. Despite differences in the overall socioeconomic characteristics of these communities, the challenges faced by the displaced populations were consistent throughout in part because our sample included those who were part of the lower socioeconomic groups in all three communities. We categorize these challenges under the categories of: (1) access to shelter (unequal access; evictions); (2) security; and (3) process of recovery (lack of voice in shelter recovery processes, lack of care by the Haitian government, and corruption).

11.4.1 Access to Shelter

Haitians displaced by the earthquake waited long for shelter and shelter-related resources (e.g., tarps) to be delivered. Approximately 1 year after the earthquake, 680,000 people remain displaced (Haiti Shelter Cluster 2011). Many of these displaced populations did not even have tents to live in, but dwell in makeshift tent-like shelters composed of long sticks, sheets/cardboard, and plastic tarp (called *anba prelas*). A community leader from Delmas explained that in the immediate aftermath of the earthquake, he and other survivors seeking shelter, "had sheets tied to 4 poles in the street…they stretched out on the concrete and prayed for rain not to fall until shelter arrived. Shelter never arrived." Staying in *anba prelas* (beneath tarps) did not provide much protection to displaced populations from such elements as the wind and rain. Some described their living arrangement as being in a "morgue, waiting to be buried." Others told us their stories of lying in water until the rain passed and keeping their children in cabinet drawers to protect them from rain.

In Haiti, international aid agencies took the lead in providing shelter-related resources after the earthquake albeit with limited or no coordination. While some camps of the displaced were served well by shelter programs of these agencies, others were left out (Rahill et al. 2014).

Some of our participants associated unequal access to shelter and shelter-related resources with social class and with inequitable distribution of resources across neighborhoods. Based on one interview conducted, a Delmas woman asserted,

> Just one person can find three to four tents. They sell them, they have so many… we find nothing…[International agencies] help them. We find none…We kept waiting for them to come and help us.

A policy maker illustrated the lack of governmental organization and shifted responsibility to those above him, while noting that determining the types and location of shelters had to take into account those who had up until then been taking advantage of a lucrative construction business:

> We are involved in urban planning, but waiting for directives from special presidential commission whose responsibility was to reflect on post January 12th event.... The focus is in preparing a code for reconstruction while making sure not to hinder what has been a dynamic construction industry.

Along with unequal access to resources, evictions emerged as an issue of access to shelter. The number of Haitians staying in camps reduced from 1.5 million in July 2010 to 171,975 in September 2013 (Haiti E-Shelter CCCM Cluster 2013). Although these numbers might be considered as a measure of the success of shelter programs in Haiti, most of the displaced persons were pushed out their camps through evictions either from government officials or from private landowners who wanted to reclaim their property after the initial shocks abated.

Community leaders and members from Delmas described the fear of evictions and the eviction process, noting that social class also featured in the speed and mode of eviction:

> It was raining recently ... 24 armed men came to evict us from the land. We reasoned with them and appealed to ... the fact that they were from the same neighborhoods and social class as we were and that there were women, children and the elderly also in the camp. They left.

In Pétion-ville, men and women who often did not originally reside in Pétion-ville, described clashes with long-term residents of the zone, noting: "People in Nerette... say, 'You guys are as good as dead. They are going to come and get you in the dead of night to evict you. You are on the field where we used to play ball'"

Likewise, the Pétion-ville men complained about residents of vacant terrains who came from lower classes and neighborhoods:

> People had found empty terrains so they mounted their tents on them, whereas the terrain was private property. The worst thing is that now the landowner comes to claim his space. So the people are obliged to shake a leg and do what they need to leave these terrains. To go where, though? There is no place to go. So that means the people return again to the streets.

In Delmas, the women mourned that international aid organizations sided with landowners, in saying that the latter provided warnings of evictions, since the earthquake itself had come without warning:

> I went to the Red Cross to ask for help because the owner of the terrain where our tents are has asked us to leave the land. The Red Cross said that "I am only here to bring water to you. The landowner is better to you than the earthquake was because as least he is giving you warning." It was as if a dagger was plunged into my heart when he said that.

11.4.2 Security in Camps

Displaced Haitians voiced significant concerns regarding security in the camps. These concerns in part had to do with lack of privacy. Such concerns were particularly relevant for women and girls who became susceptible to acts of sexual violence as they were forced to engage in personal self-care with minimal obscurity from males. Women from Delmas stated:

> I feel like I don't have a private life anymore. That's the biggest problem…When I am menstruating…Before I had a room in my house where I could take care of private women issues. Now I don't even have the money to buy sanitary napkins. Big problem for me.

Security concerns were also exacerbated since many lived next to strangers in the camps. The major complaints about strangers seemed affiliated with social status and with the personal habits of the strangers. Women from Canapé Vert complained that not only were the sleeping arrangements uncomfortable and unpleasant, but also that not having shared a long-standing mutually reciprocal trust with the strangers (*rekonèt*) led to fears that the strangers were stealing their property:

> Strangers from other areas come, you don't connect with them. It makes you ill at ease. You don't know who to trust…We sleep one on top of each other. You sleep in shifts because if the rain soaks one spot, there is only a limited area to sleep…People's feet may be in your mouth while you sleep…There are no individual beds. You just spread a sheet on the ground…There are people snoring so you can't sleep. The person next to you may smell…All my kids' clothes get lost.

11.4.3 Process of Recovery

Adding to the challenges of access to shelter and security in camps faced by earthquake survivors were challenges related to the process of recovery. These challenges involved not having a voice in shelter recovery processes, lack of care by the Haitian Government, and perceived corruption among government officials and displaced persons.

Participants in our study shared the belief that the government not only failed in making efforts to involve the masses in the recovery process but also in informing them about recovery in general and shelter and housing recovery in particular. A community leader from Pétion-ville stated, "…the government has asked us to wait for their orders." Others highlighted the fact their government does not think the masses have anything good to offer but consult foreigners regularly for matters related to Haiti. Still others noted the difficulties the masses face in reaching government officials despite their personal efforts.

Lack of voice in the shelter recovery process seems inextricably tied to the lack of social movement between classes, as the officials in charge of shelter recovery seemed most interested in receiving input from more affluent neighborhoods. Even a United Nations representative interviewed indicated that those invited to cluster meetings were those who had the means to contribute. That representative noted that in order for the masses to be heard, they need to take a firm stand that reflects their love of their country and their respect for themselves:

> A dissident voice must come from the camps that says WE WILL NOT TAKE THIS ANYMORE! The love of country is on every tongue, but only in word, not in deed. If you love your country, back up your words.

Besides lack of voice, many of our study participants raised concerns about lack of care by the Haitian Government both before and after the earthquake. A male focus group participant from Delmas lamented:

> Now we can see that the Government is not thinking about us, they never did. They have no official plan to help us out, nothing at all…It is sad, but the Haitian government just does not care about its people.

Another challenge related to the process of recovery and perceived corruption especially in the ruling classes/bodies. The masses indicated that the ruling classes/bodies took care of themselves as well as people who are connected to them (e.g., relatives and friends) with the resources collected for the masses from international donors. One policy maker, who seemed oblivious to the impact of leaders' apathy and corruption indicated:

> I think the trust in the government has improved in that those who were victims of the earthquake acknowledge that the government's means have been reduced and that it's done much for them and many live better now than before the earthquake and they're aware that the government is working on creating permanent housing. There would be many more people on the streets protesting if things had not improved for them.

Meanwhile, there had been widespread demonstrations in Port-au-Prince that same week. Community members from all enclaves in our study accused the president and other candidates of using available shelter-related resources as personal property or as incentives to purchase votes and as rationale for inactivity with respect to debris removal. Residents of Delmas described a corruption "sickness" that has permeated and is pervasive throughout the country:

> The president said to withhold the aid, closed the free hospitals so that they can make money. People are charging double what they should to rebuild…. There are people spending and wasting money on election campaigns. The first minister can't even do his job as First Minister; now he's a candidate! He never helped us. A lot of people have lost credibility. They hide all the resources at their houses to give to friends. The country is sick from the roots of its hair all the way to the tips of its fingernails. The country will never recover!

Study participants summarized the corruption process, warning that the resources do not trickle down to them because aid organizations deal only with the government officials rather than conduct community assessments or communicate with community leaders/members before distributing aid:

> IOM and USAID and the Haitian government took names, registered our names for provisional temporary permanent shelters…. These are all tricks and bluffs…They promise

> this to everyone, but no one knows exactly where they are...Our government is tricking both the people and the international aid organizations...who come to help the government. They [aid agencies] don't contact us; they deal with the government but the government knows nothing of the population's needs.... Corruption has become our heritage.

There were allegations of corruption being widespread not only among the ruling classes/bodies but also among leaders of the camps (e.g., camp committees set up by the displaced themselves).

> Each group of people who appear in the camp, it's as if you can see, it's their own business they're taking care of; meanwhile, you're suffering. Committee members come and take your names and find resources at your expense. It'd be better to have people of conscience as leaders.

A policy leader suggested that corruption persists and will continue to persist because Haitians continue to tolerate it: "There is no strong civic society. There is no dissident voice after four months! They don't take the arguments to the streets and demand for it to stop!"

There were also reports of displaced persons deceiving international aid agencies. According to a representative from such an agency, the population of Port-au-Prince increased after the earthquake. Many left their homes and came to Port-au-Prince to have access to basic needs and services (e.g., food and healthcare). Furthermore, some set up tents or lived *anba prelas* in certain camps to have access to aid:

> The camps are empty at night. They [displaced persons] leave the camps and return from time to time to see what they can get...what being is handed out...People adapt themselves and use the camps to increase their resources.

11.5 OVERCOMING THE CHALLENGES

Haitians in our study faced tremendous challenges in their tents and camps but took several steps to overcome these challenges through leadership, faith, adaptive flexibility, and social capital mechanisms that are detailed below.

11.5.1 LEADERSHIP

Community leaders demonstrated a selfless leadership and dignified approach to affecting change, thereby filling an important gap in lives of displaced Haitians. Community leaders from Delmas, for instance, initiated educational magazines detailing how to prevent cholera and civic education concerning not urinating in the streets and how to be good citizens. These leaders highlighted their obligation to Haitians as follows: "A revolution must occur even if 500,000 people die it's better than we spend all the rest of our lives suffering together. It is our obligation. There must be a revolution!"

While there was a great deal of calls for leadership and some leaders stepped in at the local level to help their fellow citizens, the majority of our town hall participants expressed reluctance to assume leadership either because they felt they would not be accepted, that their lives would be in danger, or that they would become part of a corrupt and mistrusted system:

> One element can't change a system. You can't change it from within. Maybe if the elements within a system have a collective conscience. When within the system, you're obliged to become corrupt; otherwise you either lose your place or you're killed.

11.5.2 Social Capital

Social capital, "features of social life—networks, norms, and trust—that enable participants to act together more effectively to pursue shared objectives" (Putnam 1996, p. 34), was another mechanism that helped the displaced Haitians in their shelter recovery efforts. In the context of post-earthquake Haiti, social capital enhanced access to shelter and shelter-related resources among displaced populations who had connections with the government officials or the international aid representatives. Those without connections, however, were left out on their own during the recovery process (Rahill et al. 2014).

Inequitable distribution of shelter resources among the displaced populations created tensions between those who had the right connections and those who did not (Rahill et al. 2014). There were reports of acts of violence and retaliation (e.g., cutting of tents with knives and razor blades) in the camps of the displaced that stayed in tents and were served by international aid agencies.

11.5.3 Faith

Faith and spirituality emerged as salient factors in the survivors' ability to overcome challenges. The participants' faith and spiritual perspectives mainly reflected their beliefs in what they perceived as God's ability to ensure their survival through the earthquake and to care for them after the earthquake. A great deal of debate surrounded discussions of faith, pitting, on the one hand, those who believed:

> God is grown, He does what He wants.... Faith by definition is something that is durable and firm. It is something that-when you have it, when it animates you-you will not despair for what happens.

On the other hand, there were those who asserted that viewing the earthquake through the lens of faith was natural, given that there was no precedence for such a disaster in Haiti, and given the magnitude of the earthquake, but who insisted that faith without action is inadequate:

> This earthquake that has just passed—the way it was—the magnitude it was—we don't have that tradition/historical experience...when the earthquake came, [people] were telling that the return of Jesus Christ is the end of the world—and that they had never personally witnessed the death of such a great quantity of people...The earthquake that led every Haitian to scramble and look for where their faith had been...and where they'd hidden it—well, then there is no Haitian who has faith—if that was it;

> Faith is a spiritual thing—what is palpable, what is clear, what is concrete are your two biceps; it's lending a hand to train people and educate people so that we can advance... faith—it is part of the rubric.

11.5.4 Adaptive Flexibility

Adaptive flexibility among displaced persons pertained both to personal growth stemming from the trauma of the event and to resilience in being able to resume routine activities of daily life:

> Before the earthquake, I used to be afraid of blood; but I found myself lifting people from under the debris who were covered in blood. I will never be afraid again. Nothing worse could happen than what I have seen and experienced with this earthquake.

Despite evidence of adaptive flexibility, female community members from Canapé Vert maintained that resuming normal activities did not imply that this was to a healthy level, as the resources had dwindled and the impact on people was great:

> If the person's home is not destroyed, even if it's hard for the person to find food to eat, (s)he is not too bad; but almost everyone finds something to do: those who used to go down into the city to buy oranges, mangoes, they return to doing the same thing; there is now no financing for those efforts. They live anyway. The person spends as much as (s)he knows, (s)he has. How does the Haitian proverb go again? The size of your wanga/magic/voodoo is only as big as your money.

11.6 CONCLUSION

This chapter focused on the challenges faced by Haitians who survived the 2010 earthquake and the mechanisms through which they overcame these challenges while sheltering in camps. These challenges ranged from difficulties in having access to shelter resources and in living with strangers in the camps to the top–down and corrupt nature of the post-disaster recovery process. Haitians overcame these challenges mainly through collaborating with community leaders, social capital, faith, and adaptive flexibility.

Our findings have several implications for policy makers at the international, national, and local level. *First*, there is a need for close collaboration among actors involved in shelter recovery to ensure equal access to shelter and shelter-related resources. Cluster meetings typically bring together different international and governmental actors involved in shelter recovery in places that are affected by disasters and that receive international aid. Yet, these actors need to do more in terms of working with grass-roots actors in disaster contexts (e.g., local leaders, community-based organizations) to ensure that people's voices are heard and their shelter-related concerns are addressed. Shelter-related meetings could be conducted in English and in the language spoken by the displaced (e.g., Kreyol in Haiti) and could be held in places that are more convenient to displaced people (e.g., close to the camps) versus in the offices of international aid agencies (e.g., the heavily guarded UN base in

Haiti). *Second*, policy makers could build on and strengthen the assets of displaced populations. They could initiate leadership programs at the community level, provide financial and technical support to community-based organizations, and work with religious leaders (e.g., those who lead houses of worship such as Catholic priests and Protestant pastors in Haiti) while designing and implementing shelter programs.

This chapter featured the perspectives of displaced Haitians staying in temporary shelters (tents or *anba prelas*), supplemented by the perspectives of policy makers involved in recovery processes after the Haiti earthquake. Future studies in Haiti could examine the use of temporary shelters among those who are part of higher socioeconomic groups, whose voices were not included in this study. There is also a need for comparative studies on temporary shelters, comparing the challenges faced by disaster survivors during early shelter recovery in other fragile states (e.g., Sudan, Congo). Other interesting topics for future research on fragile states include the barriers that disaster survivors face in participating in shelter recovery processes and the benefits and downsides of social capital for shelter recovery.

ACKNOWLEDGMENT

This chapter is based on research supported by the US National Science Foundation RAPID Grants #1034757 and #1034818. The findings and opinions reported are those of the authors and are not necessarily endorsed by the funding organization or those who provided assistance with various aspects of the study.

REFERENCES

Abrahams, D. 2014. The barriers to environmental sustainability in post-disaster settings: A case study of transitional shelter implementation in Haiti. *Disasters* 38(S1): S25–49.

Agar, M. 1980. *The Professional Stranger: An Informal Introduction to Ethnography.* New York: Academic Press.

Andrew, S. A., S. Arlikatti, and M. Saitgalina. 2013. Managing the impact of disaster. *Public Management Review* 15(3): 383–401.

Arlikatti, S., J. Kendra, and N. A. Clark. 2012. Challenges for multi-sector organizations in tracking and sheltering registered sex offenders in disasters. *Journal of Homeland Security and Emergency Management* 9(1), Article 27. doi: 10.1515/1547-7355.1842.

Bolin, R., and L. Stanford. 1991. Shelter, housing and recovery: A comparison of U.S. disasters. *Disasters* 15(1): 24–34.

Chandrasekhar, D., Y. Zhang, and Y. Xiao. 2014. Nontraditional participation in disaster recovery planning: Cases from China, India, and the United States. *Journal of the American Planning Association* 80(4): 373–84.

Chou, J.-S., Y.-C. Ou, M.-Y. Cheng et al. 2013. Emergency shelter capacity estimation by earthquake damage analysis. *Natural Hazards* 65(3): 2031–61.

Collier, P. 2007. *The Bottom Billion.* New York: Oxford University Press.

EM-DAT. 2015. *The OFDA/CRED International Disaster Database.* Brussels, Belgium: Université Catholique de Louvain. http://www.em-dat.net (accessed August 15, 2015).

Fothergill, A., E. G. M. Maestas, and J. D. Darlington. 1999. Race, ethnicity, and disasters in the United States: A review of the literature. *Disasters* 23(3): 156–73.

Haiti E-Shelter CCCM Cluster. 2013. Factsheet https://www.sheltercluster.org/sites/default/files/docs/Fact%20Sheet%20CCCM%20-%20Shelter.pdf (accessed September 8, 2015).

Haiti Shelter Cluster. 2011. *Shelter Cluster Needs and Gaps Analysis*. https://sites.google.com/site/shelterhaiti2010/files/SHELTER_NEED_ANALYSIS_march_2011_final3.pdf?attredirects=0 (accessed January 15, 2015).

Hooper, M. 2015. Will the city rise again? The contested geography of housing reconstruction in post-disaster Haiti. *Housing Studies* 30(7): 1016–35. doi:10.1080/02673037.2015.1006184.

Kılcı, F., B. Y. Kara, and B. Bozkaya. 2015. Locating temporary shelter areas after an earthquake: A case for Turkey. *European Journal of Operational Research* 243(1): 323–32.

Kilmer R. P., V. Gil-Rivas, R. G. Tedeschi, and L. G. Calhoun. 2010. *Helping Families and Communities Recover from Disaster: Lessons Learned from Hurricane Katrina and Its Aftermath*. Washington, DC: American Psychological Association.

Kun, P., Z. Wang, X. Chen et al. 2010. Public health status and influence factors after 2008 Wenchuan earthquake among survivors in Sichuan province, China: Cross-sectional trial. *Public Health* 124(10): 573–80.

Mileti, D. S., J. H. Sorensen, and P. W. O'Brien. 1992. Toward an explanation of mass care shelter use in evacuations. *International Journal of Mass Emergencies and Disasters* 10(1): 25–42.

Nussbaum, M. 2000. *Women and Human Development: The Capabilities Approach*. Cambridge: Cambridge University Press.

Omidvar, B., H. Zafari, and M. Khakpour. 2011. Evaluation of public participation in reconstruction of Bam, Iran, after the 2003 earthquake. *Natural Hazards* 59: 1397–412.

Paul, B. K., and D. Che. 2011. Opportunities and challenges in rebuilding tornado-impacted Greensburg, Kansas as "stronger, better, and greener." *GeoJournal* 76(1): 93–108.

Peacock, W. G., B. H. Morrow, and H. Gladwin, eds. 1997. *Hurricane Andrew: Ethnicity, Gender and the Sociology of Disasters*. London and New York: Routledge Press.

Pritchett, L., M. Woolcock, and M. Andrews. 2013. Looking like a state: Techniques of persistent failure in state capability for implementation. *The Journal of Development Studies* 49(1): 1–18.

Putnam, R. D. 1996. The strange disappearance of civic America. *The American Prospect* 24: 34–48.

Quarantelli, E. L. 1982. *Sheltering and Housing after Major Community Disasters: Case Studies and General Observations*. Columbus, Ohio: Ohio State University.

Quarantelli, E. L. 1995. Patterns of sheltering and housing in US disasters. *Disaster Prevention and Management: An International Journal* 4(3): 43–53.

Rahill, G. J., N. E. Ganapati, J. C. Clérismé, and A. Mukherji. 2014. Shelter recovery in urban Haiti after the earthquake: The dual role of social capital. *Disasters* 38(S1): S73–93.

Strauss, A., and J. M. Corbin. 1990. *Basics of Qualitative Research: Grounded Theory Procedures and Techniques*. Newbury Park, California: Sage Publications.

Streeten, P., S. J. Burki, M. U. Haq, N. Hicks, and F. Stewart. 1981. *First Things First: Meeting Basic Human Needs in the Developing Countries*. Oxford: Oxford University Press. http://documents.worldbank.org/curated/en/1982/09/6020476/first-things-first-meeting-basic-human-needs-developing-countries (accessed February 29, 2016).

The World Bank. 2011a. *Interim Strategy Note for the Republic of Haiti for CY 2012*. Washington, DC: The World Bank.

The World Bank. 2011b. *World Development Report 2011: Conflict, Security, and Development*. Washington, DC: The World Bank.

The World Bank. 2015. *World Development Indicators: Haiti*. http://databank.worldbank.org/data//reports.aspx?source=2&country=HTI&series=&period= (accessed August 15, 2015).

UNDP. 2014. *Human Development Report 2014: Sustaining Human Progress: Reducing Vulnerabilities and Building Resilience*. New York: UNDP.

World Health Organization (WHO). 2015. *Global Health Observatory: Data and Statistics*. Geneva, Switzerland: WHO.
Xiao, Y., and S. Van Zandt. 2012. Building community resiliency: Spatial links between household and business post-disaster return. *Urban Studies* 49(11): 2523–42.
Zanotti, L. 2010. Cacophonies of aid, failed state building and NGOs in Haiti: Setting the stage for disaster, envisioning the future. *Third World Quarterly* 31(5): 755–71.

12 Disaster Housing Recovery in Rural India

Lessons from 12 Years of Post-Tsunami Housing Efforts

Sudha Arlikatti and Simon A. Andrew

CONTENTS

12.1 INTRODUCTION

Despite a growing body of literature on how sustainable land-use planning and post-disaster housing recovery policies help to reduce or mitigate long-term threats of natural disasters in urban areas, there is a limited understanding of how impacted rural communities in developing countries fare over time. Moreover, little is understood about the direct and indirect effects of post-disaster housing policies and programs due to a lack of systematic analysis. This suggests that mistakes are often repeated and well-documented reconstruction experiences ignored (Ofori 2008, p. 46). Many warn of the dangers when designing and implementing "settlements and shelters as an off-the-shelf package" (Kennedy et al. 2008, p. 26). Others have highlighted the importance of disaster recovery from multiple dimensions, that is, conceptualized as an opportunity to address long-term developmental goals that are intertwined with sustainable livelihood recovery, reduction in social and physical vulnerabilities, and improving household capabilities especially in rural communities of developing countries (Haas et al. 1977; Arlikatti and Andrew 2012).

A few scholars have described recovery from a structural improvements perspective and underscored the importance of physical and material assets to survivors (Peacock et al. 1987; Bates and Peacock 1993; Zhang and Peacock 2009; Arlikatti et al. 2010). While such an examination of the built environment using measures such as the adoption of stringent building codes, better building materials, and sustainable land-use planning practices, as well as provision of new housing are important, it is not enough. The restoration and improvements to physical infrastructure is only important insofar as it facilitates the ability of affected communities to return to an acceptable post-disaster socioeconomic condition (Andrew and Arlikatti 2014). Thus, equally important is gauging beneficiaries' satisfaction in reconstruction policies and programs by examining their perceptions of household and community recovery over time (Arlikatti and Andrew 2012; Andrew et al. 2013).

This chapter aims to fill the gap in the extant literature on post-disaster rural housing recovery by summarizing the structural improvements to core housing unit designs as well as differences in perceptions of recovery by owner- and donor-driven beneficiaries of post-tsunami housing programs in South India following the 2004 Indian Ocean tsunami. It highlights the challenges faced and successes achieved by multiple stakeholders including disaster survivors in building back better and stronger, while being sensitive to sociocultural and livelihood needs of rural households. Based on field work conducted in 2005, 2008, and 2011, the authors examine post-housing recovery programs initiated by the national, state, and local governments in conjunction with local grassroots nongovernmental organizations (NGOs) and international nongovernmental organizations. The chapter focuses on the following three broad questions:

1. Are the damaged or destroyed homes built back better? (i.e., better building codes and improved disaster-resistant design standards, stringent land-use policies)
2. Are there differences in the perceptions of household and community recovery by beneficiaries of various housing programs? (i.e., owner-driven in-situ housing repair and rebuilding or donor-assisted new resettlement housing)
3. What can be learned about post-disaster rural housing policy from the post-tsunami Indian experience?

The following sections begin with a brief overview of public housing policies specifically rural housing policies to meet acute housing shortages in India since independence from the British Raj in 1947 to current times. The mechanisms for disaster response and housing recovery will be discussed as well as an elaboration of the impacts of the 2004 tsunami on the Nagapattinam District of South India. A detailed description of the research team's efforts to collect data from a longitudinal panel of respondents from seven villages at different points in time (2005, 2008, and 2011) will also be presented together with the analysis and findings underscoring the physical improvements to post-tsunami housing. This chapter also highlights the differences in perceptions of recovery by beneficiaries of owner-driven and donor-assisted resettlement housing programs. The conclusions underscore the need for national housing policies to be aligned with disaster mitigation goals instead of piecemeal efforts post disaster.

12.2 HOUSING POLICY IN INDIA

To understand disaster housing recovery in rural India, it is important to understand traditional public housing policies and settlement patterns in India that were influenced by the land tenure practices inherited from the colonial regime. As land taxes constituted the major source of government revenue (nearly 60%) for the British Raj, they adopted three different systems to collect the land tax from the cultivators of the land, based on who was given the property rights—landlord-based systems (*zamindari* or *malguzari*), individual cultivator-based systems (*raiyatwari*), or village-based systems (*mahalwart*). This distribution carried forward after India's independence continued to affect where people settled, and how they lived (Banerjee and Iyer 2005, p. 17). The post-independence era saw acute housing shortages in major cities due to industrial expansion, rapid population growth, and rural–urban migration. This resulted in an increase in the number of urban squatters and slum dwellers, a phenomenon almost unknown till the late 1950s. By the mid-1990s even with public housing subsidies, more than 50% of the urban dwellers in India lived in slum areas with substandard housing (Singh and Das 1995, p. 2477), making them vulnerable to natural disasters such as flooding and landslides. A lack of land-use planning policies and enforcement of building regulations have stifled efforts of a national disaster mitigation policy and related housing projects.

Although the national government's approach today places less emphasis on housing subsidies, the norms continue to reinforce the assumption that public housing is a means for the poor to receive tenure security and gain access to basic infrastructure that otherwise would not be available through the inflated private housing market. Thus, the production of low income housing is financed partly through cross-subsidization by public–private and nonprofit organizations (Andrew and Arlikatti 2014) wherein acquiring suitable land, clearing and providing it with basic civic amenities is initiated by state housing boards or quasi-governmental corporations and private developers or builders who are given incentives in the form of tax breaks to build subsidized housing. Alternatively, households can purchase plots of land with low interest loans and avail of housing subsidies to construct their own homes.

Post-disaster housing reconstruction projects are coordinated by the national government which provides financial assistance and mobilizes key personnel (e.g., from the Public Works Department). While the state government agencies supplement this effort, the actual implementation of the emergency response and recovery efforts fall squarely on the shoulders of district-level agencies that are subunits of each state. Individual state governments under the guidance of the District Collector's office identify partnering agencies and select housing programs that provide monetary assistance in the form of grants, or building materials and technical advice for owner-driven in-situ repairs or free housing through donor-assisted resettlement programs initiated through public–nonprofit–private partnerships.

Often, in an effort to meet the urgent housing needs of disaster-displaced populations, recovery programs may focus on replacing the physical assets such as a home and critical infrastructure and pay scant attention to social assets described as relationships and networks with neighbors and the community, psychological wellbeing, and cultural and religious needs of a community, leading to stunted recovery. Scholars have emphasized the need for post-disaster housing packages and schemes to take into account community characteristics and housing culture and norms (Barenstein and Leeman 2012) as well as a focus on livelihood establishment and psychosocial recovery (Arlikatti et al. 2014). This is crucial to the large proportion of rural poor.

While summarizing the influence of government policy on housing the rural poor in India, Athavankar et al. (2013, p. 1) noted that in 1991, nearly 3.4 million households lived in homes without legal titles and this number escalated to15 million by 2001, with 1 million being added annually. The Working Group on Rural Housing for the 12th Five-Year plan (2012–2017), estimated the total housing shortage in rural India to reach 40 million by the end of the plan period (Planning Commission, GOI 2011). Efforts are ongoing to enhance the expenditures for those living Below the Poverty Line (BPL) under the Indira Awaas Yojana—an assisted self-help housing scheme launched by the Government of India (GOI) in 1987—as part of an employment generation program. One of the most noteworthy factors of this housing scheme is that the beneficiaries have the freedom to choose the design, materials, and layout of their homes and receive housing subsidies and a loan for income generation with a low rate of interest from the GOI. However, this scheme falls short of meeting the needs of a subset of population namely poor landless laborers (Athavankar et al. 2013).

Further, though the GOI's recommendations for improving the quality of housing in rural areas include access to appropriate technological solutions and skills such as the use of "proven alternate and indigenous technologies that are cost effective and environment friendly" and an "emphasis on disaster risk reduction" (Planning Commission, GOI 2011, pp. i–iv), most states lack the incentive to meet the needs of the shelterless. Resultantly efforts across the country to address rural housing shortages are piecemeal and lack integration with public housing policies with disaster mitigation goals.

In a noteworthy effort, the GOI in its 12th Five-Year Plan (2012–2017) outlined goals to pursue faster, sustainable, and more inclusive rural growth (UNDP India 2012). This mainstreaming of sustainability as a core objective of India's rural development strategy is indeed a paradigm shift. With an annual budget of around 5000 crore* Indian Rupees (INR) approximately $733.78 million, the Ministry of Rural Development (MoRD) with the support from the United Nations Development Program (UNDP), is keen on achieving five broad outcomes—improved natural resource conservation, increased efficiency of resource use, reduced negative environmental impacts, strengthened climate resilience of communities, and contribution to climate change mitigation (UNDP India 2012, p. vii).

* 1 USD = 68.14 INR (conversion rate on Feb 12, 2016); 1 million = 1,000,000; 1 crore INR = 10,000,000 or 10 million. Hence 5000 crore INR = $733.78 million.

12.3 POST-TSUNAMI HOUSING RECOVERY

12.3.1 Background, Sample Selection, and Data Collection

On 26 December 2004, an underwater earthquake at a magnitude of Mw 9.1 on the Richer scale in northern Sumatra in Indonesia triggered a series of devastating tsunamis along the coasts of most landmasses bordering the Indian Ocean, killing more than 250,000 people in 11 countries (Andrew et al. 2013) The coastal communities were inundated with waves as high as 30 m (100 feet) destroying hundreds and thousands of homes and public buildings around the Indian Ocean, especially in India, Indonesia, Malaysia, Maldives, Thailand, and Sri Lanka.

The research reported in this chapter was conducted in the Nagapattinam District of Tamil Nadu located directly north of Sri Lanka on the south east coast of India. As of 2001, Nagapattinam District had a population of 1.5 million with most of the rural households living BPL (Census of India 2001). The district was one of the hardest-hit areas in the state of Tamil Nadu, where about 6000 lost their lives, 196,000 people were displaced, and over 28,000 were sheltered in temporary relief camps (Prater et al. 2006). Most seriously affected were households from the lower social groups and households whose livelihoods depended directly and/or indirectly on fishing activities. Compared to 10 years prior to the tsunami, household incomes from fishing activities fell from 8000–10,000 rupees/week to a mere 1000 rupees/week after the tsunami (Kumaran and Negi 2006, p. 382). Given the high population density along the Tamil Nadu coastline, the bulk of the damage was within half a kilometer from the high tide line (HTL). Settlements along the coastal belts of South India are vulnerable to natural disasters (cyclones, floods, and earthquakes/tsunamis).

The first survey was administered face-to-face in the local language Tamil, between May and July of 2005, to 1000 households, randomly selected from 16 coastal villages. The selection of villages was based on information provided by the NGO Coordination and Resource Centre set up in the Nagapattinam District Collectorate's office, which had identified 81 coastal villages as being severely impacted by the tsunami and requiring relief aid. The size of the resulting sample of 1000 was proportionate to the number of households in each of the 16 coastal villages. The interview schedule was designed to obtain detailed information on the structural characteristics of the dwellings in a manner consistent with the building materials used in India for floorings, roofing, and walls (see Arlikatti et al. 2010; Arlikatti and Andrew 2012, for a detailed enumeration). In the summer of 2008, the survey instrument from 2005 was used again in seven coastal villages with a few additional questions to gauge respondents' perceptions of household and community recovery generating useable responses from 558 respondents (only seven of the 16 coastal villages from the 2005 sample were selected for this longitudinal panel study due to funding limitations).

Based on the 2005 and 2008 responses, the quality of pre- and post-tsunami core housing unit designs were analyzed and mean differences in the size of homes and number of rooms captured. Further, the percentage change in the types of building materials used and household amenities acquired since the tsunami were computed, to demonstrate changes that might have occurred before and after the tsunami. That is, a difference of means test was conducted to analyze the differences in perceptions between beneficiaries of owner-driven in-situ reconstruction and donor-driven housing resettlement efforts.

In the winter of 2011, the research team made a final visit to all seven villages to note the physical changes 7 years since the tsunami and speak informally to the residents to get their opinion about their homes, neighborhoods, and livelihoods. It was important to gauge whether the beneficiaries of various housing programs—owner-driven *in situ* and donor-driven resettled housing had adapted to their new environment over time or if there was discontent over certain aspects of the rebuilding process. This could provide an additional qualitative understanding of ways to improve building design and performance to inform decision making in the future. The findings from the data analyses and these conversations are summarized below.

12.4 FINDINGS AND DISCUSSION

12.4.1 Assessment of Post-Tsunami Core Housing Units: Perceptions of Physical and Spatial Issues

Our findings based on the 2005 and 2008 datasets suggest that there are marked differences in the types of building materials used in the construction of core housing units prior to the tsunami and in post-tsunami rebuilding, with most changes reflecting improvements (see Table 12.1). For example, in 2004 prior to the tsunami, about 33.1% of homes used poor/weak materials building materials for floors but only 14.9% did so in 2008. The percentage increase of 32.8 households using reinforced concrete slabs or tiles as roofing material considered as strong materials, and the reduction of 33.4% households using poor/weak roofing materials such as grass/thatch/bamboo is indeed notable.

Prior to the tsunami, the average size of a home was 506 square feet but this decreased significantly to approximately 369 square feet in newly constructed post-tsunami housing because of the stipulations of the Tamil Nadu State Government, specifying maximum square footage, number of rooms, cost of housing, and selection of one of five standardized house plans. This was to maintain equity among beneficiaries irrespective of which aid organization was executing the construction. However, a majority of the homes constructed post-tsunami have at least one bedroom and a toilet within the house unlike in pre-tsunami conditions.

Although beneficiaries of the donor-driven resettlement housing programs agreed that they were safer inland, those involved in fishing expressed chagrin at the increased distances from the ocean. Villagers that did not own boats and worked as day laborers for larger boat owners said they wasted time and money going back and forth from their homes to the ocean front using public transport. This resulted in a lot of missed opportunities for day labor. Furthermore, all new settlements had houses laid out on a grid-iron street pattern with symmetrical rows and a compact plan, changing the landscape of traditional villages. It was believed that a cluster arrangement for the neighborhoods would have functioned better allowing for common open spaces to gather for religious practices, drying fish,

TABLE 12.1
Percentage Change in Building Materials Used Pre- and Post-Tsunami, $N = 558$

Elements of the Building and Materials	Before Tsunami 2004	3-1/2 Years after Tsunami 2008	% Change
Flooring			
Strong-cement/mosaic tiles	64.3	82.3	17.9
Medium-stone/brick	1.2	1.4	0.9
Poor/weak-mud/bamboo/wood	33.1	14.9	−18.2
Wall			
Strong-concrete/stone/burnt bricks	58.4	79.9	21.5
Medium-wood/unburnt brick/mud/metal	34.1	11	−22.9
Poor/weak-plastic sheet/glass/thatch	7	9	1.2
Roof			
Strong-concrete slab/roof tiles/slate	29	62.4	32.8
Medium-corrugated metal sheets	8.9	7.2	−0.1
Poor/weak-grass/thatch/polythene	87.8	36.6	−33.4

Source: From Arlikatti, S. and Andrew, S. A. 2012. *Natural Hazards Review*, Volume 13(1), 2012, 34–44, Table number 3. With permission from American Society of Civil Engineers.

Note: The shaded portions highlight the positive percentage change suggesting that more homes are being constructed of stronger and improved building materials.

and/or congregating for leisure activities. Similar views have been expressed by other rural communities in India (Barenstein and Leeman 2012). These new homes were perceived to be too small and rather inappropriate for the large extended families that is the norm in these coastal villages. They were designed with a nuclear family in mind, a rather urban centric approach, causing families to break up (see Figure 12.1).

The major task of rebuilding and reconstructing new homes was assigned by the Tamil Nadu State Government to domestic and international NGOs (Government Order Ms. 25). These organizations were asked to comply with the coastal regulation one (CRZ) notification of 1991 and Government Order Ms. 172, stating that all state government-sponsored houses would be constructed (with appropriate compensations) 200 m beyond the HTL (Government of Tamil Nadu 2005a,b). The new homes are built on stable foundations with settlements situated as close to coastal waterways wherever possible for easy access to the ocean. Large openings on the ocean side of the home have been avoided and every home has an external open staircase to access the roof and terrace floor for vertical evacuation. Efforts have also been made to plant casuarina trees in a few villages along the coastlines to serve as natural bioshields from wind and surge.

Through the informal conversations at the seven villages in 2011, three common concerns emerged—firstly, complaints about the poor quality of construction; secondly, disappointment that the government or NGOs had not returned to

FIGURE 12.1 Tarred roads, individual plots, earthquake and tsunami resistant housing, electricity, water, and sewage system provided in donor-driven resettlement housing. (Photo credit: Dr. Sudha Arlikatti, 2008.)

help with required repairs; and thirdly, the difficulties in pursuing fishing-related livelihoods. Residents were frustrated with the leaking concrete roofs in all the new housing units. They believed that the contractors had used poor quality cement which had led to the erosion of the steel reinforcing bars in the concrete slab due to weathering from the salty ocean breeze. This has caused the progressive disintegration of the roofs and severe leakages during the monsoons (see Figure 12.2).

Villagers also expressed frustrations at their inability to repair homes themselves as they were unfamiliar with modern construction materials and techniques. In the past, replacing their traditional thatched roofs was both easy and cheap and often free due to the availability of palm fronds. Those homes were also more comfortable and suited to the hot and humid climate and kept cooler. Surprisingly, they expressed their disappointment at the local government and NGOs that had rebuilt their homes for not returning to their villages on a regular basis to repair cracks and leaks and other problems that had developed in their housing units over the years. It was evident that households with higher incomes had added extensions to their homes and preferred the use of locally available building materials (see Figure 12.3).

Consistent with the literature (Lizarralde et al. 2010), this suggests that during the rebuilding phase, local government agencies need to provide technical guidance on repair and maintenance of homes to beneficiary rural communities unfamiliar with new disaster resilient building materials and designs. Such an effort can ensure "buy-in" and increase satisfaction amongst recipients. The best way to achieve true community resilience requires coordinated planning. Monitoring NGOs and private

FIGURE 12.2 Eroding of steel reinforcing bars in concrete roofs causes severe leakages, highlighting lack of government monitoring of contractors hired by NGOs. (Photo credit: Dr. Simon A. Andrew, 2011.)

contractors charged with these rebuilding efforts is also essential to maintain the standards of construction. The use of traditional and modern approaches together should be encouraged such that local resources including local craftsmen and artisans should be invited and trained by the government to use modern building materials (Andrew and Arlikatti 2014).

FIGURE 12.3 Roofs for house extensions are made of locally available thatch (of dried palm leaves) that are easy to repair and replace, preventing leakage problems during the rains. (Photo credit: Dr. Simon A. Andrew, 2011.)

12.4.2 Assessments of Housing Programs

The 2008 dataset was analyzed to determine the differences in owner-driven (give material and technical assistance to rebuild by themselves) and donor-driven (by public–NGO partnerships) housing approaches, the size of the home in 2008, damage to home from the tsunami in 2004, cash received for the replacement of household assets (in Indian Rupees), distance of home from the HTL and percentage of female, children, and elderly in the household. The data were aggregated or indices created and analyzed. Of the 558 longitudinal panel respondents, only 330 households were identified as being beneficiaries of either the donor-assisted resettlement program ($N = 138$) or owner-driven in-situ housing program ($N = 192$), respectively. About 8% of the households identified themselves as scheduled caste, 5% as backward caste, and 87% as the most-backward caste. While 16% of households worked as agricultural laborers or farmers, most of them were directly involved in fishing activities (47% boat owners and 34% laborers).

Based on the 2005 and 2008 datasets, findings suggest that beneficiaries of in-situ housing (owner-driven) tended to have larger homes (~413 square feet) but reported having received less aid for replacement of household assets such as radios, television sets, telephones, bicycles, and scooters. On the other hand, beneficiaries of the resettlement programs (donor driven) had smaller homes (~377 square feet).

To further understand how such housing arrangements and associated changes to the physical infrastructure, access to work, medical services, public safety, and aesthetics of a village might affect survivors' perceptions of household and community recovery, a chi-square analysis was conducted.

It is evident that a greater number of beneficiaries of the owner-driven in-situ housing repair, rebuilding, and retrofitting programs perceived easy access to employment, schooling, and medical services. On the other hand, about 47% of beneficiaries of the resettlement program perceived an increase in the distance to their place of employment. This was because those who lived within 200 m of the HTL were moved inland, thereby impacting the livelihoods of 87% family members involved directly or indirectly in the fisheries industry.

However, 75% did note they had better access to potable water closer to homes, 58% noted better sewage facilities, and 66% noted an improvement in their sense of safety from being relocated away from the ocean (see Table 12.2). Since titles of new homes were assigned to husband and wife (as per G.O. Ms. 172 and 774) (see Government of Tamil Nadu 2005a, 2007), the resettlement housing program provided an opportunity for young couples with children to own a home further inland where earlier they could not and also allowed women to be home owners for the first time (see Figure 12.1).

The current literature (Andrew et al. 2013; Andrew and Arlikatti 2014) suggests that a laissez faire policy on structural rebuilding following a disaster is not a sustainable solution. It will only make things worse in the short and long term for all citizens. It is important to acknowledge that post-disaster reconstruction in developing countries has experienced a shift from donor-driven approaches to owner-driven approaches (Barenstein 2010). However, when touting the benefits of the self-built or owner-driven approach, one must be cautious and acknowledge that such an

TABLE 12.2
Differences in Perceptions of Infrastructure and Quality of Services between Beneficiaries of In Situ Housing (*N* = 192) and Resettlement Housing (*N* = 138) in 2008

	Beneficiaries of...			
	In-Situ Assistance	**Resettlement Housing**	χ^2	*P*
Infrastructure				
Water supply				
Yes	127 (66.1)	104 (75.4)		
No	65 (33.9)	34 (24.6)	3.25*	0.046
Sewage systems				
Yes	41 (21.4)	58 (42.0)		
No	151 (78.6)	80 (58.0)	16.34**	0.000
Access to Services				
Schools				
Yes	174 (90.6)	106 (76.8)		
No	18 (9.4)	32 (23.3)	11.92**	0.001
Medical clinics				
Yes	90 (46.9)	47 (34.1)		
No	102 (53.1)	91 (65.9)	5.43*	0.020
Increased distance from Work				
Yes	65 (33.9)	65 (47.1)		
No	127 (66.1)	73 (52.9)	5.90*	0.015
Public Safety				
General sense of public safety				
Yes	106 (55.2)	91 (65.9)		
No	86 (44.8)	47 (34.1)	3.85*	0.05
Aesthetics				
More trees				
Yes	52 (27.1)	16 (11.6)		
No	140 (72.9)	122 (88.4)	11.77**	0.00

Source: Reprinted with permission from Springer Nature: *Journal of Housing and the Built Environment*, The effect of housing assistance arrangements on household recovery: An empirical test of donor-assisted and owner-driven approaches, Volume 28, no. 1, 2013, 17–34, Andrew, S. A., S. Arlikatti, L. C. Long, and J. M. Kendra, Table number 2, p. 27.

Note: We excluded from our final analyses, the perception of households regarding roads, electricity coverage, neighborhood crime rate, cleanliness/hygiene, and beauty, in order to conserve space. No evidence was found to suggest beneficiaries' experiences were markedly different on these aspects of built environments at the conventional statistical levels. Percentages in parentheses.

*$p \leq 0.05$ and **$p \leq 0.01$.

arrangement in itself may not be sufficient to assist the recovery process of households. As Barakat (2003, p. 33) pointed out rightly, this alternative is only "possible when labor is available, housing design is relatively simple, communities have a tradition of self-building and there are no strict time pressures."

12.4.3 Lessons Learned for Post-Disaster Rural Housing Policy

Firstly, based on past policy implementation experiences from other studies, the rural poor do not appear to understand or trust the government's efforts at trying to rebuild stronger and keep them safe (Kumaran and Negi 2006; Barenstein 2010). Government initiated housing projects are often perceived to be rushed and biased and without a thought to the loss of established traditional livelihoods. The balancing act that the government has to play can get tricky. It behooves the public sector and relief organizations to be more transparent and inclusive of community members in the design, planning, and site selection process. A caveat to this is that perceptions of distrust are found to vary depending upon recipients' socioeconomic status, gender, caste, age, and livelihood. Hence, efforts need to be inclusive of minority special needs populations who traditionally have been inadequately represented (Andrew and Arlikatti 2014).

Secondly, depending on the nature and geographical scope of disaster damage, relocation and rebuilding projects by public–nonprofit (local and international) agencies are guided by the principles of sustainable land-use practices (e.g., adherence to coastal regulatory zones requiring setback from the HTL). In the long run, this results in patterns of unequal housing development between those receiving housing assistance and those that do not. An unintended consequence of such rebuilding projects is the production of unequal distribution of post-disaster improved public housing. Consequently, rebuilding after major natural disasters in India has reinforced pre-existing social imbalances across regions as observed after the 2000 Gujarat earthquake (Barenstein 2010) and the 2004 Indian Ocean tsunami (Arlikatti et al. 2010). While the immediate provision of housing assistance following a disaster is crucial for effecting recovery, there is the potential risk of ignoring pre-disaster problems of shortage of quality housing for marginalized groups and putting them at even more risk from future threats.

Thirdly, we observed that the current post-disaster housing projects are implemented piecemeal and continue to focus on structural improvements rather than taking an integrated regional planning approach guided by disaster mitigation principles and practices. The focus is often on improving housing design, making them disaster resistant such as including an external staircase so that residents can use it to evacuate vertically in the event of surge from tsunami or floods and better building codes and materials. Such a focus on housing as a physical system fails to recognize that housing is also a living system of people from different socioeconomic, caste, religious, and cultural backgrounds coexisting together. Subsequently, the current approach puts less emphasis on community-level design, social development activities, and education on sustainable policies. Alternatively, where public–nonprofit partnerships have integrated members of the beneficiary communities into planning efforts, they have met with success in developing disaster-resistant communities while adopting vernacular architecture and designs and local building practices (Barenstein and Leeman 2012).

Finally, scarcity of rural public housing continues to be a problem in India forcing socioeconomically backward households to settle in forestlands or as nomads in squatter settlements, with substandard housing and no *pattar* or land titles. The problems these households face during disasters is multifold. There is an urgency to shift the focus of housing policies and programs from a post-disaster response and recovery orientation to one of long-term disaster mitigation and development. Although there appears to be an impetus by the MoRD to fund construction and greening of rural India under its current Five-Year Plan, what is lacking is, underscoring the need to include both structural and nonstructural disaster mitigation goals as part of the housing agenda during normal times.

In other words, we can no longer talk about providing public housing without talking about sustainable land-use planning, coastal regulations, zoning, and site selection in safe locales so that residents are safe from natural (floods, landslides, and earthquakes) and technological (chemical/nuclear plants) hazards. This must include building education and awareness, and the blending of traditional building techniques with modern technologies. In addition, design experts and engineers need to constantly come up with innovative design alternatives that marry traditional eco-friendly alternatives that are hazard resistant, but cost effective, and easy to build by the locals without over dependence on expensive materials and technology.

12.5 CONCLUSIONS

This chapter adds to the extant literature on post-disaster rural housing recovery by analyzing the physical improvements to housing and perceptions of recovery in seven coastal villages in South India following the 2004 Indian Ocean tsunami. Publications like *Hazard Mitigation: Integrating Best Practices into Planning*, edited by James C. Schwab (2010), published under the joint auspices of the American Planning Association and the Federal Emergency Management Agency, underscore the concerted efforts underway in major US cities and towns toward resiliency planning. Other scholars have suggested that city planners seek out both public and private sector entities to initiate joint disaster planning efforts to combat the spread of infectious diseases (Matthew and McDonald 2006) and the myriad challenges of effecting long-term recovery after a hurricane (Olshansky and Johnson 2010). Unfortunately, most of these studies are concentrated on cities in the developed countries of the world. Similar conversations need to be had in recognizing that prevention and preparation for these threats need to receive attention in rural communities of developing and underdeveloped countries as well. It is vital that architects and community planners work with the public, private, and the nonprofit sector groups that play a role in post-disaster recovery and rebuilding initiatives.

Land-use planning and rural housing programs with greening and sustainable development goals can serve as a vital instrument for mitigating against future threats if they allow for an active involvement of civil society. Such efforts should be cognizant of the role of social networks and livelihood preferences and constraints in rural landscapes, rather than just focusing on structural improvements. It is also vital that support for owner-driven housing programs not be limited to just monetary support but includes technical and design guidance on how rural households can build stronger and safer homes and incorporate resiliency measures beneficial to them. Public sector agencies need to facilitate the training of local masons and artisans in the use of modern materials and also have mechanisms in place (checks and balances) to oversee the work of private contractors and builders.

Alternatively, where donor-assisted resettlement packages are offered to keep the recipients out of harm's way, emphasis should be on explaining the CRZ ordinances to the rural populace in simple, easy to understand terms convincing them that relocation is for their safety and in no way a reflection of biases along the lines of caste or class. Equally important is to learn from the challenges that resettled households continue to face and also the manner in which monetary and technical resources are procured, distributed, and monitored by partnering entities. An understanding of community culture and social interactions when resettling whole villages is vital for their psychosocial recovery. The design of a home to meet the needs of a nuclear family, clearly an urban concept, needs investigation especially in communities with extended families. It is important to plan with the people in designing disaster resilient homes that cater to family needs without dividing them or alternatively create community spaces that can help foster and maintain social connections.

ACKNOWLEDGMENTS

This work was supported by a grant from the National Science Foundation (BCS0523041) and the Hispanic and Global Studies Initiative Fund from the University of North Texas. Any opinions, findings, and conclusions or recommendations expressed in this chapter are those of the authors and do not necessarily reflect the views of the National Science Foundation or the University of North Texas. We also extend our appreciation to the villagers and government officials of Nagapattinam District in South India who took the time to respond to our surveys so willingly, in 2005 and 2008; and to Drs. Walter Gillis Peacock and Carla S. Prater for initiating this research in 2005 and Drs. Himanshu Grover and Arul S. Gnana Sekar who were part of the research team then.

REFERENCES

Andrew, S. A. and S. Arlikatti. 2014. Public–private partnerships in disaster housing recovery: An examination of housing development approaches in India. In: Kapucu, N. and K. T. Liou (eds), *Disaster and Development: Examining Global Issues and Cases*, New York: Springer, 351–69.

Andrew, S. A., S. Arlikatti, L. Long, and J. Kendra. 2013. The effect of housing assistance arrangements on household recovery: An empirical test of donor-assisted and owner-driven approaches. *Journal of Housing and the Built Environment*, 28:17–34.

Arlikatti, S. and S. A. Andrew. 2012. Housing design and long-term recovery processes in the aftermath of the 2004 Indian Ocean tsunami. *Natural Hazards Review*, 13(1): 34–44.

Arlikatti, S., W. G. Peacock, C. S. Prater, H. Grover, and A. S. G. Sekar. 2010. Assessing the impact of the Indian Ocean tsunami on households: The modified domestic assets approach. *Disasters*, 34(3): 705–31.

Athavankar, A., S. Banerjee, B. K. Chakravarthy, and U. Athavankar. 2013. Conflicts in the idea of "assisted self-help" in housing for the Indian rural poor. In *International Conference on Research into Design conference proceedings*. http://www.academia.edu/13241519/Conflicts_in_the_Idea_of_Assisted_Self-Help_in_Housing_for_the_Indian_Rural_Poor (accessed January 18, 2016).

Banerjee, A. and L. Iyer. 2005. History, institutions, and economic performance: The legacy of Colonial land tenure systems in India. *American Economic Review*, 95(4): 1190–1213.

Barakat, S. 2003. Housing reconstruction after conflict and disaster. Humanitarian Practice Network Paper No. 43. London: Overseas Development Institute.

Barenstein, J. D. 2010. Who governs reconstruction? Changes and continuity in policies, practices and outcomes. In: Lizarralde, G., C. Johnson, and C. Davidson (eds), *Rebuilding after Disasters from Emergency to Sustainability*, New York: Spon Press, 149–76.

Barenstein, J. D. and E. Leeman (eds) 2012. *Post-Disaster Reconstruction and Change: Communities' Perspectives*. Boca Raton, Florida: CRC Press, Taylor & Francis.

Bates, F. L. and W. Peacock. 1993. *Living Conditions, Disasters and Development: An Approach to Cross-Cultural Comparisons*. Athens, Georgia: University Georgia of Press.

Census of India 2001. Census-2001 Data Summary, District Profile. http://www.censusindia.gov.in/2011-common/CensusDataSummary.html (accessed February 12, 2016).

Government of Tamil Nadu. 2005a. Government Order (Ms.) 25, issued January 13, 2005, Revenue (NC.III) Department.

Government of Tamil Nadu. 2005b. Government Order (Ms.) 172, issued March 30, 2005, Revenue (NC.III) Department.

Government of Tamil Nadu. 2007. Government Order (Ms.) No. 774, issued December 27, 2007, Revenue (NC.IV.2) Department.

Haas J. E., R. W. Kates, and M. J. Bowden. 1977. *Reconstruction Following Disaster*. Cambridge, Massachusetts: MIT Press.

Kennedy, J., J. Ashmore, E. Babister, and I. Kelman. 2008. The meaning of "build back better": Evidence from post-tsunami Aceh and Sri Lanka. *Journal of Contingencies and Crisis Management*, 16(1): 24–36.

Kumaran, T. V. and E. Negi. 2006. Experiences of rural and urban communities in Tamil Nadu in the aftermath of 2004 tsunami, learning from urban disasters: Planning for resilient cities. *Built Environment*, 32(4): 375–86.

Lizarralde, G., C. Johnson, and C. Davidson. 2010. *Rebuilding after Disasters: From Emergency to Sustainability*. New York: Spon Press.

Matthew, R. A. and B. McDonald. 2006. Cities under siege: Urban planning and the threat of infectious disease. *Journal of the American Planning Association*, 72(1): 109–17.

Ofori, G. 2008. Construction in developing nations: Towards increased resilience to disasters. In: Bosher, L. S. (ed.), *Hazards and the Built Environment: Attaining Built-in Resilience*, London: Taylor and Francis, 39–66.

Olshansky, R. B. and L. A. Johnson. 2010. *Clear as Mud: Planning for the Rebuilding of New Orleans*. Washington, DC: American Planning Association, Planners Press.

Peacock, W. G., C. D. Killian, and F. L. Bates. 1987. The effects of disaster damage and housing aid on household recovery following the 1976 Guatemalan earthquake. *International Journal of Mass Emergencies and Disasters*, 5(1): 63–88.

Planning Commission, Government of India. 2011. Working Group on Rural Housing for XII Five Year Plan. http://planningcommission.gov.in/aboutus/committee/wrkgrp12/rd/wgrep_iay.pdf (accessed October, 2015).

Prater, C. S., W. G. Peacock, S. Arlikatti, and H. Grover. 2006. Social capacity in Nagapattinam, Tamil Nadu after the December 2004 Great Sumatra earthquake and tsunami. *Earthquake Spectra*, 22(S3): S715–29.

Schwab, J. C. 2010. *Hazard Mitigation: Integrating Best Practices into Planning*. Washington, DC: American Planning Association.

Singh, G. and P. K. Das. 1995. Building castles in air: Housing scheme for Bombay's slum-dwellers. *Economic and Political Weekly*, 30(40): 2477–81.

UNDP India. 2012. Greening Rural Development in India. http://www.rural.nic.in/sites/downloads/NewReleases/Greening_RD_Report.pdf (accessed October 14, 2014).

Zhang, Y. and W. G. Peacock. 2009. Planning for housing recovery? Lessons learned from hurricane Andrew. *Journal of the American Planning Association*, 76(1): 5–24.

13 Planning for Housing Recovery after the 2008 Wenchuan Earthquake in China

Yang Zhang and William Drake

CONTENTS

13.1 INTRODUCTION

The catastrophic Magnitude 8.0 Wenchuan earthquake in China on May 12, 2008 and subsequent recovery presents a unique case of large-scale housing recovery. Housing recovery is arguably the most important aspect of post-disaster recovery (Zhang and Peacock 2010; Peacock et al. 2015). Housing is not only the shelter and primary investment of most residents; it is also a critical component of the local economy and social fabric (Comerio 1998; Campanella 2006). Housing recovery in particular is different from development under normal conditions (Inam 2005; Berke and Campanella 2006; Olshansky and Chang 2009). It can be best characterized as a "compression of development activities in time and in a limited space" (Olshansky et al. 2012, p. 173) which stated simply, means that planning and development happen at a much faster pace and at a much higher level of intensity during disaster recovery. However, swift action can often come at the cost of effectiveness and equity. Therefore, recovery planning also requires careful deliberation, which is usually accomplished by adopting a participatory approach to ensure that recovery decisions capture the diversity of local needs and that they incorporate invaluable local resources and knowledge.

Disaster recovery "time compression" has serious implications for participatory planning which is often considered to be a time-consuming process (Innes 2004; Maginn 2007). Recovery is a time of upheaval and change: new groups emerge in the community (Berke et al. 1993; Nelson et al. 2007; Aldrich 2010), new conflicts emerge while old ones are revived (Tierney 2001; Abrams et al. 2004) and new, "improving" ideas are considered and some old ones discarded (Schwab 1998; Godschalk 2003). There also tends to be an influx of nonlocal organizations, all clamoring to help (Quarantelli 1999), and an overall heightened sense of activism even among usually marginalized groups (Aldrich 2010).

Disaster recovery can also be a time of positive change particularly if citizens are empowered or if there are opportunities for increased and meaningful participation. Insufficient government capacity to provide information, solve problems, and provide resources during recovery could also increase demands by citizens for more resources and information. The quest for information and certainty and a shared sense of urgency in the impacted community can increase stakeholder activism (Nelson et al. 2007; Aldrich 2010), and governments may become more receptive to citizen participation during recovery. They need to mobilize citizens and stakeholders and using their networks could be an effective way to accomplish gathering intelligence from a breadth of sources, generate new ideas, and to verify and transmit accurate and timely information in a rapidly changing environment (e.g., Goodchild and Glennon 2010).

The rest of the chapter is organized as follows. We first provide an account of the impact and significance of the Wenchuan earthquake. Next, we describe our data collection procedures and the methodology employed for analysis. In subsequent sections, we review the recovery planning process and provide an assessment of housing recovery in the earthquake area. We then present a case study on housing recovery in two neighborhoods in the city of Dujiangyan. Finally, we discuss the conclusions and propose several lessons learned from this research.

13.2 THE 2008 WENCHUAN EARTHQUAKE

The Magnitude 8.0 May 12, 2008 Wenchuan earthquake was the most severe earthquake disaster in China since the 1976 Great Tangshan earthquake (see Figure 13.1) and was one of the world's most damaging earthquake disasters in recent decades. The earthquake affected an overall area of 193,051 square miles, of which 50,193 square miles (about the size of the State of Louisiana in the United States) were severely damaged (China State Council 2008a). The quake claimed over 69,000 lives and forced the temporary displacement of more than 15 million people (China State Council 2008a). Direct economic losses inflicted by the earthquake were estimated to be well over USD130 billion* (China State Council 2008a). Although the earthquake directly impacted a vast area covering 10 provinces, Sichuan province suffered the most severe damage. Overall, 76% of the counties in this province was declared damaged by the earthquake (China State Council 2008a).

* An exchange rate of 1 USD = 6.8 RMB was used in this paper.

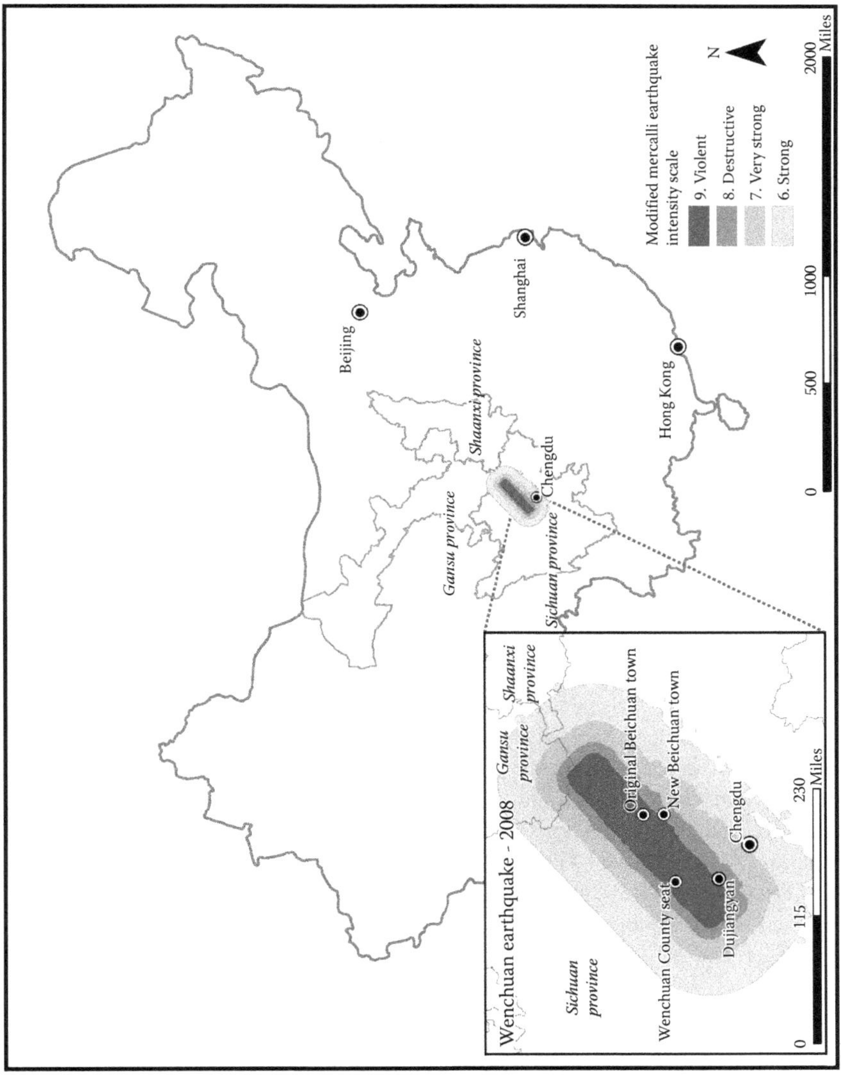

FIGURE 13.1 Location and intensity distribution of the 2008 Wenchuan earthquake in China.

About 42.8% of the total monetary damage was to housing, while infrastructure and industrial damage each accounted for about one-fifth of the total damage cost (China State Council 2008b). In Sichuan province alone, the earthquake damaged 648.0 million square meters of urban and rural residences, and directly affected 5.6 million households; this amounted to about 39% of the total urban housing stock in the disaster area and about 86.1% of the rural housing located in the severely damaged counties (China State Council 2008b).

13.2.1 Data Collection and Methodology

Our first goal is to present an overview of the planning effort by the Chinese government after the earthquake and the overall housing recovery in Sichuan Province. We relied primarily on government documents, recovery plans, annual recovery progress reports, and news reports from the major national newspapers in China. The collected information was analyzed using qualitative content analysis techniques (Marying 2001) to identify the key aspects of housing recovery planning. Specifically, we focused on developing a narrative to describe: (1) post-earthquake decision making for housing recovery; (2) the timeline of developing and approving the recovery plans; and (3) guiding principles for housing reconstruction and recovery.

Our second goal is to provide an assessment of the housing recovery, both in terms of its speed and its quality. To achieve this goal, we relied primarily on household interviews. We conducted the interviews during the summers of 2010 and 2011, when reconstruction and recovery in Sichuan Province had mostly finished (Sichuan Development and Reform Commission 2010). The semi-structured interviews included questions assessing a household's earthquake damage level, temporary housing, relocation and permanent housing, participation in recovery decision making, experiences with government recovery policies and programs, and overall satisfaction with the speed and quality of recovery. We recruited and trained nine graduate student interviewers from Sichuan University, which is 30 miles from the earthquake's epicenter, to help with the interviews. We targeted students who speak the native dialect in the earthquake area and especially those who experienced the earthquake themselves. In the field, the investigators and graduate students, in two person teams, visited random households in different neighborhoods to interview the homeowners. After each site visit, the team first entered the interviews into a standardized Excel spreadsheet, and later translated them from Chinese into English.

We interviewed 318 households in Sichuan Province. These included 278 interviews in 2011 and 40 in 2012. These households came from nine towns in three different counties—Beichuan, Dujiangyan, and Wenchuan. All experienced devastating or extensive damage during the earthquake. The locations were chosen to capture the range of urban and rural recovery issues. Three towns are within the urban area of the city of Dujiangyan, and the other six are in the surrounding rural area. The rural towns were selected to capture the varied approach to housing recovery. Four are new towns that were relocated from their pre-earthquake locations and the other two are towns that were rebuilt in their original locations.

Our third goal is to present a detailed case study of the housing recovery planning in two inner-city neighborhoods that experienced severe damage in the city of

Dujiangyan. This case study consisted of semi-structured interviews with city planning officials and residents, field observations, minutes of community meetings, and collection of relevant recovery policy and plan documents. We also interviewed a total of 11 people, including three neighborhood association leaders, five residents, and one city planning official, to gather their perceptions about citywide recovery issues and the recovery of the two particular neighborhoods included in this case study during our field research in July 2011 and July 2012. With this information, we used qualitative content analysis techniques described by Marying (2001) to identify stakeholders and interest groups in the recovery planning process; emerging interests, and conflicts between stakeholders; and the subsequent planning response. Qualitative content analysis techniques are well suited to analyzing the "manifest" (obvious) and "latent" (contextually driven, nuanced) content of texts (Marying 2001; Kohlbacher 2005). It is highly reflexive and adaptable to the context, and therefore especially suited to examining complex and evolving phenomena such as housing recovery. Research findings are reported using a narrative style.

13.2.2 Post-Earthquake (Housing) Recovery Planning

Within hours of the initial earthquake impact, the State Council set up the Headquarters for Wenchuan Earthquake Response and Relief. Nine action groups were formed to focus on different aspects of disaster response and relief (for a detailed review, see Zhang et al. Forthcoming). The National Development and Reform Commission (NDRC)* was tasked to lead the recovery planning group. Supporting agencies included the Ministry of Housing and Urban–Rural Development, three provincial governments in the affected areas, and 38 state-level entities.

The planning group first prepared a plan for managing the planning process. The *Work Plan for the National Wenchuan Earthquake Recovery Planning* (hereafter the *Work Plan*) was approved and officially issued by the headquarters on June 1, 2008. The *Work Plan* postulated the tasks, organizational structure and responsibilities, and timeline of the recovery planning in order to "streamline the recovery planning activities at different levels of government," and to "achieve better and faster post-earthquake recovery" (NDRC 2008, p. 1). It also mandated that "counties and cities in the earthquake area shall only develop recovery plans for their jurisdictions according to the national plans" (NDRC 2008, p. 2).

Following the issuance of the *Work Plan*, planning progressed largely within the set framework and timeline. The *National Master Plan for the Wenchuan Earthquake Recovery and Redevelopment* (hereafter, the *Master Plan*) was approved by the State Council on August 27, 2008. The *Master Plan* defined eight recovery principles and six objectives, and set a 3-year goal to finish the recovery.

---

* NDRC was the former State Planning Commission that directed the national development goals during the Planned Economy era in China. Today, NDRC remains the key institution that defines national development strategies and policies, including mid-to-long range planning for economic and social development, financial, investment, currency, and land policies. NDRC was a logical selection to lead the state recovery plan because in essence, recovery planning is similar to the routine 5-year state development plans made by NDRC.

One of the overarching recovery principles was the adjustment of development intensity based on a scientific assessment of the region's ecological capacity and hazard risk. The entire disaster region was divided into three recovery priority areas: (1) suitable for intense development, (2) suitable for modest development, and (3) restricted for development. The plan prescribed that pre-earthquake development patterns would be adjusted based on this new delineation of recovery area prioritization. Towns and villages located in areas not suitable for intensive development were proposed for relocation or significant downsizing. Another main objective set forth in the *Master Plan* was to use the recovery as an opportunity to expedite urbanization and industrialization of the impact area. The *Master Plan* identified housing as the highest recovery priority. It not only placed great focus on housing recovery speed, but also emphasized hazard mitigation and structural safety in the housing sector. Since the vast proportion of the disaster region was rural, the plan specifically directed that rural housing recovery should be modeled after the Socialist New Villages.*

13.2.3 Recovery Plan for Urban and Rural Housing

After the passage of the *Master Plan*, 10 specialized recovery plans† were developed and approved in the remaining months of 2008. The *Specialized Plan for Urban and Rural Housing* (hereafter, *the Housing Recovery Plan*), approved by the State Council on October 6, 2008, listed four objectives for housing recovery. These included a 3-year target to complete the transition to permanent housing, improved building standards for all new or retrofitted structures, improved neighborhood design standards, and improved infrastructure and public facilities. The plan specified yearly recovery goals for both rural and urban housing for the entire disaster area and also included detailed housing unit goals for each individual county. The estimated total cost for housing recovery was 273 billion RMB (USD 40 billion, 2008 value) including 213.6 billion RMB for building new housing units, 41.7 RMB billion for repairing and retrofitting existing structures, 9.3 RMB billion for public facilities, and 8.4 billion RMB for open space. As for implementation strategies, the plan prescribed a set of policies to facilitate housing recovery. This included grants from the central and provincial governments, government-backed commercial loans,

---

* The Socialist New Village is a neighborhood design model recommended by the Chinese national government in 2005 to reconfigure traditional rural villages. This design model primarily involves the physical "rationalization" of village environments and the modernization of infrastructure (for a detailed discussion about the rationale and policy details of the Socialist New Village, please see Guang 2010). Although the policy did not intend to threaten traditional family farms and the rural lifestyle, this has often been the outcome, because Socialist New Villages' high-density, clustered urban-style development pattern is an unwelcome change from traditional low-density, scattered rural development and housing.

† The 10 specialized recovery plans include: Public Service Facilities Recovery Specialized Plan, Urban and Rural Housing Recovery Specialized Plan, Land Use Recovery Specialized Plan, Infrastructure Recovery Specialized Plan, Industry Recovery Specialized Plan, Ecological System Recovery Specialized Plan, City/Town System Recovery Specialized Plan, Rural Area Recovery Specialized Plan, Public Service Facilities Recovery Specialized Plan, Disaster Prevention and Hazards Mitigation Specialized Plan.

innovative land-based financing tools, tax reductions or exemptions, streamlined permit and development procedures, and favorable or relaxed loan terms.

It should be noted that the planning after the Wenchuan earthquake was never a linear process with events proceeding in orderly sequence. In fact, while the organizational structure for developing recovery plans at the national level gradually took shape after the earthquake, many localities moved ahead with their own planning and recovery projects. For a brief period, recovery planning could have best been characterized as sets of parallel activities occurring at all levels of governments. Once national plans became available, local plans that were already underway had to be reconciled to fit the national plans. The reconciliation of national recovery plans and principles with local plans and implementation strategies was complicated in some cases because of local resistance to national policies (e.g., Chandrasekhar et al. 2015).

Overall, the transition to permanent housing after the initial emergency sheltering and then the temporary housing phase largely followed the schedule put forth in *the Master Plan* and *the Housing Recovery Plan*. When looking at the allocation of recovery funding, housing was the clear priority, especially in the early recovery period (as seen in Table 13.1). By the end of 2009, roughly 1.5 years after the earthquake, 91.75% of the budgeted funding for permanent housing had been allocated. It was the highest among all sectors. During that period, 1,391,000 rural houses were newly constructed, and 2,285,600 were repaired. In urban areas, 169,900 new houses

TABLE 13.1
Recovery Budgets and Realized Funding Following the Wenchuan Earthquake[a]

		Realized Funding			
Funding Areas	**Budget**	**12/31/2009**	**%**	**9/30/2010**	**%**
Urban and rural housing	32,947.3	30,230.3	91.75	31,718.4	96.27
City and town system	13,752.4	5901.9	42.92	9312.4	67.71
Rural area (agricultural) infrastructure	7881.8	7017.5	89.03	7865.6	99.79
Public service facilities	14,128.7	9297.6	65.81	11,830.7	83.74
Infrastructure	39,611.7	15,217.9	38.42	22,118.7	55.84
Industrial reconstruction	20,031.9	16,769.9	83.72	19,680.3	98.24
Market service	3432.5	2216.9	64.59	2821.5	82.20
Disaster prevention and hazards mitigation	2309.1	452.4	19.59	918.4	39.77
Ecosystem recovery	1899	589.0	31.01	938.1	49.40
Land assembly and reclamation	1130.1	312.5	27.65	629.0	55.66
Other	904.9	269.6	29.79	516.9	57.12
Total	138,029.4	88,275.4	63.95	108,349.9	78.50

Data Sources: The Master Plan, The Ten Specialized plans, Recovery Annual Reports 2008–2010.

[a] All values, measured in million USD, are in 2008 constant value. The average exchange rate between USD and Chinese RMB (1 USD = 6.8 RMB) was used to make the conversion. The Consumer Price Index published by the National Bureau of Statistics of China was used to make the 2008 constant value calculation.

were constructed and 1,334,800 were repaired (Sichuan Development and Reform Commission 2010). By September 30, 2010, 4 months after the 2-year anniversary of the earthquake, 96.27% of funding for housing construction was allocated. The transition to permanent housing was almost finished; 99.98% of rural households (3.73 million) and 98.89% of urban households (1.59 million) had moved into permanent housing by then (Sichuan Development and Reform Commission 2011).

13.3 POST-EARTHQUAKE HOUSING RECOVERY: EVALUATION

During the field investigations in July 2010 and June 2011, it was clear that physical reconstruction, particularly housing recovery had progressed at a fast pace in our study area. In July 2010, 2 years after the earthquake, most residents in the areas we visited had completed the transition to permanent housing. The conspicuous blue-roofed pre-fabricated temporary housing was hard to find in places we visited. However, progress was uneven across different communities.

In the Leigu Township in Beichuan County, many residents still resided in a large temporary housing park built alongside the highway. The village residents there indicated that they had disputes with the county government regarding the permanent housing allocation policy. Although housing projects had already finished, residents refused to move in because they felt that the allocation process was not transparent and the units assigned to them were too small. In June 2011, when we revisited this town, the temporary housing park was still there. But the changes that had occurred during the 1-year period since our last visit in 2010 were obvious. Most remaining residents who had resided there a year before had moved out. A lot of temporary housing units were either vacant or in the process of being torn down. A small group of residents, however, still resisted the move because they were not satisfied with the permanent housing units assigned to them.

The feedback from the 318 households we interviewed indicated that residents in the disaster area were mostly satisfied with the physical conditions of their permanent housing. 90.2% (287) of households said that the structural safety of their houses was better or much better than before, 94.7% (301) thought that the exterior appearance of their houses was improved, 84.9% (270) thought the infrastructure was better, and 94% (299) agreed that the transportation accessibility to their houses was better.

While residents' evaluations of the physical conditions of their houses were overwhelmingly positive, many of them, especially the rural residents, expressed negative views about other aspects of housing recovery. For villagers who were relocated into the newly constructed new Socialist Villages, characterized by higher density urban forms of "*modern*" living environments, their major complaint was that their pre-event rural life style, social networks, and traditional sources of income were all disrupted. Traditional rural living in this part of China revolved around small natural villages formed over the long history of the region. In these villages, farmers all lived close to their farmland. The traditional low-density rural houses were not only a place for villagers to live and socialize, but also a place where they grew produce for daily use. However, the concentrated *urban-style* living that emerged after the earthquake disrupted all these things that they had been used to. While most residents were aware of the government's intention to transform rural development and modernize agriculture during the earthquake recovery, they did not feel that their interests were fully considered in this process.

13.3.1 Housing Recovery: A Case Study in the City of Dujiangyan

This case features two inner-city neighborhoods in the city of Dujiangyan located in Chengdu municipality in Sichuan province that were severely damaged by the earthquake (China State Council 2008a). Tension in the neighborhoods was high and the recovery process stalled because condominium homeowners did not collectively buy into the recovery plan prescribed by the government. The rebuilding efforts progressed only after officials changed policies from a building-based approach to a community-based approach. This success was later modeled in another 179 locations across the city and was credited by the government as an important reason for fast recovery.

Dujiangyan has approximately 680,000 inhabitants (including 31,800 urban residents), and is located in the piedmont area of the Longmen mountain range, which borders it to the northwest. The Min River and its six tributaries, exiting from the steep mountain gorges, weave their way through the city area. The Dujiangyan Irrigation System has been diverting water from the Min River to the Chengdu plain almost without interruption since it was constructed in the third century BC (Cao et al. 2010). Only 48 km (about 30 miles) from the Chengdu metropolis, Dujiangyan provides water for the region's dense population and also to a vast area of fertile agricultural land (Cao et al. 2010).

Sitting very close to the fault rupture, Dujiangyan experienced devastating damage when the Wenchuan earthquake struck along the Longmen mountain fault. More than 50% of all buildings and more than 90% of residential buildings in the urban core were severely damaged beyond repair. As we noted earlier, the Chinese national government led the recovery effort and oversaw the swift development of the national earthquake recovery plans. All localities in the impacted area were required to operate in accordance with the national plans, which emphasized rationalistic planning principles, the government's resolve for a speedy physical reconstruction, and its desire to use the earthquake recovery as an opportunity to accelerate pre-existing development goals (China State Council 2008a; Abramson and Qi 2011).

To facilitate the recovery process, the central government paired up well-developed provinces from other parts of country with municipalities in the impacted area to assist with their recovery planning and reconstruction (China State Council 2008b). Under this arrangement, Shanghai and Dujiangyan formed a one-on-one assistance partnership. On June 7, 2008, the Dujiangyan city government entrusted the Shanghai Tongji Urban Planning and Design Institute to develop its "Comprehensive Earthquake Recovery and Redevelopment Plan." Data collected from the interviews indicated that the planning period lasted for months, during which time the planners held 26 input sessions, including 13 with Dujiangyan and Chengdu city officials, nine with township officials in Dujiangyan, and four with national or international planning experts. While it was evident that the planners from Shanghai maintained close communication with the various levels of government throughout the planning process, they had minimal interaction with the general public. For most residents, the first time they got involved in the planning was when the Dujiangyan city government released the final plan in October 2008.

The apparent lack of beneficiary/citizen input into recovery planning processes for Dujiangyan was not unusual within China's planning context (Yeh and Wu 1999; Ma and Wu 2005; Tang et al. 2008). While the balance of stakeholder power in planning has evolved over the recent decade with the 2004 constitutional amendment that recognizes private property rights and the quick emergence of private homeownership (Plummer and Taylor 2004; Abramson 2006), urban planning in China still typically remains a process with little social analysis and stakeholder and citizen input and negotiation. In addition, the Chinese national government's strong authoritarian approach toward recovery following the earthquake overly emphasized recovery speed, scientific planning, and acceleration of development in the impacted area. This created an uninviting political environment for localities/planners to involve citizens in the plan making process.

The official Dujiangyan comprehensive recovery plan embodied the principles of scientific planning and sought to use the earthquake recovery to achieve goals that the city had been already contemplating before the disaster. As a planning official we interviewed put it, "the whole urban core needed to be rebuilt. With the influx of support (from the national, provincial, and Shanghai governments) and favorable policies, it was a golden opportunity for a sweeping urban renewal." One of the most important aspects of the urban renewal in the plan was the reconfiguration of development alongside the long winding river network within the city. The plan highlighted the importance of riverbanks as a means to improve Dujiangyan's greenway system, control river contamination, mitigate flood hazards, and restore the river ecosystem. Based on sophisticated scientific standards for urban river ecosystem health assessment, development setbacks and design standards were stipulated for different river segments within the city boundary. Despite discrepancies in specifics, imposing riverside development controls was not a new idea to Dujiangyan. It had been included in the city's two previous comprehensive plans—the 2003 plan and the 2007 plan—before the earthquake. However, the old plans had grandfathered existing development, but the new plan required recovery projects to follow the rules. This was not a trivial difference because most riverfront land had been developed over Dujiangyan's long history, which meant a large number of pre-existing neighborhoods had to be rezoned and redesigned during reconstruction.

Our case study focused on two adjacent neighborhoods along the Liangma River near the city center of Dujiangyan. Prior to the earthquake (see Figure 13.2), neighborhood A was a middle-class community of families employed at a nearby power plant with 66 households split among three condominium units. The adjacent neighborhood B was a retirement community with 72 households of former government workers living in four condominium units. The earthquake destroyed or severely damaged every building in these two neighborhoods. The initial recovery policies pertaining to this area, prescribed in the city's recovery plan and the supplemental implementation strategies* included: (1) a significant reduction of developable land

* The policy document is the Dujiangyan Urban Housing Recovery Implementation Strategies issued by the Dujiangyan city government.

008-116: section III, clause 1.7).

FIGURE 13.2 Pre-earthquake layout of two neighborhoods in Dujiangyan, Sichuan Province, China. (Created by Yang Zhang and William Drake.)

due to the creation of a riverside green buffer (see Figure 13.2) and (see Figure 13.3) two clauses regarding housing recovery. One stated that, "... (Condominium) owners may apply for the reconstruction permit in their original location with consent from at least 2/3 of homeowners...." The other clause stated, "... owners in unrepairable buildings may choose government housing or a cash buyout ... and ... forfeit their rights to original properties..." (Dujiangyan City Government 2008, pp. 26–27).

Problems quickly emerged after the recovery plan was presented to the public in September 2008. The dispute revolved around two major issues. First, as prescribed by the policy, the reconstruction decision was building based. Property owners in a building had to decide whether to rebuild or to trade/sell to the government. Once the decision was made based on the two-third's (2/3) majority rule, everyone in the same building had to comply, including those who opposed. In neighborhood A, 51 households (77%) initially opted for either the government housing or the cash buyout. Citing socio-economic ties to the area and its riverfront location, the remaining 15 households (23%) chose to stay and vehemently opposed the government policy that they follow the stated two-third's (2/3) majority rule. In neighborhood B, most retirees knew each other and had a very strong attachment to the neighborhood. 59 households (82%) chose to stay and only 13 households (18%) opted for

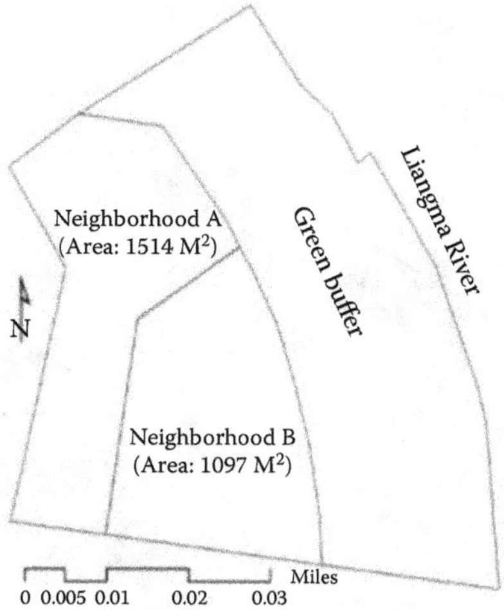

FIGURE 13.3 Initial recovery plan for the neighborhoods in Dujiangyan, Sichuan Province, China. (Created by Yang Zhang and William Drake.)

relocation. The decisions varied across buildings in both neighborhoods and owners swung back and forth between rebuilding and relocation. Second, the recovery plan left insufficient land for rebuilding houses within neighborhood B. The residents accused the government of "stealing their land" and demanded the proposed land use adjustment be reversed. Over the next 3 months, homeowners formed coalitions and tried to sway their neighbors' position so that the recovery could move forward in accordance with the government plan. With little success, they all became increasingly frustrated over their diverging interests and with the government's inability to resolve the gridlock.

Facing a tight recovery schedule, local officials proposed consolidating land that could be developed from both neighborhoods into a single development and changed the rebuilding decision from a building-based approach to a neighborhood-based one so that units could be swapped among different buildings and consolidated into fewer buildings for in-situ reconstruction. Hence, all who wished to stay could stay, and those who opted to relocate could finally relocate. Residents were asked to produce a detailed redevelopment plan on their own and the city designated a planning facilitator to provide legal and technical assistance pertaining to the consolidation and the planning process. The "cautiously elated" residents formed a homeowner recovery committee to coordinate the renewed neighborhood planning effort.

Over the next 4 months, 35 planning meetings were held. Because the consolidation required a neighborhood design that was new and unfamiliar, these meetings were always full of passionate negotiation. Nevertheless, the homeowners found a way to reconcile their differences at every step of the process, which included the initial identification of owners' intent, the resolution of differences over land use adjustments, development of a neighborhood plan, bidding by a construction firm, finance management, and overseeing construction. The final plan (Figure 13.4) included

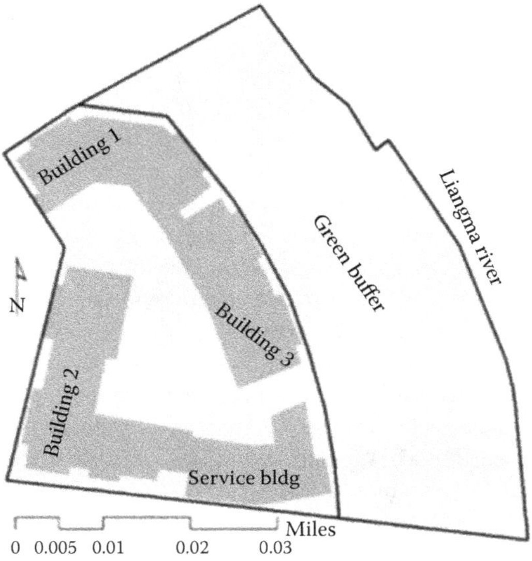

FIGURE 13.4 Final plan for the neighborhoods in Dujiangyan, China. (Adapted from Yang Zhang and William Drake.)

70 units* in three condominium complexes. On January 20, 2010, 20 months after the earthquake, the project was completed. By March 2010, most households had moved into their new, permanent homes (see Figure 13.4).

Analysis of this case revealed that the planning facilitator was crucial to the success of this participatory process. As a government advocate, he organized workshops to help homeowners understand the recovery policies and his effort was important to the implementation of the greenway buffer. In his role as a professional planner, he provided much needed legal and technical knowledge to the citizens. When homeowners presented an idea, he could assess its feasibility and suggest modifications to make the project conform to codes. The planning facilitator also provided communication between homeowners and the planning firm to ensure that their ideas were properly incorporated into the official plan. As a networked government insider, the planning facilitator was able to fast-track various review, permitting, and inspection requirements and kept the project progressing.

13.4 DISCUSSION AND CONCLUSIONS

In this chapter, we demonstrated the strengths and limitations of China's authoritarian approach toward managing housing recovery. Our research shows that planning and housing reconstruction after the 2008 catastrophic Wenchuan earthquake was fast, especially when we consider the enormous damage over a vast area caused by

* About 74 households initially decided to stay. During the planning process, four of them changed their positions and opted for the government housing or cash buyout option.

the earthquake. Two years after the earthquake, most displaced residents had completed the transition to permanent housing. The rapid housing reconstruction greatly benefited from the fact that housing recovery was deemed to be a national priority and received preferential funding allocation from the central state.

Nevertheless, our analysis challenges the notion that the Wenchuan earthquake recovery was a total success, a claim by the Chinese government that has also been contested by Chang et al. (2011, 2012). While local residents were overwhelmingly positive of the physical conditions of their houses, many of them, especially the rural residents, expressed negative views about the lack of public input in the planning phase and mass relocations. Many rural residents reported that their indigenous life styles and social networks were greatly disrupted during recovery.

The case study in two inner-city neighborhoods in the city of Dujiangyan provided a more nuanced account of housing recovery planning at the local level after the earthquake. While the planning and recovery was generally a top-down, authoritarian process, the earthquake created conditions in some communities where the Chinese government became more receptive to public participation. Similar to other cases in the world, post-disaster housing recovery must contend with the extreme concentration of activity while also utilizing the opportunities presented by the disaster to increase inclusivity in the recovery process. These are not easy tasks but our case study in China of a seemingly very top-down system suggested two lessons to better manage housing recovery.

Lesson 1: Slow is fast. Delays in housing recovery have immense consequences for the local populace. However, public participation, though seemingly time consuming, can speed up recovery in the long run (Kates et al. 2006; Olshansky and Johnson 2010; Karan and Subbiah 2011). In the post-disaster environment, people have a shared urgency for recovery and, because of this, a shared urgency to be heard. Emphasizing speed without deliberation can have the reverse effect of slowing down recovery. Taking time in the early recovery period to build key trust relations and to include residents in decision making that directly affects them can pay off in later recovery stages. Such payoff is in terms of recovery speed but also the level of acceptance among residents toward post-disaster land use adjustments and hazard mitigation strategies aimed at reducing an area's long-term disaster risk. In other words, immersive public involvement and deliberation in post-disaster housing recovery need not be a barrier to speedy and quality recovery, but a strategic tool to aid it.

Lesson 2: Bottom-up makes top-down more efficient. The value of community organizations and citizen groups is heightened during large-scale disaster and displacement events. Disaster recovery planners should make a much greater effort to build partnerships with these groups and leverage their networks for information collection, verification, dissemination, and consensus building. Such partnerships can be particularly critical to better and more effective representation of previously marginalized segments of the population.

Disasters are also associated with a heightened sense of activism (Beatley et al. 1993; Nelson et al. 2007; Aldrich 2010). New citizen groups and active opposition often arise from a sense of alienation from, or growing irrelevance to an ongoing recovery plan process. Planners' ability to quickly respond to these evolving needs of stakeholders can directly affect the housing recovery process.

ACKNOWLEDGMENTS

This material is based upon work supported by the National Science Foundation under Grant No. CMMI 1029298, 1029805; 1030332; 1030413 and the Peking University—Lincoln Institute Center for Urban Development and Land Policy under Grant No. PLC A204.

We would particularly like to thank our collaborators, Robert Olshansky, Laurie Johnson, Yu Xiao, and Yan Song. We would also like to thank colleagues and students in Sichuan University, China who provided indispensable assistance with the fieldwork in China. Finally, our thanks go out to the local residents in Sichuan Province, China for so graciously helping us in research at a difficult time in their lives.

REFERENCES

Abrams, C. B., K. Albright, and A. Panofsky. 2004. Contesting the New York community: From liminality to the "New Normal" in the wake of September 11. *City and Community*, 3(3): 189–220. Retrieved from http://socgen.ucla.edu/wp-content/uploads/2009/08/Abrams-Albright-Panofsky-2004.pdf

Abramson, D. and Y. Qi. 2011. "Urban–rural integration" in the earthquake zone: Sichuan's post-disaster reconstruction and the expansion of the Chengdu Metropole. *Pacific Affairs* 84(3): 495–523.

Abramson, D. B. 2006. Urban planning in China: Continuity and change. *Journal of American Planning Association* 72(2): 197–215.

Aldrich, D. P. 2010. The power of people: Social capital's role in recovery from the 1995 Kobe earthquake. *Natural Hazards* 56(3): 595–611. doi: 10.1007/s11069-010-9577-7.

Berke, P. and T. J. Campanella. 2006. Planning for postdisaster resiliency. *The Annals of the American Academy of Political and Social Sciences* 64: 19–31.

Berke, P. R., T. Beatley, and C. Feagin. 1993. Hurricane Gilbert strikes Jamaica: Linking disaster recovery to development. *Coastal Management* 21(1): 1–23. http://www.tandfonline.com/doi/abs/10.1080/08920759309362189?journalCode=ucmg20 (accessed March 2, 2016).

Campanella, T. J. 2006. Urban resilience and the recovery of New Orleans. *Journal of American Planning Association*, 72(2): 141–146.

Cao, S., X. Liu, and H. Er. 2010. Dujiangyan Irrigation System—A world cultural heritage corresponding to concepts of modern hydraulic science. *Journal of Hydro-Environment Research* 4(1): 3–13. doi: 10.1016/j.jher.2009.09.003.

Chandrasekhar, D., Y. Zhang, and Y. Xiao. 2015. Nontraditional participation in disaster recovery planning: Cases from China, India, and the United States. *Journal of the American Planning Association* 80(4): 373–84. doi: 10.1080/01944363.2014.989399.

Chang, Y., S. Wilkinson, D. Brunsdon, E. Seville, and R. Potangaroa. 2011. An integrated approach: Managing resources for post-disaster reconstruction. *Disasters* 35: 739–65. doi: 10.1111/j.1467-7717.2011.01240.x.

Chang, Y., S. Wilkinson, R. Potangaroa, and E. Seville. 2012. Resourcing for post-disaster reconstruction: A comparative study of Indonesia and China. *Disaster Prevention and Management: An International Journal* 21(1): 7–21.

China State Council. 2008a. *The State Overall Plan for Post-Wenchuan Earthquake Restoration and Reconstruction*. Beijing, China: China State Council.

China State Council. 2008b. *The Wenchuan Earthquake Post-Disaster Recovery and Redevelopment Pairing Assistance Plan*. Beijing, China: China State Council.

Comerio, M. C. 1998. *Disaster Hits Home: New Policy for Urban Housing Recovery*. Berkeley, CA: University of California Press.

Dujiangyan City Government. 2008. *Dujiangyan Urban Housing Recovery Implementation Strategies*. Dujiangyan, China: Dujiangyan City Government.

Godschalk, D. R. 2003. Urban hazard mitigation: Creating resilient cities. *Natural Hazards Review* 136–143. doi: 10.1061/(ASCE)1527-6988(2003)4:3(136).

Goodchild, M. F. and J. A. Glennon. 2010. Crowdsourcing geographic information for disaster response: A research frontier. *International Journal of Digital Earth* 3(3): 231–241. doi:10.1080/17538941003759255.

Guang, L. 2010. Bringing the city back in: The Chinese debate on rural problems. In *One Country, Two Societies: Rural–Urban Inequality in Contemporary China*, M. K. Whyte (ed.), Cambridge, Massachusetts: Harvard University Press, 311–34.

Inam, A. 2005. *Planning for the Unplanned: Recovering from Crises in Megacities*. New York: Routledge.

Innes, J. E. 2004. Consensus building: Clarifications for the critics. *Planning Theory* 3(1): 5–20.

Karan, P. P. and S. P. Subbiah. 2011. *The Indian Ocean Tsunami: The Global Response to a Natural Disaster*. Lexington, Kentucky: University of Kentucky Press.

Kates, R. W., C. E. Colten, S. Laska, and S. P. Leatherman. 2006. Reconstruction of New Orleans after Hurricane Katrina: A research perspective. *Proceedings of the National Academy of Sciences* 103(40): 14653–60.

Kohlbacher, F. 2005. The use of qualitative content analysis in case study research. *Forum Qualitative Sozialforschung/Forum: Qualitative Social Research* 7(1), Art. 21.

Ma, L. J. C. and F. Wu. 2005. *Restructuring the Chinese City: Changing Society, Economy and Space*. New York: Routledge.

Maginn, P. 2007. Towards more effective community participation in urban regeneration: the potential of collaborative planning and applied ethnography. *Qualitative Research*, 7(1): 25–43. doi:10.1177/1468794106068020.

Marying, P. 2001. Combination and integration of qualitative and quantitative analysis. *Forum Qualitative Sozialforschung/Forum: Qualitative Social Research* 2(1): 25–43. doi:10.1177/1468794106068020.

National Development and Reform Commission (NDRC). 2008. *Work Plan for the National Wenchuan Earthquake Recovery Planning*. Beijing, China: The National Development and Reform Commission of China.

Nelson, M., R. Ehrenfeucht, and S. Laska. 2007. Planning, plans, and people: Professional expertise, local knowledge, and governmental action in post-Katrina New Orleans. *Cityscape* 9(3): 23–52.

Olshansky, R. B. and S. Chang. 2009. Planning for disaster recovery: Emerging research needs and challenges. *Progress in Planning* 72: 200–9.

Olshansky, R. B., L. Hopkins, and L. Johnson. 2012. Disaster and recovery: Processes compressed in time. *Natural Hazards Review* 13(3): 173–8.

Olshansky, R. B. and L. A. Johnson. 2010. *Clear as Mud: Planning for the Rebuilding of New Orleans*. Chicago, Illinois: APA Press.

Peacock, W. G., S. Van Zandt, Y. Zhang, and W. E. Highfield. 2015. Inequities in long-term housing recovery after disasters. *Journal of the American Planning Association* 80(4): 356–71. doi: 10.1080/01944363.2014.980440.

Plummer, J. and J. G. Taylor. 2004. *Community Participation in China: Issues and Processes for Capacity Building*. London: Earthscan.

Quarantelli, E. L. 1999. *Preliminary Paper #286—The Disaster Recovery Process: What We Know and Do Not Know from Research*. Newark, Delaware: University of Delaware, Disaster Research Center.

Schwab, J. 1998. Planning for post-disaster recovery and reconstruction. In *Planning Advisory Service Report*, J. Schwab (ed.), Chicago, Illinois: American Planning Association, 483/484.

Sichuan Development and Reform Commission. 2010. *Wenchuan Earthquake Recovery Annual Progress Report 2009*. Chengdu, China: Sichuan Development and Reform Commission.

Sichuan Development and Reform Commission. 2011. *Wenchuan Earthquake Recovery Annual Progress Report 2010*. Chengdu, China: Sichuan Development and Reform Commission.

Tang, B. -S., S. Wong, and M. C. -H. Lau. 2008. Social impact assessment and public participation in China. *Environmental Impact Assessment Review* 28: 57–72.

Tierney, K. J. 2001. *Strength of a City: A Disaster Research Perspective on the World Trade Center Attack*. Newark, Delaware: University of Delaware, Disaster Research Center.

Yeh, A. G. -O. and F. Wu. 1999. The transformation of the urban planning system in China from a centrally-planned to transitional economy. *Progress in Planning* 51(3): 167–252.

Zhang, Y., W. Drake, Y. Xiao, R. Olshansky, L. Johnson, and Y. Song. Forthcoming. Disaster recovery planning after two catastrophes: The 1976 Tangshan earthquake and the 2008 Wenchuan earthquakes. *International Journal of Mass Emergencies and Disasters*.

Zhang, Y. and W. G. Peacock. 2010. Planning for housing recovery? Lessons learned from Hurricane Andrew. *Journal of American Planning Association* 76(1): 5–24.

14 Residential Relocation Processes in Coastal Areas

Tacloban City after Typhoon Yolanda

Kanako Iuchi and Elizabeth Maly

CONTENTS

14.1 INTRODUCTION

Relocating communities is difficult. It disrupts people's lives, burdens them financially, and erodes social networks. Because disadvantaged populations with informal land tenure are often the ones forced to relocate, they are pushed further into poverty. Effects are also felt in host communities; they experience increased job competition and added strain on public and social services as a result of accommodating newcomers, which often leads to disputes (Correa et al. 2011). Thus, both displaced people and their hosts are likely to face negative socio-economic consequences of relocation in both the short and long term (Badri et al. 2006). Experts, therefore, suggest avoiding community relocation if at all possible (Scudder 1985; Cernea 1997; ADB 1998; Jha 2009).

However, relocation in coastal areas is frequently considered after large-scale natural events—such as tsunamis and storm surges—that result in considerable losses and damages. In this context, relocation of communities away from risk is increasingly discussed as a way to protect against future losses and save lives from large-scale disasters (Kim and Olshansky 2014). Research on the usefulness of preventive relocation (see Correa 2011) which is relocation as part of the rebuilding process to prepare for future disasters is gaining attention. For instance, the Indonesian government developed a recovery master plan* 3 months after the 2004 Indian Ocean Tsunami that included a land-use plan with a 3-km coastal setback zone to regulate development (Republic of Indonesia 2005). Although this plan was adopted by the national government through Presidential Regulation No. 30 of 2005 (*Peraturan Presiden Republik Indonesia Nomor 30 Tahun 2005*), local resistance and lack of coordination among key stakeholders, including national and local governments, international donors, international nongovernmental organizations (INGOs), and communities, resulted in residents building back in place. Similarly, in tsunami-affected Sri Lanka, a presidential decree (PD) introduced a buffer zone with a maximum setback of 300 m; and people who had been living in that buffer zone were to be relocated to donor-provided permanent houses (Muggah 2008). However, tourism industry developments permitted in the buffer zone were viewed as unfair to former residents and effectively undermined the relocation efforts. In addition, the donor-driven relocation was not participatory, further alienating residents (Muggah 2008). Meanwhile, Japan is also pursuing rebuilding with strict land-use controls of coastal land after the 2011 Great East Japan earthquake and tsunami, utilizing centralized, top–down processes (Iuchi et al. 2015). In all cases, massive relocation takes time, raises social and economic concerns, and the long-term effects of preventive relocation remain unclear.

The concept of rebuilding better is also increasingly emphasized, yet adopting the concept in practice is challenging because the recovery process itself often exacerbates various existing pre-disaster problems (Wisner et al. 2004; Pyles 2007; Iuchi 2014). Issues include haphazard development, poor land management, and substandard infrastructure as a result of urbanization pressures, all of which create further vulnerabilities to natural events (Dickson et al. 2012; Esnard and Sapat 2014). In addition, inequitable financial, political, and participatory opportunities of disaster-affected populations aggravate pre-existing poverty and inequality (Bolin and Stanford 1998; Kamel and Loukaitou-Sideris 2004; Wisner et al. 2004). Studies on the impact and dynamics of the recovery processes have begun gaining more understanding, but how these dynamics function in relocation after major disasters need further research. With such understanding, the intent of this study is to examine the actual implementation of preventive relocation in recovery at the early stages

* A post-disaster interim organization, the Rehabilitation and Reconstruction Agency of Aceh and Nias (BRR: Badan Rehabilitasi dan Rekonstruksi NAD-Nias), and the Planning Agency (BAPPENAS: Badan Perencanaan Pembangunan Nasional) were responsible for developing the recovery master plan for Aceh.

and hopefully contribute to future policy inputs to reduce stresses on populations affected by disasters and to support more resilient livelihoods.

The study was initiated immediately after the landfall of Typhoon Yolanda (international name Haiyan) in November 2013, by first reviewing media sources and official documents available online to understand the extent of typhoon-related damage and devastation, as well as government responses to the event. Semi-structured interviews and informal conversations with community members, and with government officials at national, city, and local (*barangay*) levels were conducted over four fieldwork trips between March 2014 and October 2015. Official documents with statistical information on Typhoon Yolanda and housing recovery and reconstruction plans were also collected from national and local governments during these fieldwork trips. To confirm the implementation progress of relocation and rehousing reconstruction, reconnaissance surveys were carried out in the affected coastal areas as well as in temporary and permanent housing areas. Data collected were then reviewed and analyzed to structure a logical narrative. The study was supplemented by the authors' extensive past work experience on disaster risk management in the Philippines, and benefited from existing personal connections.

This chapter focuses on the first 2 years of relocation and housing efforts in Tacloban after the destruction caused by Typhoon Yolanda. The ongoing recovery process in Tacloban City entails large-scale relocation programs to move coastal residents into new permanent housing provided in the northern part of the city. This chapter discusses dilemmas faced when relocating the population away from hazardous areas, including coordination challenges that emerge while implementing rehousing and relocation, and the unintended increase in vulnerability of the relocated population as time progresses. The chapter also documents the implementation status of multiple phases of different housing recovery projects before concluding with discussing emerging issues and further challenges.

14.2 TYPHOON YOLANDA AND RECONSTRUCTION CHALLENGES

14.2.1 Typhoon Yolanda and Reconstruction Strategies

Typhoon Yolanda, one of the strongest typhoons in history, made the first of six landfalls in Guiuan on November 8, 2013. The typhoon unleashed wind speeds over 300 km/h and storm surges over 4 m, and devastated regions in its path (National Economic and Development Authority [NEDA] 2013). Damage was extreme; the government of the Philippines reported more than 6300 casualties, 1.5 million families affected, and 920,000 families displaced (Office of the Presidential Assistant for Rehabilitation and Recovery [OPARR] 2014b). Of the 1.2 million houses damaged, 600,000 were completely destroyed (NEDA 2013). Economic losses were also substantial with direct damage calculated at PhP 132.36 billion (US$3 billion*) (NEDA 2014).

* Exchange rate is calculated based on US$1 = PhP44.135 as of December 12, 2013.

Region VIII (Eastern Visayas), which includes Tacloban, was one of the hardest hit along with Region VI (Western Visayas) and Region VII (Central Visayas). Approximately 90% of affected families were from these regions (NEDA 2013; The World Bank 2014). Region VIII is historically one of the poorest in the nation; in 2012, it ranked as the third poorest (National Statistical Coordination Board [NSCB] 2013). Poverty levels in this area were exacerbated when the majority of the poor living along the coast without legal land titles lost all of their assets to the storm surge (see e.g., NEDA 2013). The poverty rate increased from 41.2% to 55.7% a year after the typhoon, making Region VIII the nation's poorest (The World Bank 2014; Gabieta 2015).

Based on an understanding that poor coastal residents were the hardest hit, the national government decided to "build back better" and published "Reconstruction Assistance on Yolanda: Build Back Better (RAY)" (NEDA 2013) within a month after Yolanda. Together with information on economic loss and recovery budgets, this document provided rebuilding principles, procedures, and institutional arrangements for recovery. Some key principles included were: (1) local governments are the principal actors for recovery, and work with the national government in coordinating with international donors and civil organizations; (2) promote recovery in partnership with the private sector; and (3) avoid hazardous zones and include necessary resettlement for future risk reduction in the rebuilding process. In December 2013, President Aquino III created the OPARR* to coordinate and implement RAY. Funds from various sources were collected including PhP 14.6 billion (US$256 billion) in December 2013 (Republic of the Philippines 2013, No. 3423) from a supplementary governmental budget, PhP 26.2 billion (US$594 million) pledged by civil organizations including about 1300 private organizations and nongovernmental organizations (NGOs), and PhP 19.36 billion (US$439 million) committed by international donors as of October 2014 (OPARR 2014a).

The national recovery plan, "Yolanda Comprehensive Rehabilitation and Recovery Plan (CRRP),"† included four cluster plans led by different national departments: (1) the Department of Public Works and Highways (DPWH) for infrastructure; (2) the Department of Social Welfare and Development (DSWD) for social services; (3) the National Housing Authority (NHA) for resettlement; and (4) the Department of Trade and Industry (DTI) for livelihood (OPARR 2014a). Among these, the resettlement cluster had the largest budget of PhP 75.67 billion (US$1.71 billion), which was approximately 45% of the total (OPARR 2014a).

14.2.2 Challenges of Coastal Housing Reconstruction

The national government initially pushed for a coastal setback. RAY called for a 40-m "no-build zone" buffer prohibiting any building construction. This concept has its root in the PD 1067, the Water Code of the Philippines (1976, PRIME-M4) that prohibits private buildings in a 40-m zone from the shore for forest areas, a 20-m

* Pursuant to Memorandum Order No. 62 of December 6, 2013.

† The CRRP included the recovery plan of 14 affected regional governments: Palawan, Masbate, Aklan, Antique, Capiz, Iloilo, Negros Occidental, Cebu, Leyte, Biliran, Eastern Samar, Western Samar, Southern Leyte and Dinagat Islands.

zone for agricultural areas, and 3-m zone for urban areas. However, actual implementation of a no-build zone became more complicated and significant concerns emerged as time passed.

In the Philippines, the president or local government can issue a declaration of calamity for a certain period of time after a devastating disaster (National Disaster Coordinating Council [NDCC] 1998). When the declaration is in effect, there are price controls to avoid inflation and no-interest loans available for recovery. In addition, the area can receive calamity funds* and foreign donations for emergency response and reconstruction. A portion of calamity funds received is often invested in the recovery of the housing sector, including temporary and permanent housing construction. Depending on the scale of devastation, disaster location, and the rebuilding stage, different procedures and actors are involved. Key actors using funds allocated to the housing sector often include national departments and agencies such as the DSWD, the DPWH, the NHA, and the Social Housing Finance Corporation (SHFC). These departments and agencies collaborate with civil society organizations, international donors, and local governments. Nevertheless, no clear framework exists for housing recovery procedures, and haphazard responses and processes have often led to unfinished projects in housing construction (Environmental Science for Social Change [ESSC] 2014).

Resettlement is not a new task for the Philippine government. The Urban Development Housing Act (UDHA) of 1992 (Republic Act [RA] 7279) designated the NHA as the primary government agency to work with local governments in providing social housing† and preparing land for relocation of underprivileged populations. People "living in dangerous areas such as esteros [coastal lagoons], railroad tracks, garbage dumps, river banks, shorelines, waterways, and in other public places as sidewalks, roads, parks, and playgrounds" (Republic of the Philippines 1992: RA 7279, pp. 23) are eligible for resettlement in social housing in safer areas. However, past experiences in many cases in Metro Manila have shown that the provision of basic infrastructure and livelihood opportunities often do not match the timing of housing allocation to residents or needs of residents. As a result, relocated individuals eventually return to familiar areas (ESSC 2014; NEDA 2014).

Housing and relocation post-Yolanda was even more challenging. The number of affected households needing assistance significantly exceeded that of past events (ESSC 2014). Supporting resettlement for all affected coastal communities seemed overly unrealistic given few successful cases from the past (NEDA 2014). In addition, the issue of setbacks was raised, including the need for scientific evidence to identify safe and unsafe zones based on geographic conditions. After a 4-month

* The calamity fund in the Philippines is a lump sum fund appropriated every year at the national level for emergency use, including aid, relief, and rehabilitation after disasters. PhP 7.5 billion (US$169.9 million) was appropriated for 2012 and 2013, and increased to PhP 13 billion (US$294.6 million) in 2014 (Department of Budget and Management [DBM] 2015; Diaz 2014).

† "Social housing" in the Philippines aims to make available "decent housing at affordable cost" for "the underprivileged and homeless citizens in urban areas and in resettlement areas" (Republic of the Philippines 1992, RA 7279, pp. 1). Programs for socialized housing "refers to housing programs and projects covering houses and lots or home-lots only undertaken by the Government or the private sector... which shall include sites and services development, long-term financing, liberal terms on interest payments, and such other benefits" (Republic of the Philippines 1992, RA 7279, pp. 6).

debate, instead of the "no-build zone," the 40-m zone was reclassified by OPARR as a no-dwell zone with adoption by local governments to be made on a case-by-case basis (OPARR 2014a).

14.3 TACLOBAN CITY: COASTAL REBUILDING THROUGH HOUSING RELOCATION

14.3.1 Tacloban City and Urban Development Trends

Before Yolanda, Tacloban City was already facing development challenges. As the first highly urbanized city in Region VIII, Tacloban is a regional economic center and attracts many people from throughout the region. Together with natural population growth, the city's population increased 2.43% from 1990 to 2010, a much higher rate than that of the national capital region (Census of Population and Housing [CPH] 2010). Located in one of the poorest regions in the country, many poor residents in Tacloban do not own land or rent in formal housing markets; instead they mainly occupy lands along shores, riverbanks, and esteros. An estimated 30,513 people or 13.8% of the city's population were living in informal settlements pre-Yolanda (Tacloban City 2012).*

To address population increase and growing urban informal settlements, there had been plans to develop Tacloban's northern agricultural areas. Plans for an Economic Zone of 237 ha in the north were already approved in 1998 (Presidential Proclamation No. 1210, 1998) to boost the regional economy (Tacloban City 2012). In addition, 124 ha of land on multiple sites, most in the north, were planned for the construction of social housing before Yolanda (Tacloban City 2012).

Tacloban was one of the cities most severely impacted by Typhoon Yolanda; 2603 people were killed or missing and 28,734 houses were totally damaged, 90% of which were in coastal areas (Tacloban City 2014b). About 28 of Tacloban's 136 barangays,† are in low-lying areas with an average elevation of 3 m, where the majority of Tacloban's informal settlers were residing (Tacloban City 2014a).

14.3.2 Rebuilding Safer: A Two-Step Plan for Relocating Coastal Families Inland

In response to the destruction and loss of lives by Yolanda, Tacloban City adopted a "no-build zone" ordinance 4 months after Yolanda, even while the national government was still discussing implementation of a 40-m setback. It aimed to "prevent repetition of [the] large number of casualties that occurred after Super Typhoon Yolanda [which] brought massive storm surges that flattened seaside communities" (Tacloban City 2014a,b, Ordinance No. 2013-12-15A). With this ordinance,

* According to the Philippines Statistics Authority, the population of Tacloban City in 2010 was 221,174 (PSA 2013).

† Barangay is the smallest administrative unit in the Philippines, often representing village, district, or ward.

Tacloban City replaced temporary "no-building zone" signage with permanent markers 40 m from the shore in 28 coastal barangays to communicate the boundary to residents.

Along with the no-build zone, Tacloban focused on relocating coastal families inland. Tacloban City planned housing relocation in two steps. In the first step, residents would move into temporary housing, locally called "bunkhouses" or "transitional shelters," as soon as these units were ready, after staying for several months in evacuation shelters such as schools, municipal buildings, or tents. Residents would then relocate to permanent housing to be built in the north of Tacloban.* When planning the two-step relocation, locations for both temporary and permanent housing were taken into consideration to reduce stress on the beneficiaries. Constructed on three sites near the city center, entry into the bunkhouses prioritized vulnerable populations, including single mothers, disabled, and elderly residents, among other evacuees. The majority of transitional shelters and permanent housing, meanwhile, was built in the north where more land is available. Locating transitional shelters and permanent housing in proximity was intended to make adjustment easier for the relocating residents (see Figure 14.1). To address the need for permanent housing in a safer area, the city's initial target was 10,000 permanent housing units in the recovery plan† (Tacloban City 2014b). Due to the limited amount of temporary housing available and the time needed to construct permanent housing, the city planned to reuse the temporary units after households moved to permanent housing to accommodate as many residents as possible.

14.3.3 Implementation of Housing Relocation: From Temporary to Permanent Housing

Typhoon-affected coastal residents began moving into temporary housing after staying in evacuation shelters‡ for a little more than a month (DPWH 2013). Evacuation shelter sites then closed before the 1-year anniversary of Yolanda in November 2014 (International Research Institute of Disaster Science 2015). Eight months into rebuilding, residents began relocating to permanent housing located in the north of Tacloban. Two years after Yolanda, the majority of typhoon-affected coastal households were living in temporary housing, including bunkhouses, transitional shelters, and other housing such as rented rooms or self-built structures. Only around

* Preparing a detailed schedule and timing of housing relocation in both temporary and permanent housing phases was difficult for Tacloban City because housing construction and procurement depended heavily on donations and support from private sector, INGOs and NGOs, as well as NHA. In addition, land use and acquisition agreements and approvals were also needed. Under such circumstances, Tacloban City's plan for housing did not focus on detailed timeframes; rather on keeping track of and understanding the actual status and counts of housing commitments and construction, while continuing to work toward provision of the target number of housing units (see IRIDeS 2015).

† The initial target for housing units was less than the calculated 14,443 households in the no-dwell zone reflecting the city's own capacity and early commitments of partners (International Research Institute of Disaster Science 2015).

‡ Evacuation shelters in Tacloban included nearby schools, municipal buildings, and tents provided by different donors and religious groups.

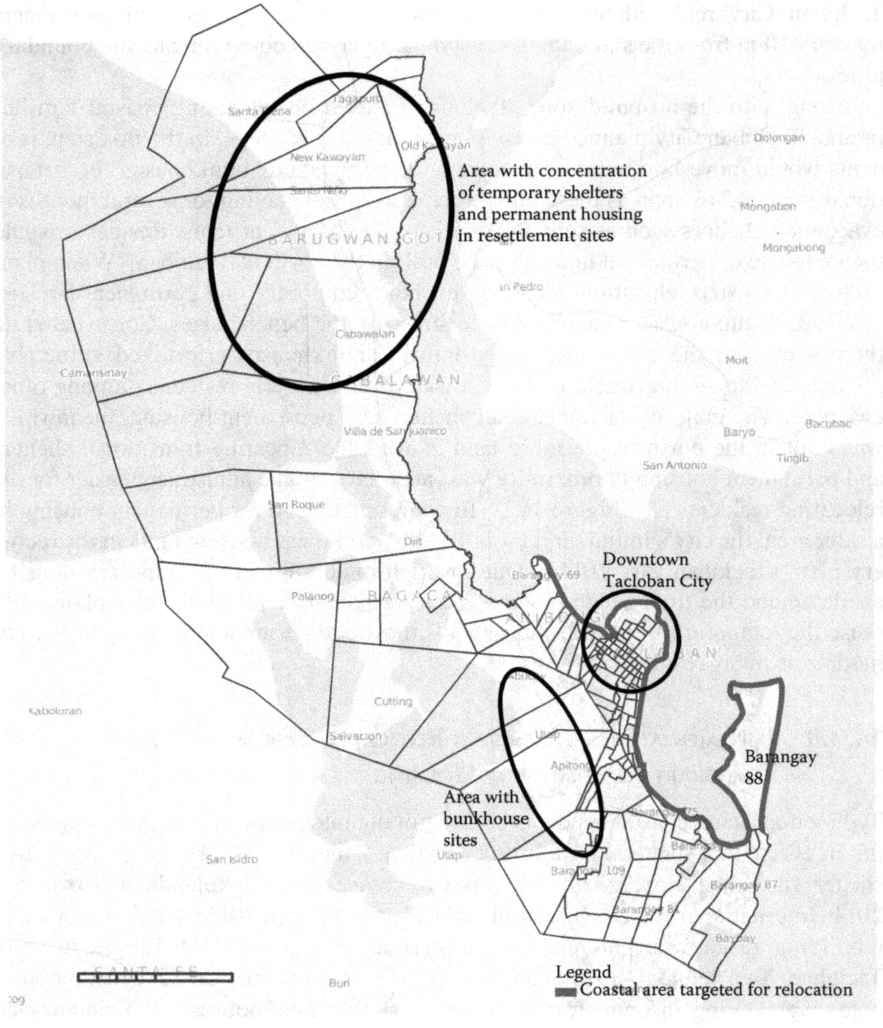

FIGURE 14.1 Map of Tacloban City showing the location of downtown, temporary housing sites, and permanent relocation sites. (Data from modified OSM Map. Open Street Map. 2013. Open Street Map: Typhoon Haiyan. http://www.openstreetmap.org/#map=15/11.2461/124.9975&layers=H [accessed February 16, 2016]).

470 households, or less than 5% of target beneficiaries, had moved into permanent houses in the relocation area (Tacloban City 2015).

Tacloban City's plan for two-step housing relocation remains the core of the recovery program, and the city continues to take the central coordination role for providing temporary and permanent housing through different combinations of support. The residents' paths to permanent housing, however, are diverging with various options that emerged as alternatives to the city's housing plan (Figure 14.2).

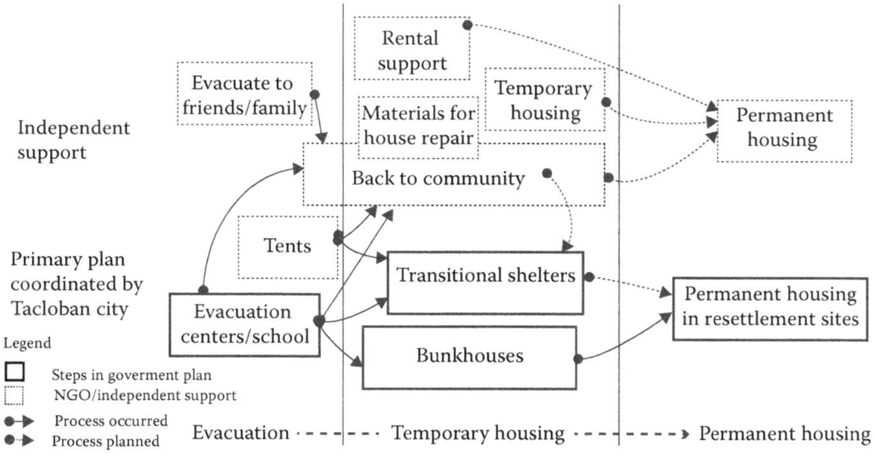

FIGURE 14.2 Coastal residents' relocation process in Tacloban.

14.3.3.1 Temporary Housing

Temporary housing support after Yolanda included: (1) bunkhouses; (2) transitional shelters; (3) rent assistance and building materials; and (4) self-built housing in former communities (see Table 14.1); 2 years after Yolanda, people are still living in each of these types of temporary housing. Multiple actors provided housing support, including the national and Tacloban City government, international and local NGOs, and residents through their own efforts. While Tacloban City is the main coordinator of temporary housing construction and management, some NGOs provided independent housing assistance without coordinating with Tacloban City. Temporary housing organized by different actors has resulted in some residents taking paths different from the city's plan. Locations and the land used for temporary housing by different actors also varied.

14.3.3.1.1 Bunkhouse Settlements

Coordinated by Tacloban City, bunkhouses were the earliest temporary housing, built by DPWH and managed by DSWD. Bunkhouses are wooden row house or barracks structures, with 12, 17.28 m^2 housing units in each building.* Two years after Yolanda, over 1000 households were still living in bunkhouses in three sites, located near the center of Tacloban City, with the farthest site about 2.5 km inland. These sites used both public and privately owned lands that were available in a short time. Residents benefited from good access to working places and schools as these sites are relatively close to the city center, although outside former neighborhoods. However, the crowded and unsanitary living conditions of bunkhouses are pressing issues for residents after living in the bunkhouses for almost 2 years.

* The nearly 250 bunkhouse units build by early 2014 were initially too small according to international standards; the calculation of 8.64 m^2 per household was later doubled to 17.28 m^2 (Official Gazette, 2014).

TABLE 14.1
Temporary Housing Types: Coordinator, Funding Sources and Activities, Location, and Land Used

Housing Types	Coordinator	Funding Sources and Activities	Location	Land Used
Bunkhouses	City	DPWH: bunkhouses provision; DSWD: welfare support	Close to city center	City government's land; land leased from private owners
Transitional shelters	City	Public agencies, private donors, INGOs, NGOs: shelter provisions	Tacloban North	City government's land; land leased from private owners
	NGO	NGOs: shelter provisions	Close to city center	Private land
Rent assistance	NGO	NGOs (i.e., CRS[a]): rental assistance	Throughout the city	Land/apartment owners, host family
Temporary housing in or near former communities	NGO/ residents	NGOs (i.e., CRS; UPA[b]): housing/ material provisions; repair support	In or near original communities	Near original land, including formal and informal inhabitation
Temporary housing in former communities	Residents themselves	Resident: self-built	Original communities	Governments' land with informal inhabitation

[a] CRS: Catholic Relief Services.
[b] UPA: Urban Poor Associates.

14.3.3.1.2 Transitional Shelter Settlements

Through partnerships between various actors such as private and public donors, INGOs and NGOs, around 950 units of transitional shelter were built in the north part of Tacloban (Tacloban North) by October 2015 (Tacloban City 2015). Most are made of bamboo with various foundations to elevate the houses off the ground, on land already owned by Tacloban City or rented from private owners. Transitional shelter sites were located mainly in the north so that residents' ongoing relocation process will be smooth. After some residents move from transitional to permanent housing, reuse of these transitional units was planned, along with the construction of additional transitional housing toward the city's target of 1500 units total (Tacloban City 2015).

14.3.3.1.3 Rental Assistance

The international humanitarian agency Catholic Relief Services (CRS), funded by the United States Agency for International Development and the US Office of Foreign Disaster Assistance, has provided the widest variety of options to support residents in the transitional housing phase. With a mission to find housing solutions close to residents' former neighborhoods, CRS's programs complemented the city's relocation efforts, including: (1) rent to own land; (2) land rental; (3) apartment rental; or (4) host family. In each option, households received 3000 pesos per month, or 72,000 pesos total for 2 years of support (CRS 2015). As it was paid in advance for 2 years, residents are still benefitting from rental assistance although CRS's program ended in December 2015. CRS supported residents from both inside and outside the no-build zone; about 60% of their 3000 beneficiaries were from the no-build zone (CRS 2015).* Since CRS's programs focused on temporary housing support, residents may face challenges in transitioning to permanent housing after their rental assistance ends.

14.3.3.1.4 Self-built Temporary Housing in Former Communities

As of October 2015, only approximately 1600 of the households targeted for relocation had moved into temporary housing† away from coastal areas (Tacloban City 2015); a majority of other affected residents returned to their former informal settlements in heavily damaged coastal areas. Although Tacloban City policy forbids construction in the no-build zone, many residents have rebuilt lightweight shelters despite the knowledge that they are forbidden to stay permanently. Interviews with barangay officials and residents indicated that some people were waiting to find out if and/or when permanent housing will be available from the city or NGO programs; some returned from temporary housing because bunkhouses were crowded and unsanitary, or transitional shelter sites were too far away.

14.3.3.2 Permanent Housing

Major permanent housing approaches include: (1) national government housing; (2) city-NGO housing; (3) NGO-independent housing, and (4) NGO-donor-social housing programs (see Table 14.2). Combinations of different actors provided housing support, including national and local governments, international and local donors, and NGOs. Funding sources also varied: for example, funding for one type of housing provision originates from the private sector while in others it comes from the national government via social housing programs. Tacloban City coordinates the overall management of beneficiaries, and collaborates closely with permanent housing construction projects by the national government and NGO partners. However, some NGO-driven housing construction programs are independent from the city's programs.

14.3.3.2.1 National Government Housing

The NHA is providing the largest share of permanent housing, with the construction of more than 13,000 units planned (Tacloban City 2015). In collaboration with Tacloban City, the NHA assesses land conditions and decides on construction sites

---

* For the 1230 dwell-zone households, CRS provided cash or building materials for on-site house repair according to damage level, along with technical guidance (CRS, 2015).

† As of October 2015, there were approximately 1000 households in bunkhouses, 600 in transitional housing, and 470 in permanent housing (Tacloban City 2015).

TABLE 14.2
Permanent Housing Types: Coordinator, Funding Sources and Activities, Location, and Land Used

Housing Types	Coordinator	Funding Sources and Activities	Location	Land Used
National government	National government and city	NHA: housing provision, land acquisition City: land provisions	Tacloban North	City government's land; purchased private land
City-NGO	City and NGO	City: land provisions; NGO (i.e., GMAKF[a], Habitat for Humanity): housing provision	Tacloban North	City government's land
NGO-independent	NGO	NGOs (i.e., UPA[b]): land acquisition and housing construction	North of city Center	Purchased private land
NGO-donor-social housing program	NGO	NGO: program coordinator, SHFC: funding provision for CMP Donors: housing construction	North of city Center	Purchased private land, using SHFC

[a] GMAKF: Global Media Alliance Kapuso Foundation.
[b] UPA: Urban Poor Associates.

and contractors for housing construction. As contractors, private developers play a large role in NHA projects; following NHA design requirements, developers acquire land, develop and build on the site, and then NHA compensates them for the completed efforts. Construction of the first NHA housing development in Tacloban North was completed in mid-2015. Other NHA funded settlements are currently in various stages of development, including site planning, ground preparation, and building construction. The NHA (2015) planned for the initial group of households to move into the earliest completed settlements by the end of 2015.

14.3.3.2.2 City-NGO Housing

For city-NGO housing, Tacloban City provides land and NGO donors prepare houses conforming to the National Building Code and Design for Socialized and Economic Housing. For instance, the Global Media Alliance Kapuso Foundation (GMAKF), a nonprofit foundation created by the Global Media Alliance (GMA), built the first housing units in Tacloban North using land that was already owned and being developed by Tacloban City when Yolanda struck. Having a site already under development fostered quick housing construction—by July 2015, GMAFK had completed all 403 planned housing units and accommodated more than 3000 residents (*Manila Times* 2015). A similar process was evident on an adjacent site; Tacloban City prepared the land for permanent housing and Habitat for Humanity constructed 200 houses. The city plans for the construction of about 1600 more housing units with similar partnerships with donors (Tacloban City 2015).

14.3.3.2.3 NGO-Independent Housing

After the initiation of government-organized housing construction, other NGOs planned smaller-scale permanent housing developments closer to the city center, and supported one-step relocation to minimize displacement and adverse impact on the livelihood of relocating residents. For instance, projects organized by Urban Poor Associates (UPA), a national nonprofit organization advocating for the rights of the urban poor, has called for housing redevelopment close to the city center due to the importance of jobs and livelihood (UPA 2015). With a consortium of supporters,* the project was initiated in August 2015, with plans to accommodate 550 households and include cooperative agriculture projects for livelihoods (Caritas 2015). UPA has already built temporary housing near residents' former coastal communities in hard-hit Barangay 88. UPA's one-step housing relocation approach has created controversy, leading residents to disagree with the city's two-step relocation process.

14.3.3.2.4 NGO–Donor–Social Housing Program

The last option combines support from various sources, with funding from the Community Mortgage Program (CMP) of the SHFC playing an important role. This program helps informal settlers attain formal land tenure and home ownership through acquiring land, after becoming members of a homeowners association with support of a SHFC-accredited community mobilizer. In Tacloban, the Brigham Estates housing development, located 7 km north of the city center, is an example of this type of housing provision. After acquiring land with the CMP, funding for housing construction comes from various sources, including the Philippine Disaster Relief Fund and crowd funding for some residents' groups.†

14.3.3.3 Emerging Issues

Two years after Yolanda, about 16% (1600 households) and 5% (500 households) of the initial target of beneficiary households‡ were still living in temporary housing, or had moved into permanent housing, respectively. In addition to people living in temporary and permanent housing provided by the government or donors, the majority of other residents from areas targeted for relocation went back to live in their original neighborhoods in self-built temporary housing.

Beyond the construction of housing, the city continues to face other coordination challenges related to infrastructure, which is delaying the actual relocation

---

* The consortium is called FRANCESCO (Pope Francis for Resilient and Co-Empowered Sustainable Communities), and includes the Canadian Catholic Organization for Development and Peace, NASSA/Caritas Philippines, UPA, the Roman Catholic Archdiocese of Palo, and the Congregation of the Most Holy Redeemer (Caritas Philippines 2015).

† To learn more about the Anibong Cluster crowdfunding on GoFundMe, visit https://bagacayhousing.wordpress.com/

‡ Over time, as housing providers committed to the construction of additional permanent housing units, the target has increased to over 15,200 (Tacloban City 2015).

of residents. At the same time, affected residents are increasingly seeing unequal opportunities, such as relocation options prioritized for residents from certain areas, and limitations leading to growing doubts about relocation. As implementation of relocation plans proceeds, some critical issues for residents' life and housing recovery have emerged.

First, although NGOs' varied assistance for temporary housing created multiple options, choices were not equally provided to beneficiaries. For instance, not all residents received equivalent information or access to rental assistance or other unique housing initiatives. Those from certain areas were prioritized for early and limited support. Depending on the type of housing they received, residents faced different problems, such as crowded and unsanitary living conditions in bunkhouses. While those in transitional shelters in the north have a more comfortable living environment with more space, they must adapt to a vastly different lifestyle. For example, they lack employment opportunities given the distance to downtown.

Second, the anticipation of moving into permanent housing has been tempered by the lack of utilities such as electricity and water; as the supply to the north has been delayed. Education is also a major concern, as additional school buildings have not yet been constructed to accommodate the influx of children, and the host barangay schools are becoming overcrowded. In the first year, some households continued to send their children back to their original schools, even though transportation costs were a significant economic burden.

Third, households currently living in temporary or permanent housing provided under the relocation scheme only represent some of those in need of housing. Most households have decided to wait back in their communities; the lengthy waiting time fosters increasing doubts about the reality of relocation. In addition, due to UPA urging one-step relocation, some barangays have requested direct relocation to permanent housing, conflicting with the city's plan, and making it difficult to convince residents to participate in two-step housing relocation.

14.4 DISCUSSION AND CONCLUSIONS

This chapter focused on the initial stage of relocation efforts and implementation status of post-Yolanda Tacloban City to explain opportunities and challenges of preventive relocation in rebuilding. Two years into recovery is too early to speculate on future outcomes, but there are several useful observations.

On a positive note, relocation processes were initiated at an early stage of rebuilding. This is rare because preventive relocation in recovery is not usually implemented, as during the time that it takes to make plans, actors start reconstruction on the ground. In Tacloban, there are several reasons behind the implementation of relocation strategies and initiatives. First, Tacloban City passed the "no-build zone" ordinance, aligning with the national reconstruction strategy, RAY, at an early stage of recovery and shared this information with coastal residents. From the very beginning, the city set a priority to relocate informal coastal residents, as they are the least privileged and most vulnerable population. Second, the local government took on the central coordination role, as called for in RAY and in the UDHA. Throughout the process, Tacloban City coordinated and advanced housing reconstruction by managing various actors representing international agencies, national governments, NGOs, and civil society organizations. So far, they have successfully built partnerships with nongovernmental actors during both the temporary and permanent phases of housing relocation, thereby leveraging varied support to provide housing to a larger population. Lastly, pre-Yolanda, the city had a general consensus and pre-existing plan to develop the northern part of the city to accommodate a growing population. This overall development direction allowed for a relatively quick initiation of large-scale relocation.

However, several concerns remain. First, although multiple actors in housing relocation provided more housing options to relocating residents, this also created confusion and difficulties in coordination. While two-step relocation out of the no-building zone was Tacloban City's main policy, the emergence of other solutions such as one-step relocation—to stay near the original neighborhoods and then move directly into permanent housing—fueled residents' growing doubts about the city's program. Second, residents in both temporary and permanent houses are becoming more vulnerable with time as their former social networks and livelihoods have been disrupted. They face urgent and unmet needs to reestablish their way of life. Basic infrastructure such as electricity and potable water systems, and public facilities such as schools are still lacking in new settlements, and the lack of economic opportunities is a serious long-term issue. Without appropriate development and strategies to support the livelihoods of both new and host-community residents, increasing competition for employment and strained social relations will negatively impact both groups.

Although earlier efforts in preventive relocation after disasters, such as in Indonesia and Sri Lanka, did not materialize, more and more disaster-stricken areas are likely to consider the types of development controls and planning processes used in Tacloban. The case of Tacloban City demonstrates that providing housing alone will not secure sustainable conditions for displaced residents. For residents to be able to recover their quality of life, it is critical that relocation is treated as a holistic effort that includes the development of social and livelihood opportunities as well as housing and infrastructure.

14.5 ACKNOWLEDGMENTS

The authors extend appreciation to those who shared their time and knowledge, especially Tacloban City, captains of coastal *barangays*, residents of Tacloban City in temporary and permanent housing as well as in their former coastal communities. We would also like to extend our gratitude to local universities, NGOs, and international organizations working on the ground. This work was supported by the funding provided by Tohoku University and JSPS KAKENHI Grant number 16H05752.

REFERENCES

ADB. 1998. *Handbook on Resettlement: A Guideline to Good Practice.* Manila, Philippines: Asian Development Bank.

Badri, S. A., A. Asgary, A. R. Eftekhari, and J. Levy. 2006. Post-disaster resettlement, development and change: A case study of the 1990 Manjil earthquake in Iran. *Disasters* 30 (4): 451–468.

Bolin, R. C. and L. Stanford. 1998. The Northridge earthquake: Community-based approaches to unmet recovery needs. *Disasters* 22 (1): 21–38.

Caritas Philippines. 2015. Pope Francis Village to give home to 550 families from Tacloban danger zones. http://www.caritasphilippines.org/2015/09/05/pope-francis-village-to-give-home-to-550-families-from-tacloban-danger-zones (accessed January 17, 2016).

Catholic Relief Services (CRS) Philippines. 2015. Urban shelter and settlement as recovery: A "menu of options" for households. *Humanitarian Exchange* 63: 36, January. Cernea, M. M. 1997. The risks and reconstruction model for resettling displaced populations. *World Development* 25 (10): 1569–1587.

Correa, E., ed. 2011. *Preventive Resettlement of Populations at Risk of Disaster: Experiences from Latin America.* Washington, DC: The World Bank.

Correa, E., F. Ramirez, and H. Sanahuja. 2011. *Populations at Risk of Disaster: A Resettlement Guide.* Washington, DC: The World Bank.

Department of Budget and Management (DBM). 2015. Calamity and quick response funds old. http://www.dbm.gov.ph/?page_id=2584#QRF.

Department of Public Works and Highways (DPWH). 2013. 2,800 families in Yolanda stricken-areas to have new homes this Christmas season. *Official Gazette.* http://www.gov.ph/2013/12/07/2800-families-in-yolanda-stricken-areas-to-have-new-homes-this-christmas-season/ (accessed May 18, 2014).

Diaz, J. 2014. Calamity fund for this year increased to P13 B. *Philstar.* http://www.philstar.com/headlines/2014/01/14/1278593/calamity-fund-year-increased-p13-b (accessed January 29, 2016).

Dickson, E., J. L. Baker, D. Hoornweg, and A. Tiwari. 2012. *Urban Risk Assessments: Understanding Disaster and Climate Risk in Cities*, ed. The World Bank, Washington, DC: The World Bank.

Environmental Science for Social Change (ESSC). 2014. *Rapid Assessment of the Performance of Post-Disaster Housing Reconstruction Approaches.* http://essc.org.ph/content/a-rapid-review-of-post-disaster-housing-reconstruction-approaches/ (accessed January 17, 2016).

Esnard, A. M. and A. Sapat. 2014. *Displaced by Disaster: Recovery and Resilience in a Globalizing World.* New York: Routledge.

Gabieta, J. 2015. Poverty worsens in Eastern Visayas NEDA says more than half of region's people now poor after "Yolanda". *Inquirer.* http://newsinfo.inquirer.net/680120/poverty-worsens-in-eastern-visayas (accessed September 10, 2015).

International Research Institute of Disaster Science. 2015. *IRIDeS Fact-Finding Missions to Philippines (Second Report).* Sendai, Japan: Tohoku University.

Iuchi, K. 2014. Planning resettlement after disasters. *Journal of the American Planning Association* 80 (4): 413–425.

Iuchi, K., E. Maly, and L. A. Johnson. 2015. Three years after a mega-disaster: Recovery policies, programs, and implementation after the great East Japan earthquake. In *Post-Tsunami Hazard Reconstruction and Restoration*, V. Santiago-Gandino, Y. A. Kontar and Y. Kaneda (eds), London: Springer, pp. 29–46.

Jha, A. 2009. *Safer Homes, Stronger Communities: A Handbook for Reconstruction after Natural Disasters*, ed. The World Bank, Washington DC: The World Bank.

Kamel, N. M. O. and A. Loukaitou-Sideris. 2004. Residential assistance and recovery following the Northridge earthquake. *Urban Studies* 41 (3): 533–562.

Kim, K. and R. B. Olshansky. 2014. The theory and practice of building back better. *Journal of the American Planning Association* 80 (4): 289–292.

Manila Times. 2015. GMAKF completes 400 houses in Tacloban. http://www.manilatimes.net/gmakf-completes-400-houses-in-tacloban/201372/ (accessed September 10, 2015).

Muggah, R. 2008. *Relocation Failures in Sri Lanka: A Short History of Internal Displacement and Resettlement*. London: Zed Books.
National Disaster Coordinating Council (NDCC). 1998. *Amended Policies, Procedures and Criteria for Calamity Area Declaration*. Manila: NDCC, NDCC Memo Order No.04 S-1998.
National Economic and Development Authority (NEDA). 2013. *Reconstruction Assistance on Yolanda: Build Back Better*. Manila, Philippines: NEDA.
National Economic and Development Authority (NEDA). 2014. *Reconstruction Assistance on Yolanda: Implementation for Results*. Manila, Philippines: Government of the Philippines.
National Housing Authority (NHA). 2015. Typhoon Yolanda rehab efforts. http://www.nha.gov.ph/news/articles/typhoon%20yolanda%20rehab%20efforts.html (accessed September 10, 2015).
National Statistical Coordination Board (NSCB). 2013. *2012 Full Year Official Poverty Statistics*. Manila, Philippines: Republic of the Philippines.
Office of the Presidential Assistant for Rehabilitation and Recovery (OPARR). 2014a. *Yolanda Comprehensive Rehabilitation and Recovery Plan*. Manila, Philippines: OPARR.
Office of the Presidential Assistant for Rehabilitation and Recovery (OPARR). 2014b. *Yolanda Rehabilitation and Recovery Efforts*. Manila, Philippines: OPARR.
Open Street Map. 2013. Open Street Map: Typhoon Haiyan. http://www.openstreetmap.org/#map=15/11.2461/124.9975&layers=H (accessed February 16, 2016).
Philippines Statistic Authority. 2013. Population of Tacloban City rose to more than 200 thousand (results from the 2010 Census of Population and Housing). https://psa.gov.ph/content/population-tacloban-city-rose-more-200-thousand-results-2010-census-population-and-housing (accessed September 20, 2015).
Pyles, L. 2007. Community organizing for post-disaster social development—Locating social work. *International Social Work* 50 (3): 321–333.
Republic of Indonesia. 2005. *Master Plan for the Rehabilitation and Reconstruction of the Regions and Communities of the Province of Nanggroe Aceh Darussalam and the Islands of Nias, Province of North Sumatera*. Jakarta, Indonesia: Republic of Indonesia, Presidential Regulation No. 30.
Republic of the Philippines. 1976. *The Water Code of the Philippines*. Manila, Republic of the Philippines, PRIME-M4.
Republic of the Philippines. 1992. *An Act to Provide for a Comprehensive and Continuing Urban Development and Housing Program, Establish the Mechanism for its Implementation, and for Other Purposes*. Manila, Republic of the Philippines, RA-7279.
Republic of the Philippines. 2013. *An Act Appropriating the Sum of Fourteen Billion Six Hundred Million Pesos (P14,600,000,000.00) as Supplemental Appropriations for FY 2013 and for Other Purposes*, Manila, RA-10634.
Scudder, T. 1985. A sociological framework for the analysis of new land settlements. In *Putting People First: Sociological Variables in Rural Development*, M. M. Cernea (ed.), 2nd edn, New York: Published for the World Bank by Oxford University Press, 148–187.
Tacloban City. 2012. *Tacloban City Comprehensive Land Use Plan*. Tacloban, Philippines: Tacloban City.
Tacloban City. 2014a. *An Ordinance Providing for a 40-Meter No-Build-Zone for Residential Housing within the Territorial Jurisdiction of the City of Tacloban*. Tacloban, Philippines: Tacloban City, Ordinance No. 2013-12-15A.
Tacloban City. 2014b. *The Tacloban Recovery and Rehabilitation Plan*. Tacloban, Philippines: Tacloban City.
Tacloban City. 2015. *Housing Projects in Tacloban City as of October, 2015*. Tacloban, Philippines: Tacloban City.

The World Bank. 2014. *Recovery and Reconstruction Planning in the Aftermath of Typhoon Haiyan (Yolanda)*. Washington, DC: The World Bank.

Urban Poor Associates (UPA). 2015. Pope Francis Housing Project. http://www.urbanpoorassociates.org/index.php (accessed September 10, 2015).

Wisner, B., P. M. Blaikie, T. Cannon, and I. Davis. 2004. *At Risk: Natural Hazards, People's Vulnerability and Disasters*, 2nd edn, New York: Routledge.

Section IV

Multiple Dimensions of Housing Recovery

15 Meta-Patterns in Post-Disaster Housing Reconstruction and Recovery

Gonzalo Lizarralde, Mahmood Fayazi, Faten Kikano, and Isabelle Thomas

CONTENTS

15.1 INTRODUCTION: LEARNING FROM PREVIOUS CASES

Sustainable reconstruction (i.e., a process of transformation that is socially just) requires identifying lessons learned from previous experiences and the careful adaptation of successful mechanisms and methods based on contextual characteristics (International Recovery Platform 2005; Lizarralde et al. 2009). Housing development after disasters can benefit from revealing common risks and avoiding recurrent mistakes (Lyons 2009; Davis, IFRC, and OCHA 2015). This chapter examines nine patterns that occur in post-disaster housing reconstruction and recovery. It reveals the conditions that typically lead to the emergence of these patterns and suggests an approach that can contribute to prevent their incidence and enhance social justice in future sustainable reconstruction processes. The identification of these meta-patterns also facilitates the transfer of lessons learned from reconstruction experiences in different contexts.

The research that supports the identification of these patterns included a comprehensive review of the literature on post-disaster reconstruction, low-cost housing, and international development. Patterns found in the literature were then validated by six case studies of reconstruction projects conducted by members of our team in Nueva Choluteca, Honduras; La Paz, El Salvador; La Tebaida, Colombia; Bam, Iran; Bousalem, Tunisia; and Canaan, Haiti.* Table 15.1 presents a summary of these projects. Patterns were then classified according to three dimensions of recovery: the built environment, socio-economic conditions, and political background (see Table 15.1).

15.2 PATTERNS IN THE BUILT ENVIRONMENT

15.2.1 Urban Sprawl and Relocation

Access to housing is one of the most important determinants of post-disaster recovery, but one of the most technically complex solutions to implement in urban contexts (UN-OCHA et al. 2008). Pressure on authorities to respond quickly to the housing needs of affected families further complicates the process (Lizarralde et al. 2009). Developing land for housing is a significant challenge for both central and local administrations. Municipalities in developing countries (even local governments in medium-size cities) rarely have the legal, financial, and administrative resources required (Gilbert 2004; Lizarralde 2014). The insufficient availability of, and capacity to use, land are additional frequent barriers (Ferguson and Navarrete 2003). Urban land is typically rare, and thus expensive, when proximate to services, infrastructure, transportation, and jobs. Naturally, it is cheaper in less suitable locations in the periphery of cities and towns (Datta and Jones 2001). This is the main reason why public organizations and NGOs tend to build low-cost housing in unserviced land and (given the impact of land value in the final outcome) seek economies of scale by building numerous units on large plots—instead of building dispersed units in small portions of urbanized land (Lizarralde 2014). Securing land in areas less subject to disaster risks is difficult even on the periphery of many cities (Harpham and Boateng 1997; Lizarralde 2008), including hazard-prone Port-au-Prince and Choluteca.

Informal occupation of land typically increases when housing shortages after disasters are not quickly met (see Figure 15.1). Yet, relocation to the urban periphery, whether induced (such as in the cases in Nueva Choluteca, Erroumani, and Razmandegan), or relatively voluntary (such as in the case of Canaan), poses several problems in the long term and is one of the most significant causes of users' dissatisfaction with post-disaster housing conditions (Lizarralde and Bouraoui 2010). First, relocated families lose the connections and proximity to friends and services

* Some of these patterns were presented by the first author in a conference paper (Lizarralde 2015).

TABLE 15.1
Description of the Post-Disaster Reconstruction Case Studies Analyzed in the Study

Project and Related Disaster	City, Country	Initiative Led by	No. of Housing Units	Start/End of the Project	Type of Housing	Location	Infrastructure Provided
Post Hurricane Mitch (1998) relocation to Nueva Choluteca	Outskirts of Choluteca, Honduras	International NGOs (more than 16)	About 2000	1999–2002	One-storey detached	Relocation 15 km away from city	Partial water, sewage, and electricity provided later in 2004
Post-earthquake (2001) rural housing by Fundasal	La Paz region, El Salvador	A local NGO	4400	2001–2002	One-storey detached	Dispersed units in rural area	None
Post-earthquake (1999) new housing project El Cantarito	Outskirts of La Tebaida, Colombia	Local NGO (funded by private donors, USAID, and Colombian Government)	952	2000–2003	One-storey row housing	Town periphery	Water, sewage, electricity, and roads
Post-earthquake (2003) relocation to Razamandegan	Outskirts of Bam, Iran	The Housing Foundation of the Islamic Republic	About 1300	2003–2006	Three to four-storey buildings	Relocation in the urban periphery	Water, sewage, electricity, telephone, gas, and roads
Post-floods (2003) relocation to Erroumani	Outskirts of Bousalem, Tunisia	The National Government	211	2004–2006	One-storey row housing	Relocation 6 km away from village	Water, sewage, electricity, and roads
Post-earthquake (2010) occupation of Canaan	Outskirts of Port-au-Prince, Haiti	Local residents (by informal land occupation) and international NGOs that provide aid	About 150,000	2010-ongoing	Informal detached transitional shelters becoming permanent housing	Land occupation about 7 Km away from the city	None by August 2015. Infrastructure is being prepared by the American Red Cross and other international agencies

FIGURE 15.1 After the 2010 earthquake in Haiti, informal occupation of land increased in Jalousie and other informal settlements in risk-prone hills in Port-au-Prince. (From Gonzalo Lizarralde.)

that constitute the social fabric that provide them access to loans, child care, affordable services, transportation, security, affordable labor, recreation, etc. (Oliver-Smith 1991; Lizarralde et al. 2009; Barenstein et al. 2010). Second, projects developed on the periphery of cities, and poorly integrated with the urban fabric are often at risk of ghettoization and stigmatization. Third, informal networks that are valuable for the local economy are typically dislocated. Fourth, transportation costs increase for low-income residents (in some cases, commuting becomes so expensive that workers prefer to sleep close to their jobs under poor conditions and occupy the houses only on the weekends). Fifth, too often, unemployment rates increase as people lose their traditional livelihoods and thus become less autonomous. Sixth, short-term construction, and long-term maintenance, of public services and infrastructure become too expensive for both beneficiaries and municipalities. Finally, most commercial activities at the household level become unproductive due to lower densities and lack of connections to the city and other urbanized areas.

15.2.2 Emphasis on Houses, Neglecting Infrastructure and Community Services

Even if safe land is made available, other challenges still exist for housing development. These include securing public funding among competitive priorities, developing programs for household savings and financing, selecting beneficiaries, and defining minimum standards for housing solutions (Gilbert 2004; Lizarralde 2008). Of course, the housing needs of affected families go beyond the need for immediate shelter. The recovery of livelihoods is crucial for achieving sustainable reconstruction

(Pomeroy et al. 2006). However, pressed by the urgency to react quickly to housing shortages, NGOs and public institutions often resort to only building houses (UN-OCHA et al. 2008). The emphasis on providing houses alone characterized reconstruction projects in Nueva Choluteca (Honduras) and La Paz (El Salvador), in which infrastructure was largely neglected (see Figure 15.2). In Canaan (Haiti),

(a)

(b)

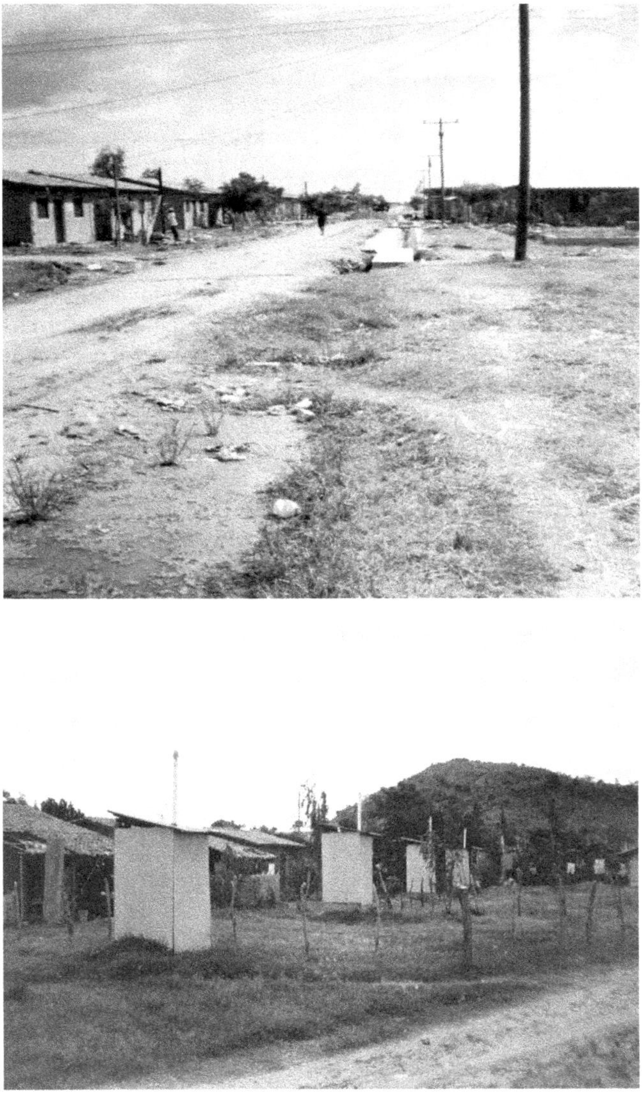

FIGURE 15.2 About 2000 houses were built in Nueva Coluteca with minimum infrastructure (a). A few organizations, such as Canadian CECI, eventually realized the importance of providing latrines and water service (b). (From Gonzalo Lizarralde.)

affected residents who occupied land informally after the disaster have received temporary shelters and aid from international agencies, but have not benefited from infrastructure, even 5 years after the first occupants moved to the area. In some cases, such as Canaan, the rush to react quickly leads organizations to build temporary shelters in hazard-prone areas, not realizing that most of them will become permanent housing. As such, Canaan keeps growing as a new urban slum increasing the footprint of Port-au-Prince with unsustainable residential development. These cases provide additional support to a well-known argument: the feasibility of housing solutions and the recovery of livelihoods is actually dependant on the suitability of infrastructure (including access to water, sewage, waste collection, electricity, and roads) and the availability of community services, such as schools, police stations, health centers, public transportation, and markets (Lloyd-Jones 2006).

15.2.3 Introduction of New Construction Technologies and Materials

When disaster strikes, it is commonly believed that new disaster-resistant construction technologies must replace local, traditional technologies. However, the introduction of new technologies causes several problems. First, local formal and informal construction companies and suppliers of materials are often ignored in the recovery process, and thus do not benefit from programs aimed at increasing efficiency or improving business practices. Second, local workers are not sufficiently employed in reconstruction, missing the opportunity to improve their skills. Third, there is often a limited transfer of construction knowledge and skills to households, and thus, later maintenance and modifications to units become difficult. Fourth, the so-called multi-hazard-resistant houses (such as the ones provided in Nueva Choluteca) ultimately preserve certain vulnerabilities, because enlargements, repairs, and upgrading of units become expensive and difficult, and thus users and local workers resume unsafe construction practices (Bouraoui and Lizarralde 2013).

15.3 PATTERNS IN SOCIO-ECONOMIC DIMENSIONS

15.3.1 Neglect of Home-Based Income Generation

NGOs and public institutions often underestimate the close relationship that exists between income generation activities and residential uses in low-income settlements. In Nueva Choluteca, Bousalem, and El Cantarito, housing units had neither the spaces nor the proper façade openings to facilitate the creation of home-based income generation activities. Informal housing solutions in most developing countries, however, integrate these two uses within a single housing unit (see an example in Figure 15.3). The ability to integrate income generation activities (such as family businesses, small workshops, rental space, and retail) within housing units is crucial for the economic sustainability of most poor families (Kellett and Tipple 2000; Gough and Kellett 2001). This integration is necessary to allow households to reduce costs associated with business development. In many cases, it also allows single parents to work while caring for children, notably allowing for women to earn an income. Informal home-based enterprises also facilitate the employment

FIGURE 15.3 Housing in low-income settlements in developing countries typically integrate residential and commercial activities, such as in this house in Martissant, Port-au-Prince, Haiti. (From Gonzalo Lizarralde.)

of unskilled individuals who often have limited possibilities of being employed in formal urban jobs.

15.3.2 Neglect of the Informal Sector

The informal construction sector is quickly transforming Canaan, Haiti, from a displaced population camp to a new permanent settlement. It is estimated that by 2015, more than USD 100 million has been invested informally by families in housing in Canaan (Kushner 2015), many times more than what has been invested by international institutions and NGOs. The informal sector is also responsible for the development of about half of the housing stock in developing countries. Most construction upgrades and additions in housing are conducted by the informal sector, notably through self-help, paid informal workers, and unpaid labor. Their participation is crucial in adapting housing units to the needs and aspirations of residents. Yet, the informal sector is rarely involved in institutionalized housing programs; a pattern unfortunately found in all the case studies presented here. This is due in part to several myths about the informal sector that still prevail. Thus, it is crucial to clarify here that informality is *not* the cause of disasters; disasters are caused by the accumulation of physical, social, economic, and political vulnerabilities (Blaikie et al. 1994). Instead, informal enterprises have some advantages that can be used in housing provision, notably their increased capacity to: (a) adapt to hostile economic environments; (b) deliver customized solutions and affordable units for the poorest families; and (c) adapt work and objectives in the project life cycle following the pace of available resources and partial commissioning. They are nonetheless constrained by significant limitations, notably their limited capacity to: (a) access financial solutions with competitive interest rates; (b) respond to disaster-resistant standards; and (c) develop comprehensive solutions for infrastructure. Given this context, the informal sector needs to be considered as an important (and unavoidable) stakeholder in housing development before, during, and after disasters (Lizarralde 2014).

15.3.3 Neglect of Socio-Economic, Cultural, and Environmental Conditions

A house not only serves as a shelter, it also *shapes* and *is shaped by* culture, social behaviors, religious beliefs, financial constraints, and the daily habits of families (Turner and Fichter 1972; Turner 1977; Kellett and Hernandez-Garcia 2013). Yet, Barenstein (2006a,b) and other specialists have shown how, in many cases, reconstruction after the 2004 tsunami in Tamil Nadu paid little attention to social, cultural, and environmental conditions, resulting in the deterioration of peoples' cultural identity and livelihood. Often, new houses do not respond to local lifestyle, economic conditions, cultural traditions, religious beliefs, and environmental characteristics. Layouts for temporary shelters in Canaan, for instance, had ignored the "Lakou," a much-valued vernacular form of clustering houses in Haiti. As shelters are transforming into permanent houses, urban layouts will become meaningless for many residents. This pattern seems to apply to developed nations too. In New Orleans, for instance, vernacular housing typologies, such as "shutguns," were suitable to local conditions and a source of pride for many local residents. Yet, since citizens and several stakeholders were not involved in defining housing types during post-Katrina reconstruction, new typologies were arbitrarily introduced (Verderber 2010). If residents do not occupy and use housing units and public space, interventions end up creating a Disneyland version of the city (Maret and Allen 2008). In Nueva Choluteca (Honduras) and La Paz (El Salvador), several families even refused to move into the new detached, rubber-stamped units provided by NGOs, while others only used them for storage. Those who moved in made numerous changes at a great cost, adding more spaces and changing the layout to adjust the space to their needs and expectations.

15.4 PATTERNS IN POLITICAL DIMENSIONS

15.4.1 Centralized Housing Provision, Corruption, and Mismanagement

Developing mass housing is a complex, financially risky, political process. Similarly, developing urban land for housing (or failing to do it) might be politically expensive. Given the stakes, servicing land, construction, and reconstruction are typically affected by high levels of corruption (Lewis 2008; Murray and Meghji 2009). Take the case of Haiti. According to Haiti Grassroots Watch, a local watchdog that monitors the reconstruction process, housing initiatives have largely suffered from corruption, mismanagement, and lengthy disputes over land ownership (Reuters 2015).

It is, therefore, common that project initiators (i.e., central authorities, municipalities, international agencies, and NGOs) seek to minimize risks of corruption, legal disputes, and mismanagement by transferring contracts to a reduced number of reliable, experienced, and recognized agencies (whether for-profit or not). This approach results in a centralized process of investment and decision making, which causes several problems in reconstruction (Lyons 2009). Agency-driven reconstruction was implemented in El Cantarito, Nueva Choluteca, Razamandegan, and Erroumani. Decisions were made based on limited information collected by leading agencies. In these and other cases, a unique housing model is built (Lizarralde et al. 2009) to optimize construction logistics and achieve economies of scale, whether through a contractor-driven approach or a self-help approach. Implementing this response requires developing large portions of land, which as we discussed above, are often scarce and expensive in desirable, fully serviced locations.

Unsurprisingly, rubber-stamped units rarely meet the needs and aspirations of (most often) heterogeneous residents. It is difficult, almost impossible, that a group of decision makers can, in a state of emergency, design, plan, and manage a unique solution for alleviating the overwhelming problems of post-disaster reconstruction within a centralized process (Lizarralde 2014). Research has shown that there are too many variables and too much information that is required to properly respond to the affected families' complex needs (Lyons 2009). This requires assessing and balancing a multiplicity of variables, including: fluctuating information about economic investment, land prices, complex cultural desires, unexpected social attitudes, controversial traditional values, day-to-day behaviors, administrative needs, complex legal procedures, interrelated infrastructure costs, recycling needs, maintenance costs, environmental considerations, and political pressures (Lizarralde et al. 2009).

Centralization of decision making is, nonetheless, sometimes necessary. The centralization of infrastructure development and operation, for instance, is often required in densely populated urban areas. Agency-driven procurement of individual low-cost housing units, however, is in many cases unnecessary and reduces the beneficiaries' capacity to make decisions that respond to their own housing and livelihood needs and expectations.

15.4.2 The "One Size Fits All Approach" and Injustices in Distribution of Resources and Services

Policies developed by institutions and agencies also often neglect the variety of households and the diversity of their needs and desires (Aysan and Oliver 1987). They typically generalize about the perceived characteristics of residents, often aggregated in what agencies indiscriminately call "the community"—members are regularly seen as being homogeneous. They, therefore, often fail to consider how policy and decisions affect different categories of residents in a distinctive manner (Aldrich 2012). In Bam, for instance, heterogeneous groups of households received the same services and resources (Fayazi et al. 2015). However, different pre-disaster conditions, such as sources of livelihood, ownership rights, and relationships with local authorities, altered their impact on household recovery. Nearly 2 years after the earthquake, for instance, pre-disaster homeowners and house tenants were given the same type of apartments in residential complexes located in Razmandegan, an area in the city outskirts (see Figure 15.4). Owning an apartment dramatically decreased the pre-disaster vulnerabilities of house tenants, and helped them recover fast.

FIGURE 15.4 Residential complex developed after the 2003 earthquake in Razmandegan in the outskirts of Bam, Iran. (From Mahmood Fayazi.)

Previous homeowners relocated to the outskirts of the city, however, saw this relocation as a significant deterioration of their living conditions given the loss of valuable connections with their communities, reduction in access to familiar services, and increases in transportation and other costs.

The "one size fits all" approach presents several difficulties. But perceptions of an unjust distribution of resources and services might also be seen as a way of exacerbating social inequalities. For instance, a significant immigration of informal settlers into disaster-affected areas occurred in Bam and has occurred in the immediate aftermath of many other disasters. In Bam, this distortion in "normal" demographic conditions led to increased demand on services and aid and created competition between local and newly arrived families. Locals perceived that it was unfair that "opportunistic immigrants" inhabited the camps of temporary houses inside the city (Fayazi and Lizarralde 2013).

15.4.3 Poor Communication and Distribution of Information

Information is one of the most useful resources that enable families to recover. Reliable and accessible information is a prerequisite to communication, which permits the articulation of needs, views, and attitudes, and allows affected families to create common meanings, narratives, and understandings (Norris et al. 2008). Housing reconstruction programs, however, often offer different levels of access to information, which consequently lead to varied levels of recovery. Our studies have found that varying and continuously changing information about land tenure, investments, and opportunities, for instance, have caused tensions among families living in Canaan. Poor communication and information in Bam made it difficult for affected residents to be aware of challenges and opportunities ahead. Rumors about the possibility of receiving funds to build new houses, for instance, led a large number of pre-disaster tenants to buy land at cheap prices in Janbazan, an area in the city outskirts. However, the municipality did not grant these new landowners permission to construct new houses in Janbazan (see Figure 15.5). Around 12 years after the

FIGURE 15.5 Informal settlement in Janbazan, developed by affected residents after the 2003 earthquake in Bam, Iran. (From Mahmood Fayazi.)

earthquake, it is estimated that more than 100 affected families still live in temporary sheltering in an informal settlement in Janbazan (Fayazi et al. 2015).

15.4.3.1 Housing as Social Justice

The previous mega-patterns (you may say, recurrent "mistakes") can be avoided. However, it requires that critical decisions be made in the interest of achieving social justice for poor, disadvantaged, marginalized, vulnerable citizens as well as children, women, and the elderly. This implies facilitating two levels of action: *individual* and *collective* agency, and therefore, requires consideration of both the enhancement of individual freedoms and the development of appropriate mechanisms of project governance.

15.4.3.1.1 Individual Freedoms

Enhancing active decision making among households has proven to be one of the most successful means to improve the performance of housing reconstruction processes. This goes beyond typical "community participation" practices in which agencies still manage resources and aid. Freedom of, and responsibility for, managing individual projects and importantly, the money itself, increases users' satisfaction and permits that investments respond more easily to their real needs and aspirations. User-driven approaches typically transfer significant decision-making power to families, so they can define the project scope, and design, manage, and finance (and in some cases even build) their own initiatives. In these approaches, each beneficiary is responsible for the planning, management, and procurement of his/her own initiative. Individual initiatives may include residential use (a house), but also, income generation activities, infrastructure, or a combination of them. Beneficiaries, therefore, assume responsibility for their own initiatives during the whole project life cycle, responding to the specific needs and expectations of their own families. Successful user-driven strategies have been developed in reconstruction processes in the Armenia region in Colombia (Lyons 2009; Lizarralde 2010) and Gujarat,

India (Barenstein 2006a,b; Jha et al. 2009). Being responsible for the direct use of resources, families tend to adopt some of the advantages of informal construction: they recycle more materials, build flexible spaces, pace construction according to their priorities, and purchase the most inexpensive resources in the market. In this way, user-driven procurement strategies overcome some of the difficulties of centralized investment and planning, and avoid the problem of having insufficient access to dynamic information regarding individual needs and expectations.

However, user-driven approaches must also avoid some of the disadvantages typically found in informal construction. Enhancing decision-making freedom, therefore, requires, steady and engaged support in information and education for affected families, as well as proper legal and administrative frameworks. Beneficiaries must also be enrolled in a financing plan in which they receive three or four progressive instalments that are approved by the same number of technical inspections at different stages of the construction. These inspections must progressively assess appropriate use of resources, disaster resistance, quality of materials, environmental concerns, etc. The approach also requires appropriate information management and attentive technical support in disaster resistance, management, contracting, etc. (Barenstein 2006a,b). It is important to emphasize that such an approach does not imply a disengagement of institutional responsibility. It demands instead a sustained engagement in planning, management, and organizational structuring, and control and supervision of construction work.

Lower housing standards can be (and indeed, are) accepted by users (see Figure 15.6), provided alternatives for incremental upgrading are available and properly

FIGURE 15.6 Despite (also, due to) having access to services and infrastructure, residents of El Cantarito made significant changes to their dwellings, proving that the original units were seen just as core units that had to be upgraded and enlarged. (From Gonzalo Lizarralde.)

planned in advance. Incremental housing solutions (including serviced core housing) optimize the participation of formal and informal stakeholders, allowing for customization and upgrading to be conducted and managed by beneficiaries. Yet, favoring incremental strategies requires careful planning of the roles of all project stakeholders, including informal builders and enterprises as well as maintenance agencies.

15.4.3.1.2 Project Governance

Housing reconstruction requires, nonetheless, more than individual actions. It also demands the development of governance mechanisms capable of integrating a multiplicity of heterogeneous stakeholders. Governance generally refers to the rules (both structures and processes) that frame the action of stakeholders in situations in which there is not necessarily one single leader, but rather a distribution of decision-making power among heterogeneous stakeholders (Reve and Levitt 1984). Governance mechanisms must allow for the debate of interests and expectations and the identification, through intense interaction between stakeholders, of collective values. Rather than eluding social responsibility (as it happens, unfortunately, quite often), various stakeholders must assume complementary roles (Lizarralde 2014).

Central governments can contribute to socially just housing development by regulating the participation of NGOs in reconstruction and development, by creating financial mechanisms that allow for decentralization of investment, and by promoting subsidized programs based on user-driven procurement and other procurement strategies that facilitate individual freedom and create collective value. Municipalities can contribute by enforcing construction codes, securing land tenure, and streamlining processes so that land can be developed for low-cost housing in areas close to services, infrastructure, and jobs. Finally, local and international NGOs and agencies can contribute by adopting strategies that go beyond traditional "community participation" approaches and instead transfer decision-making power directly to individual families, by involving informal labor and construction companies, by avoiding rapid implementation of new construction technologies (notably industrialized), and finally, by guaranteeing that housing projects include infrastructure, services, and the appropriate conditions for the development of income generation activities at the household level.

Alternative strategies to the agency-driven reconstruction must also be further explored. Cooperative housing, for example, can overcome some of the drawbacks of centralized investment and procurement. Through cooperative mechanisms, a group of families having common interests can have increased control over the design, procurement, and construction of their own projects, with the additional possibility of agreeing upon a multifamily housing building and/or collective income-generating activities (agriculture, commerce, etc.).

Unreliable governance, lack of adequate infrastructure planning, political fragmentation coupled with partisan interests, and administrative inefficiency are the major barriers for the adoption of these strategies. However, previous experiences remind us that increased individual freedoms and reliable governance mechanisms are indispensable for achieving social justice, for the long-term sustainability of the built environment, and for the prosperity of the population.

REFERENCES

Aldrich, D. P. 2012. *Building Resilience: Social Capital in Post-Disaster Recovery.* Chicago, Illinois: University of Chicago Press.

Aysan, Y., and P. Oliver. 1987. *Housing and Culture after Earthquakes: A Guide for Future Policy Making on Housing in Seismic Areas.* Oxford: Oxford Polytechnic.

Barenstein, J. D. 2006a. Challenges and risks in post-tsunami housing reconstruction in Tamil Nadu. *Humanitarian Exchange* 33: 38–9.

Barenstein, J. D. 2006b. Housing reconstruction in post-earthquake Gujarat: A comparative analysis. In *Humanitarian Practice Network Paper,* Humanitarian Practice Network (HPN) (ed.),. London: Overseas Development Institute, 44 pp.

Barenstein, J. D., P. M. Phelps, D. Pittet, and S. Sena. 2010. *Safer Homes, Stronger Communities: A Handbook for Reconstruction after Natural Disasters.* Washington, DC: The World Bank.

Blaikie, P., T. Cannoon, I. Davis, and B. Wisner. 1994. *At Risk: Natural Hazards, People's Vulnerability, and Disasters.* New York: Routledge.

Bouraoui, D., and G. Lizarralde. 2013. Centralized decision making, users' participation and satisfaction in post-disaster reconstruction: The case of Tunisia. *International Journal of Disaster Resilience in the Built Environment* 4(2): 145–67.

Datta, K., and G. A. Jones. 2001. Housing and finance in developing countries: Invisible issues on research and policy agendas. *Habitat International* 25(3): 333–57.

Davis, I., IFRC, and OCHA. 2015. *Shelter after Disaster,* 2nd edn, Geneva, Switzerland: IFRC and OCHA.

Fayazi, M., F. Kikano, and G. Lizarralde. 2015. The impacts of post-disaster reconstruction policies on different categories of households in Bam, Iran. *Paper Presented in the 7th International i-Rec Conference,* London. https://www.bartlett.ucl.ac.uk/dpu/i-rec/thematic-roundtables/roundtable-4 (accessed February 29, 2016).

Fayazi, M., and G. Lizarralde. 2013. The role of low-cost housing in the path from vulnerability to resilience. *International Journal of Architectural Research* 7(3): 146–67.

Ferguson, B., and J. Navarrete. 2003. A financial framework for reducing slums: Lessons from experience in Latin America. *Environment and Urbanization* 15(2): 201.

Gilbert, A. 2004. Helping the poor through housing subsidies: Lessons from Chile, Colombia and South Africa. *Habitat International* 28(1): 13–40.

Gough, K. V., and P. Kellett. 2001. Housing consolidation and home-based income generation: Evidence from self-help settlements in two Colombian cities. *Cities* 18(4): 235–47.

Harpham, T., and K. Boateng. 1997. Urban governance in relation to the operation of urban services in developing countries. *Habitat International* 21(1): 65–77.

International Recovery Platform (IRP). 2005. Development of a cross-disaster knowledge management kit to support better recovery learning from good practices and lessons. https://www.unisdr.org/2005/task-force/tf-meetigns/12th-TF-mtg/se5-Development-cross-disaster-knowledge.pdf (accessed August 10, 2016).

Jha, A., J. D. Barenstein, P. M. Phelps, D. Pittet, and S. Sena. 2009. *Handbook for Post-Disaster Housing and Community Reconstruction.* Washington, DC: The World Bank.

Kellett, P., and J. Hernandez-Garcia. 2013. *Researching the Contemporary City: Identity, Environment and Social Inclusion in Developing Urban Areas.* Bogota, Colombia: Editorial Pontificia Universidad Javeriana.

Kellett, P., and A. Tipple. 2000. The home as workplace: A study of income-generating activities within the domestic setting. *Environment and Urbanization* 12(1): 203–14.

Kushner, J. 2015. Following outcry, the Red Cross is shifting its priorities in Haiti. *Vice News,* August 18. https://news.vice.com/article/following-outcry-the-red-cross-is-shifting-its-priorities-in-haiti (accessed February 29, 2016).

Lewis, J. 2008. The worm in the bud: Corruption, construction and catastrophe. In *Hazards and the Built Environment*, L. Bosher (ed.), New York: Routledge, 238–63.

Lizarralde, G. 2008. The challenge of low-cost housing for disaster prevention in small municipalities. *Building Resilience: Achieving Effective Post-Disaster Reconstruction, 4th International i-Rec Conference*. Christchurch, New Zealand: i-Rec. http://www.humanitarianlibrary.org/resource/challenge-low-cost-housing-disaster-prevention-small-municipalities-0 (accessed February 29, 2016).

Lizarralde, G. 2010. Decentralizing (re)construcion: Agriculture cooperatives as a vehicle for reconstruction in Colombia. In *Building Back Better: Delivering People-Centered Housing Reconstruction at Scale*, M. Lyons and T. Schilderman (eds), London: Practical Action, 191–214.

Lizarralde, G. 2014. *The Invisible Houses: Rethinking and Designing Low-Cost Housing in Developing Countries*. London: Routledge.

Lizarralde, G. 2015. La reconstruction urbaine durable: Une approche basée sur la justice sociale. *Paper presented at Colloque Ilasouria*, Montreal, Québec.

Lizarralde, G., and D. Bouraoui. 2010. Users' participation and satisfaction in post-disaster reconstruction. *Participatory Design and Appropriate Technology for Post-Disaster Reconstruction, i-REC International Conference*. Ahmedabad, India.

Lizarralde, G., C. Davidson, and C. Johnson, eds. 2009. *Rebuilding after Disasters: From Emergency to Sustainability*. London: Taylor & Francis.

Lloyd-Jones, T. 2006. *Mind the Gap! Post-Disaster Reconstruction and the Transition from Humanitarian Relief*. London: RICS.

Lyons, M. 2009. Building back better: The large-scale impact of small-scale approaches to reconstruction. *World Development* 37(2): 385–98.

Maret, I., and B. Allen. 2008. Treme: The challenges of an equitable recovery in New Orleans. *Projections MIT Journal of Planning* 8: 191–208.

Murray, M., and M. R. Meghji. 2009. Corruption within international engineering-construction projects. In *Corporate Social Responsibility in the Construction Industry*, M. Murray and A. Dainty (eds), New York: Taylor & Francis, 141–164.

Norris, F. H. et al. 2008. Community resilience as a metaphor, theory, set of capacities, and strategy for disaster readiness. *American Journal of Community Psychology* 41(1): 127–150.

Oliver-Smith, A. 1991. Successes and failures in post-disaster resettlement. *Disasters* 15(1): 12–23.

Pomeroy, R. S., B. D. Ratner, S. J. Hall, J. Pimoljinda, and V. Vivekanandan. 2006. Coping with disaster: Rehabilitating coastal livelihoods and communities. *Marine Policy* 30(6): 786–93.

Reuters. 2015. Haiti earthquake. Reuters (January 7), Natural Disasters. http://www.trust.org/spotlight/Haiti-earthquake-2010/?tab=introduction (accessed February 29, 2016).

Reve, T., and R. E. Levitt. 1984. Organization and governance in construction. *International Journal of Project Management* 2(1): 17–25.

Turner, J. F., and R. Fichter. 1972. *Freedom to Build: Dweller Control of the Housing Process*. New York: Macmillan.

Turner, J. F. C. 1977. *Housing by People: Towards Autonomy in Building Environments*. New York: Pantheon Books.

UN-OCHA, T. Corsellis, A. Vitale et al. 2008. *Transitional Settlement and Reconstruction after Natural Disasters: Field Edition*. Geneva, Switzerland: OCHA, Shelter Centre, DFID.

Verderber, S. 2010. Five years after—Three New Orleans neighborhoods. *Journal of Architectural Education* 64(1): 107–20.

16 Post-Disaster Reconstruction

Informal Settlers and the Right to Adequate Housing

Jennifer Duyne Barenstein

CONTENTS

16.1 INTRODUCTION

Up to 50% of the urban population in low- and middle-income countries live in informal settlements. By 2030, it is estimated that their number will increase to around four billion people, or close to 50% of the world population (United Nations Department of Economics and Social Affairs [UNDESA] 2014). Informal settlements are often located on land highly vulnerable to environmental and anthropogenic hazards, which are exacerbated by poor quality of housing, water, sanitation, drainage, infrastructure, healthcare, and emergency services. Considering the inevitability of disasters affecting informal settlements and thus rendering homeless large numbers of low-income people, it is of utmost importance for national stakeholders and the international humanitarian and development community to identify durable housing solutions for urban informal settlers displaced by disasters. However, although the last decade has witnessed an increasing concern and interest in urban disasters, so far housing responses for informal settlers displaced by disasters remain poorly documented.

This chapter contributes to filling this gap by consolidating information on how governments and municipal authorities, international agencies, and nongovernmental organizations (NGOs) have engaged in reconstruction in urban areas across a wide range of disasters over the last three decades, and in particular, how they have addressed the housing needs of people who do not formally own any property. Considering that adequate housing constitutes a basic and globally recognized human right, I address the following questions: What is the influence of international rights-based legal standards and policy frameworks on housing responses post-disaster? How have reconstruction programs addressed the housing needs of informal settlers? Are disasters an opportunity for informal settlers to attain adequate housing and to enhance their resilience to disasters?

To answer these questions, I review a wide range of relevant policy documents, scientific literature, and project documents on 13 disasters that have affected urban areas in various parts of the world over the last three decades. I further draw on my own field research and project evaluations that I conducted between 2004 and 2014 in India, Indonesia, Sri Lanka, the Philippines, Haiti, and Argentina.

I start this chapter with a review of how the right to adequate housing, particularly for those displaced by disasters is defined and addressed by international legal instruments and policy documents. In doing so, I provide an analysis of how the housing needs of informal settlers were addressed in the past by international and national governmental and NGOs. To conclude, I summarize the main issues that emerged from this research and offer some general recommendations.

16.1.1 The Right to Adequate Housing in Post-Disaster Settings

The 1948 Universal Declaration of Human Rights and the 1966 International Covenant on Economic, Social and Cultural Rights recognize everyone's right to an adequate standard of living, including adequate housing. The General Comment 4 of the United Nations Committee on Economic, Social and Cultural Rights (UNCESCR) defines adequate housing with reference to seven criteria:

1. Legal security of tenure
2. Availability of services
3. Affordability
4. Habitability
5. Accessibility
6. Location
7. Cultural adequacy (UNCESCR 1991)

These criteria constitute a comprehensive checklist that is potentially of practical relevance for the definition, monitoring, and evaluation of housing strategies post-disaster: *legal security of tenure* is of upmost importance to protect people against forced evictions. The criterion, *availability of services*, underlines that the attainment of adequate housing is contingent upon the availability of safe water, sanitation, energy, and emergency services. *Affordability* refers to the fact that housing and necessary services need to be commensurate with income levels and that states should ensure the availability of housing finance mechanisms to make adequate housing affordable to all. *Habitability* refers to houses' minimum spatial and structural requirements for a safe and healthy environment. *Accessibility* means that adequate housing must be available to all those entitled to it, including socially disadvantaged groups, disabled and elderly people, female-headed households, and victims of disasters and disaster prone areas. The *location* criterion underlines that housing should be made available in places where there are livelihood opportunities, health care, education, transport, and other facilities. Finally, the standard of *cultural adequacy* recognizes that housing requirements, including considerations such as privacy and spatial organization are culturally specific.

International humanitarian and development agencies have taken a long time to recognize the human rights implications of post-disaster reconstruction. Awareness that post-disaster recovery processes pose serious human rights challenges increased following the 2004 Indian Ocean tsunami. As a result, leading international agencies supported a number of initiatives toward the development of policies and guidelines aiming to ensure the housing and land rights of informal settlers after disasters (see e.g., Habitat International Coalition [HIC] 2005; Office for the Coordination of Humanitarian Affairs [OCHA] 2007; Inter-Agency Standing Committee [IASC] 2008, 2010; Harper 2009; Mitchell 2011). The right to adequate and affordable housing and security of tenure is also being addressed by several United Nations (UN) Habitat publications, although most of them do not specifically refer to disaster situations (see e.g., UN Habitat 2010, 2011a,b).

With specific reference to CESCR's definition of adequate housing, Rolnik (2011) proposed a framework for disaster response based on the various elements of the right to adequate housing. Besides emphasizing that housing responses post-disaster should meet the criteria of affordability, habitability, accessibility, and cultural adequacy, the framework stresses that all affected persons and groups should have access to information and be able to participate meaningfully in the planning and implementation of the various stages of the disaster response and particularly, that women's participation must be ensured. It further underlines that all affected persons, irrespective of their tenure status pre-disaster, should have equal rights. In post-disaster needs assessments, major pre-disaster impediments to the realization of the right to adequate housing should be identified, as should the impact of pre-disaster situations on durable solutions and the recovery process. The broader housing situation, including unplanned and unserviced settlements, should be addressed through targeted programs in conjunction with programs for disaster response and with a focus on the most vulnerable populations. Communities and settlements, not just houses, should be rebuilt or resettled. Similarly, reconstruction should not only apply to physical structures but also include the rebuilding or setting up of basic infrastructure and services and the upgrading of settlements. Community structures and networks, to the extent that they respect international human rights standards including gender equality, should be deliberately preserved and supported. If return is impossible because the land has disappeared or there are objective safety issues preventing return, resettlement and local integration conditions must comply with international human rights standards and guidelines pertaining to adequate housing, evictions, and displacement (Rolnik 2011, pp. 22–25).

The following section examines the extent to which these various global policies, frameworks, guidelines, and instruments are reflected in national post-disaster reconstruction policies and practices.

16.2 THE REALITY ON THE GROUND: A REVIEW OF PAST RESPONSES TO THE HOUSING NEEDS OF INFORMAL SETTLERS RENDERED HOMELESS BY DISASTERS

A review of policy and project documents from a wide range of national and international governmental and nongovernmental agencies reveals that past post-disaster reconstruction programs hardly ever refer to housing as a human right and that housing responses are never designed, monitored, or evaluated with explicit reference to any housing rights-based international policy instruments. An exception is the policies and guidelines developed by the Shelter Cluster in the Philippines after Typhoon Haiyan. However, a review of the government's reconstruction policy and of a number of NGO programs shows that they had no tangible influence on the ground (GFDRR 2014; World Risk Report [WRR] 2014). Likewise, the right to adequate housing as defined by the International Covenant on Economic, Social and Cultural Rights (UNCESCR 1991) so far has hardly served as an analytical framework for research or evaluations of post-disaster programs or projects. This poses some limitations to assessing reconstruction outcomes in different urban settings with reference to their achievements in attaining the right to adequate housing (see Table 16.1). Keeping in mind these constraints, I attempt to analyze whether and how the housing rights of informal settlers were addressed in a selected number of disaster contexts summarized in Table 16.1.

As highlighted in Table 16.1, disaster responses depend on several context-specific factors. In spite of the fact that explicit reference to international rights-based policy instruments was only made by the Shelter Cluster in the Philippines following typhoon Haiyan, there are examples of disaster responses that considered the housing rights of informal settlers and/or poor renters. For example, the reconstruction program in Mexico City reflected a particular sensitivity toward poor urban tenants whose housing rights and security of tenure were severely threatened by the disaster. The government of Mexico took the politically courageous decision to expropriate the landlords of deteriorated tenement houses in which the affected people used to live before the earthquake. Its reconstruction program allowed poor tenants to become owners of an apartment in condominiums, cooperatives, or non-for-profit housing complexes, as per their preferences, thus recognizing the rights of the poor to continue living in their familiar neighborhoods where they had their social networks and livelihoods.

The municipal government of Ocotal was also committed to responding to the rights to adequate housing for informal settlers affected by Hurricane Mitch but its endeavors could not be completed due to financial constraints. There was plenty of aid after Hurricane Mitch; however, humanitarian agencies and developmental NGOs in Nicaragua preferred to have their own projects, which were less contextually appropriate and did not necessarily target the poorest. The cases of Bhachau, Santa Fe, and Jimani are also examples of local capacity and commitment to ensure the right to adequate housing to informal settlers. In contrast, large-scale central government-led reconstruction programs as those that were implemented after the earthquakes in Turkey, Iran, India, and Indonesia often neglected informal settlers and other non-land and/or home-owning categories of urban citizens or addressed

TABLE 16.1
Overview of Housing Responses for Informal Settlers and Renters in the Context of Urban Disasters in Asia and Latin America

	City, Country	Disaster	Year	Housing Reconstruction Approach toward Informal Settlers and/or Renters
1	Mexico City	Earthquake	1985	The Popular Housing Reconstruction Program expropriated highly neglected and damaged tenement houses from culpable landlords, thus enabling participatory reconstruction programs. 45,100 low-income renters became co-owners of cooperative housing units. Government project with strong involvement of local CSOs funded by the World Bank.[a]
2	Ocotal, Nicaragua	Hurricane Mitch	1998	A project initiated by the municipal government involved the relocation of displaced or vulnerable informal settlers to a well-located, well-served, and culturally appropriate settlement. This bottom–up participatory project failed to obtain support from international donors, which opted for funding top–down agency-driven projects.[b]
3	Düzce, Turkey	Marmara Earthquake	1999	The government's housing reconstruction program excluded renters and informal settlers from housing support. Only as a result of community and local CSO pressure was some support also provided to displaced non-home owners.[c]
4	Bhuj, India	Gujarat Earthquake	2001	4000 renters lost housing. Government policy instruments (financial support to landlords to rebuild rental housing and subsidies to purchase land) did not reach low-income renters and those who could not prove their status due to informal rental contracts.[d]
5	Bhachau, India	Earthquake	2001	Local CSO and NGO collaboration with municipality enabled 1300 informal settlers to obtain land titles and access to governmental housing support. Program did not reach the poorest 467 households who could not afford to pay related costs.[e]
6	Bam, Iran	Earthquake	2003	Housing support provided to homeowners with the assumption that it would restore also rental housing 2 years after the earthquake, support to former tenant households was offered conditional upon their ability to purchase a plot of land. Low-income renters could not meet this requirement.[f]

(*Continued*)

TABLE 16.1 (*Continued*)

Overview of Housing Responses for Informal Settlers and Renters in the Context of Urban Disasters in Asia and Latin America

	City, Country	Disaster	Year	Housing Reconstruction Approach toward Informal Settlers and/or Renters
7	Santa Fe, Argentina	Floods	2003, 2007, 2008	Municipality's initial intention to relocate informal settlers of flood-prone sites was abandoned in favor of DRR measures *in situ*. Where protection *in situ* was not possible relocation was voluntary and adequately supported by the local government.[g]
8	Jimani, Dominican Republic	Debris Flow	2004	The municipal authority supported the relocation of an informal settlement of 150 houses through a participatory approach and with structural DRR measures to reduce community vulnerability.[h]
9	Ampara and Hambantota, Sri Lanka	Tsunami	2004	Internationally funded reconstruction policy provided financial support to landowners to rebuild their houses *in situ*. Renters and informal settlers were relocated to NGO-built houses. Relocation sites in many cases did not meet any of the criteria that defined "adequate housing."[i]
10	Banda Aceh, Indonesia	Tsunami	2004	Housing support by government and NGOs was contingent upon ownership of land, thus excluding 70,000 informal settlers and renters. Some support was provided to the renters and informal settlers only after protests.[j]
11	Nagapattinam, India	Tsunami	2004	Large numbers of informal settlers were relocated to hazardous sites in poor quality and culturally inappropriate NGO-built houses with severe negative impacts on people's well-being.[k]
12	Port-au-Prince, Haiti	Earthquake	2010	Among the 1.5 million displaced people, 80% were informal settlers and renters. The international community primarily supported emergency and transitional shelter, revealing their unpreparedness to respond to urban disasters in poor countries characterized by high degrees of informality. Reference to international standards is increasingly made in policy and project documents, but could not be applied to durable housing solutions on a large scale.[l]
13	Philippines	Typhoon Haiyan	2013	Shelter Cluster advocated for a rights-based approach, which stands in sharp contrast with the government policy that emphasized the relocation of informal settlers of what were declared as no-build zones. Contradictions between international and national policies and lack of funding hindered large-scale housing support for informal settlers displaced by the disaster.[m]

(*Continued*)

TABLE 16.1 (*Continued*)
Overview of Housing Responses for Informal Settlers and Renters in the Context of Urban Disasters in Asia and Latin America

[a] Kreimer and Echeverría 1991.

[b] Graf, A. 2013. Unaffordable housing and its consequences: A comparative analysis of two post-Mitch reconstruction projects in Nicaragua. In Post-Disaster Reconstruction and Change: A Community Perspective, J. Duyne Barenstein and E. Leemann (eds), Boca Raton, Florida: CRC Press, Taylor & Francis Group, 195–214; Leemann, E. 2011. Housing reconstruction in post-Mitch Nicaragua: Two case studies from the communities of San Dionisio and Ocotal. In Community Disaster Recovery and Resiliency: Exploring Global Opportunities and Challenges, D. Miller and J. Rivera (eds), Boca Raton, Florida: CRC Press, 319–42; Leemann, E. 2013. Communal leadership in post-Mitch housing reconstruction in Nicaragua. In Post-Disaster Reconstruction and Change: A Community Perspective, J. Duyne Barenstein and E. Leemann (eds), Boca Raton, Florida: CRC Press, Taylor & Francis Group, 3–30.

[c] Arslan, H., and C. Johnson. 2010. Can small actors overcome the absence of state will? In Building Back Better: Delivering People-Centred Reconstruction to Scale, M. Lyons and T. Schilderman (eds), Rugby: Practical Action Publication, 263–84; Johnson, C. 2011. Creating an Enabling Environment for Reducing Disaster Risk: Recent Experience of Regulatory Frameworks for Land, Planning and Building in Low and Middle-Income Countries. Global Assessment Report on Disaster Risk Reduction, Geneva, Switzerland: UN International Strategy for Disaster Reduction (ISDR) 2; Strutz 2014.

[d] Duyne Barenstein, J. 2006. Housing Reconstruction in Post-Earthquake Gujarat: A Comparative Analysis. HPN Network Paper, No. 54, London: ODI; Taheri Tafti, M., and R. Tomlinson. 2013. The role of post-disaster public policy responses in housing recovery of tenants. Habitat International 40: 218–24.

[e] Duyne Barenstein, J. 2006. Housing Reconstruction in Post-Earthquake Gujarat: A Comparative Analysis. HPN Network Paper, No. 54, London: ODI; Unnati 2006.

[f] ReliefWeb. 2004. ACT Appeal Iran: Bam Earthquake Relief & Rehabilitation MEIN 42, rev. no. 2. Action by Churches International. http://reliefweb.int/report/iran-islamic-republic/ act-appeal-iran-bam-earthquake-relief-rehabilitation-mein-42-revision-2 (accessed March 9, 2016); Taheri Tafti, M. 2012. Limitations of the owner-driven model in post-disaster housing reconstruction in urban settlements. Paper Presented at the Proceedings of the International Conference on Disaster Management (IIIRR). Kumamoto, Japan; Taheri Tafti, M., and R. Tomlinson. 2013. The role of post-disaster public policy responses in housing recovery of tenants. Habitat International 40: 218–24.

(*Continued*)

TABLE 16.1 (*Continued*)

Overview of Housing Responses for Informal Settlers and Renters in the Context of Urban Disasters in Asia and Latin America

[g] Duyne Barenstein, J., and B. Marti Rojas Riva. 2013. Is resettlement a viable strategy to mitigate the risk of natural disasters? Perceptions and voices from the citizens of Santa Fe, Argentina. In Post-Disaster Reconstruction and Change: A Community Perspective, J. Duyne Barenstein and E. Leemann (eds), Boca Raton, Florida: CRC Press, Taylor & Francis Group, 299–324.

[h] Doberstein, B., and H. Stager. 2012. Towards guidelines for post-disaster vulnerability reduction in informal settlements. Disasters 37(1): 28–47.

[i] Duyne Barenstein, J. 2013. Post-tsunami relocation outcomes in Sri Lanka: Communities' perspectives in Ampara and Hambantota. In Post-Disaster Reconstruction and Change, J. Duyne Barenstein and E. Leemann (eds), Boca Raton, Florida: CRC Press, 215–40.

[j] Oxfam 2006; Steinberg 2007; Da Silva 2010; Steinberg and Schmid 2010; Duyne Barenstein 2013.

[k] Duyne Barenstein 2013; Duyne Barenstein, J., and D. Pittet. 2013. An environmental and social impact assessment of post-disaster housing reconstruction. The case of Tamil Nadu. In Post-Disaster Reconstruction and Change: A Community Perspective, J. Duyne Barenstein and E. Leemann (eds), Boca Raton, Florida: CRC Press, Taylor & Francis Group, 119–36.

[l] Phelps, P. 2013. Analyzing the Haiti Post-Earthquake Shelter Response and Housing Recovery: Results and Lessons from the First Two Years. Vol. 1 (Main Report) and Vol. 2 (Case Studies and Annexes). Draft for peer review, Washington, DC: The World Bank; Sherwood et al., 2014; Baptista, E., M. Treffers, and P. Giesen. 2012. Final Evaluation of the Cordaid Shelter Programme in Haiti 2010–2012. Nood: Samenwerkende Hulp Organisaties.

[m] World Risk Report (WRR). 2014. World Risk Report. Geneva, Switzerland: United Nations University-Institute for Environment and Human Security (UNU-EHS). http://ehs.unu.edu/ news/news/world-risk-report-2014.html#info (accessed March 9, 2016); GFDRR (Global Facility for Disaster Reduction and Recovery). 2014. GFDRR Annual Report 2014: Bringing Resilience to Scale. Washington, DC: Global Facility for Disaster Reduction.)

them through policies that were inadequate or insufficient. With regard to renters, there is a tendency to trust the private rental market and to assume that subsidies to owners will automatically lead to replacement of affordable rental housing. This does never appear to be the case, as was correctly understood by the government of Mexico.

The reconstruction policies in India and Sri Lanka after the 2004 tsunami and their outcomes in the cities of Nagapattinam, Ampara, and Hambantota indicate that even when the rights of informal settlers are by and large recognized and all people affected by a disaster are granted a free house, the criteria that define adequate housing are rarely met when reconstruction entails relocation. In such cases, informal settlers may be granted tenure security and given a house for free, but the availability of infrastructure and services, the quality and cultural appropriateness of the housing, and the location and accessibility of the relocation site may lead to impoverishment and social disarticulation with severe consequences for health and overall wellbeing. Land issues often constitute the main obstacle to housing resulting in displacees being relocated to remote and/or hazardous sites, as was the case in Sri Lanka and Tamil Nadu.

A wide range of publications focusing on the risks and dramatic social impacts of resettlement in relation to infrastructure development projects (Hansen and Oliver-Smith 1982; Cernea and Guggenheim 1993; Downing 1996; Cernea 1997; Scudder 2009) have led multilateral agencies such as the World Bank to introduce mandatory safeguard policies on involuntary resettlement. These policies, however, are currently weakened by reform programs (Bank on Human Rights 2015; Human Rights Watch 2015). Moreover, they do not apply to post-disaster recovery projects where the social risks of resettlement tend to be underestimated or ignored. This was the case in Indonesia, India, and Sri Lanka following the Indian Ocean tsunami. The lessons and experiences gained in relation to development-induced displacement and involuntary relocation equally apply to post-disaster reconstruction and should be carefully considered also when the aim of relocation is disaster risk reduction (DRR) (Jha et al. 2010).

16.2.1 Rights of Informal Settlers and Post-Disaster Housing

In her "framework for disaster response based on the right to adequate housing," Rolnik (2011) underlines the importance of recognizing the multiplicity of forms of tenure and to ensure security of tenure for everyone. Tenure and land rights in most countries are highly complex and their understanding requires a good knowledge of the social, cultural, historical, political, and legal context. Tenure rights are often regulated by complex sets of semiformal and informal rules that may provide a high degree of security of tenure in "normal" times also to informal settlers (Payne and Durand-Lasserve 2012). After a disaster, however, these rules may no longer apply resulting in a loss of tenure security for large numbers of people or in making it particularly challenging for reconstruction agencies to access land for displaced people. This was the case in Aceh and Haiti, where housing reconstruction projects were delayed due to land tenure problems (Etienne 2012). When there is a political will to support informal settlers in attaining adequate housing, as shown by the case of

Bhachau, Ocotal, and Jemani, it was found that municipal authorities, sometimes in partnership with local NGOs and Civil Society Organizations (CSO), are best qualified to find solutions. Also, international NGOs in particular after having been confronted with the challenges in Haiti are gradually improving their capacity to deal with informality, for example, by trusting the value of methods such as participatory community enumerations and participatory mapping for defining land rights in places where formal titles have either been lost or never existed. The reconstruction processes reviewed for this chapter indicate that the multiplicity of forms of tenure are rarely recognized in urban reconstruction programs without the pressure of local CSOs or NGOs.

Rolnik's (2011) framework further argues that all affected people should have the right to participate in various stages of the disaster response. There are several examples of good participatory planning and reconstruction projects involving informal settlers that are supported by a growing number of methods and tools. Methods such as participatory community enumeration, are often not only a means to clarify and reach consensus over informal or non-documented land rights but also to enhance community cohesion and to share visions about the future of a neighborhood. Participatory settlement planning and housing design in Nicaragua have led to houses that are culturally appropriate and in which people felt satisfied even if they had been forced to relocate. The case of Mexico City shows that high levels of participation in planning and construction through the establishment of decentralized implementation strategies is possible even in the context of mega-cities and in the framework of large-scale reconstruction programs, with results that are more likely to lead to adequate housing than top–down housing approaches. The opportunity to engage with affected communities, particularly with informal settlers and renters, was missed in large-scale reconstruction programs following the earthquakes in Turkey and Iran, whereas in India, Indonesia, and Haiti participation was sometimes ensured more or less effectively at project level depending on the implementing NGO within the framework of so-called area-based approaches (Parker and Maynard 2015). It should be emphasized, however, that participatory mechanisms sometimes underestimate the challenges posed by the social stratification and power structure of informal settlements, which are often socio-economically far from being homogeneous. This was the case in Tamil Nadu where fishing communities' *panchayats* (informal local governance institutions) had a considerable influence on some aspects of the reconstruction process. However, this relatively high level of community participation, for example, on issues like land procurement for reconstruction and the distribution of houses often led to inequities, "community-driven" forced evictions, and to a nonrecognition of the housing rights of elderly people and widows (Duyne Barenstein 2010; Duyne Barenstein and Trächser 2013; Naimi-Gasser 2013).

16.2.2 Social Vulnerabilities and Reconstruction

Theoretically, all people have a right to shelter irrespective of their pre-disaster socio-economic status, tenure, and gender (Rolnik 2011). However, with the exception of Mexico City, where the vulnerabilities of poor urban tenants were recognized and addressed in a carefully designed large-scale reconstruction program, most national reconstruction policies tend to neglect or provide inadequate support to the most vulnerable. Housing assistance post-disaster most often follows a house-for-house compensation principle, and access to compensation is generally contingent upon provable ownership of land, which leads to the exclusion of landless people. This was the case, for example, of the reconstruction policy in Aceh, Turkey, and Gujarat. Only due to massive protests by affected people, and/or to policy advocacy by local NGOs and CSOs, and after the social consequences of neglecting informal settlers and poor tenants became too obvious, were discriminating policies to some extent revised, but never to the point of ensuring equal rights to housing support. When government policies neglect inequalities and the housing needs of the most vulnerable, one would expect humanitarian agencies and international NGOs to target their projects specifically to these groups. This was the case, for example, of United Nations Development Program (UNDP) in Bam, which supported widows whose entitlements were not granted by government policy (UNDP 2008). Such examples, however, are rare. In fact, up to recently also, international organizations, including NGOs, avoided providing housing assistance to people without formal land titles. In the past, international NGOs typically avoided having to deal with the complexities of land tenure in urban areas by focusing on rural areas where land issues are less complex, even when the housing needs were primarily in urban areas (ALNAP 2012). This was the attitude, for example, of international NGOs involved in reconstruction in Gujarat, which were competing for villages to be reconstructed in rural areas while neglecting the needs of urban informal settlers and poor renters in towns (Duyne Barenstein 2006). If and when discriminations were uncovered and redressed, it was generally thanks to the initiatives of local NGOs, community-based organizations or CSOs with strong social commitments and good understandings of local contexts. Their projects, however, could not always be fully implemented due to the shortage of funds. This was the case of the NGO Unnati who supported informal settlers to regularize their land tenure so that they could access financial and technical support for reconstruction from the government in the city of Bhachau (Unnati 2006). If international agencies had recognized the need and supported these types of initiatives on a larger scale, the same type of assistance could have also been extended to informal settlers in the other three towns affected by the disaster.

Valuable experience with community-driven neighborhood reconstruction was gained by a number of international NGOs including, for example, Habitat for Humanity and Cordaid (Baptista et al. 2012; Phelps 2013). Their projects, however, were implemented in a policy vacuum, without agreed upon minimum and maximum standards. This led to overinvestments in certain neighborhoods and underinvestments in other, highlighting the risk of inequities in contexts of weak governance and entailed in so-called area-based approaches (Parker and Maynard 2015).

With the exception of Tamil Nadu, where it may not be a coincidence that the worst relocation sites were offered to scheduled castes, none of the case studies found any evidence of ethnic, religious-, or race-based discriminations. Following the earthquake in Gujarat, its government was accused by activists and the media of discriminating against Muslims and scheduled castes. Though my own research in rural Gujarat, I never found any evidence of such discriminations (Duyne Barenstein 2006; Duyne Barenstein and Iyengar 2010), while Simpson (2008) confirms that there was no such discrimination in urban areas either. In Bam, non-landowning female-headed households faced particular difficulties in achieving housing recovery; 8 years after the earthquake, these female-headed households constituted an important portion of the households still living in temporary housing (Taheri Tafti and Tomlinson 2013). It is currently a practice in many post-disaster housing projects to register the reconstructed houses in the name of husband and wife. Taheri Tafti, however, found that in urban Gujarat the policy of joint ownership between married couples was often not implemented and that many women were not aware of this policy and their related entitlements (Taheri Tafti 2012). The same situation was encountered in Tamil Nadu; when the distribution of agency-built houses was left to male community leaders (Duyne Barenstein and Trächser 2013; Naimi-Gasser 2013). Overall, the need to protect the housing rights of women has in most cases only led to the promotion of joint ownership. However, the progressive female Mayor of Ocotal went a step further by promoting the registration of the reconstructed houses in the exclusive name of the women and their children as a necessary precaution in a context where unstable relations, divorces, and female-headed households are very frequent.

16.2.3 Understanding Local Contexts

Rolnik (2011) emphasizes the importance of taking specific measures to address discrimination and to ensure the right to adequate housing for the most disadvantaged groups. This requires a good understanding of the social structure of the disaster context and recognition that informal settlements are not homogeneous. Some informal settlements are fairly consolidated and even if their inhabitants do not have formal land titles, their houses may be registered and thus enjoy a high level of legitimacy. Their inhabitants may be homeowners or renters and belong to the urban lower middle classes. This is the case, for example, in the Philippines, Indonesia, and India, where many government and private sector employees may also live in informal settlements (Porio and Cristol 2004; Duyne Barenstein and Iyengar 2010; Duyne Barenstein 2013). Other informal settlements may be located in highly hazardous sites and inhabited by very poor and socially marginalized people. These may be classified as squatters, often without any recognized entitlements to housing support. As noted earlier, the reconstruction program in Mexico City reflected a strong commitment toward urban poor tenants to restore their housing rights after the earthquake. Reconstruction programs may be considered as an opportunity to strengthen the tenure security of people with insecure tenure. It was found that when governments have the political will, it can be done and that municipal authorities are particularly qualified to implement related policies.

A final word needs to be said about the role of the different types of agencies that tend to be involved in reconstruction after natural disasters. The reconstruction cases reviewed for this chapter showed that it is very challenging to meet the housing needs of informal settlers in the context of large-scale disasters in politically fragile contexts characterized by poor governance. In order to mitigate the risk of inequities, reconstruction endeavors need to take place in the framework of policies and programs that provide guidance, define basic principles and entitlements, and establish minimum and maxim standards of assistance. Good governance is needed to solve land problems and institutional mechanisms are required to coordinate the large number of agencies offering aid (Jha et al. 2010). All these requirements were not met in Haiti and international agencies, in spite of their financial and human resources were unable to cope with the chaos, resulting in poor urban citizens still living in precarious housing or camps several years after the disaster (Levine et al. 2012; Sherwood et al. 2014). While the case of Haiti was extreme, it is unavoidable noticing that most good practices presented in this report could not be attributed to international agencies but to local governments, municipal authorities, and local NGOs. This may change in the future thanks to several important initiatives taken by agencies such as the International Federation of the Red Cross, IASC, and UN Habitat to strengthen the capacity of humanitarian and development agencies to operate in urban areas. However, an improvement is also contingent upon a change in the institutional culture of international agencies, which need to pay more attention to understanding local contexts, engage with municipalities, build alliances with local CSOs, and support local initiatives rather than ignoring and duplicating their endeavors.

16.3 CONCLUSIONS AND RECOMMENDATIONS

Housing support after a disaster should be based on the principle that all people have an equal right to adequate housing, regardless of their tenure status and housing quality before the disaster. To date, rights-based international policy instruments have hardly had any impact on housing responses post-disaster. Whether and how the housing rights of informal settlers after disasters are being addressed keeps depending on local actors and initiatives. Municipal authorities, local NGOs, and CSOs are more likely to identify the problems and to find appropriate solutions for urban informal settlers than central government and international agencies. This underlines the importance for agencies concerned about reaching the most vulnerable urban citizens to decentralize their interventions and to build new alliances with local stakeholders rather than with central government line agencies. Several examples show that reconstruction is more sustainable where affected communities are given an opportunity to take a lead in planning their neighborhoods and in solving their land problems.

Most post-disaster reconstruction programs explicitly aim at DRR. However, the approaches pursued so far tend to have a narrow view of hazards and how to address them. Solutions are oftentimes culturally inappropriate, incompatible with people's livelihoods, or entail new hazards and vulnerability. A typical example is the introduction of concrete cement-based multi-hazard resistant building technologies after earthquakes that may be unaffordable for people to maintain adequately, provide low thermal comfort, and may be incompatible with local lifestyles. Moreover, if their quality of construction is inadequate due to lack of skilled labor, contractor's vested interests, and lack of supervision and quality control, they may end up being more hazardous than pre-disaster self-built houses. Relocation is rarely a viable strategy to mitigate the risk of site-specific hazards because safe, affordable, and accessible relocation sites are generally not available for low-income people. Relocation post-disaster aiming at DRR has in most cases led to impoverishment and to affected people being exposed to new and possibly more frequent hazards. This aspect is particularly important to keep in mind because many international agencies are considering relocation as a strategy to mitigate the risk of climate change related hazards (Warner et al. 2013). It is of upmost importance that the lessons learned over the last decades with regard to the risks of development-induced relocation are applied also to post-disaster reconstruction and DRR. Whenever possible, structural and nonstructural DRR measures should be taken *in situ*. These are likely to be financially more viable and socially more acceptable. The risk of using DRR arguments to involuntarily relocate people from their homes as was attempted after the tsunami should not be underestimated and needs to be carefully monitored.

People's right to dignified housing in harmony with their culture, lifestyle, and livelihoods entails more than four walls and a roof. Far too much emphasis is generally given in defining reconstruction targets in terms of number of houses to be built and in monitoring the physical progress in construction. More importance needs to be given to qualitative and context-specific aspects of housing and to the overall habitat of human settlements. In this context, the importance of trees to provide shade and outdoor spaces is to be considered as an integral element of adequate housing. Community participation in planning and designing neighborhoods and houses is to be considered not only as a right, but is also of pivotal importance to the attainment of culturally appropriate solutions; community-driven, participatory, and owner-driven reconstruction approaches are effective also in urban contexts. Tools such as participatory mapping and enumeration are potentially very useful to ensure informal settlers land rights but need to be adapted to specific socio-economic and cultural contexts.

There is a need to better understand the culture, socio-economic context, and power structure of informal settlements and to avoid considering them as homogeneous communities. Renters are often the most neglected category of disaster-affected people, and special efforts need to be made to understand the situation of female-headed households and other vulnerable people such as elderly people.

Finally, the risk of gentrification following major investments in rebuilding and improving the infrastructure and services, and in reducing the vulnerability of informal settlements should also be considered. The paucity of detailed information on all these issues underlines the need for further investigation.

REFERENCES

Active Learning Network for Accountability (ALNAP). 2012. Responding to Urban Disasters: Learning from Previous Relief and Recovery Operations. ALNAP Lesson Paper. London:ALNAP/ODI.

Arslan, H., and C. Johnson. 2010. Can small actors overcome the absence of state will? In *Building Back Better: Delivering People-Centred Reconstruction to Scale*, M. Lyons and T. Schilderman (eds), Rugby: Practical Action Publication, 263–84.

Bank on Human Rights. 2015. The World Bank safeguards review: A critical human rights issue. Bank on Human Rights, A Coalition for Human Rights in Development Finance. http://www.conectas.org/arquivos/editor/files/Safeguards-4-pgr-General-10_17_14-2.pdf (accessed March 9, 2016).

Baptista, E., M. Treffers, and P. Giesen. 2012. *Final Evaluation of the Cordaid Shelter Programme in Haiti 2010–2012*. Nood: Samenwerkende Hulp Organisaties.
Cernea, M. 1997. The risks and reconstruction model for resettling displaced populations. *World Development* 25(10): 1569–87.
Cernea, M., and S. E. Guggenheim, eds. 1993. *Anthropological Approaches to Resettlement. Policy, Practice and Theory*. Boulder, Colorado: Westview Press.
Da Silva, J. 2010. *Lessons from Aceh. Key Considerations in Post-Disaster Reconstruction*. Rugby: Practical Action.
Doberstein, B., and H. Stager. 2012. Towards guidelines for post-disaster vulnerability reduction in informal settlements. *Disasters* 37(1): 28–47.
Downing, T. E. 1996. Mitigating social impoverishment when people are involuntarily displaced. In *Understanding Impoverishment: The Consequences of Developmental-Induced Displacement*, C. McDowell (ed.), Providence, Rhode Island: Berghahn Books, 33–48.
Duyne Barenstein, J. 2006. *Housing Reconstruction in Post-Earthquake Gujarat: A Comparative Analysis*. HPN Network Paper, No. 54, London: ODI.
Duyne Barenstein, J. 2010. Housing reconstruction in Tamil Nadu: The disaster after the tsunami. In *Community Disaster Recovery and Resiliency: Exploring Global Opportunities and Challenges*, D. S. Miller and J. D. Rivera (eds), Boca Raton, Florida: Auerbach Publications, Taylor & Francis Group, 343–62.
Duyne Barenstein, J. 2013. Post-tsunami relocation outcomes in Sri Lanka. Communities' perspectives in Ampara and Hambantota. In: *Post-Disaster Reconstruction and Change*, J. Duyne Barenstein and E. Leemann (eds), Boca Raton, Florida: CRC Press, 215–40.
Duyne Barenstein, J., and S. Iyengar. 2010. India: From a culture of housing to a philosophy of reconstruction. In *Building Back Better: Delivering People-Centred Reconstruction to Scale*, M. Lyons, T. Schilderman, and C. Boano (eds), Rugby: Practical Action Publication, 163–88.
Duyne Barenstein, J., and B. Marti Rojas Riva. 2013. Is resettlement a viable strategy to mitigate the risk of natural disasters? Perceptions and voices from the citizens of Santa Fe, Argentina. In *Post-Disaster Reconstruction and Change: A Community Perspective*, J. Duyne Barenstein and E. Leemann (eds), Boca Raton, Florida: CRC Press, Taylor & Francis Group, 299–324.
Duyne Barenstein, J., and D. Pittet. 2013. An environmental and social impact assessment of post-disaster housing reconstruction: The case of Tamil Nadu. In *Post-Disaster Reconstruction and Change: A Community Perspective*, J. Duyne Barenstein and E. Leemann (eds), Boca Raton, Florida: CRC Press, Taylor & Francis Group, 119–36.
Duyne Barenstein, J., and S. Trächser. 2013. The role of informal governance in post-disaster reconstruction and its impact on elderly people's social security in coastal Tamil Nadu. In: *Post-Disaster Reconstruction and Change: A Community Perspective*, J. Duyne Barenstein and E. Leemann (eds), Boca Raton, Florida: CRC Press, Taylor & Francis Group, 157–76.
Etienne, H. F. 2012. *Land Rights, Land Tenure, and Urban Recovery: Rebuilding Post-Earthquake Port-au-Prince and Léogâne*. Oxfam America Research Backgrounders, Washington, DC: Oxfam America. http://www.oxfamamerica.org/static/oa4/land-rights-land-tenure-and-urban-recovery.pdf (accessed March 9, 2016).
GFDRR (Global Facility for Disaster Reduction and Recovery). 2014. *GFDRR Annual Report 2014: Bringing Resilience to Scale*. Washington, DC: Global Facility for Disaster Reduction.
Graf, A. 2013. Unaffordable housing and its consequences: A comparative analysis of two post-Mitch reconstruction projects in Nicaragua. In *Post-Disaster Reconstruction and Change: A Community Perspective*, J. Duyne Barenstein and E. Leemann (eds), Boca Raton, Florida: CRC Press, Taylor & Francis Group, 195–214.

Habitat International Coalition (HIC). 2005. International Human Rights Standards on Post-Disaster Resettlement and Rehabilitation. http://www.pdhre.org/HIC-PDHRE.pdf (accessed March 17, 2016).

Hansen, A., and A. Oliver-Smith, eds. 1982. *Involuntary Migration and Resettlement: The Problems and Responses of Dislocated Peoples*. Boulder, Colorado: Westview Press.

Harper, E. 2009. *International Law and Standards Applicable in Natural Disaster Situations*. Rome, Italy: IDLO.

Human Rights Watch. 2015. *World Report 2015: Rights aren't Wrong in Tough Times*. 25th Annual World Report. https://www.hrw.org/report/2015/01/29/world-report-2015/events-2014 (accessed March 9, 2016).

Inter-Agency Standing Committee (IASC). 2008. *Human Rights and Natural Disasters: Operational Guidelines and Field Manual on Human Rights Protection in Situations of Natural Disasters*. Washington, DC: Brookings-Bern Project on Internal Displacement.

Inter-Agency Standing Committee (IASC). 2010. *IASC Strategy—Meeting Humanitarian Challenges in Urban Areas*. Geneva, Switzerland: IASC.

Jha, A. K., J. Duyne Barenstein, P. Phelps, D. Pittet, and S. Sena. 2010. *Safer Homes, Stronger Communities: A Handbook for Reconstruction after Natural Disasters*. Washington, DC: The International Bank for Reconstruction and Development, The World Bank. https://openknowledge.worldbank.org/handle/10986/2409 (accessed March 9, 2016).

Johnson, C. 2011. *Creating an Enabling Environment for Reducing Disaster Risk: Recent Experience of Regulatory Frameworks for Land, Planning and Building in Low and Middle-Income Countries*. Global Assessment Report on Disaster Risk Reduction, Geneva, Switzerland: UN International Strategy for Disaster Reduction (ISDR).

Kreimer, A. and E. Echeverria. 1991. Case study: Housing reconstruction in Mexico City. In *Managing Natural Disasters and the Environment*, A. Kreimer and M. Munasinghe (eds), Washington DC: The World Bank, 53–61.

Leemann, E. 2011. Housing reconstruction in post-Mitch Nicaragua: Two case studies from the communities of San Dionisio and Ocotal. In *Community Disaster Recovery and Resiliency: Exploring Global Opportunities and Challenges*, D. Miller and J. Rivera (eds), Boca Raton, Florida: CRC Press, 319–42.

Leemann, E. 2013. Communal leadership in post-Mitch housing reconstruction in Nicaragua. In *Post-Disaster Reconstruction and Change: A Community Perspective*, J. Duyne Barenstein and E. Leemann (eds), Boca Raton, Florida: CRC Press, Taylor & Francis Group, 3–30.

Levine, S., S. Bailey, and B. Boyer with C. Mehu. 2012. Avoiding reality: Land, institutions and humanitarian action in post-earthquake Haiti. Working paper. London: ODI HPG. http://www.odi.org/publications/6979-haiti-land-earthquake-humanitarian-cluster-camp-shelter (accessed March 9, 2016).

Mitchell, D. 2011. *Assessing and Responding to Land Tenure Issues in Disaster Risk Management*. FAO Land Tenure Manuals 3, Rome, Italy: Food and Agriculture Organization of the United Nations. http://www.fao.org/docrep/014/i2115e/i2115e00.pdf (accessed March 9, 2016).

Naimi-Gasser, J. 2013. The remembered trees: Contractor-driven reconstruction and its consequences in communities' well being in coastal Tamil Nadu. In *Post-Disaster Reconstruction and Change: A Community Perspective*, J. Duyne Barenstein and E. Leemann (eds), Boca Raton, Florida: CRC Press, Taylor & Francis Group, 137–56.

Office for the Coordination of Humanitarian Affairs (OCHA). 2007. *Handbook on Housing and Property Restitution for Refugees and Displaced Persons: Implementing the "Pinheiro Principles."* Rome, Italy: OCHA. http://www.ohchr.org/Documents/Publications/pinheiro_principles.pdf (accessed March 9, 2016).

Oxfam. 2006. *The Tsunami Two Years On: Land Rights in Aceh. Oxfam Briefing Note*. London: Oxfam International.

Parker, E., and V. Maynard. 2015. Humanitarian response to urban crises: A review of area-based approaches. IIED Working Paper, London: IIED's Human Settlements Group, July. http://pubs.iied.org/pdfs/10742IIED.pdf? (accessed March 16, 2015).

Payne, G., and A. Durand-Lasserve. 2012. *Holding on: Security of Tenure—Types, Policies, Practices and Challenges*. Geneva, Switzerland: Office of the High Commissioner for Human Rights, Research paper commissioned by the Special Rapporteur on the right to an adequate standard of living for an Expert Group Meeting on Security of Tenure, (October 22–3). http://www.ohchr.org/Documents/Issues/Housing/SecurityTenure/Payne-Durand-Lasserve-BackgroundPaper-JAN2013.pdf (accessed March 9, 2016).

Phelps, P. 2013. *Analyzing the Haiti Post-Earthquake Shelter Response and Housing Recovery: Results and Lessons from the First Two Years*. Vol. 1 (Main Report) and Vol. 2 (Case Studies and Annexes). Draft for peer review, Washington, DC: The World Bank.

Porio, E., and C. Cristol. 2004. Property rights, security of tenure and the urban poor in Metro Manila. *Habitat International* 48(2): 203–19.

ReliefWeb. 2004. ACT Appeal Iran: Bam Earthquake Relief & Rehabilitation MEIN 42, rev. no. 2. Action by Churches International. http://reliefweb.int/report/iran-islamic-republic/act-appeal-iran-bam-earthquake-relief-rehabilitation-mein-42-revision-2 (accessed March 9, 2016).

Rolnik, R. 2011. Report of the special rapporteur on adequate housing as a component of the right to an adequate standard of living A/66/270, UN General Assembly. http://www.ohchr.org/Documents/Issues/Housing/SecurityTenure/Payne-Durand-Lasserve-BackgroundPaper-JAN2013.pdf (accessed March 9, 2016).

Scudder, T. 2009. Resettlement theory and the Kariba case: An anthropology of resettlement. In *Development and Dispossession: The Crisis of Forced Displacement and Resettlement*, A. Oliver-Smith (ed.), Santa Fe, New Mexico: School of American Research Press, 25–47.

Sherwood, A., M. Bradley, L. Rossi, R. Gitau, and B. Mellicker. 2014. *Supporting Durable Solutions to Urban, Post-Disaster Displacement: Challenges and Opportunities in Haiti*. Washington, DC: Brookings Institute, International Organization for Migration.

Simpson, E. 2008. Was there discrimination in the distribution of resources after the earthquake in the Gujarat? Imagination, epistemology, and the state in western India. Non-Governmental Public Action Programme, Working Paper Series, No. 23, July. https://eprints.soas.ac.uk/5581/1/Edward_Simpson_NGPA_Paper_23.pdf (accessed March 9, 2016).

Steinberg, F. 2007. Housing reconstruction and rehabilitation in Aceh and Nias, Indonesia rebuilding lives. *Habitat International* 31: 150–166.

Steinberg, F and P. Schmid (eds). 2010. *Rebuilding Lives and Homes in Aceh and Nias, Indonesia*. ADB Urban Development Series. Manila: ADB.

Taheri Tafti, M. 2012. Limitations of the owner-driven model in post-disaster housing reconstruction in urban settlements. *Paper Presented at the Proceedings of the International Conference on Disaster Management (IIIRR)*. Kumamoto, Japan.

Taheri Tafti, M., and R. Tomlinson. 2013. The role of post-disaster public policy responses in housing recovery of tenants. *Habitat International* 40: 218–24.

Unnati 2006. Owner Driven Housing Process. Ahmedabad, India: Unnati and Basin South Asia.

UN Habitat. 2010. *Count Me in: Surveying for Tenure Security an Urban Land Management*. UN Human Settlements Programme, Nairobi, Kenya: UN Habitat. http://www.alnap.org/resource/8381 (accessed March 9, 2016).

UN Habitat. 2011a. *Global Report on Human Settlements 2011, Cities and climate change: Policy directions*, Nairobi, Kenya: UN Habitat.

UN Habitat. 2011b. *Monitoring Security of Tenure in Cities: People, Land and Policies.* UN Human Settlements Programme, Nairobi, Kenya, UN Habitat. http://www.gltn.net/jdownloads/GLTN%20Documents/monitoring_security_of_tenure_in_cities.pdf (accessed March 9, 2016).

United Nations Committee on Economic, Social and Cultural Rights (UNCESCR). 1991. General Comment No. 4: The Right to Adequate Housing (Art 11/1 of the Covenant). http://www.refworld.org/pdfid/47a7079a1.pdf (accessed March 9, 2016).

United Nations Department of Economics and Social Affairs (UNDESA). 2014. World Urbanization Prospects. http://esa.un.org/unpd/wup/ (accessed March 9, 2016).

United Nations Development Programme (UNDP). 2008. Final review: Sustainable housing reconstruction programme in Bam through community mobilization and participation. http://erc.undp.org/evaluationadmin/downloaddocument.html?docid=1838 (accessed March 9, 2016).

Warner, K., T. Afifi, W. Kalin et al. 2013. *Changing Climate, Moving People: Framing Migration, Displacement and Planned Relocation.* Policy Brief No. 8, Geneva, Switzerland: United Nations University-Institute for Environment and Human Security (UNU-EHS), June. https://collections.unu.edu/eserv/UNU:1837/pdf11213.pdf (accessed March 9, 2016).

World Risk Report (WRR). 2014. *World Risk Report.* Geneva, Switzerland: United Nations University-Institute for Environment and Human Security (UNU-EHS). http://ehs.unu.edu/news/news/world-risk-report-2014.html#info (accessed March 9, 2016).

17 Civil Society and Recovery

Nongovernmental Organizations and Post-Disaster Housing

Alka Sapat

CONTENTS

17.1 INTRODUCTION

The voluntary sector has historically played a critical role in disaster response and recovery (Arlikatti et al. 2012; Eikenberry et al. 2007; Flatt and Stys 2013; Jenkins et al. 2015; McCurry 2009; Simo and Bies 2007; Stys 2011) and their presence and numbers have grown. Voluntary or third-sector organizations encompass a range of different types of organizations and are usually referred to as nonprofit organizations (NPOs) in the United States. Nonprofit-like organizations operating outside the United States are typically referred to as nongovernmental organizations (NGOs); international NGOs focus much of their work in developing countries

(Eikenberry et al. 2007, p. 160).* Voluntary sector organizations have long been characterized as being less prone to the "poor governance" typical of states and as being closer to the people (Clark 1991; Paul and Israel 1991). These organizations often step in to serve needs and provide services and goods that governments or the private sector are unable or unwilling to provide. Philanthropic principles, high levels of commitment to missions, and flexibility have made the third sector an invaluable player in community resilience and recovery.

Understanding the role of the voluntary sector in housing recovery is important for a number of reasons: first, governments, regardless of their levels of administrative capacity, are often unable to tackle the overwhelming tasks that accompany the processes of shelter and housing recovery. NGOs have tremendous potential and are often responsible for a variety of unmet needs in housing. Second, while the third sector brings numerous assets to all phases of the disaster management cycle, there are impediments to the realization of its potential. Understanding and addressing these impediments can help improve the effectiveness of housing recovery. Finally, the role of third sector in post-disaster housing is growing (Daly and Brassard 2011) and housing is a key component of community recovery. Analyzing NGO involvement in post-disaster housing, the specific challenges that they face, and ways in which their potential can be realized is important to housing and community recovery.

This chapter seeks to address these issues and is organized into three main sections. The first section provides a brief overview of the growth of the voluntary sector and a discussion of its role in disaster housing. Next, impediments to third-sector involvement in housing recovery are discussed; these include issues such as aid volatility, impacts on communities, fragmentation, information asymmetries and internal capacity issues, competition, and the lack of oversight and mismanagement. Examples drawn from disasters around the globe are used to elucidate third-sector contributions and the challenges they face in addressing myriad and multifaceted complexities of disasters and resultant housing dilemmas. The chapter ends with some recommendations on how third-sector assets and advantages can be applied to improve housing recovery.

17.2 ROLE OF THE VOLUNTARY SECTOR IN HOUSING RECOVERY

> ...we are in the midst of a global "associational revolution" that may prove to be as significant to the latter twentieth century as the rise of the nation-state was to the

* The term nongovernmental organization (NGO) was first coined by the newly formed United Nations in 1945 in Article 71 of its Charter to acknowledge the consultative status of these organizations; in the international context, the term NGO became popular to denote voluntary organizations that are legally not part of government (Martens 2002). Within the United States, the term nonprofit organization (NPO) is mostly used, since they are provided special tax-exempt status, (501(c)(3) organizations under the US tax code) that do not distribute profits to shareholders or offer dividends. For the purposes of this paper, to match commonly used terminology, the term nonprofit organization (NPO) will be used primarily in the context of the United States, while NGO will be used in international contexts. The general terms third sector, civil society, and voluntary sector organizations will be used to refer to all organizations (NPO and NGO included) that are not statutory or profit maximizing.

> latter nineteenth. The upshot is a global third sector: a massive array of self-governing private organizations... (Salamon 1994, p. 109).

The global associational revolution as termed by Salamon (1994) has seen exponential growth since the 1970s. As McKeever and Pettijohn (2014, p. 1) document, from 2002 to 2012, the number of NPOs registered with the Internal Revenue Service (IRS) in the United States rose from 1.32 to 1.44 million; an increase of 8.6%.* The US nonprofit sector has grown faster than the private or public sector and composed 5.4% of the national gross domestic product contributing an estimated $887.3 million to the US economy in 2012 (McKeever and Pettijohn 2014, p. 1). In other countries, data on the growth of nonprofits is less clear as many countries do not have registered voluntary organizations or provide them with special tax-exempt status. However, a 2012 study shows that the nonprofit workforce, including paid and volunteer workers makes up 7.4% of the total workforce on average in 13 countries, placing it ahead of major industries such as transportation and finance (Salamon et al. 2012).

Historically, the philanthropic sector has always played a role prior to, during, and in response to disaster events. Prior to the development of formal agencies providing disaster response, NPOs such as churches, soup kitchens, the Red Cross, and other faith-based and community organizations mobilized to provide and distribute food, water, clothing, medical care, and other services to affected communities, including helping with shelter and reconstruction. Third-sector organizations play an important role in all four phases of disaster housing—emergency shelter, temporary shelter, temporary housing, and permanent housing (Quarantelli 1982). In recognition of their role and to integrate them more clearly into disaster management processes, some countries have given these third-sector organizations more formal roles in disaster response. For instance, the American Red Cross has an official role in the United States as the provider of emergency shelter. The United States Federal Emergency Management Agency also relies heavily on other nonprofits such as the Salvation Army, the National Voluntary Organizations Active in Disaster, and numerous faith-based organizations (FBOs) (Esnard and Sapat 2014; Olson 2012; Stys 2011).

The role that NGOs play in housing recovery depends on myriad factors such as their size, function, mission, and persuasion. While roles vary, the engagement of the third sector in post-disaster housing reconstruction has grown considerably, making housing one of the most well-funded sectors in recovery (Daly and Brassard 2011). Third-sector involvement in housing has been driven in part by the growth of official and private aid for housing reconstruction, the need for rebuilding post-disaster housing, its critical linkages to other forms of recovery, government cutbacks, concerns about corruption, and rising expectations of the sector in aid delivery. NPOs and NGOs bring several resources to post-disaster shelter and housing. For instance, Habitat for Humanity (HFH) plays a key role and provides housing solutions after disasters in incremental stages: (1) emergency shelters; (2) accessing or affirming

* This figure only includes registered nonprofit organizations. Since religious congregations and organizations with less than $5000 in annual revenue are not required to register with the US IRS, the total number of nonprofit organizations operating in the United States is unknown.

land rights; (3) improving transitional shelters; and (4) defining existing damaged housing or expanding new housing solutions (HFH 2015). In some cases, the role of third-sector organizations in housing reconstruction has been viewed as being highly successful (Black 2005; MacRae and Hodgkin 2011). For instance, MacRae and Hodgkin (2011) argue that the housing reconstruction program after the 2006 Yogyakarta earthquake in Indonesia was an example of one of the best reconstruction efforts completed by the humanitarian response system.

Successful participation in post-disaster housing is perhaps best exemplified by the Mennonite Disaster Service (MDS),* an FBO run by volunteers. In her rich and textured ethnographic study of the MDS, Brenda Phillips (2014) documents the critical role MDS has played in disaster response and rebuilding since 1950. Phillips (2014) notes that MDS volunteers build relationships with the communities they serve by asking what help is needed and providing it. They also address the unmet needs of the most vulnerable communities, including indigenous communities (like those in the Grand Bayou in Louisiana after Hurricane Katrina), those with special needs, and those who are uninsured or underinsured. MDS volunteers take the time to find out what end-user needs are, to suggest what has worked in other communities, and they remain involved with repairs and rebuilding over long periods of time (Phillips 2014). The MDS and numerous other organizations involved in housing reconstruction are testimony to the incredible potential of third-sector organizations. However, the engagement of voluntary sector organizations in disaster housing faces several challenges as discussed below.

17.3 CHALLENGES AND IMPEDIMENTS

> …the tough lesson for International NGOs is that housing is a complex, long-term activity, not so suitable for short-term hot-shot solutions (Davis et al. 2015, p. 11).

Some of the main challenges and impediments to third-section involvement in housing recovery include internal organizational challenges and others arising from external political, social, and economic environments.

17.3.1 Aid Flows, Aid Volatility, and Fatigue

Aid volatility, compounded by the lack of planning by NGOs and NPOs to deal with funding changes, has serious implications for long-term housing recovery. By some estimates, the median aid surge in official development assistance following disasters is 18% compared to pre-disaster flows (Becerra et al. 2012). However, pledges of aid driven by outpourings of sympathy immediately following disasters are often not kept or take time to be realized. Moreover, when media attention fades, donor interest and policy attention wanes leading to reductions in disaster aid. Aid programs are typically oriented toward short-term relief and may not link well to local needs

* The Mennonite Disaster Service is but one example of a third-sector organization that has played a critical role in housing recovery. There are countless others, both big and small who play similar roles, but are not discussed here due to space constraints.

and capacities and diverse social and economic conditions (Anderson and Woodrow 1989; Berke et al. 1993; Kartez 1991). Gaps between initial pledges and fluctuations in aid money negatively impacts NGOs. For instance, in Haiti, the initial amount promised right after the earthquake did not materialize (Beaubien 2013). After the earthquake, international NGOs began reaching the end of their budgets for response efforts and were abandoning full latrines in tent camps amidst the cholera epidemic (Arroyo 2014, p. 112; Patinet 2011). This example highlights a common problem in NGO participation in housing recovery. Typically, a large percentage of aid budgets go to response and temporary shelter, while permanent housing if built, is often incomplete, due in part to cost overruns and aid running out.

17.3.2 Negative Externalities: The Impact of NGOs and NPOs on Communities

Despite good intentions, NGO and NPO involvement in housing recovery may, inadvertently or otherwise, negatively impact communities. First, NGOs and NPOs often overlook or ignore community and individual preferences in building housing. One-size-fits-all approaches toward designing housing units may be expedient and provide economies of scale; however, they may not provide sustainable housing solutions that work and are acceptable to beneficiaries. The resulting outcome of a top–down centralized approach by third-sector organizations that neglect or ignore local conditions, preferences, and needs is housing that is not functionally or culturally appropriate (Barenstein 2006), is exclusionary, and often does not even get used by the beneficiaries for whom it is intended. Research undertaken after the 2001 Gujarat earthquake and the 2004 Indian Ocean tsunami shows that beneficiary satisfaction was greater when NGOs used owner-driven approaches, in which owners took part in the design, planning, siting, and rebuilding process; in comparison, beneficiary satisfaction was lower with donor-driven or mostly contractor-driven construction, where survivors (often resettled) were provided with fully constructed houses (Andrew et al. 2013; Barenstein 2006; Barenstein and Iyengar 2010; Lyons 2009). A note of caution here is that at times, as Twigg (2006) notes, local people themselves may reject indigenous knowledge and value "modern" building styles as symbols of development and safety; however, lax code enforcement and shoddy building practices make such construction more hazardous.

Second, the influx of aid money brought in by NGOs can have inflationary effects raising the costs of local construction materials, goods, and services (Jayasuriya and McCawley 2010; Kennedy et al. 2008; Lyons 2009). After the 2010 Haiti earthquake, NGOs were reportedly paying three to four times the local rate for rental housing and pricing out local renters (Sapat and Esnard 2013). Third, NGO involvement in housing may negatively impact local human capital by bringing in external staff or by raiding local administrative capacities (Easterly 2002; Harris 2006). International NGOs may undermine local state capacity and the capacity of local NPOs and NGOs through hiring practices (Arroyo 2014; Schuller 2009, 2012). In developing countries, middle and upper class elites, often seek employment and resources from international NGOs, usually with the aim of getting better jobs with more benefits and increased status (Hilhorst 2003); they work to support their own class and donor interests, rather than the needs of their communities (Hearn 2007).

Fourth, due to time pressures by donors to build back faster and provide numbers, NGOs and NPOs can end up marginalizing local needs, preferences, and skills. Time compression, as discussed in Chapter 5, can lead to unsynchronized flows of information, funding, and capabilities, resulting in housing that can be substandard or fall short of beneficiary needs and expectations. The lack of time is also a key challenge in coordinating community-based activities in post-disaster reconstruction (Hayles 2010).

17.3.3 Internal Capacity Issues and Information Asymmetries

NGOs with extensive experience in rebuilding such as HFH and MDS are typically successful in shelter and housing provision, but most NGOs and NPOs lack prior housing and building experience (Davis et al. 2015). The lack of capacity and information asymmetries between international NGOs and local communities has several ramifications. First, NGOs often experience hurdles as they may not understand the local building process, be conversant with contractors in the field, or understand the political ramifications involved with reconstruction. Sourcing materials for reconstruction, whether following donor- or owner-driven construction approaches, may be problematic due to the lack of organizational knowledge of local procurement practices, corruption in contracting, competition for limited supplies and resources, and lack of government support (Chang et al. 2011). Housing structures that are poorly designed and constructed can result when NGOs lack the requisite expertise and knowledge of suitable local uses of space and materials (Barenstein 2006).

Information asymmetries may also lead international NGOs to overlook or neglect the availability of indigenous and/or locally available materials. In studies of major disasters with extensive housing losses, it has been found that:

> there have been enough resources from indigenous and salvaged materials to rebuild nearly three-quarters of the housing to pre-disaster standards. Indeed, for houses rebuilt to a structurally safer standard, the same materials can be used in over 90 per cent of cases.... Yet, authorities and agencies responsible for handling relief and reconstruction efforts have repeatedly overlooked these resources... (Davis et al. 2015, p. 44).

For some third-sector organizations involved in shelter and reconstruction after disaster, the question of building standards and their lack of knowledge and confusion about them have also posed a problem. After the 2004 tsunami and March 2005 earthquake, an Agence d'Aide à la Coopération Technique Et au Développement (ACTED) official in Nias, Indonesia noted: "For people like me that work in the field, it would be useful to know what the international standards are that we should follow during the reconstruction. Some organizations refer to the Sphere Project, others to the UNHCR Emergency Handbook or to the more recent Hyogo Framework for Action" (Guarnacci 2012, p. 80).

Problems may be compounded when humanitarian work following natural disasters is layered over the displacement of populations due to conflict (Boano 2009).

International NGOs that are not conversant with the conflict may, through their distribution of housing resources or resettlement of communities and populations, inadvertently or carelessly exacerbate underlying conflict or ethnic and social tensions as occurred after the 2004 tsunami in Sri Lanka (Harris 2006). Communication can be another problem. Local beneficiaries may receive disjointed or incorrect information about NGO initiatives and NGOs may not communicate information correctly, which can lead to inequitable outcomes. As documented in Chapter 14, not all barangays in the Philippines received equivalent information about rent assistance programs by NGOs (Iuchi and Maly 2016). Finally, information asymmetries in expectations can lead to international NGOs assuming that local or national governments will provide the basic infrastructure needed for the adequate functioning of the housing that NGOs build. However, when the political or economic will and/ or the capacity of governments are limited, these unrealistic expectations result in the provision of unsuitable housing due to the lack of infrastructure, such as water, sanitation, or transportation to places of livelihood.

17.3.4 Competition and Collaboration

A fourth set of challenges that arise is the level of competition and collaboration among third-sector organizations. Disasters attract aid money and a larger percentage of it is increasingly going to the third sector, particularly in areas where trust in government institutions is low and where fears of corruption and mismanagement by political entities prevail. The resulting outcome is that there are larger numbers of NGOs and NPOs who are responding to disasters. For instance, there were 300 new international NGOs operating in Sri Lanka in 2005, which was a four-fold increase over pre-tsunami numbers (Harris 2006, p. 2); that number increased to 615 organizations by 2007 (Boano 2007, p. 243). The vast numbers of NGOs and NPOs responding to disaster can provide enormous resources to deal with a disaster, but these numbers also raise problems with regard to coordination and the increased competition among them. Boano (2009, p. 6) notes that after the 2004 tsunami in Sri Lanka, the lack of coordination between international NGOs resulted in transitional shelters that took different shapes, formats, quality, materials, methods, and standards depending on donor requirements and the money and expertise available to them. The resulting disparity in shelter types created social tensions and led to shelters unsuited to local climates or that were poorly built. Similarly, the lack of coordination among NPOs providing assistance to displaced survivors of Hurricane Katrina in Austin, Texas led to some survivors receiving services from multiple agencies, whereas others received none (Gajewski et al. 2011).

Problems of coordination are compounded when competition among third-sector organizations also occurs for resources such as local partnerships and personnel. Case in point is the "bidding war" that ensued in Sri Lanka with different agencies competing with each other to secure the best local NGO to partner with; local and humanitarian agencies noted that interagency rivalry over territory, partners, personnel, and projects was a serious threat to effective relief and reconstruction (Harris 2006, p. 5).

17.3.5 Lack of Oversight and Weak Governance

The lack of oversight contributes to problems in third-sector coordination and other obstacles to effective recovery. First, the lack of local or regional capacity to allocate roles for third-sector organizations can lead to duplication or excessive concentration of resources in some areas and none in others. It may also lead to a plethora of local and international third-sector organizations of various sizes, budgets, ambitions, and commitment. The resultant congestion of humanitarian space might be difficult for local governments to monitor and coordinate (Boano 2009; Harris 2006). For instance, there were so many NGOs who were present in Haiti after the 2010 earthquake, that it was dubbed the "NGO Republic" (Klarreich and Polman 2012). A large percentage of these were unregistered and government officials had no mechanisms to monitor or coordinate the NGOs' work (Farmer 2011).

Second, with respect to housing, problems can arise when there are no housing authorities or planning agencies within countries or states, land rights and land tenure are unclear, or if there is no pre-disaster planning for post-disaster housing which includes clear guidelines on NGO partnerships for housing recovery. For instance, in the Trincomalee district in Sri Lanka, following the 2004 tsunami, the central government dealt with six different international NGOs to build permanent housing with no prior coordination or negotiation; the outcome was 349 permanent homes on one site built with different designs, methodologies, and time frames, increasing disparities and social tensions (Boano 2009, p. 777).

The lack of oversight is often accompanied by corruption and mismanagement within disaster-affected countries, muddying post-disaster reconstruction processes. Corruption makes it hard to procure the appropriate resources for reconstruction, increases accountability concerns with respect to donors, and leads to reduced levels of trust, which in turn precludes the development of much-needed partnerships between third-sector organizations and local, regional, and national government entities. The lack of monitoring and mismanagement can further attenuate downward accountability and enhance power differentials between aid organizations and government agencies. Power asymmetries render it difficult for governments to hold errant organizations accountable even when problems surface (Arroyo 2014). A case in point is the problem reported on housing promised but not delivered by the Red Cross in Haiti. While the Red Cross received millions of dollars in funding after the 2010 earthquake and claimed to have provided homes to over 130,000 people, media investigations disclosed that only a handful of homes were built (Elliott et al. 2015).

17.4 CONCLUSIONS AND RECOMMENDATIONS

> To accompany someone is to go somewhere with him or her, to break bread together, to be present on a journey with a beginning and an end (Farmer 2011).

While third-sector organizations play a unique role in housing recovery due to their commitment, resources, and networks, their effectiveness can be positively enhanced in some of the following ways.

First, NGOs and NPOs need to pay more attention to the sustainability of their interventions in housing reconstruction, particularly when working in developing countries. International NGOs working in these countries are often seen as instruments of neo-liberal regimes that foster a culture of dependency (Schuller 2007). Top–down and centralized approaches that incorporate local participation mostly as sweat equity need to be changed and authentic participation from communities, while difficult to achieve (Davidson et al. 2007; Twigg 2006) needs to be adopted in planning and providing transitional, and permanent housing. While communities and local NGOs within developing countries may lack resources and have attenuated capacities after disaster, international NGOs engaging in reconstruction need to apply sustainability practices (Telford and Cosgrave 2007) to reconstruction. In particular, mechanisms to help build local capacity and expertise in post-disaster reconstruction are needed, including setting aside dedicated funding for such programs (Clinton 2006). The capacity is needed for many things: to be able to rebuild, survey existing resources, and know where to source them. For instance, organizations such as Architects without Frontiers follow strategies such as working closely with local communities and educating and training them to foster self-sufficiency (Black 2005). Paul Farmer, head of the Partners in Health, an NGO that has worked for over 25 years in Haiti, while lauding international aid efforts, argues that the "the international humanitarian effort could have done more to accompany the local authorities in charge of direct relief and reconstruction" (Farmer 2011, unpaginated).

Second, the third sector needs to do more than focus on the physical buildings or houses they build. Homes are cultural, social, psychological, economic, political, and even historical spaces. Rather than a one-size-fits-all approach, developing long-term relationships, understanding local political and economic environments, societal and cultural norms, accompanying infrastructure needs, and end-user preferences is critical to successful housing recovery and is related to concepts such as accompaniment. As discussed earlier, MDS does this with volunteers who are extremely dedicated, who respect and know the communities that they work in intimately, and who go back year after year to help, developing relationships, understandings, and networks with the communities they serve (Phillips 2014).

Third, NPOs and NGOs engaging in housing recovery need to develop adaptive resilience and build their own organizational capacities and expertise in housing, particularly at the local level. Pre-planning and adoption of disaster readiness and response plans are needed for the organizations themselves. During Hurricane Katrina, a large percentage of local NPOs reported extensive organizational damage and struggled to survive (Jenkins et al. 2015), and many international NGOs responded (Eikenberry et al. 2007). Since local nonprofits are the ones who will remain in the community while national or international NPOs and NGOs typically move on to the next disaster, local NGOs need capacity in the housing and reconstruction sector and to develop pre-disaster plans for procurement of reconstruction materials and personnel. More adaptability and flexibility (Von Meding et al. 2009), better dissemination of lessons learned, and knowledge management of volunteers and employees for organizations that have fluid employment patterns can bolster internal organizational capacities (Hayles 2010) to deal with the large number of challenges that occur in housing recovery.

Fourth, voluntary sector organizations at all levels also need to find appropriate policy venues to build partnerships in the communities where they work. While generalizations are hard to make, in cases where there is strong state capacity at the national level from which resources are dispersed, it may be better for nonprofits to build partnerships with agencies at national levels to acquire resources needed for housing reconstruction. For instance, in response to Hurricane Katrina, Jenkins et al. (2015) find that those nonprofits that developed networks with federal and state-level agencies were better able to adapt and survive. However, in fragile states with weak governance mechanisms, it may be more beneficial for NGOs and NPOs to focus their efforts at local government levels. In the case of Bachhau in Gujarat, local NGOs and other civil society organizations worked with the municipal governments to overcome land tenure issues and developed housing for informal settlers after the 2001 earthquake (Barenstein 2006, 2010).

Finally, better coordination and oversight of third-sector organizations in housing reconstruction is needed. This can be achieved by improved coordination and communication mechanisms among aid organizations and pre-disaster planning for disaster response and recovery agencies. Integrated versus compartmentalized or silo approaches to funding by donors (e.g., avoiding separate funding for housing, water, sanitation, etc.) would also lessen coordination problems in housing and community recovery (Hayles 2010).

Looking ahead, the increasing intensity and frequency of disasters, exacerbated by climate change, will further expand the role that NGOs will play in post-disaster housing recovery. Understanding both the problems and potential of third-sector involvement will be critical to improving overall outcomes of recovery that are so dependent on housing.

ACKNOWLEDGMENTS

The concepts and ideas presented in this chapter evolved from research supported by the US National Science Foundation Grants Nos. CMS-9813611, CMMI-0726808, CMMI-1034667, and CMMI-1162438. The findings are not necessarily endorsed by the NSF. Any opinions, findings, and conclusions or recommendations expressed in this material are those of the author and do not necessarily reflect the views of the National Science Foundation.

REFERENCES

Anderson, M. D. and P. J. Woodrow. 1989. *Rising from the ashes: Developing Strategies in Times of Disaster.* Boulder: Westview Press.

Andrew, S. A., S. Arlikatti, L. C. Long, and J. M. Kendra. 2013. The effect of housing assistance arrangements on household recovery: An empirical test of donor-assisted and owner-driven approaches. *Journal of Housing and the Built Environment* 28(1):17–34.

Arroyo, D. M. 2014. Blurred lines: Accountability and responsibility in post-earthquake Haiti. *Medicine, Conflict, and Survival* 30(2):110–32.

Arlikatti, S., K. Bezboruah, and L. Long. 2012. Role of voluntary sector organizations in posttsunami relief: Compensatory or complementary? *Social Development Issues*, 34(3): 64–80.
Barenstein, J. D. 2006. Housing reconstruction in post-earthquake Gujarat: A comparative analysis. Humanitarian Practice Network (HPN) 54, April. http://www.odihpn.org/index.php?option=com_k2 &view=item&layout=item&id=2782 (accessed September 20, 2015).
Barenstein, J. D. and S. Iyengar. 2010. India: From a culture of housing to a philosophy of reconstruction. In *Building Back Better*, M. Lyons, T. Schilderman, and C. Boano (eds), London: Practical Action, 163–88.
Beaubien, J. 2013. What happened to the aid meant for Haiti? *National Public Radio*, February 28. http://www.npr.org/sections/health-shots/2013/02/28/172875646/what-happened-to-the-aid-meant-to-rebuild-haiti (accessed September 10, 2015).
Becerra, O., E. Cavallo, and I. Noy. 2012. Foreign aid in the aftermath of large natural disasters. Working Paper No. IDP-WP-333, Inter-American Development Bank, Washington, DC, August 2012. http://publications.iadb.org/bitstream/handle/11319/4056/Foreign%20Aid%20in%20the%20Aftermath%20of%20Large%20Natural%20Disasters.pdf?sequence=1 (accessed September 20, 2015).
Berke, P. R., J. Kartez, and D. Wenger. 1993. Recovery after disaster: Achieving sustainable development, mitigation and equity. *Disasters* 17(2):93–109.
Black, F. 2005. After the flood: Architects without frontiers in Sri Lanka. *Architectural Review Australia* 92:34–5.
Boano, C. 2007. Dynamics of linking reconstruction and development in housing and settlements for forced migrants in post-disaster situations. PhD Dissertation, Oxford Brookes University. United Kingdom: Oxford University.
Boano, C. 2009. Housing anxiety and multiple geographies in post-tsunami Sri Lanka. *Disasters* 34(3):762–85.
Chang, Y., S. Wilkinson, R. Potangaroa, and E. Seville. 2011. Donor-driven resource procurement for post-disaster reconstruction: Constraints and actions. *Habitat International* 35(2):199–205. http://dx.doi.org/doi:10.1016/j.habitatint.2010.08.003 (accessed September 20, 2015).
Clark, J. 1991. *Democratizing Development: The Role of Voluntary Organizations*. West Hartford, Connecticut: Kumarian Press.
Clinton, W. J. 2006. *Lessons Learned from Tsunami Recovery: Key Propositions for Building Back Better*. New York: Office of the UN Secretary-General's Special Envoy for Tsunami Recovery.
Daly, P. and C. Brassard. 2011. Aid accountability and participatory approaches in post-disaster housing reconstruction. *Asian Journal of Social Science* 39(4):508–33.
Davidson, C. H., C. Johnson, G. Lizarralde, N. Dikmen, and A. Sliwinski. 2007. Truths and myths about community participation in post-disaster housing projects. *Habitat International* 31(1):100–15.
Davis, I., P. Thompson, and F. Krimgold, eds. 2015. *Shelter after Disaster*, 2nd edn. Geneva, Switzerland: International Federation of Red Cross and Red Crescent Societies (IFRC) and the Office for Coordination of Humanitarian Affairs (OCHA).
Easterly, W. R. 2002. *The Elusive Quest for Growth: Economists' Adventures and Misadventures in the Tropics*. Cambridge, Massachusetts: MIT Press.
Eikenberry, A. M., V. Arroyave, and T. Cooper. 2007. Administrative failure and the international NGO response to Hurricane Katrina. *Public Administration Review* 67(1) (Special Issue):160–70.
Elliott, J., ProPublica, and L. Sullivan. 2015. How the Red Cross raised half a billion dollars for Haiti and built six homes. *National Public Radio*, June 3. http://www.propublica.org/article/how-the-red-cross-raised-half-a-billion-dollars-for-haiti-and-built-6-homes (accessed September 20, 2015).

Esnard, A.-M. and A. Sapat. 2014. *Displaced by Disaster: Recovery and Resilience in a Globalizing World.* New York: Routledge Press.

Farmer, P. 2011. Partners in help: Assisting the poor over the long term. *Foreign Affairs,* June 28. http://www.foreignaffairs.com/articles/68002/paul-farmer/partners-in-help (accessed September 20, 2015).

Flatt, V. B. and J. J. Stys. 2013. Long term recovery in disaster response and the role of non-profits. *Oñati Socio-Legal Series* 3(2):346–62.

Gajewski, S., H. Bell, L. Lein, and R. J. Angel. 2011. Complexity and instability: The response of nongovernmental organizations to the recovery of hurricane Katrina survivors in a host community. *Nonprofit and Voluntary Sector Quarterly* 40(2):389–403.

Guarnacci, U. 2012. Governance for sustainable reconstruction after disasters: Lessons from Nias, Indonesia. *Environmental Development* 2:73–85, April. http://dx.doi.org/doi:10.10.1016/j.envdev.2012.03.010 (accessed September 1, 2015).

Habitat for Humanity (HFH). 2015. About habitat for humanity's disaster response. *Habitat for Humanity's Disaster Response.* http://www.habitat.org/disaster/about (accessed September 8, 2015).

Harris, S. 2006. *Disaster Response, Peace and Conflict in Post-Tsunami Sri Lanka. Part I: The Congestion of Humanitarian Space.* Working Paper No. 16, Department of Peace Studies, University of Bradford, Bradford, United Kingdom. http://www.eldis.org/go/home&id=31605&type=Document (accessed September 20, 2015).

Hayles, C. S. 2010. An examination of decision making in post disaster housing reconstruction. *International Journal of Disaster Resilience in the Built Environment* 1(1):103–22.

Hearn, J. 2007. African NGOs: The new compradors? *Development and Change* 38(6):1095–110.

Hilhorst, D. 2003. *The Real World of NGOs: Discourses, Diversity and Development.* London: Zed Books.

Iuchi, K. and E. Maly. 2016. Residential relocation processes in coastal areas: Tacloban city after typhoon Yolanda. In *Coming Home After Disaster: Multiple Dimensions of Housing Recovery.* A. Sapat and A-M. Esnard (eds), Boca Raton: CRC Press, 209–227.

Jayasuriya, S. and P. McCawley. 2010. *The Asian Tsunami: Aid and Reconstruction after a Disaster,* 1st edn, Cheltenham: Edward Elgar Publishing Limited.

Jenkins, P., T. Lambeth, K. Mosby, and B. Van Brown. 2015. Local nonprofit organizations in a post-Katrina landscape help in a context of recovery. *American Behavioral Scientist* 59(10):1263–77.

Kartez, J. D. 1991. Planning for cooperation in environmental dilemmas. *Journal of Planning Literature* 5(3):226–37. http://dx.doi.org/doi:10.1177/088541229100500302 (accessed September 20, 2015).

Kennedy, J., J. Ashmore, E. Babister, and I. Kelman. 2008. The meaning of "build back better": Evidence from post-tsunami Aceh and Sri Lanka. *Journal of Contingencies and Crisis Management* 16(1):24–36.

Klarreich, K. and L. Polman. 2012. The NGO Republic of Haiti. *The Nation,* October 31. http://www.thenation.com/article/170929/ngo—republic—haiti (accessed September 20, 2015).

Lyons, M. 2009. Building back better: The large-scale impact of small-scale approaches to reconstruction. *World Development* 37(2):385–98, February. http://www.sciencedirect.com/science/article/pii/S0305750X08001472 (accessed September 20, 2015).

MacRae, G. and D. Hodgkin. 2011. Half full or half empty? Shelter after the Jogjakarta earthquake. *Disasters* 35(1):243–67.

Martens, K. 2002. Mission impossible? Defining nongovernmental organizations. *Voluntas: International Journal of Voluntary and Nonprofit Organizations* 13(3):271–85.

McCurry, R. A. 2009. *Dependence on Non-Profits during Major Disaster Relief: A Risky Dilemma.* Washington, DC: The George Washington University Homeland Security Policy Institute.

McKeever, B. and S. Pettijohn. 2014. *The Nonprofit Sector in Brief 2014: Public Charities, Giving, and Volunteering.* Washington, DC: Urban Institute.

Olson, L. L. 2012. Of hell and high water: Longitudinal case studies of the internal and external recovery efforts of non-governmental organizations after Hurricane Katrina. PhD dissertation, George Washington University, Washington, DC.

Patinet, J. 2011. Managing water, sanitation and hygiene in Port-Au-Prince: How do we get out of the emergency phase? *Humanitarian Aid on the Move* 7 (February, Special Issue: Haiti):26–8.

Paul, S. and A. Israel, eds. 1991. *Nongovernmental Organizations and the World Bank.* Washington, DC: The World Bank.

Phillips, B. 2014. *Mennonite Disaster Service: Building a Therapeutic Community after the Gulf Coast Storms.* Lanham, Maryland: Lexington Books.

Quarantelli, E. L. 1982. *Sheltering and Housing after Major Community Disasters: Case Studies and General Conclusions.* Columbus, Ohio: Ohio State University, Disaster Research Centre.

Salamon, L. 1994. The rise of the nonprofit sector. *Foreign Affairs* 74(3):109–22, July/August.

Salamon, L. M., S. W. Sokolowski, M. A. Haddock, and H. S. Tice. 2012. *The State of Global Civil Society and Volunteering: Latest Findings from the Implementation of the UN Nonprofit Handbook.* Working Paper No. 49. Baltimore, Maryland: Johns Hopkins Center for Civil Society Studies.

Sapat, A. and A.-M. Esnard, 2013. Interviews by authors with Haitian-American NGOs. Boca Raton, Florida, June.

Schuller, M. 2007. Invasion or infusion? Understanding the role of NGOs in contemporary Haiti. *Journal of Haitian Studies* 13(2):96–119.

Schuller, M. 2009. Gluing globalization: NGOs as intermediaries in Haiti. *PoLAR: Political and Legal Anthropology Review* 32(1):84–104. http://dx.doi.org/doi:10.1111/j.1555-2934.2009.01025.x (accessed September 20, 2015).

Schuller, M. 2012. *Killing with Kindness: Haiti, International Aid, and NGOs.* New Brunswick, New Jersey: Rutgers University Press.

Simo, G. and A. L. Bies. 2007. The role of nonprofits in disaster response: An expanded model of cross-sector collaboration. *Public Administration Review* 67(s1):S125–42.

Stys, J. J. 2011. *Non-Profit Involvement in Disaster Response and Recovery.* Prepared for the Center for Law, Environment, Adaptation and Resources (CLEAR). Chapel Hill, North Carolina: University of North Carolina School of Law. http://www.google.com/url?http://www.law.unc.edu/documents/clear/publications/nonprofit.pdf&sa=U&ved=0-ahUKEwjvtY76x6DLAhVIKCYKHWPcAUoQFggFMAA&client=internal-uds-cse&usg=AFQjCNG30V4xjFzi_UexVzKQt-uDBRt63Q (accessed February 29, 2016).

Telford, J. and J. Cosgrave. 2007. The international humanitarian system and the 2004 Indian Ocean earthquake and tsunamis. *Disasters* 31(1):1–28.

Twigg, J. 2006. Technology, post-disaster housing reconstruction and livelihood security, Disaster Studies Working Paper 15, Benfield Hazard Research Centre, London. http://practicalaction.org/post-disaster-reconstruction-2 (accessed February 29, 2016).

Von Meding, J. K., L. Oyedele, and D. J. Cleland. 2009. Developing NGO competencies in post-disaster reconstruction: A theoretical framework. *Disaster Advances* 2(3):36–45.

18 Pre- and Post-Disaster Conditions, Their Implications, and the Role of Planning for Housing Recovery

Gavin Smith

CONTENTS

18.1 INTRODUCTION

Housing-related issues are among the most complex, intertwined, and impactful aspects of disaster recovery (Bates and Peacock 1987; Bolin 1986; Bolin and Stanford 1991; Quarantelli 1982; Welsh and Esnard 2009). While early research suggests that the larger process of recovery follows an orderly sequencing of activities (Haas et al. 1977), this chapter recognizes that housing recovery is fraught with uncertainty and conflict and differential outcomes are based on a number of pre- and post-disaster conditions (Peacock and Ragsdale 2000; Smith 2011). Pre-disaster conditions include the type (e.g., permanent, rental, and public housing) and condition (e.g., quality of construction, maintenance, adherence to codes and standards) of housing (Bolin 1994; Comerio 1998; Comerio et al. 1994); its location relative to hazards (Bolin and Stanford 1988); the financial standing of residents (Berke et al. 1993; Bolin and Stanford 1988; Rubin 1985); local government experience dealing with past disaster recovery housing issues (Anderson and Woodrow 1989; Phillips 1993); as well as numerous demographic factors (e.g., race, gender, and education) that influence the nature of disaster recovery assistance received (Bolin and Bolton 1983; Morrow and Peacock 2000; Peacock et al. 2014).

Post-disaster conditions include the level, type, and distribution of disaster impacts at the household level (Cutter et al. 2014; Peacock et al. 1987); the quality of formal resource delivery frameworks (e.g., grants, loans, and insurance) (Comerio 1998; Lubell 2006; Peacock et al. 1987; Wu and Lindell 2004); the degree to which plans reflect locally based housing needs (Comerio 2014; Iuchi 2014; Oliver-Smith 1990; Smith 2011); the presence of autonomous and kinship-related assistance (Bolin and Trainer 1978); and the individual and collective capacity of federal, state, and local government officials to address housing issues within the larger sphere of disaster recovery (Berke et al. 1993; May 1989; Oliver-Smith 1990).

The brief description of pre- and post-disaster conditions provides an instructive lens that guides the remainder of this chapter. First, I focus on unpacking the complexities of pre- and post-disaster conditions through planning-based housing policies within the United States to highlight the currently unrealized potential of pre-disaster recovery planning (see also Smith and Wenger 2006). Efforts to plan in the aftermath of a disaster, while common in practice, can result in a return to pre-event conditions that further vulnerable, inequitable, and economically unsustainable development (Geipel 1982; Peacock and Ragsdale 2000; Smith 2011; Smith and Wenger 2006). Plans developed in the aftermath of disasters can succeed under the right conditions and should support spontaneity, improvization, and adaptation to the conditions that emerge, including a window of opportunity to affect change (Kendra and Wachtendorf 2006, pp. 325–326; Smith 2010, p. 7, 2011). Case studies provide examples of ways to better catalyze the latent and unrealized value of recovery planning and inform a concluding set of recommendations, including proposed changes to national disaster recovery policy in the United States.

18.2 DISASTER RECOVERY PLANS AND HOUSING POLICIES

Planning for disaster recovery remains an important, albeit underutilized process (Smith 2010, 2011; Smith and Wenger 2006), including its application to housing-related problems (Welsh and Esnard 2009). This is gradually changing in the United States with the advent of the National Disaster Recovery Framework, which encourages local governments to develop pre-disaster recovery plans and the National Disaster Housing Strategy (NDHS), which encourages states to develop Housing Solutions Task Forces to aid local governments address housing issues. As this process begins in earnest, it is useful to discuss housing policies that should be included in recovery plans in the United States and in other countries.

It is important for good plans, including those addressing disaster recovery, to include a set of interrelated components, referred to in the literature as plan quality principles (Baer 1997; Berke and Godschalk 2009). Internal principles include: (1) a clear vision that defines the themes and intent of the plan; (2) a set of goal statements that reflect future desired conditions and are closely linked to the plan's vision; (3) a fact base describing current and future conditions in the study area; (4) a set of policies intended to guide public and private decisions and designed to achieve associated goals; (5) a process to carry out or implement the plan; (6) a clear monitoring and evaluation process; (7) a strong participatory component spanning the planning process; (8) a means to ensure inter-organizational coordination; and (9) mutually reinforcing linkages between the plans vision, goals, and policies. External principles include: (1) organizational clarity and plan legibility and (2) a description of how the plan complies with existing local regulations as well as state and national laws and programs (Berke and Godschalk 2009).

For the purpose of this chapter, I focus on housing-related fact bases and policies in recovery plans. A fact base should include a pre-event housing inventory and assessment and draw from the findings of damage assessments conducted after an event occurs. Specific policies should address emergency sheltering and temporary housing and long-term and permanent housing, drawing on a housing typology originally developed by Quarantelli (1982).

18.2.1 Pre-Event Housing Inventory and Assessment

A housing inventory and assessment describes the condition and location of the study area's current and future housing stock. Characteristics described in this assessment should include the age (in order to determine the codes and standards in place when the structure was built); condition (e.g., quality of construction and maintenance); and type of housing (e.g., permanent, rental, seasonal, and multifamily, including public housing and special needs facilities). In addition to understanding how structures are built, it is important to understand where current and proposed housing stock is located, in particular, relative to natural hazards.

The housing assessment helps to establish a baseline from which a local government can begin to understand hazard risk and vulnerability (in concert with a community's hazard identification and risk assessment found in their local hazard mitigation plan) as well as guide pre-event outreach and help to predict the differing needs that may occur after a disaster strikes. For instance, the presence of rental units suggests reaching out to property owners and tenants, to inform both parties about grants or loans that may be available to them before or after a disaster. In the case of landlords, most assistance comes in the form of loans, whereas tenants may be eligible for relocation assistance should they be displaced. The process should also assess other multifamily units, including public housing. Findings should inform the involvement of organizations such as Community Development Corporations, other quasi-governmental housing agencies, nonprofits, and private developers. Given the difficulties of identifying firms that are willing to engage in the financing or repair and reconstruction of low income housing, and the potentially compounding effects of increased rents in some affected areas following disasters, policies and associated financial strategies should be developed to ensure that an adequate number of these units are repaired or rebuilt.

18.2.2 Post-Event Damage Assessments

Damage assessments should also undergird good recovery plans and associated policies. They help to capture the deleterious effects of events on individual structures, their spatial distribution, and help to determine whether damages are sufficient to merit state and federal assistance. The effective, timely, and equitable distribution of housing assistance should be informed, in part, by the results of the damage assessment, including the collection of time sensitive or "perishable" data such as high-water marks and debris fields associated with floods and forensic information tied to building performance relative to hazard forces such as high winds, storm surge, ground motion, and fire. The development of sound processes should be developed beforehand, accounting for the difficulties of accurately assessing the number and severity of damages and accurately conveying these findings. The development of defensible procedures can counter the influence of political interests and those who stand to gain from exaggerated losses through additional federal assistance and insurance claims or underestimated losses as a means to assure potential businesses and investors (Comerio 1998, pp. 37–38).

The accurate assessment of damages across differing housing types and household characteristics can help to pinpoint local needs relative to post-disaster recovery programs and their associated eligibility requirements. If gaps are identified between the type of damages and local needs, states, local governments, and other stakeholders, like nonprofits, foundations, community groups, and quasi-governmental organizations can use this information to provide targeted assistance. The effective use of this information benefits from the development of strong inter-organizational relationships which facilitate the sharing of information regarding the types of damages, the nature of assistance available across these groups, and the development of coordinated resource distribution strategies (Berke et al. 1993; Smith 2011). It is also incumbent on local governments to foster relationships with nongovernmental aid providers as the majority of damages sustained at the local level do not merit federal assistance (National Emergency Management Association 1998; Smith 2011, p. 12).

Another way in which the results of the assessment can help to inform recovery is through the identification of the personnel/staffing needs required to deliver information to applicants, including the possible deployment of housing counselors who can decipher and explain how differing programs work across the larger assistance network and who is eligible to apply for them. If needs exceed available resources at the local level, state and federal disaster assistance cadres may be deployed to assist. Prior studies have shown, however, that damage assessments often fail to account for local capacity, including the use of indigenous knowledge of local housing needs to inform recovery policy in the United States and abroad (Ganapati and Ganapati 2009, p. 51; Oliver-Smith 1990, 1991; Smith 2011, pp. 244–245).

The damage assessment process also involves conducting substantial damage determinations, which are used to ascertain whether pre-established damage thresholds have been exceeded. If this occurs, property owners must comply with current codes and standards during the repair and reconstruction process. Complying with codes can result in a significant cost to the property owner. Informing affected parties of these requirements beforehand may encourage the individual to undertake risk reduction initiatives on their own if they can afford the additional costs and they clearly understand how the benefits of taking action may be realized over time (Mileti 1999, pp. 137–143). The assessment of code compliance and permitting after a major disaster can also prove daunting to local building officials, and as such, recovery plans should identify the means to quickly increase staff after a disaster to assist with the additional workload.

An important, but often overlooked part of the damage assessment process is to evaluate the performance of hazard mitigation measures relative to "non-mitigated" structures. Often referred to as losses avoided studies, these initiatives monetarily tabulate expected damages and associated costs for events of differing magnitudes and compare it to the damages that were "avoided" due to the implementation of hazard mitigation measures beforehand (Smith 2015, pp. 294–295). In practice, damage assessment protocols rarely include procedures to calculate losses avoided. Instead, the process tends to be focused on determining whether a jurisdiction is eligible to receive an emergency or major disaster declaration and the associated relief the declarations entail, including that which is tied to a range of emergency, temporary, long-term, and permanent housing programs.

18.2.3 Emergency and Temporary Housing Policies

Emergency and temporary housing policies should be flexible; account for local capabilities and factors that are subject to change over time; and span a variety of housing types available such as emergency shelters, hotels, apartments, friends' and relatives' homes, and Federal Emergency Management Agency (FEMA)-provided campers and mobile homes. Emergency and temporary housing policies should also recognize both informal and formal housing solutions provided by individual families, nonprofits, federal, state, and local governments, and others as identified.

The transition from temporary to permanent housing can take years to achieve following major disasters (Peacock et al. 1987) and housing trajectories are shaped by the type of housing sought and the demographic characteristics of those seeking it. Significant temporary housing needs may also exist for contractors tasked with debris management, housing repair and reconstruction, grants management, insurance settlements, environmental restoration, or other activities following major disasters. The development of temporary housing policies to address these and other issues is often unplanned for at the local level, which can lead to significant challenges in not only housing displaced individuals but also those tasked with rebuilding replacement housing after a disaster strikes.

Policies should also address the identification of temporary housing sites (including supporting water, sewer, electrical, and transportation infrastructure). Care should be taken during the assessment of potential sites to consider the distance from places of employment and schools, the ability to provide public transit to and from the area if needed, and its location relative to known hazards. Policies may include the construction of multifamily housing for those initially dislocated by a disaster, temporary workers, or units that can transition to permanent housing over time (see Figure 18.1).

The construction and management of larger group sites, small sites, and siting units on private property all require addressing differing, sometimes contentious issues in the immediate aftermath of a disaster. The failure to discuss and plan for these issues beforehand can cause further conflict (Erikson 1978; Smith 2011, pp. 266–268). For instance, placing group sites in a neighborhood can raise concerns among local residents, and tenants of these group sites tend to be stigmatized. The identification of larger group sites (particularly in post-disaster settings) can

FIGURE 18.1 Multifamily housing design and construction techniques intended to address a range of post-disaster recovery housing needs. This multifamily housing complex in Seattle, Washington was erected in less than 6 months by six workers and a crane. Pre-fabricated wall, floor, and roof parts arrive ready to assemble. While intended for permanent residents and renters, its rapid deployment, durability, and sustainability features enable it to house those displaced by a disaster or workers tasked with post-disaster recovery and reconstruction. (Photo: With permission from CollinsWoerman.)

be difficult to identify due to available land (some of which may be used as debris staging areas), suitable supporting infrastructure, and public opposition. Locating group sites in places like vacant industrial or public parks can create transportation challenges for those living there, raise environmental justice issues, or engender conflict among those who seek to protect the use of parks as a place for recreation or contemplation after disasters.

Group sites are often identified and constructed quickly in the aftermath of major disasters that render a significant number of homes uninhabitable. The process typically includes identifying a location that requires minimal preparatory work, and has access to power, water, and sewer hook ups. Units are placed on pads in close proximity to one another (as seen in Figure 18.2). The individual placement of units on a property owner's land represents an alternative approach and can help to facilitate recovery as this allows the owner to be adjacent to the site while home repairs, insurance-based assessments, and post-disaster permitting procedures are undertaken. This approach can prove difficult for FEMA, state, and local government officials to manage as units may be scattered throughout a jurisdiction, thereby affecting maintenance and monitoring efforts (see Figure 18.3).

18.2.4 Long-Term and Permanent Housing Policies

Like many complex recovery issues, housing policy necessitates working with members of the larger assistance network, including federal and state agencies, nonprofit

FIGURE 18.2 Post-disaster Temporary Housing Group Site following the 2011 Joplin Tornado (top left), including bus stop (bottom left) and tornado shelter (top right). Image of destroyed home, including notes thanking volunteers (bottom right). (Photos: Gavin Smith.)

FIGURE 18.3 Temporary housing unit placed on a homeowner's lot as they rebuild their coastal Mississippi home following Hurricane Katrina. (Photo: Gavin Smith.)

BOX 18.1 MISSISSIPPI ALTERNATIVE HOUSING PROGRAM

Following Hurricane Katrina, the State of Mississippi was awarded $246,000,000 to design, construct, and deploy three temporary housing types: the Mississippi Cottage, the Mississippi Park Model, and the Green Mobile (ultimately called the Eco-Cottage), collectively known as the Mississippi Alternative Housing Program (MAHP). The modular units were intended to offer alternatives to mobile homes and campers typically used by FEMA to temporarily house disaster survivors. Improvements included the use of International Residential Code construction standards, a more efficient use of interior space, the use of materials that did not emit formaldehyde, a covered front porch, the ability to affix the larger Mississippi Cottage and Green Mobile units to a permanent foundation once the steel transportation undercarriage was removed (see Figure 18.4), and the ability to reuse the units in future disasters (Smith 2014, p. 349).

Following a housing design workshop and a competitive selection process, modular home builders were selected. Once the units were constructed they were delivered to a staging area. The MAHP units were then deployed to group sites and individual lots where they replaced FEMA-provided temporary housing. Over time, the units were sold to individuals, nonprofits, and developers, some of which have become permanent housing on the Mississippi coast, while others were purchased for use as accessory dwelling units or hunting camps. While widely recognized by tenants as a significant improvement over FEMA-provided temporary housing (Maly and Kondo 2013, p. 502), two

FIGURE 18.4 Mississippi Cottage, purchased post-Katrina and elevated on an individual's lot. (Photo: Gavin Smith.)

issues unique to the alternative housing program were identified. Some local official noted that they might actually be "too nice" and this could serve as a disincentive for those living in the units to "move on with their lives" and seek permanent housing (Smith, G. 2007. Personal communication with mayors in coastal Mississippi). The two and three bedroom Mississippi Cottage units, which were designed to replace the use of FEMA-provided mobile homes (and could become permanent housing once the wheeled undercarriage was removed) were slightly smaller than 1000 square feet, which was the minimum size requirement for permanent housing in many Mississippi coastal communities (Maly and Kondo 2013, p. 506).

The physical design of the MAHP units served to address a number of important issues including improved tenant satisfaction and livability, enhanced durability, and the flexibility to adapt the units based on individual preferences, needs, and local standards. Yet, the total number of units that ultimately served as a bridge to permanent housing were small relative to demands as expressed by tenants (Maly and Kondo, 506–507). Nor did FEMA adopt this approach on a permanent basis, instead reverting to the use of campers and mobile homes following subsequent disasters (Smith 2014, p. 359) (see Figure 18.2, top left). The unwillingness of FEMA to adopt a new approach to temporary housing may be due to a number of factors including: (1) the agency and staff are reluctant to change long-standing methods as evidenced by their common refrain that FEMA is "not in the business of providing permanent housing," (2) the large inventory of temporary housing units already purchased and warehoused for future use, (3) concerns expressed by manufactured housing industry lobbyists about altering the status quo, and (4) the agency was not involved in the design and deployment of the units and as such did not have ownership of the process (Smith 2011, pp. 359–360).

aid organizations, community development corporations, and private sector organizations. Planners need to address broader community issues that may be present before a disaster, like poverty and access to decision-making efforts (Geipel 1982), and go beyond a "project-based approach" to housing reconstruction that embraces local involvement (Ganapati and Ganapati 2009, p. 42). For instance, some hazard scholars have lamented an approach to disaster recovery driven by private sector interests (Freudenberg et al. 2009; Klein 2007; Peacock et al. 2000). In many cases, these arguments fail to recognize the important roles the private sector plays in repairing and reconstructing housing (Smith 2011, pp. 175–176). They also pick up debris, design and rebuild damaged infrastructure, finance reconstruction, and administer grants for local governments (Comerio 1998; Smith 2011, pp. 157–159, 165; Sylves 2008, pp. 163–168). Yet, the private sector is rarely invited to participate as stakeholders in the pre- and post-disaster recovery planning process, even in those cases in when they are hired to write such plans (Smith 2011, pp. 187–191). The failure to develop inclusive recovery plans, to include groups like the private sector, can hinder innovation, like that shown in Figures 18.5 and 18.6.

FIGURE 18.5 Neighborhood development using Mississippi Cottages purchased after Katrina for adaptive reuse. Mississippi Cottages, the largest experimental designs created by the State of Mississippi, were purchased by a private developer after they were used to house disaster survivors following Hurricane Katrina. In this case, they have been stacked on top of one another, creating multistory housing. (Photo: Gavin Smith.)

FIGURE 18.6 Adaptive expansion and elevation of Mississippi Alternative Housing Project home. This image is representative of the power of multi-institutional collaboration. The original unit (Mississippi Cottage) was funded by a Congressional appropriation, designed and deployed by the state working in concert with the private sector, and its expansion and siting on an elevated foundation was undertaken by Habitat for Humanity and other nonprofit organizations. (Photo: Gavin Smith.)

BOX 18.2 STATE OF NORTH CAROLINA DISASTER RECOVERY HOUSING PROGRAMS

Following Hurricane Floyd, which struck in 1999, the State of North Carolina created 22 state recovery programs to address gaps in federal assistance, including several that sought to further hazard mitigation objectives targeting housing. The programs were developed as a result of extensive conversations with local communities following what proved to be the worst disaster in the state's history. One of these programs, the State Acquisition and Relocation Fund (SARF), provided up to $75,000 in addition to federal funding used to purchase flood-damaged structures at their pre-disaster fair market value. Once acquired, the home was demolished and the land returned to open space, thereby reducing future losses. In many cases, the homes slated for acquisition had been flooded repeatedly and were in poor condition. The additional funding provided by the state further incentivized participation in this voluntary program and significantly increased the likelihood that these residents had the means to move out of the floodplain and into a home that was of comparable size but in good condition (Smith 2011, pp. 56–58; 2014, pp. 206–207).

Since Hurricane Floyd and Hurricane Fran, which had struck the same area just 3 years before, over 5000 homes have been acquired in one of the largest single-state acquisition programs in the United States. While the program decreased flood risk, it further reduced the limited amount of low income housing in the area, a long-standing pre-event condition facing much of Eastern North Carolina. In an effort to alleviate this problem, the state also developed a program that sought to build new low income housing subdivisions to replace many of the units that were lost, but due to limited funding and a lack of interest at the local level, the program proved less successful than SARF and was unable to significantly address the deficit of affordable housing (Smith 2014, p. 207).

Kinston, North Carolina was one of the hardest hit communities following both Hurricanes Fran and Floyd and the city's actions highlight the merits of pre-event planning for post-disaster recovery. Following Hurricane Fran, the city developed an application to acquire over 360 flood-prone homes, including a mobile home park. Given the complexities of the grant program and inexperienced federal, state, and local officials, it took 1 year to approve the application (Smith 2011, p. 65). Kinston was in the process of implementing the acquisition program when Floyd struck 3 years later. In the interim, however, the city had developed a pre-disaster recovery plan, which included an assessment of other flood-prone homes that ultimately served as the basis for a grant application containing more than 600 structures proposed for acquisition should future funding become available. The plan also sought to guide future development away from hazardous areas, encourage housing reinvestment in the town center (Call Kinston Home), train those displaced by the flood in housing repair skills in partnership with the local community college (Housing and Employment Leading People to Success), and identify open space options for land that was slated for acquisition. When Floyd struck, the city submitted an application to the state and FEMA which was approved 1 week after the disaster, thereby substantially speeding up the housing recovery process, while at the same time incorporating hazard mitigation, and implementing several pre-identified goals (Smith 2011, p. 65).

The complexities of these and other examples provided throughout this chapter highlight the importance of planning for post-disaster housing recovery at the federal, state, and local levels. The true power of planning is achieved when planning principles work in tandem, mutually reinforcing one another as part of a coordinated whole. In the case of North Carolina, the 22 state programs remain one of the most comprehensive set of recovery policies and programs developed to address gaps in federal assistance (Smith 2011, p. 57). Yet, the state did not develop an associated state recovery plan to systematically coordinate these initiatives or account for some key local conditions. As a result, the vision of the governor, the extensive outreach conducted by state officials to identify local needs, and the development of state programs to address them, fell short of its intended target. Important factors hindering desired outcomes included: (1) the lack of a pre- or post-disaster state recovery plan, (2) varied levels of coordination across state agencies tasked with the administration of new recovery programs, (3) conflicting state program objectives, and (4) further overwhelming local officials who were already struggling to administer federal disaster recovery programs (Smith 2011, p. 57).

18.3 CONCLUDING THOUGHTS AND RECOMMENDATIONS

A community's vision of recovery is often to return to what was in place before the disaster rather than explore alternative futures, even if the past is characterized by high risk, inequity, and degraded environmental and economic systems. The choices made by communities directly impact a range of housing-related issues and outcomes. One of the values of pre-event planning for post-disaster recovery involves providing a process-oriented approach that allows stakeholder groups to take the time required to contemplate policy options. Plans also provide a procedural and legally enforceable mechanism to implement policies derived from thoughtful and inclusive deliberation.

This means investing more in pre-disaster recovery capacity building initiatives through enhanced training efforts, providing funds to help local governments develop pre-disaster recovery plans, and engaging states and local governments (Smith 2011). Key aims should be to create flexible national policies that foster pre-event collaboration across broad networks while accounting for the realities of post-disaster spontaneity and adaptation. In the United States, this would mean strategies such as operationalizing the NDHS (FEMA 2009). For instance, while FEMA discusses the use of "innovative forms of interim housing," the agency has returned to the use of campers and mobile homes after the US Congress invested more than $400,000,000 in the development of improved alternative housing. Operationalizing this element within the larger national housing strategy should include working with architects to improve the design of temporary units, drawing on lessons derived from experimental approaches developed in Mississippi, Louisiana, and Alabama following Hurricane Katrina. An additional consideration should include exploring new design-related approaches to group sites, including those that may transition to permanent neighborhoods. Involving national, as well as state and local officials, nonprofits, and the private sector are vitally important to develop a coherent and actionable housing strategy.

At the state level, recommendations include increasing the role of states as local government capacity builders, and developing state recovery housing policies and programs to address gaps in federal housing assistance. This may include developing pre-disaster cadres of building officials that can deploy to hard hit areas to assist local officials conduct damage assessments, substantiate damage determinations, and review permit requests. Other examples include the development of state-level recovery planning guidance to include checklists intended to assess the degree to which local plans address emergency, temporary, long-term, and permanent housing. These actions should coincide with the creation of a state Housing Solutions Task Force, as suggested in the NDHS (FEMA 2009). A review of state recovery plans have found, however, that they focus on the administration of federal programs and policies that do not necessarily reflect local housing needs and conditions (Sandler and Smith 2013; Smith and Flatt 2011). These findings suggest the need to foster a greater commitment to state recovery planning, in part, by federal support as well as a willingness to solicit and act on state input before and after disasters. As shown in the North Carolina and Mississippi examples, states can push for changes in federal housing policy or adopt new state policies to address gaps in post-disaster federal housing assistance. Yet, the lack of a state recovery plan can limit the overall effectiveness of new programs.

Local governments are key players in housing recovery as they possess unique tools, capabilities, and an in-depth awareness of local conditions as evidenced by Kinston, North Carolina. In that case, the development of a disaster recovery plan was used to accomplish multiple aims. These included relocating flood-prone housing, adopting green infrastructure strategies, and guiding future development away from flood hazard areas. Additional examples worthy of emulation at the local level include the utilization of pre-event housing assessment data and post-disaster damage assessment information to inform local policies and plans and applying land use tools and planning procedures to emergency, temporary, and long-term housing policy and programs.

The complexities of housing recovery require developing a vertically integrated national strategy that allows collaboration and innovation to thrive across the broad network of stakeholders and to develop a set of cohesive policies addressing local conditions, needs, and capabilities (Smith 2011). This also means building and sustaining the collective capacity of networks identified during the recovery planning process as well as developing actionable pre-disaster recovery plans that proactively tackle the myriad housing conditions identified in this chapter.

REFERENCES

Anderson, M. and P. Woodrow. 1989. *Rising from the Ashes: Development Strategies in Times of Disaster.* Boulder, Colorado: Westview.

Baer, W. C. 1997. General plan evaluation criteria: An approach to making better plans. *Journal of the American Planning Association* 63(3): 329–45.

Bates, F. L. and W. G. Peacock. 1987. Disasters and social change. In *The Sociology of Disasters*, R. R. Dynes, B. Demarchi, and C. Pelanda (eds), Milan, Italy: Franco Angeli Press, 291–330.

Berke, P. and D. R. Godschalk. 2009. Searching for the good plan: A meta-analysis of plan quality studies. *Journal of Planning Literature* 23(3): 227–40.

Berke, P., J. Kartez, and D. Wenger. 1993. Recovery after disaster: Achieving sustainable development, mitigation, and equity. *Disasters* 17: 93–109.

Bolin, R. C. 1986. Disaster impact and recovery: A comparison of black and white victims. *International Journal of Mass Emergencies and Disasters* 4: 35–50.

Bolin, R. C. 1994. *Household and Community Recovery after Earthquakes.* Boulder, Colorado: University of Colorado, Institute of Behavioral Science, Program on Environment and Behavior.

Bolin, R. C. and P. Bolton. 1983. Recovery in Nicaragua and the USA. *International Journal of Mass Emergencies and Disasters* 1(1): 125–52.

Bolin, R. and L. Stanford. 1991. Shelter, housing and recovery: A comparison of US disasters. *Disasters* 15(1): 24–34.

Bolin, R. C. and L. Stanford. 1988. The Northridge earthquake: Community based approaches to unmet recovery needs. *Disasters* 22(1): 21–38.

Bolin, R. C. and P. A. Trainer. 1978. Modes of family recovery following disaster: A cross-national study. In *Disasters: Theory and Research*, E. L. Quarantelli (ed.), Beverly Hills, California: Sage, 233–47.

Comerio, M. 1998. *Disaster Hits Home: New Policy for Urban Housing Recovery.* Berkeley, California: University of California Press.

Comerio, M. 2014. Housing lessons from Chile. *Journal of the American Planning Association* 80(4): 340–50.

Comerio, M. C., J. D. Landis, and Y. Rofe. 1994. *Post-Disaster Residential Rebuilding.* Working Paper 608. Berkeley, California: University of California, Institute of Urban and Regional Development.

Cutter, S. L., C. T. Emerich, J. T. Mitchell, W. W. Pieqorsch, M. M. Smith, and L. Weber. 2014. *Hurricane Katrina and the Forgotten Coast of Mississippi.* New York: Cambridge Press.

Erikson, E. H. 1978. *Everything in Its Path.* New York: Simon and Schuster.

Federal Emergency Management Agency (FEMA). 2009. *Disaster Housing Strategy.* Washington, DC: FEMA. www.fema.gov/news-release/2009/01/16/national-disaster-housing-strategy-released (accessed February 29, 2016).

Freudenberg, W., R. Gramling, S. Laska, and K. Erickson. 2009. *Catastrophe in the Making: The Engineering of Katrina and the Disasters of Tomorrow.* Washington, DC: Island Press.

Ganapati, N. E. and S. Ganapati. 2009. Enabling participatory planning after disasters: A case study of the World Bank's housing reconstruction in turkey. *Journal of the American Planning Association* 75(1): 41–59.

Geipel, R. 1982. *Disaster and Reconstruction: The Fruili (Italy) Earthquake of 1976.* London: Allen and Unwin.

Haas, J. E., R. Kates, and M. Bowden. 1977. *Reconstruction Following Disaster.* Cambridge: MIT Press.

Iuchi, K. 2014. Planning resettlement after disasters. *Journal of the American Planning Association* 80(4): 413–25.

Kendra, J. M. and T. Wachtendorf. 2006. Community innovation and disasters. In *Handbook of Disaster Research*, H. Rodriguez, E. Quarantelli, and R. Dynes (eds), New York: Springer, 316–34.
Klein, N. 2007. *The Shock Doctrine: The Rise of Disaster Capitalism*. New York: Henry Holt and Company.
Lubell, J. 2006. Housing displaced families. In *Rebuilding Urban Places after Disaster: Lessons from Katrina*, E. L. Birch and S. Wachter (eds), Philadelphia, Pennsylvania: University of Pennsylvania Press, 168–84.
Maly, E. and T. Kondo. 2013. From temporary to permanent: Mississippi cottages after Hurricane Katrina. *Journal of Disaster Research* 8(3): 495–507.
May, P. 1989. Disaster recovery and reconstruction. In *Managing Disaster: Strategies and Perspectives*, L. Comfort (ed.), Durham, North Carolina: Duke University Press, 236–54.
Mileti, D. 1999. *Disasters by Design: A Reassessment of Natural Hazards in the United States*. Washington, DC: Joseph Henry Press.
Morrow, B. H. and W. G. Peacock. 2000. Disasters and social change: Hurricane Andrew and the reshaping of Miami? In *Hurricane Andrew: Ethnicity, Gender, and the Sociology of Disaster*, W. G. Peacock, B. H. Morrow, and H. Gladwin (eds), Miami: Florida International Hurricane Center Laboratory for Social and Behavioral Research, 226–42.
National Emergency Management Association and Council of State Governments. 1998. *Report on State Emergency Management Funding and Structures*. Lexington, Kentucky: National Emergency Management Association and the Council on State Governments.
Oliver-Smith, A. 1990. Post-disaster housing reconstruction and social inequality: A challenge to policy and practice. *Disasters* 14: 7–19.
Oliver-Smith, A. 1991. Success and failures of post-disaster resettlement. *Disasters* 15(1): 12–23.
Peacock, W. G., W. Killian, and F. Bates. 1987. The effects of disaster damage and housing aid on household recovery following the 1976 Guatemala earthquake. *International Journal of* Mass *Emergencies and Disasters* 5(1): 63–88.
Peacock, W. G., B. H. Morrow, and H. Gladwin. 2000. *Hurricane Andrew: Ethnicity, Gender, and the Sociology of Disaster*. Miami, Florida: International Hurricane Center Laboratory for Social and Behavioral Research.
Peacock, W. G. and A. K. Ragsdale. 2000. Social systems, ecological networks and disasters: Toward a socio-political ecology of disasters. In *Hurricane Andrew: Ethnicity, Gender,* and the *Sociology of Disaster*, W. G. Peacock, B. H. Morrow, and H. Gladwin (eds), Miami, Florida: International Hurricane Center Laboratory for Social and Behavioral Research, 20–35.
Peacock, W. G., S. Van Zandt, Y. Zhang, and W. Highfield. 2014. Inequities in long-term housing recovery after disasters. *Journal of the American Planning Association* 80(4): 356–71.
Phillips, B. D. 1993. Cultural diversity in disasters: Sheltering, housing, and long-term recovery. *International Journal of Mass Emergencies and Disasters* 11: 99–110.
Quarantelli, E. 1982. General and particular observations on sheltering and housing in American disasters. *Disasters* 6: 277–81.
Rubin, C. B. 1985. The community recovery process in the United States after a major natural disaster. *International Journal of Mass Emergencies and Disasters* 3(2): 9–28.
Sandler, D. and G. Smith. 2013. Assessing the quality of state disaster recovery plans: Implications for policy and practice. *Journal of Emergency Management* 11(4): 281–91.
Smith, G. 2010. Disaster recovery in the United States: Lessons for the Australasian audience. Special Issue of the *Australasian Journal of Disaster and Trauma Studies*. Natural Hazards Planning in Australasia. ISSN: 1174-4707, Volume 2010–1.

Smith, G. 2011. *Planning for Post-Disaster Recovery: A Review of the United States Disaster Assistance Framework*. Washington, DC: Island Press.

Smith, G. 2014. Applying hurricane recovery lessons in the United States to climate change adaptation: Hurricanes Fran and Floyd in North Carolina, USA. In *Adapting to Climate Change: Lessons from Natural Hazards Planning*, B. C. Glavovic and G. Smith (eds), New York: Springer, 193–229.

Smith, G. 2015. Creating disaster resilient communities: A new hazards risk management framework. In *Hazards Analysis: Reducing the Impact of Disasters*, J. Pine (ed.), 2nd edn, Boca Raton, Florida: CRC Press, 281–308.

Smith, G. and V. Flatt. 2011. *Assessing the Disaster Recovery Planning Capacity of the State of North Carolina*. Research Brief, Durham, North Carolina: Institute for Homeland Security Solutions.

Smith, G. and D. Wenger. 2006. Sustainable disaster recovery: Operationalizing an existing agenda. In *Handbook of Disaster Research*, H. Rodriguez, E. L. Quarantelli, and R. R. Dynes (eds), New York: Springer, 234–57.

Sylves, R. 2008. *Disaster Policy and Politics: Emergency Management and Homeland Security*. Washington, DC: CQ Press.

Welsh, M. G. and A.-M. Esnard. 2009. Closing gaps in local housing recovery planning for disadvantaged displaced households. *Cityscape: A Journal of Policy Development and Research* 11(3): 195–212.

Wu, J. Y. and M. K. Lindell. 2004. Housing reconstruction after two major earthquakes: The 1994 Northridge earthquake in the United States and the Chi-Chi earthquake in Taiwan. *Disasters* 28: 63–81.

19 Anticipating and Overcoming Regulatory and Legal Barriers during Rebuilding and Resettlement

John Travis Marshall, Adrienne La Grange, and Ann-Margaret Esnard

CONTENTS

19.1 INTRODUCTION

Disasters frequently change the physical landscape of communities in fundamental ways. While the tragic loss of life profoundly affects communities, one of the deepest scars that disasters leave is the destruction of neighborhoods: thousands of homes splintered by tidal surge or fierce winds, or long strings of city blocks festering in floodwaters. A major disaster's damage is typically overwhelming: tens of thousands of damaged rental and homeowner housing units, millions of square feet of unsafe office and retail space, shuttered health clinics, and wrecked community centers.

The result, however, is often the same. Within hours of a disaster's onset, tens or hundreds of thousands of families may have no home to which to return. The emphasis then shifts to funding for infrastructure, housing, and neighborhood reconstruction.

In this chapter, we focus on three main types of legal and regulatory issues important to communities interested in cultivating a robust housing environment. The first two types are (i) relocation of residents from hazardous areas and (ii) identification and removal of land title barriers to land acquisition and housing (re)development. Although these two issues by no means represent an exhaustive list of legal or regulatory considerations, they point to general areas of vulnerability that have played significant roles in undermining housing redevelopment following recent crises and disasters. Examples and solutions are drawn from various disasters around the globe (including the 2004 Indian tsunami, 2005 Hurricane Katrina, and the 2010 Haiti earthquake) to illustrate the central importance of each of the legal or regulatory issues for post-disaster housing recovery in particular.

An easily overlooked key to community resilience is adopting legal strategies that pave the way for efficient, equitable, and fair implementation of housing and community development projects. Thus, this chapter's third focus is what communities can do to cultivate and reform critical legal infrastructure before disaster ever strikes. Given the importance of anticipating, developing, and implementing relocation programming, for example, we examine strategies in countries such as Hong Kong, which though not generally in the crosshairs of natural disasters, has extensive experience with relocation of squatter settlements. Further, we highlight discrete strategies, policies, and frameworks that can be used by governments and international institutions to promote effective and inclusive housing and community development programs. These legal tools include imposing a small fee for public filing of real estate documents to raise funds for addressing low-income land owners' land title deficiencies, incorporating a capital absorption framework into local government housing and community development policies to help insure optimal investment of scarce public and philanthropic redevelopment funds, and enacting land use laws that help communities adapt to repeated challenges posed by natural hazards, such as statutes mandating rolling coastal easements or coastal development setbacks.

19.2 RELOCATING RESIDENTS FROM HAZARDOUS AREAS

Relocation of residents from unsafe locations or substandard housing is a critical consideration and potentially important opportunity in a community's post-disaster recovery journey but one thwart with complexities. In the United States, communities have struggled to develop housing programs that allow for fair, efficient, and effective large-scale relocation of vulnerable residents. Local, state, and national governments have generally favored community recovery that subsidizes rebuilding homes within a disaster's footprint (Nelson 2014). The reason relocation has largely been side-stepped is not only its expense, but also that US laws make even small-scale relocation a major logistical challenge (Marshall et al. 2016). Local zoning codes and comprehensive plans generally do not include provisions recognizing the need for post-disaster relocation of neighborhoods. State constitutions and statutes closely guard private property rights, sometimes making it difficult for local governments to acquire blighted, storm-damaged properties for redevelopment efforts including relocation projects (Marshall 2015). Further, when residents are relocated as part of a federally funded housing initiative, federal law requires compliance with highly technical notice and compensation procedures (US HUD 2014). Despite these obstacles to relocation and resettlement, threats from sea-level rise and climate change suggest the importance of advancing government initiatives aimed at incremental pre-disaster relocation and resettlement.

Relocation can also be complicated by a government's poor formulation and administration of post-disaster resettlement restrictions. The impacts to coastal communities around the globe from tsunamis and other weather disasters provide a glimpse into the dilemmas of regulating and/or enforcing coastal zone development policies (e.g., building setback limits and "no-build" coastal buffer zone) in highly populated communities with acute land shortages (Shaw and Ahmed 2010). After the Indian Ocean tsunami of 2004, the Sri Lankan Government instituted no build zones within 100–200 m of the high tide line. However, such setbacks could not be enforced because relocation of several hundred thousand households with livelihoods linked to the coast was not feasible (Shaw and Ahmed 2010). There were accusations that the setbacks were arbitrary and were not applied uniformly. For example, hotels were exempted from the ban on new building within the setback limit, thereby resulting in accusations by fishing communities that this amounted to a land grab for tourism projects and other more lucrative endeavors (Shaw and Ahmed 2010). In the end, Government Order 172 relaxed mandatory relocation and made it optional for residents within 500 m of the high tide line to relocate. Bristol (2010) also focused on land rights and land grab concerns in the tsunami-impacted coastal areas of Thailand. She warned that communities must plan for disaster, but that they must also be prepared for the aftershocks of development that follow. She also drew our attention to a statement made by the Tourist Board of Sri Lanka which typified the development response to the tsunami: "[i]n a cruel twist of fate, nature has presented Sri Lanka with a unique opportunity, and out of this great tragedy will come a world class destination" (Bristol 2010, p. 138).

The reality is that post-disaster land redevelopment in hazardous areas is intensely political. Formulating a successful relocation program is a complex endeavor because the government must manage a highly detailed, resident-by-resident, process of evaluating potential claims and then of valuing residents' homes and businesses. A major difficulty for home owners and owners of businesses that participate in voluntary resettlement is that even generous financial compensation may not enable them to reestablish themselves in another home and neighborhood. This issue can be compounded in the case of large-scale disasters where many households, with similar compensation packages and benefits, enter the housing (or other) real market at a similar time. The reality is that more people there are seeking to purchase or rent new housing (or purchase or rent new business premises) the greater will be pressure on available supply. Many tenants entering the rental market at the same time are likely to cause rapid rent rises as suitable supply is consumed. This can lead to a rapid deterioration in the real and perceived value of cash compensation and undermine the objectives of providing subsidies and assistance to help victims reestablish their households or their businesses.

19.3 "CLEAR" LAND TITLES AS CRITICAL BUILDING BLOCKS FOR STABILIZING AND REDEVELOPING NEIGHBORHOODS AND CITIES

The haphazard appearance of neighborhood recovery is often described as a gap-tooth or jack-o-lantern recovery, evoking an unattractive or even frightening picture of once-occupied neighborhood homes now empty or missing. There are a number of explanations for the patchy character of neighborhood recovery in disaster-impacted communities. Some families lack necessary homeowner or flood insurance, as discussed above. Other homes may have been occupied by elderly residents who could not manage the logistical burden of rebuilding their damaged residence. But one of the most common impediments to neighborhood rebuilding is that homeowners lack clear title to their residence (Glauber and Zisser 2013). Local governments are often oblivious to neighborhood redevelopment delays caused by clouded title to residential property. With major disaster recovery programs managed by federal and state agencies, it may be years before local governments learn about a family's ineligibility for public or private disaster recovery funds. By that time affected families' homes can be seen to lag far behind their neighbors in reconstruction or repair. Those lagging homes slow overall community recovery efforts.

Landowners who do not have legal title to their homes (or "real property") do not have a clear claim to legal ownership of real property that could stand against the right of anyone else to claim the property. As a practical matter, this means that landowners do not have ownership evidenced by a deed, court judgment, or will that is recorded in the public records establishing their ownership. The reasons homeowners lack clear title are many, but most often stem from extenuating family circumstances (Alexander 2007; McCarthy-Brown and Waysdorf 2009; Glauber and Zisser 2013). Children and grandchildren are living in homes owned by parents or grandparents who are deceased. Parents have purchased a home for their children but they never transferred title to children. A married couple jointly purchased a home and later divorced, leaving only one former spouse in the home.

Resolving title problems ordinarily requires the assistance of legal counsel and often necessitates filing legal actions (Glauber and Zisser 2013). Many families cannot afford a lawyer following a disaster where their resources are committed to covering the basic costs of family subsistence. But failure to address these title issues often scuttles families' efforts to rebuild their homes. Government disaster aid programs, private bank loans, and much of the nonprofit and philanthropic funding used by families to rebuild is disbursed contingent on homeowners showing clear title to their homes and thus the ability to convey clear title to third parties.

Title problems are more complex in countries without such records, systems, or basic land ownership laws. The fragility and informality of the land tenure system and land ownership laws in countries like Thailand and Indonesia, for example, became particularly evident after the 2004 Indian Ocean tsunami. Brown and Crawford (2006) noted that less than 10% of the land in Aceh, Indonesia was officially registered before the tsunami, and land transfers were predominantly informal and locally recorded. Furthermore, tsunami disasters expose the fragility of records and documentation. In North Sumatra and Aceh, 10% of the land books were lost, and in Sri Lanka, an estimated 90% of people who suffered extensive property damage lost all of their legal documentation (Brown and Crawford 2006, p. 7). A similar dilemma was presented in post-earthquake Haiti, which according to Castor (2012) had only 5% of land that was surveyed, registered, notarized, publicly filed, and verified in accordance with local and national law. Other scholars have discussed these informal methods of land acquisition, transfer, and titling in Haiti (Olshansky and Etienne 2011; Ferreira 2013). For both Thailand and Haiti, investment decisions were stalled by the lack of formal land tenure and land ownership systems. Specifically, post-disaster rebuilding and reconstruction of permanent housing and infrastructure were slowed or halted as international aid organizations sought proof of land ownership (Brown and Crawford 2006; Kennedy 2012; Ferreira 2013). The fragility of land tenure systems is further complicated by long-term collective leasing arrangements and vague squatter laws with citizens living on state-owned lands with livelihoods that are coastal/sea based, but where post-disaster reconstruction initiatives are fueled by economic development and tourism interests. After the 2004 Indian Ocean tsunami, Thailand's "Sea Gypsy" community made legal claim to the land that they had inhabited for decades, and started rebuilding their houses without government approval despite simultaneous and intensified efforts to clear land for tourist resorts (Brown and Crawford 2006).

Relocation planning and title clearing services represent two types of pre-disaster legal interventions that could help eliminate barriers to a quick, efficient, and equitable post-disaster recovery. The focus of the third part of this chapter, which follows immediately, is five additional ideas for legal interventions to help facilitate not only better long-term disaster recovery, but also sound redevelopment practices during non-disaster periods.

19.4 REPRESENTATIVE APPROACHES TO USING LEGAL AND POLICY TOOLS TO OVERCOME BARRIERS TO EFFICIENT, AND EQUITABLE HOUSING AND COMMUNITY DEVELOPMENT

There is no "one size fits all" approach to ensuring successful disaster resilience. As noted by Esnard and Sapat (2014, p. 187) in their discussion of crosscutting dilemmas faced by countries across the globe seeking to address population displacement and relocation issues, "generalizations may not always be instructive, given complex and diverse processes unique to each country." This is even more pertinent in the case of legal and regulatory solutions and strategies.

19.4.1 Anticipating and Responding to Potential Mass Relocation

Despite limited exposure to disasters in recent years, Hong Kong's experience of more than 40 years with relocating and resettling residents in new housing—provides a valuable narrative for understanding the challenges and opportunities associated with proactive relocation efforts in high density and high valued megacities. This has not always been the case however. The Hong Kong Government began to provide large-scale public housing from 1954 after a large-scale fire in the Shek Kip Mei squatter settlement on Christmas Eve in 1953 left 53,000 people homeless (Smart 1992, p. 33). The government's view was that it was cheaper to build affordable, simple resettlement housing for those affected by the fire than provide emergency relief, and so, as Hong Kong's public housing narrative goes, the public housing program was born.

Hong Kong has successfully dealt with its main exposure to natural disasters, namely fires, flooding, and landslides, but the government has continued to be intensively involved in developing and implementing land acquisition and resettlement policies. The demolition and redevelopment of the city's obsolete housing stock is a complex task as a consequence of the city's high density construction and multi-ownership of most private sector buildings. Hong Kong's land acquisition and resettlement policies have, therefore, evolved from responses to natural disasters (such as fires, flooding, and landslides) to policies to redevelop obsolete housing stock. Principles and policies developed to mitigate potential future losses from natural disasters have informed general policies regarding housing development. Hong Kong has long been vulnerable to landslides caused by heavy rain because of the unstable nature of the territory's soil and its undulating topography. Over the last four decades, the government has implemented widespread slope stabilization practices and landowners (leaseholders) are legally responsible for both periodic slope inspection and maintenance. Slopes that are deemed particularly vulnerable are required to be inspected annually to ensure that slope stabilization measures are in a good state of repair. In the mid-1970s, two landslides that resulted in the death toll of about 150 people, led to an expansion of government efforts to stabilize slopes (Choi and Cheung 2013). The government has also developed sophisticated tools to minimize damage to people and property from landslides, such as the quantitative risk assessment techniques to assess natural hillside hazards (Hong Kong Geotechnical Engineering Office 2012). Hong Kong's extensive land reclamation over the decades has been undertaken in manners that minimize the risk of flooding from the sea. While low-lying areas of low intensity development in the New Territories do experience flooding in heavy rains, at this stage of Hong Kong's urban development this can be classified as an inconvenience rather than a disaster. Sea-level rise and climate change pose new threats to the city, including many of Hong Kong's new towns (with populations of many hundreds of thousands), which are built on low-lying reclaimed lands that are vulnerable to rising sea levels (Francesch-Huidobro 2015; Francesch-Huidobro et al. 2016).

Hong Kong's experience with large-scale redevelopment projects involving resident relocation suggests at least four related programmatic challenges: (a) developing a compensation scheme that fairly assigns value to the properties of both residential and commercial occupants; (b) providing for relocation of so-called informal occupants of properties targeted for acquisition; (c) addressing the secondary effect of relocating residents and businesses in an environment where there is a limited supply of residential and commercial units available for lease or purchase; and (d) meeting the needs of the city's most vulnerable residents who may be subject to relocation including the poor and the elderly (La Grange and Pretorius 2016). For an in-depth discussion of post-disaster housing responses for informal settlers in several other countries, please refer to Chapter 16 by Barenstein (2016). The author asks and addresses the salient and related question of whether disasters present a window of opportunity for informal settlers to attain adequate housing and to enhance their resilience to disasters.

19.4.2 Redevelopment Safeguards

The Asian Development Bank (ADB 2010) has developed a series of "redevelopment safeguards" to guide assistance and compensation decisions associated with land (re)development projects. Among the redevelopment safeguards are the following goals, including: avoiding and minimizing involuntary resettlement; restoring livelihoods to previous levels; conducting appropriate resettlement planning through a survey or census of displaced persons; conducting meaningful consultation with affected people, including paying specific attention to the needs of vulnerable groups; establishing grievance redress mechanisms; restoring livelihoods following redevelopment; resolving tenure issues; ensuring integration of resettled persons economically and socially into their host communities; providing appropriate transition support and development assistance and civic infrastructure and community services; preparing a resettlement plan that presents entitlements in a transparent way and incorporating a resettlement/compensation schedule; and monitoring and assessing resettlement outcomes. While these principles (and others) have been developed by the ADB to apply to land acquisition and resettlement projects, many of the principles would also provide an outline for departure in developing equitable assistance and compensation to families in cases of disaster (ADB 2010).

19.4.3 Nominal Surcharge as a Solution to the Clear Title Problem

Communities cannot afford to wait until after a disaster to learn whether its neighborhoods include significant numbers of families that lack title to the home where they live. Clouded title to property can mean that hundreds or thousands of families cannot establish ownership of their property and, thus, may be disqualified from receiving government money offered to rebuild or purchase their homes (Glauber and Zisser 2013). Instead, they must take steps before disaster strikes to identify families who may lack clear title and to connect them with legal services necessary to rectify the legal deficiencies. Funded by a nominal surcharge imposed each time a document is recorded in a local government's property records, cities should establish an interface between local land records databases and existing robust databases that track information on a resident's voter registration, homestead exemption from property taxes, or payment of property taxes or business tax for rental properties. The information gleaned from crosschecking ownership and tax or voting data can determine if the current residents own the property, if they rent the property, or if the residents may be living in a home to which they do not have clear title. Local governments can then both monitor possible incidence of clouded land titles and contact owners in order to connect them with legal services necessary to address title issues. Even if a homeowner declines a city's offer to assist, the city will have a database to help identify those neighborhoods whose recovery may be delayed by higher incidence of title problems. Further, the city will be able to request assistance immediately following a disaster to aid affected families so that they experience little delay in receiving government disaster aid.

19.4.4 Capital Absorption Framework

It is tempting to conclude that disaster recovery funds, together with a range of willing private, nonprofit, and government partners, can make long-term recovery happen. Scholars have shown, however, that money and willing partners to manage long-term recovery are necessary, but certainly not sufficient predicates to recovery (Olshansky and Johnson 2010). Critical to recovery are ample time and opportunity for "thoughtful and deliberate" coordination of recovery efforts (Olshansky and Johnson 2010, pp. 217–19). A central part of this deliberative process concerns the development of safe, equitable, and efficient housing and community development resources—and doing so with relatively limited funding.

The City of New Orleans and the New Orleans Redevelopment Authority together had access to less than $500 million to help promote long-term housing and community development projects following Hurricane Katrina (Hammer 2012a; Marshall 2014). Unfortunately, the price tag for comprehensively addressing *only* those housing and community development needs exceeded $1 billion in US dollars (Carr et al. 2008). In short, the public sector money available to seed the city's recovery efforts was far less than was needed. These circumstances required the city to work with state, federal, nonprofit, private, philanthropic, and charitable organizations to cobble together necessary funding to advance essential city redevelopment projects. Although the city appears to have made a number of solid investments in long-term recovery programs (Barnes 2015), there were early redevelopment opportunities that were poorly vetted (Brescia et al. 2012; Hammer 2012b). Mindful of the city's missed recovery opportunities, the Ford Foundation and Living Cities, Inc., which is an international philanthropic effort led by the world's largest foundations, combined forces in 2012 to craft a framework—the New Orleans Capital Absorption Framework—to help make the best possible redevelopment decisions with the city's shrinking disaster recovery resources (Greater New Orleans Foundation 2013).

Based on a model developed for Baltimore, Cleveland, Detroit, Newark, and the Twin Cities, the Capital Absorption Framework is intended to serve as a vehicle to help communities pursue development projects that meet their needs and that leverage all available resources to help critical development projects succeed (Hacke 2014). Although this framework is being developed to aid cities' housing and community development decisions, its value is not limited to that context. It is a helpful pre- and post-disaster legal and planning tool because it addresses the problems associated with ensuring that relevant stakeholders are identified and included in pre-disaster planning efforts as well as post-disaster rebuilding decisions (Smith et al. 2013). Scholarship on long-term recovery indicates that local government deployment of recovery aid tends to be reactive and fails to be collaborative.

The Capital Absorption Framework is designed to guide a city's day-to-day development decisions toward more collaborative stakeholder decision making while a city is functioning under normal, nonemergency circumstances (Hacke 2014). Based on a formal system of seeking and obtaining input from neighborhoods, financial institutions, nonprofits, philanthropy, and other local stakeholders, the Capital Absorption Framework model aims to ensure that public investment in housing and community development projects is made only after stakeholder feedback is provided on a proposed housing and community development project. The goal of this Capital Absorption Framework review process, which would ideally be grafted into a local government's policies and procedures for allocating and awarding public sector subsidy funds, is that the Framework would result in housing and community development projects that better serve a community (Greater New Orleans Foundation 2013; Hacke 2014).

The Capital Absorption Framework also serves as instrument for making sure that relatively scarce funds for housing and community development projects are invested wisely—in times of crisis or amid the day-to-day challenges of neighborhood transformation (Greater New Orleans Foundation 2013). Following a catastrophic disaster, the pool of funds to complete the recovery projects is entirely insufficient to meet the reconstruction needs. Many homeowners lack sufficient property or hazard insurance coverage (Bayot 2005). Those with coverage often see their payouts reduced by coverage exclusions. Philanthropic and private donations fill only a small (albeit crucial) gap in development proformas. Government recovery funding is, by itself, completely insufficient (New Orleans Redevelopment Authority [NORA] 2010). The challenge in this environment is to promote successful, equitable, fully responsive post-disaster development. That means fostering development projects that not only fill clear post-disaster needs for new housing, retail, and community assets, but building those resources at a time and in a location that aligns with community needs. It also means ensuring that projects have the broad-based financial, legal, and community backing necessary to navigate often demanding post-disaster development terrain. In addition to New Orleans, Living Cities is piloting capital absorption initiatives in Denver, Los Angeles, and San Francisco (Hacke et al. 2015), but this initiative is still in the process of being implemented in New Orleans.

Up to this point, the legal strategies set forth in this chapter primarily encompass housing or community redevelopment tools. In other words, the preceding discussion concerns law-related tools to help facilitate neighborhood redevelopment, whether in the post-disaster long-term recovery setting or where a town, city, or region is pursuing a general goal of community development. The next section applies more narrowly to legal strategies to address a natural hazards; it focuses on coastal communities subjective to catastrophic flooding and storm surge.

19.4.5 Natural Hazard Adaptation: Representative Legal Tools

The wall of water that slammed Thailand's coast following a December 2004 Indian Ocean earthquake swept away thousands of residents, fishermen, and tourists (Waldman 2004). The storm surge caused by Superstorm Sandy was the overwhelming reason for loss of life and loss of property along the New York and New Jersey coasts (Hurricane Sandy Rebuilding Task Force 2013). These catastrophic coastal events, which have been shown to be repetitive in nature, point to the need for legal interventions to help coastal communities adapt to natural hazard risks, such as storm surge or tsunami waves. This section focuses on development setbacks and rolling easements, which establish demarcation lines for coastal construction, for shore zone planning and management, and viable approaches for holding back the sea (Titus 1998, 2011; Grannis 2011; Mitsova and Esnard 2012; Siders 2013).

Coastal setbacks are used to keep landowners from building structures too close to potential coastal hazards such as storm surge (ActionAid 2006; Juergensmeyer and Roberts 2012). To accomplish this objective, coastal setbacks cover a much wider strip of land than would commonly be seen in a normal residential context. Unfortunately, coastal erosion is a continuous process that is sometimes accelerated by natural hazards. To promote the state's or the local government's goal of providing a necessary and ample buffer between the shoreline and coastal development, local or state lawmakers should consider revisiting and revising setbacks every several years to ensure they are providing baseline protection for property owners and local and state governments (Siders 2013). This periodic recalibration of setbacks allows for local governments to take stock of the gradual but constant threats from sea-level rise and coastal erosion (Siders 2013).

A rolling easement is a regulatory tool that allows property owners to place building structures near vulnerable areas but prohibits armoring of the shoreline and other structural protection measures, thus preventing protection from rising sea levels (Titus 1998; Grannis 2011). Variations of rolling easement management practices have been adopted by the states of Oregon, Texas, Rhode Island, Maine, and North and South Carolina in the United States (Grannis 2011). Laws establishing rolling easements also frequently require coastal property owners to remove structures that encroach on the easement and mandate coastal property owners to provide formal written disclosure of the rolling easement's existence to individuals to whom they may sell their coastal property. Government-imposed initiatives to restrict coastal building are also common outside the United States. The use of so-called development buffer zones has, however, been particularly controversial where the restrictions impede the ability of low-income families to maintain or reestablish livelihoods that demand easy access to coastal waters (ActionAid 2006).

While development setbacks and rolling easements represent two important legal tools for mitigating coastal hazards, implementing these tools often comes at a high cost. After all, these tools can lead to expensive challenges to restrictions that prevent property owners from developing prized coastal lands. Given the potentially high price tag that might attach to these tools and the funding constraints faced by almost all local governments, it is important to acknowledge that these legal interventions are not, by themselves, the solution. Instead, it may make sense to supplement these tools with new statutes that discourage development in flood hazard areas. Such laws have been promoted by the European Union and adopted as regulations in countries such as Spain (Ponce 2013). These supplemental tools might also include passing laws that taper or end government subsidy for flood insurance for coastal property owners. In short, such laws call for any government backed flood insurance protections to reflect the actual risk associated with potential storm or erosion-related casualties to coastal properties (Juergensmeyer and Roberts 2012).

Overall, these legal and policy tools demonstrate a range of interventions governments can consider to increase community resilience to shocks and stresses.

Successful transferability of strategies is not guaranteed, and will have to be customized accordingly. At the same time, it is also a mistake to compartmentalize legal strategies for promoting critical legal reforms in the wake of disaster. Solutions and strategies should not be restricted to disaster-ravaged communities, particularly where a culture of pre-disaster mitigation and preparedness is weak or absent.

19.5 CONCLUSION

Following a catastrophic disaster, a community's long-term recovery depends on a community's robust housing recovery. A community that fails to rebuild its neighborhoods well may effectively deny full recovery to those who, due to delays in neighborhood recovery, never succeed in returning home. But the stakes for a community are also high because an anemic housing recovery also jeopardizes a community's continuing prosperity as a center of commerce or culture. One of the most important ways a community can increase its chance of making a strong recovery from crisis or disaster is by taking steps prior to crisis or disaster to write better regulations and eliminate legal impediments. These legal interventions facilitate prudent redevelopment tools, such as programs anticipating the need for resident relocation (Nelson 2014), ensuring more equitable redevelopment (ADB 2010), and facilitating stakeholder collaboration among potential developers, funders, and residents of new housing (Greater New Orleans Foundation 2013). These legal interventions also eliminate barriers to redevelopment caused by the inability of residents to show clear title to the land they occupy (Glauber and Zisser 2013). Looking forward, legal interventions can allow communities to adapt to the risks posed by natural hazards that pose the greatest threat to their region, such as sea-level rise, coastal storms, or tsunamis (Grannis 2011; Siders 2013). Among the greatest challenges of disaster recovery are rebuilding homes and simultaneously resettling the thousands of residents who fled near and far to find shelter with family or friends. By crafting housing redevelopment plans and standards that facilitate fairer, more inclusive, more predictable, and more collaborative housing recovery, communities can codify critical keys to quicker and more equitable rebuilding in the wake of crisis and disaster.

ACKNOWLEDGMENT

We wish to acknowledge Georgia State University's Comparative Urban Research Partnership Initiation Grant for the funding that enabled this book chapter collaboration.

REFERENCES

ActionAid International. 2006. *Tsunami Response: A Human Rights Assessment*. http://www.alnap.org/resource/5581 (accessed February 29, 2016).

Alexander, F. S. 2007. Louisiana land reform in the storms' aftermath. *Loyola Law Review* 53: 727–61.

Asian Development Bank (ADB). 2010. *Legal and Regulatory Framework for Land Acquisition and Resettlement in the Hong Kong SAR*, TA-6285-REG: Strengthening Country Safeguard Systems (Consultancy Report Prepared by Adrienne La Grange).

Barenstein, J. 2016. Post-disaster reconstruction: Informal settlers and the right to adequate housing. In *Coming Home After Disaster: Multiple Dimensions of Housing Recovery*, A. Sapat and A.-M. Esnard (eds), Boca Raton: CRC Press, 245–262.

Barnes, S. 2015. *Impact Analysis on Housing Disaster Recovery Programs 10 Years after Katrina and Rita*. Prepared for the Louisiana Office of Community Development-Disaster Recovery Unit and the City of New Orleans, Baton Rouge, Louisiana: Louisiana State University, Division of Economic Development. http://measuringrecovery.lsu.edu/ (accessed February 29, 2016).

Bayot, J. 2005. Payouts hinge on the cause of damage. *New York Times*, August 31. http://www.nytimes.com/2005/08/31/business/payouts-hinge-on-the-cause-of-damage.html?_r=0 (accessed February 29, 2016).

Brescia, R. H., E. A. Kelly, and J. T. Marshall. 2012. Crisis management: Principles that should guide the disposition of federally owned, foreclosed properties. *Indiana Law Review* 45: 305–41.

Bristol, G. 2010. Surviving the second tsunami: Land rights in the face of buffer zones, land grabs and development. In *Rebuilding after Disasters: From Emergency to Sustainability*, G. Lizarralde, C. Johnson, and C. H. Davidson (eds), Abingdon: Spon Press, 133–48.

Brown, O., and A. Crawford. 2006. *Addressing Land Ownership after Natural Disasters: An Agency Survey*. Winnipeg, Canada: International Institute for Sustainable Development. http://www.iisd.org/pdf/2006/es_addressing_land.pdf (accessed February 29, 2016).

Carr, J. H., H. B. Marcus, S. N. Jagpal, and N. Kutty. 2008. *In the Wake of Katrina: The Continuing Saga of Housing and Rebuilding in New Orleans*. Washington, DC: Joint Center for Political and Economic Studies, Health Policy Institute. http://70.32.93.32/sites/default/files/InTheWakeofKatrina.pdf (accessed February 29, 2016).

Castor, A. 2012. *The Haitian Cadastral System: The Case of the Commune of Aquin: Revealing the Opportunities and Challenges*. Opening remarks and welcome conference proceedings, Aquin, Haiti: Aldy Hotel, December 14. http://www.hrdf.org/files/rapport-conference-cadastre-aquin-dec-14-2912-english.pdf (accessed February 29, 2016).

Choi, K. Y., and R. W. M. Cheung. 2013. Landslide disaster prevention and mitigation through works in Hong Kong. *Journal of Rock Mechanics and Geotechnical Engineering* 5(5): 354–65.

Esnard, A. M. and A. Sapat. 2014. *Displaced by Disasters: Recovery and Resilience in a Globalizing World*. Boca Raton: Routledge Press, Taylor & Francis.

Ferreira, S. 2013. Haiti's road to reconstruction blocked by land tenure disputes. *Reuters Online*, January 26. http://www.reuters.com/article/2013/01/26/us-haiti-land-idUSBRE90P0BM20130126 (accessed February 29, 2016).

Francesch-Huidobro, M. 2015. Collaborative governance and environmental authority for adaptive flood risk: Recreating sustainable coastal cities. *Journal of Cleaner Production* 107: 568–80.

Francesch-Huidobro, M., M. Dabrowski, Y. Tai, F. Chan, and D. Stead. 2016. The governance of climate adaptation in flood-prone delta cities: Bridging the gap between spatial planning and flood risk management, in press. *Progress in Planning*. http://www.sciencedirect.com/science/article/pii/S0305900615000628 (accessed February 29, 2016).

Glauber, D., and D. Zisser. 2013. Innovative post-disaster community-based housing strategies. In *Building Community Resilience Post-Disaster*, D. R. Gilmore and D. M. Standaert (eds), Chicago, Illinois: American Bar Association, 371–89.

Grannis, J. 2011. *Adaptation Tool Kit: Sea-Level Rise and Coastal Land Use: How Governments Can Use Land Use Practices to Adapt to Sea-Level Rise*. Washington, DC: Georgetown Climate Center.

Greater New Orleans Foundation. 2013. *Capital Absorption in New Orleans*. New Orleans, Louisiana: Greater New Orleans Foundation, September.
Hacke, R. 2014. Letting the dollars land. *Shelterforce*, March 26. http://www.shelterforce.org/article/print/3652/ (accessed February 29, 2016).
Hacke, R., D. Wood, and M. Urquilla. 2015. *Community Investment: Focusing on the System*. Troy, Michigan: The Kresge Foundation. http://kresge.org/sites/default/files/Kresge-Community-Investment-Focusing-on-the%20System-March%202015.pdf (accessed February 29, 2016).
Hammer, D. 2012a. NORA makes deadline for federal anti-blight grant spending. *Times Picayune*, February 14. http://www.nola.com/politics/index.ssf/2012/02/nora_makes_deadline_for_federa.html (accessed February 29, 2016).
Hammer, D. 2012b. Pontchartrain Park rebuilding effort may lose key financing. *Times Picayune*, May 25. http://www.nola.com/katrina/index.ssf/2012/05/pontchartrain_park_rebuilding.html (accessed February 29, 2016).
Hong Kong Geotechnical Engineering Office, Civil Engineering and Development Department. 2012. *Terrain in Hong Kong*. http://hkss.cedd.gov.hk/hkss/eng/natural_terrain.aspx (accessed on February 16, 2016 in English).
Hurricane Sandy Rebuilding Task Force. 2013. *Hurricane Sandy Rebuilding Strategy: Stronger Communities, A Resilient Region*. http://portal.hud.gov/hudportal/documents/huddoc?id=HSRebuildingStrategy.pdf (accessed February 29, 2016).
La Grange, A., and F. Pretorius. 2016. State-led gentrification in Hong Kong. *Urban Studies* 53(3): 506–23.
Juergensmeyer, J. C., and T. C. Roberts. 2012. *Land Use Planning and Development Regulation Law*, 3rd edn, St. Paul, Minnesota: West Academic.
Kennedy, B. 2012. *The Haitian Cadastral System: The Case of the Commune of Aquin: Revealing the Opportunities and Challenges*. Conference Proceedings: Background of Cadaster, Aquin, Haiti: Aldy Hotel, December 14. http://www.hrdf.org/files/rapport-conference-cadastre-aquin-dec-14-2912-english.pdf (accessed February 29, 2016).
Marshall, J. T. 2014. Weathering NEPA review: Superstorms and super slow urban recovery. *Ecology Law Quarterly* 41: 81–130.
Marshall, J. T. 2015. Rating the cities: Constructing a city resilience index for assessing the effect of state and local laws on long-term recovery from crisis and disaster. *Tulane Law Review* 90: 35–74.
Marshall, J. T., R. M. Rowberry, and A.-M. Esnard. 2016. Core capabilities and capacities of developer nonprofits in post-disaster community rebuilding. *Natural Hazards Review*, in press.
McCarthy-Brown, S., and S. L. Waysdorf. 2009. Katrina disaster family law: The impact of hurricane Katrina on families and family law. *Indiana Law Review* 42: 721–65.
Mitsova, D., and A.-M. Esnard. 2012. Holding back the sea: An overview of shore zone planning and management. *Journal of Planning Literature* 27(4): 446–59.
Nelson, M. 2014. Using land swaps to concentrate redevelopment and expand resettlement options in post-hurricane Katrina New Orleans. *Journal of the American Planning Association* 80(4): 426–37.
New Orleans Redevelopment Authority (NORA). 2010. *Transition Report* (on file with authors).
Olshansky, R. B., and H. F. Etienne. 2011. Setting the stage for long-term recovery in Haiti. *Earthquake Spectra* 27: S463–86.
Olshansky, R. B., and L. A. Johnson. 2010. *Clear as Mud: Planning for the Rebuilding of New Orleans*. Chicago, Illinois: American Planning Association.
Ponce, J. 2013. Land use planning and disaster: A European perspective from Spain. In *Disaster and Sociolegal Studies*, S. Sterett (ed.), New Orleans, Louisiana: Quid Pro Books, 41–69.

Shaw, J., and I. Ahmed. 2010. Design and delivery of post-disaster housing resettlement programs. *Case Studies from Sri Lanka and Indi*, Report 6.

Siders, A. 2013. *Managed Coastal Retreat: A Legal Handbook on Shifting Development Away from Vulnerable Areas.* New York: Columbia Law School, Columbia Center for Climate Change Law.

Smart, A. 1992. *Making Room: Squatter Clearance in Hong Kong.* Hong Kong: The University of Hong Kong.

Smith, G., D. Sandler, and M. Goralnik. 2013. Assessing state policy linking disaster recovery, smart growth, and resilience in Vermont following tropical storm Irene. *Vermont Journal of Environmental Law* 15, 66–102.

Titus, J. G. 1998. Rising seas, coastal erosion, and the takings clause: How to save wetlands and beaches without hurting property owners. *Maryland Law Review* 57: 1281–398.

Titus, J. G. 2011. *Rolling Easements.* Washington, DC: United States Environmental Protection Agency Climate Ready Estuaries (US EPA). http://www.epa.gov/sites/production/files/documents/rollingeasementsprimer.pdf (accessed February 29, 2016).

United State Department of Housing and Urban Development (US HUD). 2014. *Community Development Block Grant Disaster Recovery (CDBG-DR) Toolkits: Homebuyer Property Acquisition Checklist.* Washington, DC: US HUD. https://www.hudexchange.info/programs/cdbg-dr/toolkits/#hb (accessed February 29, 2016).

Waldman, A. 2004. Thousands die as quake-spawned waves crash onto coastlines across Southern Asia. *New York Times*, December 27. http://www.nytimes.com/2004/12/27/world/asia/thousands-die-as-quakespawned-waves-crash-onto-coastlines-across.html?_r=0 (accessed February 29, 2016).

Index

D

H

V

W

Y

For Product Safety Concerns and Information please contact our EU representative GPSR@taylorandfrancis.com
Taylor & Francis Verlag GmbH, Kaufingerstraße 24, 80331 München, Germany

www.ingramcontent.com/pod-product-compliance
Lightning Source LLC
Chambersburg PA
CBHW070549270326
41926CB00013B/2248
* 9 7 8 1 0 3 2 2 4 2 2 8 6 *